COLD WAR CONSTRUCTIONS

The Political Culture of United States Imperialism, 1945–1966

A VOLUME IN THE SERIES

Culture, Politics, and the Cold War

Edited by Christian G. Appy

COLD WAR
CONSTRUCTIONS

The Political Culture of
United States Imperialism,
1945–1966

Edited by

CHRISTIAN G. APPY

The University of Massachusetts Press
AMHERST

LIBRARY OF CONGRESS CATALOGING-IN-PUBLICATION DATA
Cold war constructions : the political culture of United States
imperialism, 1945–1966 / edited by Christian G. Appy.
p.   cm.—(Culture, politics, and the cold war)
Includes bibliographical references and index.
ISBN 1-55849-217-8 (cloth : alk. paper).—ISBN 1-55849-218-6 (pbk. : alk. paper)
1. United States—Foreign relations—1945–1989.   2. Cold War.   3. United States—
Politics and government—1945–1989. 4. United States—Foreign relations—
Developing countries.   5. Developing countries—Foreign relations—United States.
6. Political culture—United States—History—20th century.   7. Imperialism—
United States—History—20th century.   I. Appy, Christian G.   II. Series.
E744.C636   2000
327.73′009′045—dc21
99-37765
CIP

British Library Cataloguing in Publication data are available

For Barry O'Connell

Contents

Acknowledgments

THE INSPIRATION for this collection came from Clark Dougan, senior editor at the University of Massachusetts Press. Working with him on this project, and all the volumes in "Culture, Politics, and the Cold War," has been a great pleasure. Clark is a superb editor, a gifted historian, and a wonderful friend.

Ella Kusnetz skillfully directed the book through the production process and Michael Burke did a great job of copyediting, both tasks especially difficult and crucial in a work of multiple authorship. Thanks, as well, to Lynda Stannard for preparing the index.

My greatest debt is to the contributors—Mark Bradley, Jim Fisher, John Foran, Kevin Gaines, Van Gosse, Tina Klein, Jonathan Nashel, Andy Rotter, Penny Von Eschen, and Wendy Wall. It was an honor and a joy to work with such dedicated, supportive, and intellectually exciting colleagues. We are all grateful to historians Marilyn Young and Frank Costigliola for their thoughtful reviews of the manuscript.

As an undergraduate at Amherst College, I once complained to my mentor about the isolation of academic work. Barry O'Connell taught me that scholarship not only builds on the labor of others, but can be truly collaborative, and take us to sources, subjects, and convictions that live far beyond the walls of libraries. For that, and his friendship, I dedicate this book to him.

Cold War Constructions

The Political Culture of United States Imperialism, 1945–1966

Introduction
Struggling for the World

The reality is that the only alternative to the communist World
Empire is an American Empire which will be, if not literally
world-wide in formal boundaries, capable of exercising decisive world control.

James Burnham, *The Struggle for the World* (1947)

By 1947, former Trotskyist James Burnham was moving quickly
along a political trajectory that would soon make the once radical philosophy professor a leading ideologue of the right wing. Even before the
Korean War broke out in June, 1950, Burnham believed World War III had
quite literally begun. Paul Nitze agreed. As deputy director of the State
Department Policy Planning Staff, Nitze was principal author of National
Security Council 68, a top secret memorandum that was among the most
crucial Cold War blueprints to militarize the United States in opposition to
the Soviet Union. According to NSC 68 (April 1950), nothing less than a
massive National Security State (including a tripling of military spending)
would prevent the Soviet Union from carrying out its "fundamental design"
"to impose its absolute authority over the rest of the world." Whether or
not the United States mobilized sufficiently would depend, Nitze argued,
on the "recognition by this Government, the American people, and all free
peoples, that the cold war is in fact a real war in which the survival of the
free world is at stake."[1]

Such apocalyptic language was not confined to secret memoranda or the
pages of William Buckley's National Review, the right-wing journal James
Burnham would join in 1955. It was, in fact, a staple of public discourse in
the early Cold War. President Dwight Eisenhower began his first inaugural
address in 1953 with a stark evocation of a world divided between two hostile and irreconcilable enemies: "We sense with all our faculties that forces

of good and evil are massed and armed and opposed as rarely before in history. This fact defines the meaning of this day."[2]

Holy war rhetoric was common enough, but Burnham's explicit call for a global American Empire remained something of a novelty. The denial of imperial ambition has been a hallmark of American ideology, as critical to dominant conceptions of national identity as individualism, opportunity, and classlessness.[3] And, just as upward mobility was most celebrated when individual opportunities were profoundly circumscribed by the rise of industrial capitalism, so, too, the denial of empire became most vociferous as the United States became a dominant global power. American imperialism has succeeded in part because of the ability of its exponents to insist that real empire was a product of Old World greed, religious or ideological absolutism, and decadent corruption. The New World, in this view, was constructed not as an extension of European imperialism, but in opposition to it, a land of freedom from the control of foreign tyrants. By the early years of the Cold War, U.S. policymakers, drew on this long tradition of anti-imperial rhetoric to argue that freedom was everywhere endangered by a red imperialism of unprecedented power and ambition that was headquartered in Moscow.

James Burnham's call for "world control" was brazenly explicit, but the underlying impulse was widely shared in Cold War Washington. By the 1950s, virtually everyone in authority insisted that the threat of Soviet imperialism required the United States to assume world leadership and global responsibility—the key phrases by which American policymakers at once denied imperialism and enacted it. Sometimes Cold War policymakers conceded that the United States had crucial strategic concerns around the world that warranted overseas military bases and troop deployments. It was even politically acceptable to point out the importance of vital resources in other lands and the necessity of protecting international markets. But the American Century was more typically broadcast as a philanthropic endeavor to share the blessings of freedom and democracy. In 1965, President Johnson insisted that "we want nothing for ourselves" in Vietnam. Empire remained an American pejorative as the imperial quest for global control carried on apace.[4]

Common to virtually all American officials was a rhetoric of global competition in which the United States, as leader of the "Free World," was pitted in a world threatening struggle with the "Slave World" of Communist tyranny. So, too, was the view that the Cold War would last indefinitely. As late as the mid-1980s, few Americans predicted that the "long, twilight struggle" of Kennedy's inaugural address would end before the millennium, much less before the end of the decade. Even so, the Cold War lasted almost half a century, cost Americans almost $10.5 trillion in military expenditures alone, and destroyed millions of lives around the world.[5] The struggle encompassed not only the entire surface of the earth, but its underground resources and its outer space. It embraced economics, ideology, religion, education, family life, sports—who can name a realm of human endeavor untouched by Cold War competition?

Appropriately, the thirteen original essays in this volume include an enormous range of topics—travel literature, diplomacy, Broadway musicals, foreign aid, propaganda programs, covert operations, journalism, expatriot activism, lobbyists, philanthropy, and more. They are written, in part, out of the faith that now is a propitious moment to study the Cold War anew. The era's habits of mind, economic burdens, military and nuclear weapons, and physical, psychological, and environmental legacies, may remain with us for years to come, but as the formal end of superpower conflict recedes farther into the past, we have reason to hope for interpretations that scrutinize the unchallenged assumptions of the lived experience.

There is, however, little reason to expect that the post–Cold War era will produce a unitary explanation of the global struggle. Indeed, the Cold War itself played an important role in generating profound intellectual suspicion of any single interpretation that promises mastery of a subject. As Tom Engelhardt has written, the very presence of atomic weaponry challenged the idea that anything could truly be mastered, least of all one's "enemies." A nuclear war would be devastating to all sides; it would, in fact, render all conventional boundaries meaningless. Nor could Cold War ideologies be mastered or contained (how do you even identify a communist?). While superpower leaders may have wanted global control, Cold War realities subverted all traditional narratives of victory.[6] The following essays reveal many Cold War scripts and actors, an enormous variety in the ways the "struggle for the world" was perceived and engaged. And many of these essays make abundantly clear that the Cold War was, as much as anything else, a competition over discourse, a "struggle for the word."

The common goal of this collection is to address the connections between domestic political culture and U.S. Cold War foreign policy. Cultural and literary historians have led the way in teaching their colleagues that all experience is historically constructed. Terms like Cold War, Free World, and containment are not fixed, immutable terms, but are created within particular historical and cultural contexts and are subject to contention and

change over time. These scholars further argue that discourse has ideological resonance that extends well beyond conventional associations. For example, in a pathbreaking study of the political culture of the Cold War,
Elaine Tyler May argued that the American policy of containment abroad
may be equally useful as an explanation of the tightly contained ideals of
middle-class family life in the 1940s and 1950s. Just as the United States
tried to contain communism around the world, domestic ideology attempted
to contain men, and especially women, within narrow boundaries of permis-
sible thought and behavior.[7]

We need to go farther in our efforts not only to examine the connection
between domestic and foreign events but to explore as well the specific
relationships between politics and culture. The ideas that culture is inherently political (that it is embedded in, and expresses, relations of power)
and that all political struggles are culturally constructed (embedded in systems of value and meaning) are not especially new. Only recently, however,
have scholars begun to produce works that develop both insights.

While cultural historians have enriched and enlarged our understanding
of politics, the political significance of their subjects is not always sufficiently
assessed. Furthermore, a good deal of cultural scholarship has tended to
obscure the life and death actualities of human experience beneath a web
of textual interpretation. For their part, diplomatic historians have been
perhaps the slowest of all scholars to adopt insights beyond their discipline.
As a result, dozens of books and essays on American foreign policy during
the Cold War are virtually oblivious to the possibility that policy-making,
intelligence-gathering, war-making, and mainstream politics might be profoundly shaped by a social and cultural world beyond the conference table
and the battlefield. Largely unfamiliar with the work of literary and cultural
critics, many diplomatic historians have read their documents too literally
and assume the events they describe can be understood as unmediated,
objective realities rather than dynamic historical constructions.[8]

This collection seeks to illuminate the ways in which U.S. political culture
has shaped specific foreign sites of Cold War conflict. Mark Bradley argues
that U.S. Cold War policies toward Vietnam cannot be fully understood
apart from the cultural conceptions that developed in the decades before
World War II, an Orientalist portrait of the Vietnamese that depicted them
as passive, lazy, immature, untrustworthy, and vulnerable to outside control.
As William Bullitt reported, "The Annamese are attractive and even lovable,
but essentially childish." Such views were amazingly impervious to the
contrary evidence provided by the Viet Minh's extraordinary resistance to

French control, and provided a set of cultural assumptions that fueled U.S. intervention. Bradley's work challenges scholars of the Cold War to explore the prewar roots of postwar policy.

Christina Klein analyzes the cultural construction of Asia in the late 1940s and 1950s. Postwar middlebrow culture, she argues, "formulated a utopian vision of cross-racial and cross-national community that served as a reward for Americans' ideological, financial, and political support for the Cold War in Asia." Focusing on the *Saturday Review,* the Christian Children's Fund, and the musical *South Pacific,* Klein shows how the figure of white adoptive motherhood was central to the promotion of U.S. global expansion. This essay raises the possibility that the political culture of U.S. postcolonial imperialism has been shaped as much by popular constructions of international family ties as it has by westerns, war movies, and figures of aggressive masculinity such as John Wayne.

Andrew Rotter uses the occasion of a 1951 U.S. wheat loan to India to analyze the cultural values and assumptions that shaped Indo-U.S. relations. He goes beyond the surface of political debates to examine the cultural differences on both sides that gave diplomatic gestures deep and often unintended significance. For example, the tradition of *dana,* or "royal giving," is based on a keen sense of proper relations between people of different social positions. According to *dana,* subordinates should neither ask for help nor express gratitude when a gift is given. Many U.S. policymakers and diplomats were appalled by the apparent unwillingness of India to act like a humble and grateful supplicant. When John Foster Dulles told the embassy staff in New Delhi that Indians would "come crawling on their hands and knees" if the United States offered economic assistance in turn for Cold War loyalty, he was not only arrogant, but utterly ignorant of Indian culture. As Rotter points out, however, diplomatic success did not necessarily depend on westerners adopting Indian manners. The best-received westerners were men like Chester Bowles who addressed Indians with respectful informality, from a cultural position well outside Indian norms. They did not presume to have a place within the Indian social hierarchy.

Wendy Wall focuses her study of Cold War propaganda on U.S. efforts to defeat Communist candidates in the Italian elections of 1948. Thousands of Italian Americans engaged in a massive letter-writing campaign to persuade overseas friends and relatives to vote against the left and embrace "the American way of life." Though promoted as a spontaneous, grass-roots upwelling, the campaign was orchestrated by a coalition that included journalist Drew Pearson, Italian-American leaders (including many former supporters of Mussolini), and the Truman administration. An early example of "public diplomacy," the "Letters to Italy" campaign was inspired by the 1947 "Friendship Train" and would, in turn, inspire dozens of similar efforts throughout the Cold War. Wall's essay shows how Cold War propaganda sought not only to demonize communism, but to build a consensus about American national identity.

Penny Von Eschen examines State Department programs designed to win African Cold War allegiance and to gain greater access to vital strategic minerals. Her analysis of African American "goodwill ambassadors" offers persuasive evidence that they were not malleable agents of United States policy. "Jambassadors" like Louis Armstrong were sent to Africa as symbols of racial and democratic progress in the United States, but they may have done more to inspire pan-African solidarity and Cold War nonalignment than uncritical loyalty to the West. For example, when the United States Information Service celebrated Harry Belafonte's "crusade for American-ism," the Gold Coast *Daily Mail* hailed it as a "crusade for Africanism." Von Eschen's work encourages us to explore the complex meanings and unin-tended consequences of state-sponsored cultural programs.

Jonathan Nashel provides a new interpretation of modernization theory by placing it in a larger cultural context. He argues that it was not only a powerfully influential conceptual framework among academics and poli-cymakers, but reached a much broader audience as the "civil religion" of Cold War liberals. Alongside figures such as Walt Rostow, Robert McNa-mara, and David Lilienthal, Nashel offers a fresh reading of the best-selling novel *The Ugly American*. While sharing the technological and marketplace zeal of modernization theorists, this popular prescription for third world development recommended starting with small-scale, localized capitalist development led by ambassadors of Americanism with an appreciation of local customs—a kind of Peace Corps of modernizers. Nashel shows how these apparently benign ideas led, in Vietnam, to "little more than the terror-bombing of peasants."

John Foran takes up the CIA-orchestrated coup that overthrew Iranian prime minister Muhammad Musaddiq in 1953. Developing a "third world cultural studies perspective," Foran weighs the impact of mass media in producing the "structure of feeling" in which the coup was conceived and executed. He argues that Henry Luce's *Time* magazine did not simply parrot the conventional wisdom of the political establishment. Rather, *Time*'s Orientalist construction of Musaddiq as a "demagogic, emotional, child-like fanatic" who had become a "Communist dupe" served as an important catalyst for covert intervention. By contrast, *Time*'s construction of the Shah Mohammad Reza Pahlavi as a pro-Western modernizer was a kind of "Orientalism-in-reverse." Foran's work should inspire a rethinking of the media's role in shaping Cold War policy.

The "success" of the coup in Iran helped to inspire the CIA plot to overthrow the democratically elected government of Jacabo Arbenz in Guatemala. My essay on the coup begins with a sketch drawn by Eisenhower on the morning after the overthrow. This "Guatemalan doodle" is emblematic of a self-reflective, and Americo-centric worldview that was useful to policymakers who struggled to create convincing narratives that bore little resemblance to Guatemalan reality. Even so, official storytellers, including a remarkably compliant media, faced a number of significant literary challenges. How, for example, could they construct a fictional "mass uprising" in Guatemala without also celebrating third world revolution in general? And how could the United States take credit for a Cold War victory for which it had already denied responsibility? Strained as these narratives were, the official claim that Guatemala represented a Communist threat to the Western Hemisphere went virtually unchallenged.

In his essay on the Vietnam Lobby, James Fisher argues that the primary advocates of U.S. support for Ngo Dinh Diem were "liberal internationalists, socialists, and assorted figures on the 'non-Communist Left.'" These men constructed, and believed in, a myth of Diem as a cultural democrat. Diem's dictatorial rule of South Vietnam from 1954 to 1963 eventually became an embarrassment to the leftists who had championed him, yet Fisher makes the case that the Lobby's efforts advanced a "liberal culture" in the United States. Their campaigns on behalf of liberal, pluralist internationalism helped to give political legitimacy not only to a variety of left perspectives, but to "Catholic anti-Communists [like John Kennedy] eager to embrace a complex world that the McCarthyites had reviled." According to this provocative thesis, the Vietnam Lobby contributed to disaster abroad, but served to enrich political culture at home.

Van Gosse explains the surprisingly wide-ranging, if short-lived, American support for Fidel Castro and the Cuban Revolution. "At no other point in the post-1945 period did so many ordinary Americans unabashedly embrace a foreign insurgency of fatigue-clad, gun-toting rebels." Gosse attributes the "seemingly anomalous pro-Castroism," in part, to a pre–Cold War tradition in U.S. popular culture that romanticized Latin American insurgency. The fact that Batista's Cuba had a reputation as "the whorehouse of the Caribbean" also predisposed many journalists and liberals to support a revolution that seemed to offer a non-Communist alternative. Added to the mix was a 1950s youth culture that attracted many young American men to the bearded revolutionaries of the Sierra Maestra. Along the way, Gosse analyzes the ways in which Yankee *fidelismo* reflected important class and racial perceptions of Castro. This essay offers striking evidence that the political culture of the period was not nearly as conservative, conventional, or compliant as many interpreters have suggested.

Kevin Gaines shows how African American expatriates such as Julian Mayfield were moved by the example of Ghanaian independence to a radical and international conception of black power in the late 1950s. While most conventional treatments of the early Cold War emphasize black moderation on matters of foreign affairs, Gaines provides persuasive evidence that African American expatriates struggled, against great odds, to develop an independent and international politics founded on black liberation. This assertion of black power was threatened by a narrower civil rights agenda largely imposed by Cold War orthodoxy. Gaines thereby reverses the textbook view that the civil rights movement was undone by the rise of black power and reveals a dynamic political culture among African American activists in the early Cold War.

Now, almost a full decade removed from the Cold War, we can still feel its constraints in the poverty of our political imagination. Since the collapse of the Soviet Union, the West, as Jonathan Schell has put it, "is like a person who has won $50 million in the lottery and then declares, 'Wonderful— now I can redecorate my living room!' Why not buy a whole new house?"[9] Schell's "new house" is the abolition of nuclear weapons, just one of many proposals that the end of the Cold War has made more plausible yet still, to most Americans, barely imaginable. In so many ways we have failed to grasp the freedom and opportunity history has conferred. These essays help us understand not only the iron cage of Cold War ideologies, but the various ways people acted to uphold and resist them. Perhaps they can also help us imagine peaceful and nonimperial ways to struggle for the world.

PART ONE

Foreign Relations

Slouching toward Bethlehem
Culture, Diplomacy, and the Origins of the Cold War in Vietnam

MARK BRADLEY

A T THE NOVEMBER 11, 1943, meeting of the State Department's Subcommittee on Territorial Problems, Kenneth P. Landon, as he listened to a discussion of the future role of the Great Powers in determining the postwar political status of Vietnam, remarked that he

> could not help thinking of the colored gentleman in the Civil War who had been chided for not enlisting. In reply, he asked his interlocutor whether he had ever seen a dog fight and if so whether he had ever seen the bone take sides. . . . [A]s the colored people had been the bone in the case of the Civil War it was assumed by many that the Oriental peoples were the bone of contention in the controversy under discussion.

Landon questioned whether this was actually the case, adding that while "it might be true temporarily it was nevertheless possible that the bone might have feelings about itself and might at some later date even become a dog." [1]

Some seven years later Vietnam once again occupied the attention of policymakers in Washington. On January 19, 1950, the People's Republic of China recognized Ho Chi Minh's Democratic Republic of Vietnam (DRV) and began to provide military advisers, equipment, and supplies for the DRV's ongoing war against the French. Within days, the Soviet Union joined China in extending its recognition of the Ho Chi Minh government. The American response was swift, with the Truman administration announcing its recognition of the French-backed Associated States of Vietnam led by the former Vietnamese emperor Bao Dai on February 3, 1950. By the end of the year, the administration had pledged more than $100 million in military and economic aid to the French and Bao Dai government for their fight against the DRV. The Cold War had come to Vietnam.

To borrow Kenneth Landon's analogy, existing scholarship on the origins of the Cold War in Vietnam has largely viewed Vietnam as a bone pushed and pulled by the political and economic aspects of American power. While the explanatory variables offered in these works are diverse—ranging from the potential instability of Western Europe to the need for a liberal capitalist trading order in the Pacific, the vulnerability of Southeast Asia with the rise of Mao's China, or the domestic political threat of McCarthyism at home— they share a common focus in asserting that realist geopolitical imperatives were the centerpiece of American policy.[2] This emphasis on the political and economic dimensions of power, however, obscures the essential role of cultural forces in conditioning American policy toward Vietnam.

As early as the period between the two world wars, American policymakers began to construct a series of culturally based images of Vietnam that came to play a pivotal role in decision making after 1945. These American images, filtered through a prism of racialist and Orientalist assumptions like those expressed by Kenneth Landon, were almost always unfavorable. The Vietnamese appeared to most American observers as a primitive and inferior people. French colonial rule was judged to be an administrative, economic, and moral failure, in sharp contrast, many Americans argued, to the successes of U.S. colonial policy in the Philippines. And expressions of Vietnamese nationalism were dismissed as the work of external, often Soviet, agents. Yet an unwavering belief in the ability of superior American political, economic, and social models to cross cultures increasingly convinced many policymakers that Vietnam could be reformed, a sentiment that shaped efforts to remake Vietnamese society in the American image during World War II and in its aftermath.

Along with challenging the primacy of interpretations that stress geopolitical imperatives in policy making, this exploration of American relations with Vietnam also seeks to advance a more rigorous approach to analyzing the place of cultural forces in U.S. diplomacy during the early Cold War period. Culture, as Clifford Geertz has suggested, is a notoriously slippery and elusive concept.[3] Too often the study of culture and diplomacy, when informed by the postmodern and pluralist sensibilities of contingent meanings, leaves itself open to well-deserved criticism. As one leading realist scholar of post-1945 American foreign relations recently argued, the sometimes opaque relativism of postmodern approaches to the cultural dimension of foreign relations can divert "attention from questions of causation and agency."[4] Alternatively, more traditional efforts to link culture and international order, such as Samuel P. Huntington's thesis that culture *writ large* serves as the only significant fault line for the actions of actors in the international arena, risk a similar reductionism and analytical imprecision.[5]

By exploring the cultural vocabularies embedded in American discourse on Vietnam, this essay aims to reveal the patterns of ideas, beliefs, fears, and aspirations that shaped American power and its Cold War strategic vision. In making policy toward Vietnam, American diplomats were engaged in a broader attempt to define the proper and desirable workings of international order for themselves, the nation, and the peoples they encountered overseas. The almost instinctual values and norms embedded in this horizon of choices[6] were often implicit and are sometimes difficult to tease out of the received historical record. But a close reading of the language and rhetoric by which policymakers framed their choices can retrieve these assumptions and force them to the forefront.[7] Within the interstices of the often contested articulation of national self-identity and world order, American aspirations in Vietnam reflected the powerful influence of a wider European colonial discourse and cultural attitudes toward morality, poverty, and race at home that first emerged in the interwar period. If the Cold War in Vietnam began in 1950, much of its immediate and enduring character lay with these persisting assumptions that made up the American vision of the postcolonial state in Vietnam.

The Interwar American Construction of French Indochina

"Backwaters of Empire in French Indo-China" was an apt title for American journalist Gertrude Emerson's 1923 account of her first experiences in Vietnam.[8] Like much of Southeast Asia beyond the Philippines, Vietnam received little public attention from most Americans in the interwar period. Nor did Vietnam hold much political and economic significance for the United States. Yet it did attract journalists like Gertrude Emerson as well as a number of scholars, missionaries, and travel writers throughout the interwar period. The works of these authors, along with the reports of U.S. consular officials in Saigon, provided the first sustained body of American commentary on Vietnamese society, French colonialism in Vietnam, and Vietnamese nationalism.[9]

Most interwar accounts of Vietnam began with an examination of what one observer termed "Annamite psychology."[10] With very few exceptions, the Vietnamese were found wanting. "Lazy," "primitive," "liars," and "effeminate" are the most common descriptions of the Vietnamese that emerge in these accounts. "Natural laziness," wrote Virginia Thompson in the most comprehensive American study of Indochina before World War II, "keeps the Annamite in a state of chronic poverty and often vagrancy." For Thompson, the "Annamite's total lack of initiative" characterized all important aspects of Vietnamese life, a view reflected by most observers including American consul Leland L. Smith, who reported to Washington in 1924 that the "Annamites as a race are very lazy and not prone to be ambitious."

An image of Vietnamese society and culture as primitive also emerges in these accounts. The veteran Asia correspondent Mona Gardner, in a 1939 book chronicling her travels throughout Southeast Asia, summarized a common view of living conditions in Vietnamese villages: "houses . . . were layers of desiccated mud, and might have been fashioned just slightly after the Stone Age. . . . Inside everything was sliding down as though the earth were drawing these people and their few possessions back unto it." Similarly, the journalist Gertrude Emerson was struck by the "groups of flimsy thatched hovels often standing in stagnant waters" that she observed in Vietnamese villages during her 1924 journey through northern Vietnam. "Annamites at best are never clean," Virginia Thompson claimed, "but sickness shows up this trait in its most revolting form. To have his pulse taken, the patient clothed in be-vermined rags extends a grimy fist covered with layers of dust." Almost all indigenous cultural practices drew contempt from American observers. Thompson's view that "native eating" illustrated "general negligence" and "indelicacy" was echoed in accounts of diplomats like Leland Smith who, in upcountry trips, described the preparation of an "exceedingly Annamite meal" which he "could not eat (having seen it prepared)."[11]

Along with perceptions of the Vietnamese as lazy and primitive, many American observers argued that the Vietnamese were, by nature, liars. "[L]ying does not trouble the Annamite conscience," one observer reported in a discussion of indigenous government. "Facts makes little impression on . . . a chaotic state of mind." The Vietnamese "flair for imaginative lying," according to many of these observers, pervaded indigenous society.[12] Many authors also criticized Vietnamese men for their lack of virility and military prowess. Gardner considered them to be "weak husks of men" whose "faces are long and thin, and so delicately featured that it is difficult to tell a man from a woman" as "the women put their thin flat bodies in the same identical clothes . . . as their men wear." Others commented on the "puerile vanity" of Vietnamese men, discussing the reticence of most Vietnamese to join local militias, and what one observer called "the conspicuous absence of epic virility" in Vietnamese literature.[13]

The explanations American observers offered for the deficiencies they perceived in Vietnamese society reveal both their reliance on European Orientalist representations of colonized peoples as well as prevailing views of poverty, morality, and race at home. In part, interwar Americans turned to French sinological scholarship on Vietnam which highlighted the deleterious effects of Chinese civilization on Vietnamese culture. Drawing upon influential works by such French scholars as E. Luro, who argued that "Annamite civilization in its present state has preserved the archaic forms long discarded in China,"[14] Americans came to view Vietnam as a fossilized "little China." Vietnam's monarchy, administration, legal codes, and family structure were seen as "servile" copies of their counterparts in China and further evidence of Vietnam as an imitative and static society.[15] Similarly, American renderings of the absence of virility among Vietnamese men drew upon a substantial body of French writing on Indochina that characterized Vietnamese men as effeminate "boys " who were indistinguishable from women and that dismissively rendered indigenous troops as *"soldats mamzelles."*[16]

The American embrace of French writings on Vietnam placed American perceptions of the Vietnamese in the larger European Orientalist tradition by which, as Edward Said and other post-Orientalist scholars have argued, the European colonial powers formulated essentialist differences between immutable non-Western and dynamic Western cultures as a tool to reinforce European political and cultural mastery.[17] Interwar American observers frequently used the term "Oriental" both to explain the inadequacies of Vietnamese cultural practices and to contrast them with the more progressive West. Virginia Thompson makes frequent reference to such rhetorical figures to account for a number of the weaknesses she and others identified in Vietnamese society. For example, the Vietnamese were "indifferent" farmers, Thompson argued, because of an "age-old Oriental prejudice" against manual labor and "a life so impregnated with ritual and static . . . philosophy that it makes antique methods meritorious simply because they are old." The deprecatory image of Oriental somnolence also emerged in the observations of other Americans, like Mona Gardner, who suggested that the Vietnamese "seem too finally bred, as though the long civilization behind them has made them tired, too tired to change, and that in the process strong emotions and passion have been drained from them."[18]

If the appropriation of Orientalist discourse allowed interwar authors to universalize their disparaging critiques of Vietnamese society, it also prompted American observers to locate the deficiencies they perceived in Vietnamese society within Vietnam's tradition as a cultural borrower. Viewed as cultural imitators rather than innovators, the Vietnamese attracted considerable American opprobrium, suggesting the presence of subtle, hierarchical distinctions within the largely negative view of Oriental civilizations. For many Americans, Vietnam was not only a smaller China but a lesser civilization as well.[19] American observers often followed French interpreters to argue that China was "infinitely more disciplined and cultured" than Vietnam. The widespread perceptions of Vietnam as a second-rate Oriental nation helped Americans to explain what they believed to be the particularly conservative and immutable character of Vietnamese society. By viewing the Vietnamese as dedicated preservers of appropriated cultural forms with no indigenous civilization of their own, many American authors echoed Virginia Thompson's comment that "the Annamite is the enemy of all change . . . the tranquil observer and defender of law and custom."[20]

American interpretations of Vietnamese society, following another common discursive practice of Orientalist writings in Europe, also reflected concerns about state and society at home. Several scholars of European colonialism have noted what they term the "embourgeoisement" of Western images of colonized peoples, arguing that descriptions of the colonial "other" corresponded to existing patterns in the metropole, particularly anxieties about the moral standards of the rapidly expanding working classes in Europe and middle class obsessions with family organization, sexual standards, medical care, and moral instruction.[21] Though these interconnections for American images of non-Western peoples have yet to receive sustained scholarly attention, cultural studies of the United States in the 1930s, the decade when the majority of interwar American observers of Vietnam were writing, suggest that white middle-class Americans increasingly embraced a conservative vision of family and social structure.[22] The conservative moral climate of the1930s may help to account for the seeming obsession of Americans with the "lack of comfort" in homes, "drab" clothing, "indelicate" eating, "primitive" medical practices, and the "general negligence" they found in Vietnam, as well as the use of such tropes as laziness and lying to denote Vietnam's poverty and perceived vagrancy.

The fascination of American observers with Vietnam's poverty may also have had its origins in a domestic context. Most of the interwar American reporting on Vietnam took place in the 1930s, when an enormous body of travel literature emerged that chronicled the impact of the Great Depression in the United States. Works such as Edmund Wilson's *American Jitters,* Sherwood Anderson's *Puzzled America,* and the photographs of Depression-era life by Walker Evans and Dorothea Lange for the New Deal's Farm Security Administration were exposés of rural poverty and the human costs of joblessness in industrial cities.[23] These works may have provided the initial impetus for many of the American journalists and writers who came to Vietnam and equipped them with a conceptual vocabulary for reporting on what they found in Vietnam. The shared experience of worldwide depression and their observations of Vietnam, however, served to reinforce rather than to blur the prevailing perceptions of a progressive American society and a backward Vietnam. Whatever the difficulties facing Americans in the 1930s, conditions in Vietnam seemed far worse to most observers and required an interpretation that transcended the nature of the contemporary international economy.

Perhaps the most common explanation for the inadequacies interwar Americans found in Vietnam was the interconnection between climate and race. The "inferiority of Annamite mental development," Virginia Thompson argued in a passage typical of the period, was a result of tropical climate:

> A more subtle effect of climate upon Annamite psychology is their inability to receive sharp, clear-cut impressions. Perhaps it is the brilliant sunshine that has weakened their sensory reactions along with their will power. The Annamite dreams a perpetual melancholy reverie uncontrolled by any critical faculty. His thinking is confused and indecisive . . . incapable of separating the essential from the trivial.[24]

In discussing issues of race, American interwar observers had no need to turn to European Orientalist models given the pervasive racialism in nineteenth-century America and the use of Social Darwinism and perceptions of African and Native American inferiority to describe the peoples white Americans encountered in the Caribbean and the Philippines in the late nineteenth and early twentieth century.[25] Rarely, however, did American writers draw attention to these intellectual and cultural legacies. More commonly interwar Americans drew on French accounts to lend authority to their racialist conceptions of the Vietnamese. For instance, Virginia Thompson made reference to the work of Paul Giran, a French colonial administrator who served in Vietnam in the late nineteenth century, to support her claims that climate was "a major influence on native character." Giran's 1904 text, *Psychologie du peuple Annamite*,[26] presents a hodgepodge of racial interpretations for Vietnamese inferiority, including an illustrated cranial analysis that purported to explain the less developed Vietnamese brain by reference to the effects of tropical climate.

The persistence of racial and climatic theories in the American discourse on Vietnam may be illustrative of wider trends in white American thought on non-Western peoples in the 1920s and 1930s. Studies of the resurgence of nativism in the 1920s and unchanging interwar perceptions of African Americans indicate a highly charged domestic racial climate.[27] Highly suggestive of the continuing links between domestic racial attitudes and interwar American perceptions of the non-Western world is a 1924 Yale University survey of eminent American diplomats, missionaries, and scholars who were asked to rank the civilizations of the world based on climatic and racial characteristics. One hundred was considered the highest level of civilization, and most of the West was ranked in the ninetieth percentile. Central America and South America were ranked in the fortieth percentile. Vietnam was ranked at thirty-five, just above Africa.[28]

A second element of the American interwar discourse on Vietnam focused on the nature of French colonial rule. Mona Gardner's contention that "French colonization is poor, uneconomical, and inordinately selfish" accurately captures the vociferous American criticism of French colonial policies and French disregard for the welfare of the Vietnamese. The French administrative structure in Vietnam was criticized for its overcentralization and financial disorganization, as was the "excessive growth" and inefficiency of the colonial bureaucracy. The French settler population drew American scorn as "besotted and whoring *colons* who lived with a maximum of ease and a minimum of exertion." French efforts to develop Vietnamese agriculture for the world market, to construct a modern infrastructure of roads and railway lines, and to establish discriminatory tariffs also received strong American censure.[29]

American observers attacked French political, economic, and social policies for overtaxing Vietnamese society and marginalizing them in the colonial bureaucracy.[30] They also voiced disapproval of many aspects of colonial labor, educational, and medical policies. For example, most observers noted that labor standards in colonial Vietnam were far below the standards of other colonized territories. Americans often pointed to the ill treatment and dangerous working conditions of Vietnamese mine and plantation workers, describing incidents of torture by French overseers, the prevalence of disease, and the provision of meager salaries and inhuman living conditions.

Several observers in the mid-1930s claimed there was "a wide-spread feeling among the Annamite masses that a New Deal [was] not only due, but overdue."[31]

Significantly, American critiques of French colonialism were not a reflection of broad anticolonial sentiment. No American in the interwar period suggested that improvements in Vietnamese society would come without the firm guidance of a Western power. Rather, American observers believed that the French had not met what they viewed as the proper responsibilities and obligations of a colonial power to better the lives of a people whose racial characteristics and physical environment rendered self-improvement improbable, if not impossible. In offering this critique, American rhetoric recalled the common British, French, and Dutch practice of celebrating their own achievements in the colonies—and denigrating the practices of other European powers—to construct and promote national identity and exceptionalism in the metropole.[32]

Most Americans who came to Vietnam would have agreed with the conclusions of a report on French colonial rule in Indochina prepared by Philippine governor general Dwight F. Davis after his 1931 visit to the colony:

> The poverty of the average native . . . is very apparent. . . . The native people are considered useful for the purpose of labor and, with that end in view, their welfare is not entirely neglected but little effort is made to improve their mental condition or to give them any real voice in government. . . . The underlying principle of all governmental activities is to develop the country economically for the benefit of France.[33]

The implicit contrast to the selfishness and incompetence Davis ascribed to the French, of course, was American self-perceptions of the success of U.S. colonial policies in the Philippines. The contrast between French and American colonial policies infused American writing on Vietnam, with American efforts in the Philippines approvingly regarded as maintaining "native individuality" while promoting "native development" and making American colonial models "as little odious" as it was possible for colonialism to be.[34] In this way, American interwar critiques of French colonialism served to reinforce American national identity as an exceptional power by suggesting that American practices offered potentially more instructive models than those of the French for remaking Vietnamese society.

Vietnamese radical nationalism shaped the third and final aspect of the interwar discourse on Vietnam. Most Americans attributed the rise of anti-French and nationalist sentiment among the Vietnamese to failed French colonial policies which impoverished the rural peasantry and frustrated the ambitions of Vietnamese elites.[35] But if Americans were critical of the French policies that had produced indigenous discontent, they were far from champions of Vietnamese nationalism. Orientalist and racialist categories shaped their unfavorable assessments of Vietnamese nationalism. Most interwar American observers regarded nationalist leaders as selfish, dishonest, and vain. Indigenous anticolonial elites, they believed, were "hampered by an Oriental psychology" that produced self-defeating "mutual jealousies" and allowed for the "mismanagement of funds."[36]

American observers attributed the emergence and organization of most large-scale anticolonial protest movements in Vietnam to the work of external agents. American diplomats and other observers wrongly contended that most incidents of anticolonial agitation in Vietnam during the interwar period were directed by Soviet or Chinese agents.[37] Drawing upon their derisive perception of Vietnam's permeability to foreign influence, however, Americans believed that any successful effort to surmount what they termed the "natural" obstacles to effective anticolonial nationalist organization had to come from exogenous forces. Just as the Chinese had shaped Vietnamese society some thousand years earlier, Americans argued, Marxism now found fertile ground in an imitative and unreflective society.[38]

World War II and the American Vision of Postwar Vietnam

Had it not been for the outbreak of the Pacific war in 1941, interwar American perceptions of Vietnam might best be viewed as little more than a historical curiosity. But as war with Japan heightened the geopolitical significance of French Indochina for the United States, the perceptual legacies of the interwar period came to inform wartime American policy toward Vietnam. By dislodging French colonial authority in Vietnam, Japanese wartime occupation of Indochina during World War II presented the United States with the opportunity to shape the creation of an independent postwar Vietnamese state.[39]

Just a few months after the Japanese attack on Pearl Harbor, President Franklin D. Roosevelt expressed doubts about French colonial rule in Indochina and initiated plans to place Vietnam under some form of international trusteeship. By mid-1942, discussions were under way within the State Department on possible forms of international supervision for the development of indigenous political and civil society in postwar Vietnam. From

1942 onward, Roosevelt vigorously pressed members of the wartime alliance to support trusteeship, winning the support of Chiang Kai-shek at the Cairo conference and of Stalin at Teheran.

Embedded in these wartime efforts were the central elements of the American construction of Vietnam that had emerged in the interwar period: unfavorable images of a "primitive" and "backward" Vietnamese society, vociferous critiques of French colonial policy in Vietnam, and an unwavering belief in the applicability of American institutions and values across cultures. These shared assumptions were essential in shaping the outlook of Franklin Roosevelt and his diplomatic advisers who framed the American vision of postwar Vietnam. If the Vietnamese were innately incapable of self-government and French rule had done almost nothing to correct these deficiencies, the dislocations of the Pacific war appeared to most wartime policymakers to offer the opportunity to arrest the stagnation of Vietnam's civil society by providing the Vietnamese with tutelage in superior American political, economic, and social models.

Three critical assumptions guided Franklin Roosevelt's wartime discussions of trusteeship and his vision of the postwar independent Vietnamese state: the failure of French colonial rule, Vietnamese inability to govern themselves, and the necessity of tutelage in American models to inform the slow process of Vietnamese development. Roosevelt saw French rule in Vietnam as a particularly egregious example of colonial failure. Acting solely in their own economic self-interest, Roosevelt argued on one occasion, the French had done nothing to "improve the lot of the people." In a meeting with Stalin at the Teheran conference in November 1943 where he won the support of the Soviet leader for trusteeship, Roosevelt told Stalin "that after 100 years of French rule in Indochina, the inhabitants were worse off than they had been before." It was a refrain that he would repeat many times in wartime discussions of trusteeship for Indochina with the Chinese, the British, and the Soviets.[40]

Like prior American observers of Vietnam, Roosevelt's hostility toward French policy in Indochina was not so much opposition to colonial rule itself as a sense that the French had not upheld the obligations of a colonizing power. In one of his earliest statements on French colonialism in Vietnam, Roosevelt observed in May 1942 that "the French did not seem to be very good colonizers." French conduct in Indochina, he suggested, "was at considerable variance with the general practice of Great Britain and the United States to encourage natives to participate in self-government to the limit of their abilities."[41] Roosevelt made explicit some ten months later the critical role French failure to reform Vietnamese society played in his assessment of Indochina's future, arguing "that we must judge countries by their actions and that in that connection we should all avoid any hasty promise to return French Indo-China to the French."[42]

Roosevelt's firm belief that the Vietnamese were unable to govern themselves also shaped his plans for trusteeship in Vietnam. In part, Roosevelt argued that the failed policies of the French had left the Vietnamese unprepared for self-governance. But his perception of Vietnamese political immaturity was also refracted through the same Orientalist prism that had guided the interpretations of interwar American observers of Vietnam. To Roosevelt, indigenous Vietnamese society was one that needed external improvement. His use of the word *naturally* to introduce his assertion that the Vietnamese were not yet ready for independence is instructive. Roosevelt's direct knowledge of indigenous Vietnamese society was extremely limited. In one of the few instances in which he described the Vietnamese, Roosevelt called them "people of small stature, like the Javanese and Burmese," who were "not warlike," a comment that recalls the negative interwar American perception of Vietnam as a feminized and weak society permeable to outside influence. [43]

Perhaps most important, Roosevelt's vision for postwar Vietnam was shaped by his certainty that American political, economic, and social models were essential in guiding Vietnam's gradual evolution toward independence and self-government. Roosevelt's argument that the success of American policy in the Philippines demonstrated that there was "no reason why it should not work in the case of Indo-China" illustrates his faith in the universality of American models and the ease of their cross-cultural transfer. It was a faith that Roosevelt expressed on many occasions. In a November 1942 radio address on American policy toward colonial territories, Roosevelt argued: "I like to think that the history of the Philippine Islands . . . provides . . . a pattern for the future of other small nations and peoples of the world. It is a pattern of what men of good-will look forward to in the future—a pattern of a global civilization."[44]

But Roosevelt's emphasis on the gradual evolution in the Philippines toward full independence suggests he saw the process of political and social development in Asia as a slow one. In Roosevelt's view, some forty-five years would elapse between the coming of American rule to the Philippines and independence. In 1900, Roosevelt argued, not only were the Philippines unprepared for independence, but a date could not "be fixed when they would be." Even after thirty-three years of efforts to build public works and provide education in "local, and finally, national governmental affairs," Roosevelt continued, both American and Philippine elites agreed in 1933 that the Philippines would not be "ready for independence" until 1945. As Roosevelt suggested in his November 1942 radio address, only after the "fulfillment of physical and social and economic needs" and tutelage in "the various steps to complete statehood" could the Philippines enjoy self-government.[45]

The lessons of the American experience in the Philippines often informed Roosevelt's presentation of a timetable for trusteeship in Vietnam. In conversations with Chiang Kai-shek and Stalin later in 1943, for instance, Roosevelt raised the Philippine analogy to suggest that trusteeship "would have the task of preparing the people for independence within a defined period of time, perhaps 20 to 30 years." As he told a group of reporters accompanying him on his return from the Yalta conference in 1945, "The situation there [in Indochina] is a good deal like the Philippines were in 1898. It took fifty years for us to . . . educate them for self-government."[46]

While President Roosevelt worked to advance his sometimes nebulous plans for international trusteeship in Indochina, members of the State Department's postwar policy planning staff began to craft their own proposals to prepare Vietnam for independence and self-government. The final recommendations of State Department postwar planners favored a more limited role for the United States in Vietnam's future development than the one envisioned by Roosevelt and reflected a somewhat different assessment of the geopolitical forces acting on Indochina. But their deliberations on the necessity for political, economic, and social change in Vietnam reflected the same assumptions that guided Roosevelt's plans for trusteeship as well as his insistence that American models could best guide Vietnam's future development.

The most sustained wartime discussion of Indochina policy in Washington took place in the Subcommittee on Territorial Problems, one of many committees in the State Department's vast postwar policy planning apparatus. In meetings held in November of 1943, the subcommittee took up the question: "Should Indo-China be restored to French sovereignty, with or without conditions?" Its regular membership was supplemented for these discussions with representatives from the Division of Far Eastern Affairs and several members of the policy planning research staff who were to serve as area specialists.[47] None of these specialists had particular training on Vietnam, but three of them—Kenneth P. Landon, Amry Vandenbosch, and Melvin K. Knight—did bring some knowledge of Southeast Asia and

French colonialism. Landon, a former missionary in Thailand for ten years, had recently joined the State Department's Office of Southwest Pacific Affairs. Vandenbosch, a University of Kentucky political scientist who was the leading American scholar on Indonesia, and Knight, an economic historian who had published works on French colonial rule in North Africa, were members of the research staff.[48]

The subcommittee initially took up a review and discussion of working papers prepared by Vandenbosch and Knight on French colonial practices in Indochina and the capabilities of indigenous peoples to govern themselves. In their critical assessments of French colonialism and Vietnamese society, which met with general agreement among the members of the subcommittee, Vandenbosch and Knight echoed the views of President Roosevelt and the thrust of interwar American commentary on Vietnam.[49] Most subcommittee members believed that French practices in Vietnam "fell short of the standards set by most of the other Western European powers." French bureaucracy in Indochina, Melvin Knight told the committee, was marked by "inefficiency" and "corruption".[50]

French economic policies in Indochina were also criticized as selfishly serving "the interests of the mother country" rather than "the colonies." Although Knight noted that efforts to build railroads and other public works projects "had contributed greatly to the prosperity of the area," he argued that indigenous peoples had seen little of the benefits as they were burdened by ever higher tax burdens to support the development of the French export economy. Recalling interwar American critiques of French tariffs in Indochina, Knight suggested that the injustices of French protectionist policies undermined both the development of the colonial economy and the improvement of indigenous economic welfare.[51]

Along with its critique of French administrative and economic practices, the subcommittee also shared the views of Roosevelt and interwar American observers of French Indochina that the Vietnamese were not yet ready for independence. Their perceptions of Vietnamese political immaturity, like those of FDR, were partially grounded in perceptions of the failures of French colonial rule. Amry Vandenbosch told the subcommittee that the French had made no effort to prepare the "natives" under their rule for self-government. Melvin Knight, revealing his own limited knowledge of colonial Vietnam, noted his surprise that "the native population had no knowledge of the French language and apparently did not have any understanding of France and the French."[52]

French unwillingness to prepare the Vietnamese for eventual self-government, subcommittee members argued, marked a sharp departure from what they believed to be prevailing colonial norms. Vandenbosch told the subcommittee that the "Dutch had done much better by their colonies than had the French" as "the Indonesians had made more rapid progress in the direction of self-government under the Dutch than had the populations of Indo-China under the French." A sense of the superiority of American policies in the Philippines also shaped the subcommittee perception that French failure to guide Vietnamese political development had violated a fundamental obligation of colonizing powers. Assistant Secretary of State Adolph A. Berle, one of the subcommittee members, observed that "self-government, as was indicated by our experience in the Philippines, de-pended . . . on the policy which the government pursued."[53]

Although it emerged more elliptically in their deliberations, the subcommittee's perceptions of Vietnamese political immaturity also rested upon interwar Orientalist assumptions of Vietnam as an inferior and imitative "little China." In a discussion of Vietnam's "backward political development," Melvin Knight told subcommittee members that "it was doubtful whether the Annamites . . . would have been any better off had the French not taken them in hand." Vandenbosch called French rule the "glue" that held Vietnam together, adding that "it would not be possible to conduct any government in this area" without it.[54] Many members of the subcommittee assumed the Chinese had dominated Vietnam's precolonial history and political traditions, reinforcing their sense that Vietnamese society lacked traditions of indigenous governance. Beyond "the patriarchal family which had been the dominating social force up to the time of the French arrival," Knight argued, there had been "no organized system of government . . . to establish public order." When asked if the Vietnamese had put up any opposition to French conquest, Knight, unaware of vigorous if unsuccessful Vietnamese efforts in the late nineteenth century to oppose the French presence, replied that "these areas had been protectorates of China and it was . . . from the Chinese that the main objections had come." Other committee members, such as Adolph Berle, believed the Vietnamese "were Chinese for the main part."[55]

The subcommittee's contemptuous perceptions of Vietnamese nationalism did not reassure them that Vietnam was capable of self-government. Members of the subcommittee expressed sympathy with the frustrations that had produced nationalist sentiment in Vietnam as they believed French colonial policy had done little to advance Vietnamese political or socioeconomic welfare. But their unfavorable perceptions of nationalist politics reinforced their sense that the Vietnamese lacked the abilities necessary to immediately govern themselves. As Vandenbosch told the subcommittee, the nationalist movement was "limited" to a small number of educated elites who were unable to win the support of the peasant masses. Nationalist leaders, he observed, were "split by factional strife and [an] inability to formulate a constructive program acceptable to a wide following." Reflecting the interwar American emphasis on the innate deficiencies of the Vietnamese character, Vandenbosch suggested that "violence, mismanagement of funds, dishonesty and petty bickering . . . characterized most of the nationalist organizations."[56]

Most policymakers in the State Department came to favor regional commissions, colonial charters, and annual reports rather than international trusteeship as the vehicle to effect their envisioned reforms of French colonialism and Vietnamese society. But the fundamental assumptions guiding their proposals, like Roosevelt's plans for trusteeship, were infused with sharp critiques of French colonialism, perceptions of powerful barriers within Vietnamese society to self-government, and a sense of the importance of American models for Vietnam's future political development. Taken together, the shared outlook that joined Roosevelt's advocacy of trusteeship and the deliberations of State Department planners marked the emergence of a fully articulated American vision of Vietnam and its postwar development.

For these American policymakers, U.S. prescriptions for the transformation of Vietnam marked a revolutionary break from the French colonial past. But this emerging vision of postcolonial Vietnam may not have proved as sharp a departure from prevailing colonial norms as American rhetoric sometimes suggested. The certainty that American approaches to colonial tutelage differed sharply from French ideas and practices obscured essential commonalities between French conceptions of themselves as "fathers" to their Vietnamese "children" and American self-perceptions of what one scholar has termed "benevolent assimilation."[57] Continuing American suspicions of Vietnamese capacities to assume the responsibilities of independence and the gradual process through which Americans believed their own ideals and institutions would animate political, economic and social change in Vietnam rested in part upon the racialist and nationalist premises common to the Orientalist discourse of most colonial powers.

In this very important sense, American plans to remake Vietnamese society remained subsumed and shaped by the wider Western ideology of empire. While the French *mission civilisatrice* and the rhetoric of French governor-generals that "a father does not abandon his children" may have been unconvincing to contemporary American observers, the unwavering assertion by wartime American policymakers that Vietnam needed a New Deal implied that Vietnamese society did not so much require independence as a new father in the American image.

Culture and the Origins of the Cold War in Vietnam

Wartime efforts to transform the American vision of Vietnam's future into policy encountered serious and ultimately insurmountable obstacles. By the spring of 1945, the United States had retreated from its efforts, abandoning plans for the international supervision of Vietnam's transition to independence and acquiescing to the return of the French to Indochina. Much of the existing historiography on American policy toward Vietnam after 1945, shaped by a focus on geopolitical imperatives of the Soviet-American rivalry, argues that the post–World War II period marked a sharp break with wartime plans for trusteeship as the United States came to support French efforts to reassert its control of Vietnam and wrest power from the Vietnamese Communists and their supporters in Moscow and Beijing. [58]

Yet the language and rhetoric through which American diplomats articulated policy toward Vietnam between 1947 and 1955 reveal the persistence and centrality of cultural forces in decision making. The American vision of Vietnam that had emerged during the interwar period and the Second World War—unfavorable perceptions of Vietnam, French colonialism, and Vietnamese nationalism, and the sense that Americans could do better—fundamentally framed the horizon of choices through which postwar American policymakers sought to meet the perceived challenges of the early Cold War period in Vietnam.

For many American diplomats in the late 1940s, communism posed a particular threat in Vietnam because of the same fundamental weaknesses in Vietnamese society identified by earlier American observers. Diplomatic reporting on Vietnam rendered the Vietnamese Communists as passive, uninformed, and vulnerable to outside control. "The Annamese are attractive and even lovable," William C. Bullitt told members of the State Department's Division of Philippine and Southeast Asian Affairs in 1947, "but essentially childish" It was a characterization that echoed U.S. consular reporting from Saigon and Hanoi. "Few of the Annamites are particularly industrious," the American consul in Saigon claimed, nor were they noted for their "honesty, loyalty or veracity." "Most Vietnamese," the American

vice-consul in Hanoi reported to Washington, "do not really understand"
the meaning of communism nor "would they care if it was thoroughly explained to them." Given the susceptibility of the Vietnamese to outside direction, most American diplomats darkly warned that the result of a French
defeat by Ho Chi Minh's forces would be a Vietnamese government "immediately run in accordance with dictates from Moscow." As Robert Fulson,
the American consul in Saigon in 1950, argued, "I, personally, am fully convinced that he [Ho Chi Minh] . . . is the head of the Soviet Fifth Column
in Indochina."[59]

By the late 1940s, these attitudes toward the Vietnamese Communists
had become almost unshakable. The ability of the Vietnamese to hold their
own against the French on the battlefield during this period, as well as a
series of Vietnamese military victories beginning in 1950, might have
prompted American observers to modify their conceptions of the Vietnamese as a backward, lazy, and incompetent people unable to rise to the challenges of constructing and maintaining an independent state.[60] American
perceptions of the Chinese Communists in this period did undergo something of a transformation. At the beginning of the Korean War, many American policymakers saw the Chinese as an "unaggressive, nonmechanical and
unmartial" people whose "comic opera warriors" were no match for sophisticated Western armies. But after Chinese intervention in the Korean conflict these images shifted quite radically. The Chinese became a fierce and
threatening mass whom Americans like General Douglas MacArthur, in a
speech before Congress in 1951, termed "excellent soldiers, with competent
staffs and commanders."[61]

A similar reassessment of the Vietnamese Communists never took place.
Despite considerable evidence of Vietnamese Communist military prowess
and strategic sophistication, American reporting was refracted through the
prism of unfavorable assumptions about the Vietnamese and the French
that had shaped the interwar and World War II visions of Vietnam and denied any real agency to the Vietnamese. American diplomats, military officers, and intelligence operatives emphasized the critical role of the Chinese
Communists and the French in commenting on the substantial victories
gained by the Vietnamese Communist military in a series of campaigns
launched against French positions near the Chinese border in the fall of
1950. Reflecting the persistence of the idea that Vietnamese society was
particularly permeable to external control, many analysts argued that Vietnamese military victories reflected Chinese Communist military direction
of its Vietnamese puppets and suggested continued Vietnamese permeabil-

ity to external control. An assessment prepared by the CIA in late December 1950, for example, claimed: "The Chinese Communists have been training and equipping large numbers of Viet Minh [Vietnamese Communist] troops in China and are supplying . . . considerable amounts of matériel. . . . [They] give the Viet Minh a distinct superiority over present French forces." American observers also suggested that Vietnamese victories provided further evidence of the failure of French policies in Vietnam rather than signs of Vietnamese capabilities. As another American military analysis of the border campaigns argued, the French "have failed in Indochina to provide adequate political and military leadership, to develop sound military plans, and to utilize properly their military resources."[62]

If the broader cultural assumptions that informed interwar American commentary and official wartime discourse on Vietnam made it impossible to view the DRV as anything other than a servile tool of Moscow and Beijing, they also shaped the response of the Truman administration to French moves beginning in 1947 to put forward Bao Dai as a credible nationalist alternative to Ho Chi Minh and the Vietnamese Communists. These French efforts, which became known as the Bao Dai solution, culminated in the Elysée Agreement of March 1949 through which the French pledged to grant eventual Vietnamese independence but continued to hold responsibilities for such essential matters as foreign relations and defense. The agreement did not specify a time when Vietnam would receive its independence; in the meantime it stipulated that Vietnam would join Laos and Cambodia as "associated states" within a broader French Union that was controlled from Paris. Bao Dai returned to Vietnam in July 1949 to lead this nominally independent Vietnamese state.

Throughout the late 1940s, many American diplomats were critical of Bao Dai and the terms by which the French intended to organize his new government. American diplomats judged Bao Dai and the figures who would form a part of his cabinet through the same unfavorable prism by which they had judged Vietnamese radicals. Bao Dai and his compatriots appeared to most American observers as naive and incapable of governance. As one diplomat commented from Hanoi in June 1948 on the installation of the Nguyen Van Xuan government in what was an initial phase of the Bao Dai solution, the "expressions on the faces of both the participants and the spectators gave one the impression that the whole thing was a rather poorly managed stage show, with the actors merely going through the motions. The appearance of Xuan, his stocky figure clothed in mandarinal robes which he quite obviously did not know how to handle, almost succeeded in introducing a note of low comedy. Gilbert and Sullivan came to mind."[63]

American diplomats were also critical of the continuing limitations the French appeared to impose on Vietnamese independence, reflecting a continued belief that American political ideals and institutions rather than French colonial models best served the development of the postcolonial state. In 1948 and 1949, many policymakers in Washington along with diplomats in Paris, Hanoi, and Saigon argued that French plans for the Bao Dai solution were a "continuation of parade puppets such as French have produced over past two years." They insisted that France should provide assurances for full Vietnamese independence "to dispel Vietnamese distrust of the French, split off adherents of Ho" and "materially reduce hostilities." Only "with concrete evidence that the French are prepared to implement promptly the creation of Vietnam as free state . . . with all the attributes of free state," Secretary of State George C. Marshall argued, could a potential Bao Dai government succeed. In the face of persisting French unwillingness to accede to these American views, many policymakers in 1948 and 1949 believed that the United States should not "be committed in any way to approval" of the Bao Dai solution until the French undertook a "liberal and enlightened policy." As late as December 1949, Secretary of State Dean Acheson continued to question the viability of a Bao Dai regime, arguing that the French must provide a "timetable leading to independence" and immediately show evidence of a mechanism to implement it.[64]

Although Chinese and Soviet diplomatic recognition of Ho Chi Minh's DRV prompted the swift American recognition of the French-backed Associated States government led by Bao Dai in February 1950, the ensuing partnership between Bao Dai, the French, and the United States was an increasingly fractious one. Tensions emerged almost immediately over the political, economic, and social construction of the new Vietnamese state, shaped in large measure by the assumptions of innate Vietnamese incapacities and the failures of French colonial policies that had guided American policymakers since the interwar period. Beginning in the fall of 1950, the Truman administration began to voice doubts about the capabilities "of the Vietnam Govt and its leadership to inspire support." A National Intelligence Estimate prepared by the Central Intelligence Agency (CIA) somewhat dryly suggested that Bao Dai's "qualities of leadership" were "hitherto unrevealed." Exercised about Bao Dai's extended absences from Vietnam and his indifferent leadership, Secretary of State Acheson instructed the American diplomats in Saigon to inform him that the "US Govt does not regard him as indispensable to contd existence and growth in stability" of Vietnam and that he must "display an unusually aggressive leadership and courage." Policymakers also expressed dissatisfaction with French policies, including "deficient French generalship" and colonial controls of the economy that deprived Vietnam of its "economic liberty." But a larger problem, most Americans agreed, was that "[c]oncessions to nationalist sentiment, leading toward full sovereignty for the Bao Dai Government, have been forthcoming so slowly and with such seeming reluctance on the part of the French" that the government had not "won a strong nationalist following in any quarter."[65]

Persistent dissatisfaction with the Bao Dai government and French policies toward Vietnam continued to shape American discussions of Vietnam after 1950. American diplomats maintained their unfavorable assumption of the Vietnamese capacity for self-government. Writing from Hanoi in 1952, one exasperated American diplomat characterized Bao Dai's new prime minister, Nguyen Van Tam, as a "puppet, 'cop' and sadist" and the rest of his cabinet as composed of "reactionaries, criminals, assassins" and "men of faded mental powers." As increasing amounts of American military and economic aid entered Vietnam, American scorn for French colonial methods and the assurance that American models would best guide the construction of the Vietnamese state also intensified and provoked bitter disputes between French and American officials on how American aid dollars in Vietnam would be spent.[66]

With the French defeat at Dien Bien Phu in 1954, the Eisenhower administration was free to pursue the realization of the American vision for Vietnam without interference from the French. As they did so, unfavorable perceptions of the Vietnamese and the certainty that American political ideals and institutions served as universal models continued to shape the perceptions of the newly organized Ngo Dinh Diem government in the mid-1950s. They faced their first test in what is known as the sect crisis in the spring of 1955. In late March 1955, the Cao Dai and Hoa Hao, sectarian religious movements with substantial popular support in southern Vietnam, joined with the gangsterlike Binh Xuyen organization that controlled Saigon's police force in a United Front to demand the reorganization of Ngo Dinh Diem's government. In the confrontational style that characterized many of Diem's responses to his political opponents, Diem refused to consider the Front's demands. Eisenhower's personal envoy in Vietnam, General J. Lawton Collins, acting on instructions from Secretary of State John Foster Dulles, insisted that the only solution to the crisis was for Diem to broaden his cabinet, but he despaired at Diem's intransigence. As Collins reported to Dulles in a cable from Saigon, "I told Diem that he must learn how to handle strong men who disagree with him since the knack of governing consists largely in that skill."[67]

For American observers, Diem's unwillingness to emulate American models of governance to solve the sect crisis was a continuing reflection of Vietnamese political immaturity. As Collins told Dulles, "We are not dealing here with fully rational, educated, unbiased Westerners. The Prime Minister of this country must know how to direct men who are highly venal, and who have not learned to subordinate their selfish interests for the good of the country." Many Vietnamese, he added "simply cannot handle these mental adjustments." To Collins and other American diplomats, these weaknesses were a result of the "oriental psychology" of Diem and his ministers.[68] Collins's assessment of Diem eventually prompted him to recommend to Dulles that the United States withdraw its support of the Diem government. Initially the Eisenhower administration resisted, but by late April of 1955 Dulles cabled the American embassy in Saigon to inform them of American plans to replace Diem and reorganize the South Vietnamese government. The policy reversal was short-lived. Faced with Diem's decisive victory in late April battles with United Front troops, Dulles once again shifted American policy, cabling the Saigon embassy in early May to reaffirm American support for Diem. It was a decision that would hold until Diem's ouster in an American-backed coup in 1963. But relations between the United States and Diem, like its partnership with the Bao Dai government before him and its relationship with the Nguyen Cao Ky and Nguyen Van Thieu governments in the 1960s, were fractious and strained, in large measure because of the culturally based assumptions that made up America's vision of postcolonial Vietnam.

✢   ✢   ✢

In 1920, as interwar observers unconsciously began to construct what would underlie American policy toward Vietnam after 1945, the Irish poet William Butler Yeats wrote:

> Things fall apart; the centre cannot hold;
> Mere anarchy is loosed upon the world. . . .
> Surely some revelation is at hand;
> Surely the Second Coming is at hand. . . .
> [N]ow I know

That twenty centuries of stony sleep
Were vexed to nightmare by a rocking cradle,
And what rough beast, its hour come round at last,
Slouches towards Bethlehem to be born?[69]

Many American diplomats in the interwar period shared the twin sensibilities embedded in Yeats's poem of revulsion at the chaos and carnage unleashed by the First World War and optimism that a better and more hopeful future was imminent. American diplomats, bankers, businesspeople, writers, and missionaries of the 1920s believed the time had come to assert a distinct vision of international order which should supersede the European norms that had produced the anarchical forces of war in 1914. Their efforts focused on transforming political, economic, and cultural relations in Europe.[70] But interwar commentary on Vietnam suggests this vision of a new Bethlehem also had an incipient global dimension whose center belied the lingering potency of the European order it sought to supplant. If the outlines of what Yeats might term the "rough beast" waiting to be born emerged in the interwar period, these expansive notions of international order continued to shape American efforts to define its global mission after 1945.[71]

To view American relations with Vietnam and other non-Western states solely through the geopolitical lens of the Cold War obscures such essential and broader cultural forces. American policymakers in the period after 1945 seldom paused to explicate the premises that lay behind their perceptions of the Vietnamese and the role they believed American models should play in the construction of a new political community in Vietnam. Nor were these ideas ever fundamentally challenged. The Orientalist and racialist discourse that framed American perceptions of Vietnam during the interwar period and World War II remained essential starting points for American policy toward Vietnam in the early Cold War period. Americans continued to classify and define the Vietnamese in a way that signaled American power and superiority. At the same time, the growing American sense of mission to remake Vietnamese society in its own image joined American postwar policy in Vietnam to interwar European colonial efforts to transform the immutable, stagnant, and primitive "oriental."

Vietnam, of course, was not alone among non-Western states in providing the central battleground for the Cold War. Yet much of the existing scholarship on American relations with Latin America, Africa, the Middle East, and South Asia after 1945, like that on Vietnam, also takes the Cold War rivalry with the Soviet Union as a primary explanatory variable.[72] As the Vietnamese case suggests, however, the political and economic dimension of American power only partially reveals the nature of U.S. perceptions and aims. Slouching toward Bethlehem, American Cold War diplomacy remained rooted in the persisting legacies of the European Orientalist tradition and the articulation of a cultural construction of international order.

Family Ties and Political Obligation
The Discourse of Adoption and the Cold War Commitment to Asia

CHRISTINA KLEIN

Crisis in Asia

IN THE EARLY YEARS of the Cold War, Asia "exploded into the center of American life," as James Michener phrased it in *Life* magazine.[1] Asia seized center stage in the nation's political consciousness around 1950, and it held that position until the last helicopter lifted off from the roof of the Saigon embassy in 1975. The first crisis came in 1949, when the United States "lost" China to Mao Zedong's Communists, and others piled up in quick succession thereafter. In 1950, civil war erupted in Korea when Stalin's proxies in the North attacked America's clients in the South. In 1954, the French lost their colonial hold on Indochina and ceded northern Vietnam to Ho Chi Minh, who promptly created the second Communist state in Asia. In 1955 and again in 1958, tensions with China threatened to turn into war over the offshore islands of Quemoy and Matsu. Throughout the decade, anticolonial revolutions and Communist insurgencies wracked Burma, Malaya, and the Philippines. It appeared to many that Moscow was preparing to grab all of Asia, and that Stalin would soon add millions more potential soldiers to the 800 million he already controlled in the Soviet Union, Eastern Europe, and China. When Americans looked East during the 1950s, they saw the majority of the world's population and a wealth of strategic resources teetering on the brink of Soviet control—and they felt the global balance of power in danger of tipping permanently against the United States.

As a result, Asia increasingly became the focal point of United States foreign policy. On the military front, the United States occupied Japan from the end of World War II until 1952, waged war in Korea from 1950 through 1953, built a string of military bases in Japan, Korea, and the Philippines, and after 1954 gradually replaced French forces in South Vietnam. At the political level, the United States entered into alliances with Japan, South Korea, Taiwan, the Philippines, South Vietnam, Cambodia, Laos, Thailand, and Pakistan, and launched nation-building projects in Japan and South Vietnam. Economically, the U.S. poured billions of dollars of foreign aid into Japan, South Korea, Vietnam, and Thailand, promoted private capital investment and corporate expansion throughout Asia, exported American-produced goods and services, and imported Asia's raw materials. This network of policies demanded an unprecedented level of political obligation to Asia on the part of the American public, which supported these efforts with their tax dollars and their blood.

In the early years of the Cold War, however, it was not at all clear that Americans would support these expansionist foreign policies. Although the Truman administration urged Americans to embrace their new global "responsibilities" and "commitments," it feared that many were unwilling to do so. George Kennan, director of the State Department policy planning staff and architect of Truman's containment policy, expressed doubts about American's capacity for "world leadership." He feared that Americans had lost their sense of "community" and were becoming "bewildered and anxious because they are trying to solve as individuals problems which they could solve only by a collective approach." Kennan worried that the expanding mass media exacerbated this social "disintegration." By rendering "recreation passive and vicarious rather than active and immediate," the press, radio, television, and movies provided only "a vast fog of recreational stimuli which demand nothing of the individual, develop nothing in him, and tend to atrophy his capacity for self expression." The result, potentially disastrous, was a "paralysis of the sense of responsibility and initiative."[2]

To help win consent for the global expansion of American influence, policymakers explained it in terms of collective security, which the National Security Council categorized as the "guiding principle" of U.S. foreign policy throughout the Cold War. Strictly speaking, collective security denotes a system of universal obligation, such as the United Nations, in which all nations agree to join forces and resist an act of aggression by any other state; it was thus a misnomer for the smaller regional alliances, such as the Southeast Asia Treaty Organization, that it was used to describe during the Cold War. Commentators have described collective security as a fundamentally "utopian" ideal that emphasized the nation's membership in a community and that entailed the "extension of the sense of social responsibility across the frontiers of the state." During the Cold War, policymakers consciously misapplied the concept as a way to harness collective security's utopian ideals to their foreign policies, and they described their allies in Asia not just as members of a "world community," but in affective terms as "best friends" and "family." Collective security, then, was not simply a foreign policy, but an ideological construct that underwrote the global expansion of U.S. power.[3]

While political leaders could cultivate a sense of obligation to Europe by appealing to a shared Western identity, they recognized that this sense of commitment would not extend automatically to the less familiar nations of Asia. In 1950, ambassador to India Loy Henderson expressed regret for this weaker sense of obligation yet deemed it "only natural," since "most people of the United States or their ancestors migrated from Europe." By pointing to the role of immigration in legitimating international allegiances, Henderson cast the problem of political obligation to Asia as a problem of family: Americans did not feel bound to Asians because they have rarely belonged to the same families and thus shared few of the ties of culture, religion, and language that families knit across oceans and generations. Henderson saw the family as an incubator of knowledge and he linked the absence of family ties to Americans' "deficiency of knowledge and understanding" about Asia, a lack that he deemed a serious "handicap" in the achievement of U.S. policy goals. In making this argument, Henderson raised, albeit inadvertently, the specter of American racism: Americans had few family ties to Asia in 1950 because the United States began restricting Asian immigration on racial grounds in 1875 and cut it off entirely in 1924. He thus identified a set of interconnected obstacles to a popular sense of political obligation to Asia: absent family ties, ignorance about Asia, and a history of racism.[4]

Over the course of the Cold War, Americans did commit themselves to Asia, as the host of political, military, and economic initiatives mentioned above indicates. My question is, given the obstacles that Loy Henderson identified, how was that obligation cultivated? How were Americans educated about Asia in such a way that they overcame their history of racial antipathies and lack of family ties? How was the paralysis of public responsibility that Kennan so feared surmounted? For diplomatic historians, the standard answer has been that the sudden outbreak of the Korean War jolted Americans into awareness of the Soviet threat to Asia and thus automatically generated the necessary support for expensive—and expansive—foreign policies. Coming from a cultural studies perspective, I want to focus

instead on the role of culture and look at how a national identity was constructed that figured Americans as protectors of Asia while denying any imperial aspirations.[5]

This essay argues that middlebrow culture played a crucial role in culti-
vating a sense of political obligation to Asia. Middlebrow producers took on
the task of educating Americans about Asia that Henderson and so many
others deemed essential; in the process, they imaginatively resolved the barriers to obligation that could not be so easily remedied in the political realm.
While the effects of seventy-five years of anti-Asian immigration laws could
not easily be undone, middlebrow culture symbolically created the family
ties with Asia that these laws had prevented from existing in reality. At the
same time, these cultural producers offered Americans ways to see themselves as participants in their nation's foreign policies and in the construction of a new arrangement of global power. My focus will be on three representative middlebrow texts: the *Saturday Review* magazine, a series of
Christian Children's Fund advertisements published in the *Saturday Review*, and the Rodgers and Hammerstein musical show and film *South Pacific*. By producing images and narratives of joint American-Asian families,
these texts imaginatively created and sustained the ties to Asia that many
Americans felt already committed them to Europe. They produced the cultural counterparts to the policies of collective security.[6]

Middlebrow Culture

As a "total war" of competing ideologies rather than a conventional one of
military battles, the Cold War demanded the marshaling of all the informa-
tional and educational resources of American society. Secretary of State
Dean Acheson, in a 1950 speech on U.S.-Asian relations, pushed the state
into the background and exhorted the press and other social and cultural
institutions to enlist themselves in the struggle for American hearts and
minds. He argued that the achievement of America's goals in Asia depended
on the extent to which the nation's foreign policies "grow out of the fundamental attitudes of our people," and he called on American social and cultural leaders to help express popular attitudes that would support America's
policy aims in Asia. If these attitudes "are to be effective," Acheson said,
they "must *become articulate* through all the institutions of our national
life . . . —through the press, through the radio, through the churches,
through the labor unions, through the business organizations, through all
the groupings of our national life" (emphasis added). Although he used a

passive verb construction so as to avoid calling for the production of outright propaganda, Acheson clearly urged social and cultural institutions to pro-mote—to render "articulate"—the premises of the Cold War in Asia.[7]

Middlebrow culture, more than any other stratum of cultural production, responded to the atmosphere of Cold War crisis and heeded Acheson's call. The term "middlebrow" came into wide use during the 1950s, most force-fully by the New York intellectuals who used it pejoratively to criticize what they saw as the dominant culture of the Cold War consensus. Dwight Mac-donald, warning that "there is slowly emerging a tepid, flaccid middlebrow culture that threatens to engulf everything in its spreading ooze," charged middlebrow cultural producers with abandoning the intellectual's role of social critic and embracing rather than challenging conventional wisdom. The New York critics condemned middlebrow culture for eschewing "au-thentic," individual experience and instead driving their audiences toward a predetermined response: through relentless editorializing and moralizing, and by manipulating audiences' emotions, middlebrow texts confined their viewers and readers to a single, "appropriate" response. Among the targets of such attacks were Pearl Buck, James Michener, the *Saturday Review,* and Rodgers and Hammerstein.[8]

Advocates of middlebrow culture didn't deny the charges levied against them, but rather recast them in the more positive language of public service and popular education. Joseph Wood Krutch defended the *Saturday Re-view,* one of the most frequently vilified middlebrow venues, on precisely these grounds: "And, of course, it will be labeled by the superior as middle-brow. What else can a journal devoted to criticism and education afford to be? After all, only middlebrows are interested in education. . . . Lowbrows don't want it and highbrows are certain they don't need it." In defending middlebrow culture as educational, Krutch brought to light what its critics never mentioned: that Buck, Michener, and other icons of middlebrow cul-ture provided information about America's relations with the rest of the world, especially Asia. At a moment when much high culture and criticism tended to focus on the psychological workings of characters or the formal qualities of the medium, middlebrow culture constructed a complex global imaginary that linked the United States to nations and peoples around the world.[9]

Recent cultural historians have charted an evolution in twentieth-century culture, from the socially and politically engaged art of the Depres-sion and war years to a postwar art that celebrated the individual, alienated artist. A focus on middlebrow culture disrupts this neat narrative: it contin-

ued many of the political concerns of New Deal and Popular Front art—
especially the utopian vision of multiracial community—but reoriented
them from a domestic to an international, specifically Asian, context and
enlisted them firmly within the Cold War's anti-Communist, rather than
antifascist, project.[10]

The Saturday Review

The *Saturday Review,* under the editorship of Norman Cousins, wholeheartedly took on the task of educating Americans about their new postwar
role as leaders of the "free world." A graduate of Columbia University's
Teachers College, Cousins embraced the role of public educator and continued the founding editor's vision of the magazine as "like a modern university." Sympathetic to Marxism in his youth, after the war Cousins rejected
communism, like so many other intellectuals, and devoted himself to the
cause of world federalism. During the immediate postwar years he used
the magazine to promote an internationalist stance, and editorials regularly
appealed to readers to reject isolationism, make a "mental reconversion to
a fundamentally changed world," and accept their "responsibilities towards
a bankrupt, starving world." To encourage this education in international
affairs, Cousins devoted a great deal of space to reviewing and promoting
the legion of popular and scholarly books on Asia published during the
decade.[11]

Cousins echoed Acheson's call for the mobilization of all levels of American society to produce the necessary popular "attitudes" toward Asia. The
magazine called upon cultural producers to help educate the country about
its new global obligations via "every form by which knowledge is transmitted, through the printed word, the spoken word, the movies, the radio, the
newspapers, the magazines." If America was to survive the revolutionary
upheavals in Asia, the average citizen needed to be re-formed by "all the
institutions which mold the individual: home, school, church, library, newspaper, radio, theatre must cooperate to educate him to the understanding
that he can no longer be a citizen only of his own country; he must become
a citizen of the world." Cousins identified "commitment" to other nations as
the attitude which Americans needed to adopt in order to ensure American
"world leadership and world influence."[12]

Over the course of the 1950s, that "commitment" took concrete form in
a network of metaphors centering around familial love. Appearing frequently in articles, editorials, and book reviews devoted to Cold War politics

under headlines such as "They Love Us for the Wrong Reasons," love emerged as a significant political language for U.S.-Asian relations. Cousins gave this political discourse of familial love its clearest expression in an editorial about a group of disfigured Hiroshima survivors, dubbed the Hiroshima Maidens, whom the *Saturday Review* arranged to come to the United States for free reconstructive plastic surgery. In quoting their nurse's explanation of why Americans are so generous to a former enemy, Cousins offered a vision of America bound to Asia through ties of familial love: "Suppose . . . that some people have a philosophy of life which enables them to regard all human beings as belonging to a single family. Even though they might not actually know each other, even though they might live thousands of miles apart, they might still believe in their closeness to one another and in their duty to one another. The same love that members of a family feel for one another can be felt by these people for all others, especially for those who are terribly in need of help."[13]

Cousins here follows Acheson's directive to help "articulate" the "attitudes" that will support American policies in Asia. Using plastic surgery as a metaphor for the "reconstruction" of postwar Japan, Cousins casts the relationship between the United States and Japan in the familial terms of one member feeling "love" and a sense of "duty" to another family member who is "terribly in need of help." Japan, as the most industrialized nation of Asia and the prime location for U.S. military bases, was the strategic Asian prize that had to be kept out of the Communist sphere at all costs. As such, it was the first Asian nation to which the United States committed substantial postwar aid, and the occupation and reconstruction of this former enemy was promoted as a model of American selflessness, as proof of America's benign global aspirations. In addition to figuring the economic aid of reconstruction, the familial rhetoric also works as a model for the postwar principle of collective security by constructing a "natural" relationship of hierarchy within identity. As in collective security arrangements that bound "free nations" together under the leadership of the United States, the family Cousins invokes casts the United States as the healthy and strong family member that can provide the "help" that others in the family need. Cousins's "single family" philosophy, which he ascribes to all Americans, subsumes the complex economic and security bases of the U.S.-Japan relationship to a purely personal affective bond that deflects all charges of American self-interest.

In addition to teaching the reader about the relationship between America and Japan, which it figures as a relationship between individuals rather than states, the editorial "solves" the problem of America's racially exclusive immigration laws. It frees the idea of "family" from its biological roots and dependence on physical proximity and makes it a function of sentiment instead. Asians do not actually have to enter the United States in order to become tied to Americans through family bonds; instead, the American family, and the love and aid that goes with it, can extend out beyond the borders of the nation. This idea of a multiracial, multinational family repudiates the history of American racism without the difficulties of putting that position into practice at the level of social and political policy.

In formulating and disseminating a discourse of familial love to explain and legitimate America's political commitment to Asia, the *Saturday Review* helped resolve a mini-crisis in American national identity. The rejection of isolationism that began with World War II demanded a reconceptualization of "America" as an international player. Henry Luce, when he urged that the United States intervene in Europe in 1941, articulated the need to redefine America in a way that reflected the nation's new global power: "As America enters dynamically upon the world scene, we need most of all to seek and to bring forth a vision of America as a world power which is authentically American and which can inspire us to live and work and fight with vigor and enthusiasm." After the war, many feared that Washington's emphasis on anticommunism at home and abroad was leading toward the deadend of a purely negative national identity. As Raymond Fosdick, Acheson's Far East consultant, phrased the problem in 1949: "it seems to me that too much thinking in the [State] Department is negative. . . . We are *against* Communism, but what are we *for*?"[14]

The struggle for the allegiance of Asia—and the need to win popular American support for that struggle—sent political, business, and cultural leaders scrambling to define "America" and what it stood for in such a way that it would appeal to Asians and Americans alike. In the process, they discovered that many of their traditional terms of self-definition did not internationalize very well: in 1951, the National Security Council dismissed "democracy" as a term of appeal for Asians because it had "too often been associated with the privileged white man and the memories of colonial exploitation"; in 1952 *Harper's* magazine found "capitalism" had become a dirty word that called up visions of nineteenth-century exploitation; and that same year *The American Scholar* rejected "individualism" and "private enterprise" as tired slogans that perpetuated a false impression of Americans as lonely, isolated materialists. Norman Cousins predicted in the *Saturday Review* that the nation's global power would remain "incomplete" until

Americans developed "a firm foundation of clearly defined national purpose reinforced by the great ideas and ideals which can inspire and animate not only our own people but the peoples of the world."[15]

In his *American Scholar* essay, which *Reader's Digest* condensed and reprinted, Bradford Smith offered a solution to this problem remarkably similar to the one put forth by Cousins in his Hiroshima Maidens editorial. "Teamwork" should be America's defining concept, he wrote, because "in its origin, 'team' means family. That comes close to expressing the too-long ignored, yet traditional, American ideal of men joined together in a common effort. If we can make men feel that this is what we stand for, we shall have offered an ideal to arouse those who now float apathetically in an eddy between two tides of ruthless collectivism and selfish individualism." In the pages of these middlebrow magazines, "family" emerged as a flexible concept that could communicate the ideals of "common effort" and shared interests in such a way as to appeal to Americans wary of expensive commitments and to Asians wary of Western imperialism. A broadly inclusive metaphor, it captured a range of internationalist positions, from support for the United Nations and world federalism to advocacy of collective security and free trade.[16]

By personalizing U.S.-Asian relations in terms of familial love, Cousins and other magazine writers reinforced Washington's efforts to repudiate accusations of imperialism and self-interest. Communist and nonaligned leaders regularly accused America of harboring imperial aspirations in Asia and of reducing Asians to pawns in its struggle with the Soviet Union. Washington sought to deflect these charges by emphasizing the *personal* roots of U.S. policy: Acheson, in a 1950 speech entitled "The Relations of the People of the United States and the Peoples of Asia," denied that American policy toward Asia was "a mere negative reaction to Communism," and insisted that "our real interest is in these people as people . . . not . . . as pawns or as subjects for exploitation." In making love the motivation for U.S. action around the world, Cousins likewise denied military force and economic coercion, and offered instead a depoliticized and demilitarized image of the United States that enabled Americans to exert power around the globe with a clear conscience.[17]

Far from anomalous, this intense personalization—and sentimentalization—of U.S. foreign policy was common political rhetoric throughout the 1950s, arising out of the Cold War need to delegitimize all systematic analyses based on collectivities such as class. The individual was seized upon as the constitutive feature that distinguished America from Communist states;

yet the individual had also become an emblem of Western selfishness, especially in the eyes of Asian intellectuals. The personalization of international relations continued the focus on the individual as the only legitimate unit for social and political analysis, but broadened it out to mean the relationship between individuals rather than the solitary and self-interested actions of a single individual. This sentimental discourse increased under Eisenhower, who insisted that "every international problem is in reality a human one" and promised that global tensions could be eased through the "sympathetic understanding of the aspirations, the hopes and fears, the traditions and prides of other peoples and nations."[18]

This sentimental discourse drew on well-worn traditions of imagining U.S.-Asian relations. Beginning in the mid-nineteenth century and continuing deep into the twentieth, American missionaries in China and Japan encouraged their fellow Christians to feel a bond of sympathy with Asia. Enormously influential in shaping political and popular attitudes, these missionaries did much to create the sense of a "special relationship" between the United States and China, which figured America as a defender of China against foreign aggression and an altruistic guide to democracy and modernization. Pearl Buck and Madame Chiang Kai-shek, along with other promoters of China from both the political left and right, carried these ideas into the 1930s and 1940s, when China suffered under Japanese attack and became America's ally in the Pacific war. So when Norman Cousins and others employed the language of love to talk about Cold War geopolitics, they tapped into a deep reservoir of positive American self-identification.[19]

Christian Children's Fund

In its mission to educate Americans about their new global obligations, the *Saturday Review* openly exhorted readers to accept their "responsibilities towards a bankrupt, starving world" and employed a metaphorical language of family that rendered morally indefensible any shirking of these obligations. The Christian Children's Fund, in a series of advertisements published in the pages of the *Saturday Review* during the same years that Cousins urged global commitment, took this educational and rhetorical strategy one step further. Fine-tuning the logic of familial love, the advertisements cast the relationship of Americans to Asians in parental terms and made an appeal to the reader to take a specific action that would commit them personally to Asia.

Presbyterian minister Dr. J. Calvitt Clarke founded the Christian Children's Fund (originally the China's Children Fund) in 1938 to raise money for Chinese children orphaned and rendered homeless by the Sino-Japanese war. Clarke's fund-raising innovation was to appeal to prospective American donors by representing their relationship with the children they sponsored as one of "adoption." Americans responded so enthusiastically to this logic of "adoption" that CCF was able to expand its operations throughout Asia, and the world, in step with the Cold War; by 1955 it had an annual budget of $1.8 million and supported children in fifteen Asian countries, many of them refugees from Communist China and North Korea.[20]

In the late 1950s, CCF and its "adoption" program garnered public acclaim as a successful strategy for fighting Asian communism. In 1957 and 1958, Clarke received awards and commendations from the anti-Communist governments of Japan, Taiwan, and South Korea. In 1956, Universal Pictures released *Battle Hymn,* a Korean War film based on the true story of Air Force colonel Dean Hess, who, as the Communists moved in on Seoul in 1950, evacuated nearly one thousand CCF orphans to an off-shore island, whereupon CCF staff arranged their "adoption." The film was followed in 1957 by the publication of John C. Caldwell's *Children of Calamity,* an organizational history of CCF that included a foreword by Pearl Buck, and in 1961 by a second history, Edmund Janss's *Yankee Si!,* which CCF sent out to each sponsor. Janss dedicated his book "To those who have helped make America loved" and emphasized CCF's role in stemming the spread of Asian communism. Describing "adoptees" as "tiny ambassadors" for America, Janss compared CCF sponsor dollars to the billions of dollars in military aid then pouring into Southeast Asia and remarked that "[t]he best investment dollar-for-dollar, however, will be the tangible love sent by Americans who 'adopt' Asia's babies." This public promotion of CCF efforts helped make Clarke's strategy of "adoption" a familiar way for millions of Americans to imagine their relations with Asia.[21]

CCF's print advertisements were their most significant pedagogical device: they appealed to the reader to take a specific action that would commit them personally to Asia. Published in the pages of magazines, they seared the idea of "adoption" into millions of Americans' minds as an effective means to fight the Cold War. Written by Clarke, the advertisements kept pace with the changing focus of the Cold War, offering children from Taiwan, Korea, and India to American readers. Instead of merely *feeling* a familial tie to the people of Asia, which Cousins's editorials encouraged, these advertisements urged readers to act on their feelings and become "parents" to an Asian child.

A typical advertisement from 1952 works by first provoking the reader's anxiety about communism and then offering parenthood as a means to defuse it (Fig. 1). A photograph of a middle-aged white man and woman holding a "hunger limp" Indian baby dominates the advertisement; beneath the caption "Am I My Brother's Keeper?," Dr. Clarke takes the reader on a three hundred-word, first-person tour through the trouble spots of the Cold War—India, Korea, Japan, Germany. Clarke figures the menace of communism, and the failures of democracy, in terms of decimated families: in Japan, orphanages are full of GI babies "deserted by their American fathers"; among Korean refugees, "[t]here is hardly a family not broken, fathers taken prisoner or shot, mothers abused and carried off or left dead behind a broken wall"; among refugees from East Germany, "[f]ew families escaped intact. Children, parents, wives and husbands shot down or dragged off to labor camps." The logic undergirding this advertisement, and much of CCF's promotional material, is that family breakdown, whether caused by Communists, war, or poverty, leads to hungry children, hungry children are susceptible to Communist promises of a better future, thus hungry children threaten the security of Americans. As Clarke concludes in the last line of his tour, "The hungry children of the world are more dangerous to us than the atom bomb."[22]

The advertisement invokes the twin paralyzing anxieties of the Cold War—communism and the atomic bomb—only to offer an easy solution. It concludes by inviting the reader to "adopt a child . . . for ten dollars a month" in any of the fourteen countries in which it runs orphanages. The advertisement thus resolves imaginatively what cannot be so easily resolved politically: while the average individual can't protect America from the atom bomb, the advertisement suggests that, for a modest sum, he or she can save Asia. The advertisement invites the reader to save himself from atomic war, and the child from communism, by extending the American family out into the world. The photograph of the white couple holding the starving child makes this solution easy: it offers a ready-made subject position and visual model of global responsibility which the reader can step into through the simple act of writing a check.

An advertisement from 1954 employs a slightly different strategy (Fig. 2). Under a menacing headline—"This Picture is as DANGEROUS as it is PITIFUL!"—it presents a picture of a stern, well-fed Asian man holding an emaciated, naked Asian child on his knee. The text warns that this image—not just the hungry child alone—"threatens to take from us all that we hold most dear—life, liberty and pursuit of happiness." Like the earlier adver-

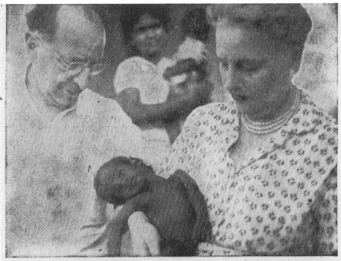

Am I My Brother's Keeper?

IN INDIA I asked myself this question when I saw thousands of homeless sleeping in the streets of Calcutta and Bombay. When I saw half starved children and "hunger limp" babies like the one above.

IN KOREA (My schedule did not permit me to examine the 28 orphanages in which CCF assists Korean children). There is only ugliness and misery in Korea. Wandering refugees, little ragged children, destroyed homes. There is hardly a family not broken, fathers taken prisoners or shot, mothers abused and carried off or left dead behind a broken wall. A destroyed country of rubble, rags, disease, hunger and human misery.

IN JAPAN in the Elizabeth Saunders Home for GI babies, deserted by their American fathers, and 18 other CCF orphanages, all over-crowded.

IN GERMANY where I saw some of the several million people who are refugees in their own country. Those who escaped from East Germany won their freedom at great cost. Few families escaped intact. Children, parents, wives and husbands shot down or dragged off to labor camps. Those who escaped are destitute. They can't find work and have inadequate food and shelter.

The sick little children of India, the wandering orphans of Korea, that flaxen haired German miss, who saw her father killed, does God charge me with their plight? I have returned from overseas with the realization that the Communists care enough to make very successful capital of democracy's failures and with the strong conviction that we Americans can not close our eyes or stop our ears to the cry of a hungry child anywhere in the world — black, brown, yellow or white. The hungry children of the world are more dangerous to us than the atom bomb.

CCF assists children in 97 orphanages in the following countries: Borneo, Brazil, Burma, Finland, Formosa, Indonesia, India, Italy, Japan, Jordan, Korea, Lapland, Lebanon, Malaya, Okinawa, Pakistan, Philippines, Puerto Rico, United States and Western Germany. You can adopt a child in any of these countries for ten dollars a month and the child's name, address, picture and information about the child will be furnished. Correspondence with the child is invited. Smaller gifts are equally welcome. God sees not the coin but the heart that gives it.

For information write to:

Dr. J. Calvitt Clarke
CHRISTIAN CHILDREN'S FUND, INC.
RICHMOND 4, VIRGINIA

FIG. 1. "The hungry children of the world are more dangerous to us than the atom bomb." Courtesy Christian Children's Fund.

This Picture is as DANGEROUS as it is PITIFUL!

The ominous significance of this picture is that it threatens to take from us all that we hold most dear—life, liberty and the pursuit of happiness. Not only in South Korea, where this picture was taken, but in India and other *democratic* countries, millions awoke this morning hungry. They will be hungry all day and will go to bed hungry. To bed?—Millions of them after working all day will sleep in the streets at night. They have no home. They can't even afford a few feet of space in some vermin infected shack without sanitary arrangements of any kind.

The road to communism is paved with hunger, ignorance and lack of hope. Half of the school age children living in the world today do not attend school. If they did, they would be too hungry to study. What does a man, woman or child, without a roof over their heads, with no personal belongings whatever, save the rags wrapped around them, tormented with the inescapable lice, always hungry and above all facing only hopeless tomorrows—what do such have to lose if they listen to communist propaganda? Their resentment may any day ignite the spark that will explode the hydrogen bomb.

The misery of human beings is the most powerful weapon in the hands of the communists. It just can't go on. The world can't exist half stuffed and half starved. The rumble that is growing in intensity around the world is not the rumble in overfed stomachs. It is the fearsome and dangerous rumble in the empty stomachs of the world.

Christian Children's Fund did something about the boy in the picture. It fed him and saved his life and will give him schooling and teach him a trade. It assists children in 170 orphanages in the 27 countries listed below. Established in 1938, it is efficient, practical, economical, conscientious and Christian. It helps children regardless of race, creed or color.

For Information write: Dr. J. Calvitt Clarke

CHRISTIAN CHILDREN'S FUND, INC.
RICHMOND 4, VIRGINIA

☐ YES! I want to do what I can to help the starving, homeless children of the world. I wish my gift to be used in the country circled below:

Borneo Brazil Burma Finland
Formosa France Free China
Greece Hong Kong India
Indochina Indonesia Italy
Japan Jordan Korea Lapland
Lebanon Macao Malaya
Mexico Okinawa Pakistan
Philippines Puerto Rico
United States Western Germany

Enclosed is my gift of $_____
I would also like to make a regular contribution of $_____ per month, for one year. _____

☐ I am interested in your work. Please send me additional information

NAME_____

ADDRESS_____

CITY_____ ZONE_____

STATE_____

REMEMBER: All Gifts Are Deductible From Income Tax

FIG. 2. "The misery of human beings is the most powerful weapon in the hands of the communists." Courtesy Christian Children's Fund.

tisement, this one links starving children to communism—"The road to Communism is paved with hunger, ignorance and lack of hope"—and nuclear war—"Their resentment may any day ignite the spark that will explode the hydrogen bomb." The text under the photograph interprets the image for the reader by identifying "the misery of human beings" as "the most powerful weapon in the hands of the Communists." Together, the image and text invoke the threat that an Asian man—a Communist—will assume the paternal obligation of feeding this starving child and thus manipulate him into accepting communism. Like the earlier advertisement, this one also appeals to the reader to step into the world of the photograph, only this time to displace the Asian man as parent to the Asian child.[23]

The Christian Children's Fund program of "adoption" invited Americans to participate in the Cold War struggle for Asia in a number of different ways. The advertisements conclude on a note of vigorous assent and a pledge to take action: at the bottom of the page, the advertisement offers a box for the reader to check off that says "YES! I want to do what I can to help the starving, homeless children of the world," with a blank space to fill in for the amount of money the reader will include. CCF newsletters and books were full of stories of individuals making quiet, yet heroic, efforts to save children from poverty, starvation, and the consequences of communism. Adopting a child made the reader a participant in this large, dramatic historical struggle, and because CCF asked the sponsors to support the child for at least a year, adoption entailed a commitment rather than just a gesture.

In one sense, the advertisements figure participation in terms of consumption: for ten dollars a month, the reader can purchase a child, protection from communism, and relief from a sense of political powerlessness. John C. Caldwell captures this sense of adoption as commodity consumption in his book *Children of Calamity*, in which he describes the cables CCF headquarters in Virginia regularly sent to the Hong Kong office. They sound like nothing so much as department store back orders: "Need 4,000 more children!," "Rush me 500 orphans," "Need 200 Koreans, 10 Japanese mixed-blood, 50 Chinese, 10 Arabs." The advertisements make purchasing a political act, and purchasing the idea of the family becomes a mechanism for creating ties between the United States and Asia.[24]

The "adoption" process also opened a route to participation in terms of education. In checking the "YES" box and "adopting" a child, the reader expressed a willingness to learn more about the country in which the child resided. The exchange of information played an important role in the "adoptive" relation. American "parents" and their "adoptees" exchanged personal narratives, letters, and photographs, thereby fostering an individual bond of intimacy that incorporated the Asian child, emotionally and textually, into the American family. This new family thus became a two-way site of education: the parents learned about the misery that communism bred, and the child learned about the material abundance and personal generosity that the free world offered. In the absence of widespread awareness about Asian history, culture, and language, the mechanism of the adoptive family worked to produce knowledge about a part of the world that Washington saw as the primary arena of the Cold War.

Finally, to "adopt" a child was to participate in U.S. foreign policy, as the State Department recognized when it created the Advisory Committee on Voluntary Foreign Aid to oversee CCF and other similar programs. At the most abstract level, one can see the donation of funds—the unequivocal "YES!"—as an affirmation of willingness to fight communism in Asia. CCF's emphasis on feeding the hungry also meshed with the logic of American food aid to Asia. When India faced widespread famine in 1950, Ambassador Henderson urged Washington to send shipments of wheat, arguing that it offered not only a way to communicate America's concern for the people of Asia (particularly important at a time when the United States was under attack for killing Asians in Korea), but also an opportunity to depict the United States as a nonimperial nation motivated by generosity and not just anticommunism. CCF advertisements reinforced the logic of this aid effort and provided an opportunity for Americans to participate in it at the individual level.[25]

The participation that CCF offered linked pleasure to political obligation by opening up the idea of the family to anyone who was interested. At a time when the nuclear family was privileged throughout American culture as the ideal form of personal relations, and when people who did not marry and have children were stigmatized as selfish or perverted, the opportunity to "adopt" a child offered parenthood to all those excluded from this family ideal. And indeed, testimonials on the pleasures of "parenthood" by childless and unmarried individuals formed a staple of CCF literature.[26]

South Pacific

Hollywood in the 1950s picked up on the pervasiveness of adoption as a device for representing American relations with Asia. Korean War combat films such as *Steel Helmet* (1951), for instance, largely followed the estab lished formula of the World War II combat film, with their primary generic innovation being the hero's adoption of a Korean child as proof that he has accepted his responsibilities in the war. One of the most popular films to use adoption to explain U.S.-Asian relations during the 1950s was *South Pacific* (1958). *South Pacific*, of course, was not explicitly about the Cold War. Yet its narrative readily invites comparison with the evolution of political relations among the United States, France, and Indochina in the years after 1949. Collapsing past and present, the film used World War II to narrate the U.S. assumption of French colonial obligations in Indochina, from the initial infusions of economic assistance in 1949 to the gradual U.S. replacement of French forces after their defeat at Dien Bien Phu in 1954.[27]

Cultural critics of the 1950s often cited Rodgers and Hammerstein's *South Pacific*, like the *Saturday Review*, as the epitome of middlebrow culture, mocking its "orotund sentimentalities" and "liberalistic moralizing." Like the Christian Children's Fund, *South Pacific* was advertised in the *Saturday Review*, and like the magazine and the advertisements it shared the logic of family ties as a tool to imagine America's postwar relations with Asia. *South Pacific* took Cousins's overarching rhetoric of familial love and the Christian Children's Fund's particularized figure of the adoptive parent and narrativized them, put them into motion across time and space, and expressed them through song and dance—and as a result disseminated them to millions more Americans than the *Saturday Review* or the Christian Children's Fund could ever hope to reach. *South Pacific* educated Americans by telling them a story about fully articulated characters whose anxieties and contradictions are raised and explored before being resolved in a coherent, unifying ending.[28]

Much of *South Pacific*'s significance derives from its phenomenal popularity. James Michener wrote *Tales of the South Pacific* in 1945 while stationed as a naval officer in the New Hebrides, and in 1947 the collection of sketches won the Pulitzer Prize for fiction. In 1949, Rodgers and Hammerstein turned the stories into the musical show *South Pacific*, which ran on Broadway for five years, won the Pulitzer again for drama, toured nationally and internationally for several years more, and continued for decades as a staple of regional, community, and high school theater productions. The show's original cast album, one of the first popular 33⅓ rpm long-playing records, sold one million copies and held the number one position on the charts for sixty-nine weeks, while the sheet music sold an additional two million copies. The show proliferated throughout other media as well: magazines and newspapers published interviews with the stars, *Life* gave it a big

photo spread, and the new medium of television broadcast a Sunday mati-
nee live. Even before the movie rights were sold, *South Pacific* earned
profits exceeding $5 billion. In 1958, Twentieth Century–Fox released
South Pacific as a film musical which garnered three Academy Award nomi-
nations and won for best sound. The soundtrack album, displacing the original cast album, stayed in the U.S. top ten for two years, including fifty-four
weeks in the number one spot, and became the biggest-selling soundtrack
of the decade with sales of five million. What these figures show is that from
1949, the year the United States "lost" China to the Communists and began
financially supporting the French war in Indochina, through the end of the
1950s, when the United States was nation-building in South Vietnam to the
tune of $150 million a year, *South Pacific* saturated American culture
through a multitude of media, educating millions of Americans about their
roles and responsibilities in Asia.[29]

Like Norman Cousins, *South Pacific*'s author was well suited to take on
this role of popular educator. A 1929 graduate of Swarthmore College,
James Michener earned a master's degree in education from Colorado State
College of Education and began, but never finished, a Ph.D. program at
Harvard's Graduate School of Education. He devoted the better part of the
1930s to teaching English and social studies to high school students and
publishing articles in education journals, with a year spent lecturing at Harvard. In 1941, he left academia to become an editor of textbooks at Macmillan, a job to which he returned after his wartime stint in the Pacific.[30]

The success of *South Pacific* turned Michener into the nation's foremost
popular expert on Asia. It gave him the financial freedom to write full-time,
and he spent the 1950s producing an abundance of articles, essays, short
stories, and novels about Asia, a number of which became successful movies. Critics hailed Michener for his "educational entertainment" and applauded him for helping to dispel the dangerous ignorance about Asia.
Newsweek announced in 1954—the year that the United States began replacing the French in Vietnam—that "never has there been such need as
now for Americans to know their Asiatic enemies and respect their Asiatic
friends." It went on to praise Michener as the foremost popular interpreter
of Asia to Americans and singled him out as the man responsible for "intro-
duc[ing] the world of the trans-Pacific into almost every American home."
When President Ford awarded Michener the Medal of Freedom in 1977,
he commended him as an "author, teacher and popular historian" who had
"expanded the knowledge . . . of millions." Michener's biographer captured
his appeal to the education-minded middlebrow audience when he de-

scribed Michener's readers: "Trying to improve themselves, if even pain-lessly, Middle Americans have likened Michener's books to a seminar, and read them as a way of continuing their education. In turn, Michener has become one of the most cherished teacher-authors of all time."[31]

In his role as popular educator, Michener largely promoted Washington's views on Asia throughout the 1950s. Over the course of the decade he wrote a novel promoting the official reasons why Americans should fight in Korea (*The Bridges at Toko-Ri,* 1953, which the *New Republic's* critic dismissed as sounding too much like a Voice of America broadcast), altered his first *Reader's Digest* article on the Korean War to suit Defense Department pro-paganda needs, narrated a State Department–sponsored TV series titled *Appointment in Asia,* and at the behest of Washington helped weed out suspected Communists from the Asia Foundation, a private organization that sent aid to Asia. He accepted numerous invitations from State Depart-ment officials, ambassadors, and members of foreign governments to visit and write about their specific concerns in Korea, Japan, Thailand, and other Southeast Asian nations, to the extent that, according to his biographer, "it was difficult at times to separate Washington's interests from Michener's work." Praising his combined literary and political efforts, Hawaii congress-man Daniel Inouye described Michener in 1962 as "one of our most effec-tive anti-Communist weapons in the worldwide struggle." Michener himself credited America's postwar expansion with creating his audience: "I pub-lished my books at the precise time when Americans were beginning to look outward at the entire world rather than inward at themselves. . . . Had I come along fifty years earlier, when America was isolationist, I doubt if any-one would have bothered much with my writing."[32]

As one of the most ubiquitous narratives about Americans in Asia pro-duced during the postwar years, and as the first installment of Michener's cultural-educational empire, *South Pacific* bears a closer look. The show and the movie (the latter a faithful adaptation of the former) focus on two love stories culled from Michener's collection of nineteen sketches. The narrative revolves primarily around Ensign Nellie Forbush, an enthusiastic young nurse from Little Rock, Arkansas, stationed in the South Pacific dur-ing World War II. Nellie falls in love with Emile De Becque, a wealthy, sophisticated, and considerably older French plantation owner. After ac-cepting his proposal of marriage, she discovers to her horror that he had previously been married to a Polynesian woman and fathered two children, thereby confronting Nellie with what she calls in the sketches a "nigger" problem: "Emile De Becque had lived with the nigger. He had nigger children. If she married him, they would be her step-daughters." Feeling that "a man who had lived openly with a nigger was beyond the pale," she calls the marriage off. Only when De Becque embarks on a life-threatening mission for the American military does she realize her love for him is more powerful than her prejudice, and when he returns alive she welcomes him back and accepts his children as her own.[33]

The subplot follows a similar racial line and tells the story of Joe Cable, a Marine lieutenant who falls in love with the beautiful daughter of Bloody Mary, an entrepreneurial Tonkinese with an eye out for an American son-in-law. Sharing Nellie's racial antipathies, Cable initially refuses to marry Liat; although love eventually overwhelms his racism as well, he dies on the mission with De Becque before he can marry her.

As this brief synopsis indicates, the narrative goes to great lengths to repudiate American racism, and Rodgers and Hammerstein went so far as to include a musical number, "You've Got to Be Taught," that condemns racism as a perverted pedagogy. Antiracism occupied a contradictory place in the Cold War political landscape, serving as a marker of both Communist sympathies and dedication to the anti-Communist cause. On the one hand, anti-racist activism indicated a continued adherence to 1930s-era radical politics and was used by HUAC investigators as evidence of subversive beliefs. On the other hand, the disavowal of race prejudice became a staple of official Cold War discourse, necessitated by close international attention to America's racial segregation, lynchings, and insults to dark-skinned visiting foreign dignitaries. Policymakers found that these incidents provided fuel for Communist charges of American imperialism and they feared that they would delegitimize the United States in the eyes of those nonwhite, decolonizing nations whose allegiance the United States was trying to gain. Secretary of State Dean Acheson went so far as to assert that "racial discrimination in the United States remains a source of constant embarrassment to this Government in the day-to-day conduct of its foreign relations; and it jeopardizes the effective maintenance of our moral leadership of the free and democratic nations of the world." The Truman administration viewed racial discrimination as so detrimental to its foreign policies that by 1948 it began filing amicus curiae briefs in support of civil rights cases before the Supreme Court.[34]

In *South Pacific*, love stands as the only force capable of eradicating racism. Not all kinds of love have equal value, however. Within the film's logic, romantic love conquers racism and leads to its renunciation, but only parental love offers a model of stable interracial relations. Endorsing parental over sexual love as the preferred affective relation between Asians and Americans, the film kills off Cable before he can marry Liat, while clearing all obstacles to Nellie's love for her Asian stepchildren. Like the Christian Children's Fund advertisements, the film offers parental love as a way to assert cross-racial alliance, while containing the racial anxieties of miscegenation or potentially inverted racial hierarchies provoked by interracial marriage. Parenthood maintains the racial hierarchy by mapping racial differences onto the natural hierarchy of age; marriage, as a more egalitarian relationship between adults, runs the risk of leveling that hierarchy—or, should the nonwhite partner seize the upper hand, inverting it altogether.

South Pacific's final scene enacts the logic of adoption as political obligation. The film culminates in a scene of family formation in which Nellie accepts De Becque's Asian children as her own, a scene easily recognizable from Christian Children's Fund advertisements as a primal act of Cold War obligation. Visualizing a structure of alliance in which French and American characters join together as partners in charge of dependent Asians, this last scene narrativizes America's emerging role in Southeast Asia: it presents an innocent young American stepping awkwardly but eagerly into a French imperial outpost and becoming parent to Asians who are biologically and culturally the offspring of an aging French colonialist.

Set at De Becque's plantation, the final scene presents Nellie, having overcome her racism, nervously awaiting De Becque's return so she can tell him she will marry him and become mother to his children. The scene opens with Nellie looking out over the ocean with the children and pointing out to them all the different kinds of American ships as they steam off to attack the Japanese. The historical moment is precise—the film has made clear that this attack represents the turning point of the Pacific War, the moment when the United States launches the offensive that will lead to Japanese defeat. The scene thus presents us with the origins of America's postwar domination of Asia and the Pacific. Yet it also represses this military power as soon as it invokes it: even as Nellie describes the military capabilities of each ship, the camera turns away from them and Nellie tells the children that the soldiers will now be largely absent from the island.

As part of this deflection away from militarism, Nellie exercises greater authority in this scene as a mother than she has in the rest of the film as a military officer and nurse. No longer a "knucklehead," as she described herself earlier, Nellie acts for the first time with an air of responsibility. After commanding the children to do her bidding even in her absence, Nellie puts a hand on each one's head and "playfully" forces them into their seats

FIG. 3. Nellie Forbush and the children. *South Pacific*, 1958. Courtesy Museum of Modern Art/Film Stills Archive.

at the lunch table. Yet even as she uses physical force, she justifies it with an appeal to love: "Now you have to learn to mind me when I talk to you, and be nice to me, too. Because I love you . . . very much." Repudiating her racism and declaring maternal "love" in its place, Nellie steps into a position of colonial power and for the first time exerts "moral leadership"—backed up with physical force—over France's Asian progeny.

De Becque soon returns and joins them at the table, thereby completing the family circle. In her role as mother and moral leader, Nellie gathers the French and Asian characters around her in a relation of sustenance and unity. Enacting the logic of foreign aid in the largest sense, Nellie bestows her healthy sexuality upon the graying De Becque in a transfusion of life-giving energy. On the more literal level she does precisely what the Christian Children's Fund advertisements urged readers to do: she feeds hungry people, doling out soup from a generous tureen to her Asian dependents and her French partner. The final shot visualizes the principle of collective security as it shows Nellie and De Becque joining hands and encircling and containing their small Asian children as they gaze lovingly into each other's

FIG. 4. Nellie Forbush, Emile DeBecque, and the children. *South Pacific, 1958.*
Courtesy Museum of Modern Art/Film Stills Archive.

eyes. Finalizing the film's drawn-out process of family formation, this shot
presents a vision of cross-racial, cross-national commitment made in terms
of the family. This family represents the ideal of America's post-1949 aid
programs to Indochina: it invigorates an aging and weary France, gives provincial America access to France's colonial-based wealth and prestige, and
maintains the childlike Asians in a condition of security and dependence.

The final shot of the film extends into the Pacific at large the scene's
vision of a French-American-Indochinese family alliance. Lingering on the
tableau of the French and American parents containing and protecting their
children within their arms, the shot continues in a long, arcing crane shot
that pulls up and back to conclude on a vista of a Pacific seascape. In contrast to the opening shot of the scene, in which a similar ocean view was full
of American warships, this patch of Pacific is free of a military presence,
as if the family had not only superseded the military but also rendered it
unnecessary. The magnificent upward sweep of the shot suggests not just
the success of the family formation that has just been completed, but also
its expansive potential and its broad applicability throughout the Pacific.

The difference between the opening and closing shots of the Pacific in the scene works to suggest a historical development in the American presence in the Pacific—formerly based on military power, it will now be exercised through "familial" values of nurturing aid and mutual protection. Pushing military power literally and figuratively into the background, the scene visualizes the logic of Cousins's editorials: familial love, not global military power, explains America's postwar presence in Asia.

At the same time that this scene figures the pre-1954 Franco-American alliance in Indochina, it also envisions the post–Dien Bien Phu supersession of France's colonial position by America. For although De Becque stands as an equal parent in this family partnership, and as the father perhaps even the head of the family, it is clearly Nellie who, by virtue of her youth and energy, will raise the children and guide them into adulthood. The children may run to greet their father at his return, but it is Nellie who commands their obedience. The book makes Nellie's future even clearer by showing De Becque wooing Nellie with a vision of the future in which she is wealthy and America is powerful. "I have a lot of money saved," he tells her. "I will die before you, Nellie, since I am older. . . . But if you like the islands then, you will have no need to fear hunger or poverty. And if you have children, they will be growing up. By that time there will be an American base here. Your little girls will have fine American young men to choose as husbands." De Becque seduces Nellie by offering her a vision of a Pacific in which America has wealth and prestige, a vision he makes even more appealing by casting in terms of an all-white, all-American family. Instead of the European colonial heritage of racial mixing, Nellie's adoption of De Becque's Asian children becomes merely a stepping stone on the way to extending the *real* American family across the globe.[35]

Nellie's transition from nurse to mother presents domesticity as an expansionist ideology that gave women a role in the nation's assertion of global power. Her trajectory enacts in miniature the postwar migration of millions of women out of military and defense jobs and back into the home. Nellie joined the Navy to escape the confinement of Little Rock and marriage, and her energy and desire to have new experiences are potentially rebellious. She does indeed escape Little Rock, but not domesticity—the film redirects her energies into the service of the nation by channeling it into a domestic sphere that encompasses the world. By giving Nellie—as wife and mother, not as military officer—a role in the expansion of America's global power, the film helps contain the potential discontent of real women who resented their ouster from well-paying jobs. Nellie also assuages wartime fears, sparked by Philip Wylie's charges of "Momism," that the American wife and mother posed a threat to national security. The Cold War, as a battle of ideas, gave new value to Mom's "natural" qualities of nurturing, sustaining, feeding, and exercising moral authority through love and gentle persuasion.[36]

This final scene "articulates" a vision of America in Asia that supports America's policies there. The United States is allied with France and supporting and sustaining France's Asian offspring. France has done its work of defending the world from "bullies," and now it is America's turn to exert authority, which will be done on the basis of "love," not force. As the military asserts American power in Asia in the background, Nellie asserts the feminine, domestic power of love and nurture in the foreground: America's job in Asia is to love, feed, and support. While World War II was won on the basis of American military strength, the Cold War, as a struggle for allegiances, demands the skills of a parent, not those of a soldier. At a moment when the United States was seeking both to influence Asia and to enlist popular American support for that effort, the rhetoric of familial virtues and obligations works to express both sides of the dilemma. It offers a stable vision of how America got involved in Southeast Asia, what our responsibilities there would be, and how we should relate to the other players. It figures America as parents bound to Asia through the disciplining love that demands obedience.[37]

Read this way, *South Pacific* seems to be a straightforward work of ideological expression. But this final scene illustrates how the discourse of representing American relations with Asia in terms of the family also carried a powerful idealistic, even utopian, element. George Kennan, in 1949, feared that Americans would be unable to meet the long-term demands of the Cold War because they had lost their "sense of belonging" and collectivity due to the breakdown of American families and communities. *South Pacific*, and especially the final scene, combats Kennan's despair, and helps restore Americans' sense of belonging and thus of power, by offering its millions of viewers the exquisite pleasure of feeling oneself a member of a community.[38]

The final scene is clearly a moment of community formation. At the level of plot, it forms an international community that transcends the potentially divisive boundaries of race, nation, and generation. The form of the scene—a musical number—constructs a more complex community that expands to include the viewer. The number begins when the children ask Nellie to sing a song for them. In requesting this particular song—"Dites Moi"—the children invite Nellie into their family, since the song is one that the children usually sing with their father. As Nellie sings, she enters this community by literally adopting the language of colonialism—the words of the song are French. The viewer sees the work of community formation in progress: Nellie, not always sure of the words, struggles to remember them, as De Becque and the children help her. As the means of inclusion, the song binds the disparate individuals together as a family for the first time, and as Nellie, the children, and De Becque sing, they affirm their unity with each other. At one point in the film an American officer asks De Becque the quintessential Cold War question, the same one that the State Department's Raymond Fosdick asked in 1949: "I know what you are against, but what are you for?" This final scene gives the film's answer: America is "for" collective security—a cross-racial, multinational community built around shared interests.

At a deeper level, the number opens this community up to include the audience by allowing it to join in the song. The song sounds more like a school sing-along than a polished showtune, and out of its four lines of basic French, two repeat. The viewer, having heard the song in an earlier scene, can't help but at least mentally hum along. The utopian act of participating in a larger community is exactly the pleasure that Cousins's editorial and the Christian Children's Fund advertisements offer to their readers. In a frightening world of atomic bombs and menacing communism, they all offer an ideal of reaching out across the boundaries of race and nation and joining a community of like-minded people by helping and feeding them. The musical number enhances this ecstasy of communion because by its very nature it is a moment when characters articulate their innermost feelings without any danger of reproach or humiliation. The final number is an idealized moment of unadulterated and transparent communication among Americans, Europeans, and Asians—what the United Nations had promised, but clearly failed, to deliver.[39]

At yet another level, the musical numbers create an even larger imagined community among the millions of Americans who, over the course of the decade, saw *South Pacific* on Broadway or in the movie theater, who listened to the soundtrack or cast album at home, who produced the music themselves from the sheet music, or who sang and danced in the myriad local theatrical productions. In singing along with the catchy show tunes, they joined each other in a community grounded in the expression of feeling, in participation in a pleasurable activity. Through these utopian moments of imaginary community formation, millions of Americans committed themselves—if only for the duration of a song—to the ideals that Nellie Forbush expressed, the ideals of overcoming racism and building a family that included French allies and Asian dependents. As millions of Americans purchased *South Pacific* at the movies, on a record, or in high school auditoriums, they expressed their consent in a fashion similar to those people who checked the boxes of the Christian Children's Fund advertisements and "adopted" an Asian child. They purchased a vision of themselves in relation to Asia, one which "articulated" a "fundamental attitude" undergirding American policies in Asia.[40]

This interpretation of *South Pacific* begs the question of chronology, since the Cold War and American aid to Indochina could not have been in Michener's mind when he wrote *Tales of the South Pacific* in the final months of World War II. Yet the anticolonial revolution that erupted in Indochina after the war is latent in Michener's stories, most concretely in the figure of Bloody Mary, the Tonkinese mother in search of an American son-in-law. In his 1992 autobiography, Michener describes the real Bloody Mary, a Tonkinese worker he encountered on a French plantation in the New Hebrides. Her name derived not from her penchant for chewing betel nuts, as in the film, but from her outspoken "advocacy of Tonkinese rights" and "strong resistance to exploitation." Tonkin, of course, was the colonial name for what would become North Vietnam, and this Bloody Mary was a "potential revolutionary" committed to returning there after the war in order "to oppose French colonialism." As America's involvement in Vietnam escalated into war during the 1960s, Michener wondered if American leaders realized that "the enemy they were fighting consisted of millions of determined people like Bloody Mary." Michener repressed Bloody Mary's revolutionary tendencies while writing his tales, and transformed her anticolonial politics into a romantic story of family formation.[41]

Already in 1945 Michener saw that the postwar years would entail an increased American presence in the Pacific, and he wrote *Tales of the South Pacific* in part to ease the way for that expansion. He wanted to correct any negative impressions about the Pacific that the war produced: "If America was committed to the retention of bases in the Pacific, then many Americans would have to live in that region, and living there would not be as bad if silly preconceptions were not allowed to prejudice first judgments." Writing his tales as promotional literature for expansion, he pointed out that "the standards of living and enjoyment were greater than comparable standards in many parts of the States." Nellie thus becomes a kind of international suburbanite, the first in a projected flow of postwar Americans who will spread American influence by reproducing American homes and families, and an American standard of living, around the globe.[42]

Nellie's adoption of De Becque's Asian children solved America's "race problem": it proved that Americans were not irredeemably racist and that they could overcome their prejudices and live in harmony with nonwhite people around the world. *South Pacific* did not stand alone in advocating cross-racial adoption. In June 1958, the *Saturday Review* awarded its Anisfield-Wolf Award in Race Relations to Jessie Bennett Sams for her memoir *White Mother.* In her book, Sams, a black woman, lovingly recalls her own and her sister's experience of being adopted and raised by a white woman. Pearl Buck, a member of the judging committee, saw this act of adoption as a kind of missionary salvation and conflated American blacks with overseas "savages": "In the deep South, a white lady, a lady of distinction, took into her care two small Negro girls, so underprivileged they might have been savages in a wild land." Buck read the memoir as offering a solution to the nation's, and the world's, problem of racial conflict, and she went so far as to advocate cross-racial adoption as a course of action that all concerned Americans could take: "When any American asks the question of what he—or she—can do to bring an end to prejudice in our country and in the world, that one has only to read 'White Mother.' The answer is there. You do what the white mother did. There are children everywhere in deep need of love and faith and opportunity. The dearth is in white mothers and fathers. I am not saying too much when I declare that were we all to follow in the footsteps of this one white mother, we would need not ask how to achieve peace on earth. Peace would be here."[43]

The choice of Buck to announce this award served, like *South Pacific,* to link African Americans and Asians together as equivalent racial Others whom Americans must somehow incorporate. Beginning with the 1931 publication of *The Good Earth,* her novel about Chinese peasant life, and continuing through World War II, Buck had been America's popular expert on Asia before Michener. She was also a proponent of cross-racial adoptions: herself the adoptive mother of several Asian-American children, she established Welcome House, an agency devoted to arranging the adoption of children fathered by American servicemen in Asia, whom established agencies refused to accept. Buck viewed these adoptions as political as well as personal acts. In a 1952 *Saturday Review* story about Welcome House, she claimed that U.S. policy had failed in China and allowed the Communists to take over not because of insufficient support for Chiang Kai-shek, but rather because there were not enough Americans who understood the similarities and differences between Chinese and Americans. She proposed the mixed-race children available for adoption through Welcome House as "key children" who could help prevent similar losses of Asian nations to communism in the future. By defining the race problem as a "dearth . . . in white mothers and fathers," Buck promoted white parenthood, especially white motherhood, as the solution to the problem of racial conflict, and by extension, the problem of communism.[44]

James Michener and lyricist Oscar Hammerstein, the authors of *South Pacific*, shared Buck's belief in adoption as a means to eradicate racism. These three middlebrow cultural producers, all of whom played major roles in introducing Americans to Asia, knew each other as neighbors in Bucks County, Pennsylvania. In 1949, Michener approached Hammerstein for his help in supporting Welcome House; Hammerstein agreed, and when his daughter Alice adopted a baby girl, he became one of the first grandfathers of a Welcome House child. He later cowrote a show with his son-in-law, *With the Happy Children*, that sought to promote goodwill and understanding about Welcome House among their Bucks County neighbors. Michener also adopted two boys from Welcome House with his second wife, but for some reason it did not work out and they "returned" them. Norman Cousins also adopted an Asian child, a Japanese girl orphaned at Hiroshima, although not through Buck's organization. This shared practice of adoption among Hammerstein, Buck, Michener, and Cousins shows that these cultural producers, so important in educating Americans about Asia during the 1950s, sought to promote their social and political views not only at the level of their art, but also in their own lives. They strove to model their political beliefs as social practice, and so demonstrate to other individual that they could do the same.[45]

In 1957 Hammerstein, Buck, and Michener got together again, this time to write a book about racism in America, a "short, unhysterical, profound and unequivocal statement concerning America and the race problem." Each author wrote a chapter—Hammerstein, "Dear Believer in White Supremacy," Buck, "The Effect of Prejudice upon the Individual," Michener, "Prejudice Is Wrong"—before the publisher backed out of the project.[46]

The "white mother" that Buck, Michener, and Hammerstein invoke in their writing as a model for the U.S. presence in Asia, and who is a member of each of their families to varying degrees, simultaneously disavows and insists on racial difference. On the one hand, the ability to love a child of a different race, take him into your family and raise him as your own does imply a certain willingness to transcend the cruder assertions of racial difference and purity that were still common and socially acceptable in the 1950s. On the other hand, the image of the white parent to the nonwhite child has long worked as a central trope in imperial discourses for the "natural" relations of hierarchy and domination among the races. As a figure that reappears over and over again in the lives and work of American cultural producers committed to the Cold War, the "white mother" of the 1950s can be read as a figure for America's desire to act in Asia not through force but through the distinctly maternal power to shape the consciousness of emerging nations and their leaders.[47]

Conclusion

The middlebrow discourse of cross-racial adoption, by integrating Asian children into American families, symbolically integrated Asia into the postwar American economy. Throughout the postwar period, the middle-class, suburban family served, both materially and discursively, as the symbol, proof, and engine of America's unsurpassed economic power. Along with the burgeoning defense industries, consumer spending on housing, furniture, appliances, cars, and other domestically oriented durable goods drove the postwar economic boom that made the United States the strongest economy in the world. The American mother, as the primary purchaser of consumer goods, performed a key economic function. Narratives of "adoption," by extending the American family and the suburban ideal out into Asia, symbolically integrated Asia into this economic engine as a source of raw materials and a market for American-produced consumer goods: when the American mother adopted an Asian child, she purchased Asia in miniature and brought it into the sphere of the American economy.

Collective security in general, and foreign aid in particular, aimed to bring the developing nations of Asia into the American-dominated world capitalist economy by channeling their economic growth along lines complementary to the United States. Aid policies for South Vietnam in particular seemed intent on proving the applicability of American ideology and institutions to developing nations by remaking that nation along the lines of suburban America. In 1955, Washington established a commercial-import program as the main mechanism for delivering nonmilitary aid to South Vietnam, and by 1957, as much as two-thirds of the goods brought into South Vietnam were American-produced consumer goods. One visitor to Saigon noted that "the stores and market places are filled with consumer goods; the streets are filled with new motor scooters and expensive automobiles; and in the upper-income residential areas new and pretentious housing is being built." This aid raised the urban elites' standard of living in South Vietnam to artificially high levels, but did little to induce actual economic development. Saigon in the late 1950s, its residents armed with American stereos and water skis, bore the material signs of an American suburb.[48]

Washington's policies of nation-building in South Vietnam drew support from the logic of political-obligation-as-parenthood that middlebrow culture constructed during the 1950s. Through nation-building, Washington sought to construct in South Vietnam a viable, non-Communist nation that would stand, in Senator John F. Kennedy's words, as the "cornerstone of the Free World in Southeast Asia." The role of the United States, as a mature democracy, would be to nurture the newly born South Vietnam and help it walk the fine line between colonialism and communism. Middlebrow culture helped pave the way for nation-building by making available an idealistic logic of obligation that President Diem's supporters could draw on to explain and legitimize their policies.

Kennedy relied on this logic of adoption in a 1956 speech to the American Friends of Vietnam. In articulating Washington's deep commitment to the Diem government, he used language that would have been comfortingly familiar to the millions of *South Pacific* viewers: "If we are not the parents of little Vietnam," said Kennedy,

> then surely we are the godparents. We presided at its birth, we gave assistance to its life, we have helped to shape its future. As French influence in the political, economic and military spheres has declined in Vietnam, the American influence has steadily grown. This is our offspring—we cannot abandon it, we cannot ignore its needs.[49]

The middlebrow discourse of parenthood and adoption provided a set of terms, images, and narratives that made America's increasing commitment to Asia seem natural, legitimate, and morally sound—and thus palatable to the millions of voters and taxpayers who had to pay the bill. These imaginary U.S.-Asian families met many demands of the Cold War. They created a sense of community with people about whom Americans knew little but had to financially assist; they offered relief from fears of nuclear war; they gave re-domesticated women a role in the national project of global expansion; they confirmed that Americans were neither racists nor imperialists. Perhaps most important, they gave millions of Americans a sense of personal participation in the Cold War. In all these ways, producers of middlebrow culture constructed the American commitment to prevent Asia from falling to communism not just as an obligation, but also as a source of pleasure. The white mother became an iconic figure for postwar national identity, a distinctly nonimperial representative of America's new global power. Through her ministering love, she knit together the exemplary America of the white, suburban middle class and the politically contested regions of Asia.

Feeding Beggars
Class, Caste, and Status in Indo-U.S. Relations, 1947–1964

ANDREW J. ROTTER

T HE HUNGER BEGAN in the south of India, in early 1950, with the failure of the monsoon. Gradually it crept north, as drought struck the populous Hindi belt, including the states of Uttar Pradesh, Bihar, and Bengal. To this region then came floods that wiped out what food crops remained. Reports of hunger, malnutrition, and starvation reached the capital of New Delhi, mocking the promise of Prime Minister Jawaharlal Nehru that India would be self-sufficient in food grains by the end of 1951, and reviving memories of the killing famine of 1943, when three million Indians had died. In mid-December, Nehru swallowed his considerable pride and directed India's ambassador in Washington—his sister, Vijayalakshmi Pandit—to ask the U.S. government to supply India with two million tons of wheat.

Secretary of State Dean Acheson, who received the request, promised to "explore the situation urgently and thoroughly," though he noted that the magnitude of the request meant that congressional action would be required. After a month of study, the State Department concluded that the request should be honored. President Truman met with key members of Congress on February 6 and found overall sympathy for India's request. The president formally requested the aid, a grant of $190 million, on February 12, and days later supporters of the proposal in the House and Senate introduced bills that would give the Indians food.

But the bills got stuck. Some members of Congress argued that India should be required to trade strategic materials, among them manganese, beryl, mica, and monazite, to the United States in return for the wheat. Others claimed that the Indian government had squandered opportunities to alleviate the suffering of its people when it refused to reconcile with its rival Pakistan, which had offered India food. And why, a few House members asked, should the United States help a country that was led by a Communist (Nehru), that consorted with the Soviets and Chinese Communists, and that refused to back the United Nations in its battle against Communist aggression in Korea? Finally, even some of those willing to provide food for India felt that the aid should come as a loan, not a grant. India, they said, could afford to pay for its food, and if it had to do so it would behave more responsibly in the future.

The administration tried to rally the pro-aid forces. At a March 29 press conference, Truman urged Congress to pass the legislation. Friends of India in the House watered down a Senate amendment that called upon India to repay a portion of its debt to the United States with strategically important manganese and monazite, so that the final version of the food bill called for repayment in part by "materials required by the United States," without mentioning what the materials might be. Nehru cooperated too, though through gritted teeth. He sent word that he would prefer a loan to a grant of food, anticipating that the terms of the former would be less onerous to India than the exactions the Americans would expect following a gift. Nehru also signaled that he would not object to using nonatomic strategic materials to help pay off the loan. The food loan bill, finally rewritten by a House-Senate conference committee, then passed the House on June 6 and the Senate on June 11; Truman signed it on the 15th.[1]

It had been an unexpectedly hard fight, but the Truman administration had won. American food would be sent to feed hungry Indians. U.S. officials, especially Ambassador Loy Henderson, had hoped that the aid would create sympathy among Indians for American foreign policy positions. Since congressional action was favorable, since the *outcome* of the process was good, they had reason to believe that a grateful Nehru would reevaluate his suspicions of the materialistic Americans.

That is not what happened. Instead, as Robert McMahon has written, "the long delay, the intemperate statements of certain legislators, and the crude efforts to use the specter of imminent starvation had left deep scars" on the Indo-U.S. relationship. Despite the insistence of the State Department that it was attaching no "political strings" to the food bill, Indian officials were never convinced that the Americans were engaged in an act of altruism. There was the discussion of tying the loan to sales by India of strategic materials. The Americans also sought changes in Indian foreign policy generally as payment for their largesse. Members of the House chastised Nehru for provoking Pakistan over the disputed state of Kashmir. The Indian refusal to support the U.S. position in the Korean War also drew fire. "India has proved to us that it is not our friend in the Korean struggle," said Wisconsin Republican Alvin O'Konski. "We are going to look like a bunch of stupid jackasses if we pick that nation and give them a gift of $190,000,000."[2]

There was something more. During the Wheat Loan debate, American friends and foes alike of food aid represented India metonymically as a beggar, or as a country full of beggars. As the Truman administration began to gear up its campaign for the Wheat Bill in January 1951, Acheson requested from the embassy in New Delhi materials that would reveal to Congress the extent of India's distress. Send us, Acheson wrote, "any graphic material distressed areas present or past including revealing photographs" of the afflicted. The secretary also asked for the embassy's "best estimate probable deaths, other suffering, reduced nat[ional] and local caloric intake, short-run and long-run effects, if emergency requirement not met." In April and May, with the Wheat Bill mired in committee, the *Washington Post* cartoonist Herblock scathingly depicted congressional opponents of aid as overfed plutocrats who demanded that Indians meet certain conditions before they would provide food. Herblock sympathized with India, but in each cartoon he represented India as a famished supplicant. Opponents of aiding India used the beggar image less sympathetically. Congressman Edward E. Cox insisted that any food sent to India was likely to be wasted. India, said Cox, had 180 million sacred cows, 136 million sacred monkeys, and "10,000,000 sacred or professional beggars—and all these sacred things will have a first claim on any wheat that may be procured by money lent to India."[3]

It was true, of course, that there were beggars in India, and that their ranks had been swelled by victims of the famine. To use graphic pictures of starving Indians seemed logical to Herblock and other Americans who wished to help. Nevertheless, there the image was: India-as-beggar, an outcaste, powerless and humiliated. The representation of India as a beggar, even for a magnanimous purpose, dismayed Indians because of what it seemed to say about the status of their country. Following his receipt of Acheson's request for illustrations of India's distress, Ambassador Henderson, along with the embassy's agricultural counselor, Clifford Taylor, met with K. M. Munshi, the food minister, and Vishnu Sahay, the food and agriculture secretary. Taylor asked Munshi to estimate the number of deaths that would result from the anticipated grain shortfall. Munshi refused to do so. Publicizing famine, even in the United States, would undermine his efforts to prevent starvation in India. Photos of the starved would provide "evidence [of] his failure," and would "create panic" that would greatly complicate his work. So Taylor answered his own question—he thought India might have an "extra 1 million or 2 million deaths"—to which Sahay responded that "this was as good a reply as could be made." Left unmentioned was the Indians' discomfort over the subject itself, the depiction of Indians as beggars, dependent on others for help.[4]

Nehru had always decried what he saw as the Western determination to turn India into a nation of beggars, with himself as chief supplicant. Beggars were outcastes, and they had, thought Nehru, forsaken their pride, the very thing that was essential for a truly independent India. In late 1946, Nehru wrote to his ambassador in Washington of his hopes that India would remain friendly with the United States. "Nevertheless," the prime minister added, "I should like it to be made clear that we do not propose to be subservient to anybody and we do not welcome any kind of patronage. . . . There is no need whatever to appear as suppliants before any country." At Bhopal in June 1954, Nehru told his audience that the country would develop only if people worked hard: "They [were] not going [to] beg for assistance from other countries because he did not want [the] people of this great land [to] become beggars." Speaking to a British reporter in the early 1960s, the prime minister stressed the importance of a country's approach to foreign assistance. "The ways and means of giving aid are far more important than the amount of aid given," he said. "Some countries think that they can buy up a country by giving aid, and even when they do not think that, like the Americans, they want to tear every shred of self-respect away from the countries before they give aid. You either have to crawl before them, toe their line at the United Nations, or beg them to save you from starvation or political chaos." India would refuse aid given as "charity or blackmail."[5]

Nehru was a sensitive man, and he was offended by American characterizations of his country during the Wheat Bill debate. Still, India had got its wheat. The Truman administration had acted in good faith, compromising with its congressional opponents when it seemed necessary but in general staying on course. Indians were starving. The United States would provide starving Indians with food. It was foolish, even petty, to obsess about the ways in which some Americans had described Indians during the discussion of the bill, for actions spoke louder than words, name calling was part of the political process, and the behavior of a few boors meant nothing, finally, at the end of the day. But while Americans focused on the outcome of the Wheat Loan debate, Nehru could not forgive Americans for the humiliations they heaped on India during the debate itself, during the process, that is, of making what turned out to be a positive decision. Why was there such an enormous difference in perspective between Americans and Indians?

The answer is that ideas about class, caste, and status affected the way Americans and Indians saw their places in the world, and by extension the places of their nations, during the period of Nehru's prime and foreign ministry, 1947 to 1964. Ideas about class and caste shaped American and Indian worldviews, and in that way conditioned relations between the United States and India—how policymakers in both nations approached the Wheat Loan episode, for example. One's social system and where one stood in it influenced how one thought about and acted toward others. The apprehension of others through the prisms of class and caste led to misunderstandings that are excruciating to contemplate even now. And yet, like these other perceptions, those based on class and caste were not always damaging: they help us understand not only the failures of the Indo-American relationship but also some of its successes.

There were no more pervasive or profound American images of India than those involving the caste system. In his classic survey of American attitudes toward China and India, Harold Isaacs noted that the typical American was "horrified by the rigidities of Indian caste," which established for Americans "an immediate barrier of incomprehensibility, a first and powerful impulse of rejection." Any Indian criticism of American society met with a rejoinder about caste. While Indians who met Americans rarely defended caste, they pointed out that the American social system was so fluid that it destabilized human relationships and washed away all sense of community. Or, said Indians, the gap between rich and poor in the United States was in fact a good deal wider than the defenders of the American class system cared to admit, and the American boast that anyone could make it to the top was empty. In the end, Indians claimed, there wasn't much difference between the two social systems. In October 1961, the Madras *Hindu* ran an ad for the Hollywood film *Tammy Tell Me True,* in which a college professor (played by John Gavin) is seduced by Tammy (Sandra Dee), a Mississippi riverboat girl turned student. "A Hilarious Delight!" burbled the ad. "It's just like a fisherman's daughter from Adyar Beach attending a Madras college!"[6]

It was not quite the same, really. The *Hindu's* analogy called forth any caste prejudices held by the paper's readers, for as much as they were poor people, the fisherfolk of Adyar were more securely members of a subcaste, or *jati,* that was unlikely to be represented at a Madras college in 1961. The comparison would have been more apt had Sandra Dee been black, and her seduction of John Gavin thus a violation of a fundamental social taboo, not merely the transgression of class boundaries. This distinction bids us grapple with the necessarily imperfect definitions of the words *caste, class,* and *status. Caste* is a system of social classification made up of largely fixed social stations, in which membership is conferred by birth, and in which rank is hierarchical and reinforced by proscriptions against commensality (sharing food) and intermarriage. *Class,* too, is a system of social classification, a way of ranking people by some combination of education, social aptitude, and especially wealth. Gerald D. Berreman has summarized the difference between caste and class: "In a caste system an individual displays the attributes of his caste because he is a member of it. In a class system, an individual is a member of his class because he displays its attributes." There is in theory no individual mobility within a caste system, while mobility is theoretically possible in a class system. Finally, the word *status* means standing, the regard with which one is held by others. The relationship between status and caste is direct: caste confers status. The relationship between status and class is more complicated. While in some societies wealth brings social regard it does not always, and modest means do not always confer low status.[7]

To Americans, the most fascinating, perplexing, essential, and abhorrent feature of India has always been the caste system. This is true in large part, one suspects, because the rigidity of caste stands in sharp contrast to the marvelous flexibility Americans claim for their own social system. Contrast this, said Americans, with India, where people were stuck in a particular social station because of an accident of birth. Caste in India, Harold Isaacs concluded, was for Americans "the symbol of ultra stratification and . . . a symbol for all the elements in Hindu society which retard the country's advance."[8]

Nothing disturbs a thoughtful Hindu more than false generalizations about Indian caste. Western misunderstandings of caste take several forms. Westerners have tended to focus on the four great castes of Hindu society, rather than on *jati,* the smaller and more various subcastes with which Indians themselves are more likely to identify. Nor is the contrast between the supposed social rigidity of Hindu caste and the apparent fluidity of the American class system as great as it seems at first glance. The American system does not permit perfect mobility, while Hindu caste does not absolutely prevent it. What was forbidden in theory could nonetheless occur: lower subcastes could move up the social ladder if they could appropriate the rituals of more exalted groups. M. N. Srinivas called this process "Sanskritization," pointing out that a low subcaste could rise in the hierarchy "by adopting vegetarianism and teetotalism, and by Sanskritizing its ritual and pantheon"—by imitating, in other words, the high-caste Brahmins. Finally, westerners have allowed their fascination with caste to delude them into thinking that caste *is* India, or at minimum that caste determines all that happens there. As the anthropologist Arjun Appadurai has put it, Western discourse has "essentialized" and "totalized" caste, making it the fundamental institution of India and expecting that it represented the whole of Indian society. Instead, Indians identify not only with their subcastes but with their families and villages, among other loci of authority.[9]

And yet, despite the efforts of the independent Indian government legally to expunge caste from national life, *jati* has remained important to the identity of Hindus. The psychologist Sudhir Kakar has written, *"jati* has become a dirty word to be mentioned only in a covert whisper." But Kakar notes that even modern Indians often identify with a subcaste. A civil servant told Kakar that he "took pride in stories" that members of his subcaste, the Khatris, "did not intermarry or interdine with the Aroras. . . . I used to take pride that Khatris are, by and large, good-looking and have a fair complexion, without bothering about the fact that I possessed neither. I know I do not possess any attributes of the warrior class, yet I cling to the dogma of being a warrior type of yore, of being a ruling type with all the obligations of conduct that go with it."[10]

Jawaharlal Nehru led the fight against caste injustices. But Nehru was descended from Kashmiri Brahmins, a caste association he never fully jettisoned. Observers often attributed Nehru's thinking to his caste standing. One of Nehru's biographers concluded that Nehru "remains a Brahmin with everything that this status connotes." Nehru himself admitted as much. "India clings to me as she does to all her children, in innumerable ways," he wrote, "and behind me lie, somewhere in the subconscious, racial memories of a hundred, or whatever the number may be, generations of Brahmins. I cannot get rid of . . . that past inheritance."[11]

Let me suggest several ways in which American and Indian ideas about class, caste, and status affected relations between the United States and India. First, Americans tend not to assign certain behaviors to particular classes, believing as they do that there are no permanent classes, just the democratic universe to which all are supposed to belong. This is not the case in India. The position one holds within a *jati* entails certain social expectations to which one must conform. One must, in other words, play a role. While what you say in India matters very much, how you say it, and how you behave generally—how you play your social role—matters more. Behavior is an act of self-presentation, absolutely critical as a reflection and affirmation of proper place in the hierarchy. How you act toward others indicates your position in relation to theirs. Thus, at the proper time and with the right people, one must show (toward an equal) politeness, grace, and tact, or (toward an inferior) strength and firmness, or (toward a superior) humility and respect. In his study of a north Indian village, G. Morris Carstairs noticed that "formality of demeanour was highly esteemed. The exchange of courtesies of speech and gesture appropriate to each other's age and caste was a habitual and enjoyable activity. At such times, people spoke with confidence and dignity as if good manners had power to neutralize all that was uncertain and inimical in a shifting world"—and by affirming the integrity of the hierarchy, "good manners" in fact did have such power. The requirement that behavior indicate proper place created acute sensitivity among *jati* and laid the basis for social injury should behavior fail to conform to *jati* position.[12]

The idea that behavior was a reflection of proper place applied as well to India's relations with foreign nations. *How* Americans and others acted toward Indians and India had an enormous impact on India's policy. In October 1953, G. S. Bajpai, governor of Bombay state and former secretary general at the Ministry of External Affairs, told the U.S. consul in Bombay that "tact must characterize all of America's work in India. . . . No matter how imaginative Americans are in seeing *what* is to be done and *how* things should be done, they must bear in mind that they are dealing with someone else's country when they operate abroad. Hence, along with their consummate imagination and ability, Americans must have consummate tact." This was something that U.S. policymakers had trouble understanding.[13]

Again and again, Indian officials objected to the way their American counterparts said and did things, rather than to what they said and did. Discussing U.S.-India relations in general with Assistant Secretary of State for African, Near Eastern and South Asian Affairs George McGhee in November 1950, Ambassador Pandit complained that Nehru was "disturbed by the 'pressure' which the U.S. seemed to apply to India in efforts to win India over to U.S. views." McGhee asked Pandit to cite an example of such "pressure." Had it something to do with relations with the Soviet Union? The United Nations' decision to send troops across the 38th parallel in Korea? Possible United States arbitration of the Kashmir problem? None of these specifically, replied the ambassador; it was rather "the urgency which seemed to characterize our approaches to the Indian Government." Indians, she said, "liked to think things out and did not like to feel they were being rushed into making decisions." Nehru himself resented the presumptuousness of Americans in India—"we have had quite enough of American superiority," he snapped in mid-1953. The rise of American power since 1945 "made [the Americans] look down on almost every country, friend or foe, and they have developed a habit of irritating others by their overbearing attitudes."[14]

What types of behavior, of self presentation, led to misunderstandings in Indo-U.S. relations? We start small, looking at what might be called the gestures of diplomacy. The word "gesture" has two meanings. First, it is a nonverbal cue, a part of body language—a wave of the hand, a crossing of the legs, a raised eyebrow. Second, a gesture in a more general sense is a small but symbolically weighted act, intended (according to a dictionary) "for effect or formality." A gesture of this sort is a little act of kindness (say) that one does for someone as an indication of support or sympathy.

Americans have seldom concerned themselves with the subtleties of body language. Studies of the phenomenon are treated with amusement, the property of counterculture faddists who cannot be convinced that body movements are usually random, and that people say what they wish to say with words. Gesture in its second definition is also a suspect concept in the United States. A synonym for it might be "token," and Americans hold it to be a substitute for a more effective action. To make a gesture is to lack full commitment to the person at whom the gesture is aimed, and thus to lack sincerity. As a type of behavior, gesture does not indicate anything about place or standing in a supposedly fluid society. The idea that gestures are meaningless extends to diplomacy. During a low point in U.S.-India relations in mid-1950, Secretary of State Acheson had a talk with Ambassador Pandit. As Acheson recorded the conversation, Pandit said that she was "pretty sure" of America's friendship for India, but added that the Indian people were "disappointed" in the "lack [of] any concrete evidence thereof." The ambassador "urged repeatedly some IMMED gesture demonstrating . . . our . . . good will for India." Acheson explained that the U.S. government was "not adapted [for a] gesture type approach [to] serious problems." He could "not believe [that] longterm Indo-AMER relations [were] dependent on small *ad hoc* gestures."[15]

Acheson was wrong. For Indians, gestures in both physical and symbolic senses were important as indications of proper place and manifestations of correct behavior. Again, *how* something is presented has great meaning in

India. Body language reflects one's regard for another; whether one feels affection, pleasure, scorn, or distaste can be read in movements and postures. As Alan Roland has observed, "closeness need not necessarily be verbalized, but can often be conveyed simply by a glance or smile—reflecting the strong non-verbal communication of emotion in Indian relationships." Indians are attuned to read the messages of the body, including those broadcast by American statesmen: those, like John Foster Dulles, who sat stiffly cross-legged and did not smile, and those, like Chester Bowles, who once abandoned formality, and a jacket and tie, to help a fisherman haul in a net.[16]

Indians believe not only that human society is hierarchical, but that the international system is too. On a scale of power, some nations rank higher than others, and nations should conduct themselves according to their place in the hierarchy. India, Nehru acknowledged, was "not a Power that counts" in 1947. A newly independent nation, India must address the world appropriately. India would be humble for now, as befit a new and weak nation. But Indians also felt that stronger nations had obligations to them. Power and status were not the same thing; even nations (like India) that lacked power overall must be treated with respect. As Nehru knew, Brahmins were not always the strongest or wealthiest Indians. Members of the Kshatriya caste were warriors, charged with fighting the state's enemies, while Vaishyas—merchants and farmers—often had more money than anyone else. Independent India might be likened temporarily to a poor Brahmin, physically unprepossessing, struggling to make ends meet, but deserving nevertheless of the formal civility to which those of his social rank were entitled. Superior powers must never presume superior status: indeed, because Indians were willing to accept inferior power, their proper place, their superiors must allow them to save face. Do not sell us short, the Indians told the world. While India's diplomacy must have "its full complement of good manners and courtesy"—these were India's obligations—India was "in no mood to be patronised" by the powers, "much less to suffer threats" or be "bullied."[17]

In fact, the United States frequently did ignore India, which undermined India's status and sense of place. Resentment over their alleged mistreatment led Indian officials to demand (or plead for) due consideration on a variety of issues:

1. *Don't patronize us—we are entitled to high status in the United Nations.* From the founding of the United Nations in 1945, Indians saw the organization as a forum in which they could compete with the great pow-

ers. The Indian delegation quickly asserted itself when it raised for discussion the matter of apartheid in South Africa, and through the years the Indians continued to court controversy, frequently damaging relations with the United States. Prior to the UN session in the fall of 1946, Nehru wrote to M. C. Chagla, a newly appointed delegate: "We want to make a splash at this General Assembly meeting." This India did. Its representatives were elected to all six of the UNO's commissions, and India's delegation promoted its views with asperity. The probability that Indian behavior might put others off did not deter Nehru from advocating for principle. "I am . . . anxious to make the world feel that we have got a will of our own," he wrote the delegation. "I do not want to function on the sufferance of anybody. If any nation or group of nations wants to be tough with us, we can be tough with them also. . . . I have no doubt this has displeased many people, but it is about time they knew that they have to deal with a new India which will not tolerate the old practices"— the masquerade of subservience dictated by the powers prior to independence.[18]

2. *Don't insult us — our representatives deserve respectful treatment when they visit the United States on official business.* Racism could be a serious problem for Indian visitors to the United States. The Indians perceived smaller but nonetheless stinging insults as well. On Nehru's first visit in the fall of 1949, a businessman thoughtlessly remarked that Nehru was lunching with men worth twenty billion dollars. State Department officials unthinkingly addressed Ambassador Pandit as "Madam Pandit," a holdover from the heyday of Madam Chiang Kai-shek. ("Why do you call me Madam?" the ambassador, who despised Madam Chiang, snapped at a State Department official one day. "I'm Mrs. Pandit.") In the mid-1950s, U.S. policymakers found themselves fielding complaints from official Indian visitors that the $12 per diem paid by the U.S. government was inadequate to cover the Indians' expenses, and it was much lower than the sums granted to Indians in the Soviet Union and China. Was this not further evidence of American scorn for Indians as supplicants in the land of the wealthy?[19]

3. *Don't behave with arrogance when you come to our country.* Despite the insults Indians thought they faced in the United States, many Indians found the freedom of American life liberating. Americans could be refreshingly unconscious of class and caste boundaries; the backslapping familiarity that so offended Nehru and other Brahminical types rather charmed Indians who chafed under a system where social position was

formalized and frequently fixed. One of these was M. K. Mehta, who was in 1959 the chief instruments engineer at India's Bhilai steel plant. Mehta had lived in the United States between 1938 and 1946, attending college and then working for General Motors. He returned to India, worked for General Motors in Bombay for a year, then for a variety of enterprises before settling in at Bhilai, a Soviet-built plant whose staff included many Russian advisers. In an April 22, 1959, conversation with David S. Burgess, the labor attaché at the U.S. embassy in New Delhi, Mehta recounted with fondness his eight years in America, where he was "always treated as an equal" by his associates at college and work. But things were different when he returned to India after the war. He received a lower salary than American engineers doing exactly the same work at the Bombay GM plant. The Americans in India had "an air of superiority," and "looked down on him as an Indian." They spent their astronomically high salaries "rather recklessly," and they shuttered themselves away in air-conditioned homes, to which they seldom invited Indians. The wives of the American engineers were just as bad: "A woman who had to dump out her own garbage in the States became a lady of high society in India and an administrator of many household servants." Mehta contrasted this with the behavior of the Russian advisers at Bhilai. Their salaries were modest, they lived humbly, they treated their Indian counterparts as equals, and any who made trouble were promptly sent home. "In my opinion," concluded Mehta, "the Russians are the most effective engineers in India. If I had my way, I would commission them to help us build other steel plants and other factories." The Americans, Mehta declared, "would not change their habits."[20]

4. *Above all, the Indians pleaded with the Americans, let us know, in some small way, that we can expect your favor and count on your help.* Again and again, American officials, who were (like Dean Acheson) skeptical that gestures had any lasting significance, were urged by Indians to signal that they cared about India, that they wanted to help, and that they liked Indians as people. In June 1950, C. R. Srinivasan, the president of the All-India Newspaper Editors Conference, told the State Department's Elbert Mathews "that what was necessary to reverse the [anti-American] trend of Indian opinion was some act or gesture by the United States which would have dramatic impact on the emotional people of India"— a bit of economic aid, for example. The British high commissioner in Delhi, Sir Alexander Clutterbuck, told Donald Kennedy, the U.S. chargé d'affaires, in September 1954 that Nehru "would not be pushed around"

by the Americans, and that Indian officials resented that Americans "sounded off" while they were in India. "There was also the question of 'saving face,'" Kennedy noted, "and Sir Alexander was of the opinion that this was of more importance than we gave it." But in his summary of the conversation, Kennedy omitted reference to Clutterbuck's comments, in all likelihood dismissing the Indian need for "saving face" as a matter unworthy of serious concern.[21]

In the realm of behavior, the way in which one party treats another, gratitude has a critical function. Americans regard gratitude as a natural response to an act of kindness or generosity. If one appreciates what another has done for her or him, one expresses gratitude. It is a way of evening the exchange between the two parties: the donor gives something of value to the recipient, and the recipient returns thanks for the gift having been made. Gratitude comes in return for some tangible commodity—often material, but sometimes emotional—that the donor is perceived as having given up. I have sacrificed, the donor implies. You, the recipient, must acknowledge that I have done so by repaying the debt you have incurred with the coin of gratitude.

The Indian view of gratitude is different. It is shaped by a tradition of *dana,* which means, roughly, "royal giving." *Dana* is based on a mutual understanding of proper place and the set of obligations that are predicated on the social positions of the parties involved. The queen, prince, or any powerful and wealthy superior should feel obliged to give to those less powerful and wealthy. He or she is by definition a donor, expected by all parties to be generous. No recipient should have to ask the donor to give, but if asked the donor should give without hesitation and unstintingly. A superior who refuses to give, who gives only grudgingly, who gives only because it benefits him or her, or who attaches conditions to the gift, has violated the obligations of the donor, and may be castigated or spurned by the recipient.

The obligations of the subordinate in a relationship based on *dana* are of a negative sort. If a subordinate is forced to ask a superior for help the subordinate is embarrassed, and loses status. The relationship is, after all, already rigged against the subordinate, since the individual who is asked for help is presumably of higher status than the person doing the asking. But the negative obligation incurred most forcefully by the *dana* subordinate is that s/he *not* express gratitude for a gift. To do so would so skew the relationship in favor of the donor that it would humiliate the recipient. Donors must not expect thanks for doing what *dana* requires them to do.

And so, when the government of independent India found itself needing assistance from the United States, it was faced with the unhappy prospect of having to ask for help, and then having the Americans expect thanks for the help that it was their obligation to provide. Having to ask was excruciating; being told to ask by well meaning but naive American officials was humiliating in the extreme. In April 1950, Ambassador Loy Henderson queried G. S. Bajpai about the parlous state of Indo-American relations—strangely so, thought Henderson, given the attention the United States had lavished on India. Bajpai replied that Indians had the impression that Americans helped others only when there was something to be gained, and that, for example, while India had had to grovel before American authorities when requesting food aid, nations that professed a commitment to the U.S. side in the Cold War had found the Americans far more accommodating. "Indians," Bajpai told Henderson, "were accustomed [to] regard expressions of friendship as empty unless they were accompanied by acts of generosity." Eleven years later, Vice President Lyndon Johnson barnstormed through several Indian villages. At one stop, he asked an elderly peasant what he would like President Kennedy to do for him. Nothing, the old man replied. Who knew what kinds of obligations he would incur, and how much status he stood to lose, by accepting a gift from this remote and apparently powerful man?[22]

When Americans expected Indians, like Johnson's peasant, to ask them for boons, when they publicized their help or expected Indians to be grateful for it, they were taking advantage of their already superior position in the relationship and abusing the protocols of *dana*. Americans expected gratitude when they bestowed favors on India and were affronted when it was not forthcoming. In November 1954, following the creation of the Southeast Asia Treaty Organization (SEATO), Secretary of State Dulles, the organization's architect, wondered "whether we ever attempted to make an asset out of the fact" that the United States had armed SEATO nations against attacks by Communists alone, thereby absolving the members of the organization of the need to act should Pakistan, a participant in the pact, invade India. "So far as I am aware," Dulles added, "there has never been any indication by India of appreciation for our position in this respect." (When Dulles had visited India in 1953, he reportedly told the New Delhi embassy staff and other American representatives that the way to handle Indians was to "make them come to you." "Why," Dulles had said, "if we just tell them to get on our side for foreign economic assistance, they will come crawling on their hands and knees.")[23]

Indian officials were unwilling to suspend the mutual obligations of *dana*. Time and again, Indians asked for things bluntly because it was so hard for them to ask, failed to accept things graciously, or simply refused to ask outright for that which both sides knew they wanted. In December 1950, the *Times of India* editorialized that India would be grateful for American help. "But any attempt to give [aid] negotiations the appearance of a bargain for concessions and alliances will be resented and resisted in this country," the paper cautioned. "Esteem is lost when asked and bargained for." Sarvepalli Radhakrishnan, the renowned philosopher who was India's vice president from 1952 to 1962, clarified the Indian position for a U.S. official in June 1952:

> We resent your continuous publicizing of your own achievements. You are a strong country, and should be able to make concessions to our current psychology. It is we who need building up. . . . You don't need this building up. Keep yourselves in the background and help us to grow, by helping us to feel a sense of pride in our progress. By publicizing yourselves, you deprive us of the psychological help which is so vital to us at this stage of our development.[24]

This was a condition the Americans did not understand, though Radhakrishnan overestimated American feelings of self-confidence during the early 1950s. Probably Americans, too, needed some "building up." In either case, they could not help pushing themselves awkwardly into situations that called for tact. Lyndon Johnson, in India in 1961, thought he had found a way to help a people who were reluctant to ask for favors: he would take a physically handicapped child back to the United States for medical treatment. The symbolism of this act—the advanced United States would help a victim of backwardness whose afflictions were beyond the abilities of his fellow Indians to cure—was appalling to the Indian government, which objected to John Kenneth Galbraith. The ambassador put a stop to Johnson's plan, though of the Indians he remarked in his diary, "I think they are too sensitive."[25]

This discussion of *dana* brings us full circle, back to the Wheat Bill controversy of 1951. Throughout the debate over the food grains legislation, American policymakers were struck, and clearly annoyed, by Nehru's refusal to thank them for their exertions. Loy Henderson wrote from New Delhi that when the food aid issue came up, Nehru "did not . . . express any hopes on the subject or any appreciation of the efforts on India's behalf of the United States Government." (It was "a little humiliating," Nehru told his chief ministers, "to wait in this way for favours to be bestowed upon us.") An American writer named Edgar Mowrer visited Nehru in March 1951. "Nehru appeared bent forward and glum," Mowrer reported. "Expression: underlip protruding, chewing on something like gum and obviously expecting to accomplish an unpleasant duty. I countered by giving him greetings from his sister in Washington and telling him of a slight effort which I made to help them get their wheat. . . . He remained glum." Later in the conversation, Mowrer commented that the United States had received very little help at the United Nations from several countries, including India. At this, "Nehru flew into a temper." "The way in which you are handling our request for grain is insulting and outrageous," he stormed. "I can tell you that if we go through centuries of poverty and if millions of our people die of hunger we shall never submit to outside pressure." When Nehru announced that he would rather have a loan than a grant, he justified his preference with the argument that the grant bill led "practically to converting India into some kind of semi-colonial country." "I realize completely," he said, "the consequences of our refusal of this gift. Nevertheless, I cannot bring myself to agree to this final humiliation." Members of Congress could not understand why the Indian prime minister was so touchy, but they put it down to churlishness and ingratitude and voted for a loan instead. Over two decades later, Loy Henderson had sour memories of Nehru's behavior. Nehru would "at times consent to accept American aid," said Henderson, "but when he did so it was usually with reluctance and without grace or gratitude."[26]

The Wheat Bill affair marked a low point in Indo-U.S. relations, one of many during the Nehru period. But there were good moments, too. Some of these resulted from a coincidence of Indian and American views on world events. More often, Indo-U.S. relations improved incrementally because of a warm meeting between Nehru and some U.S. official, because of a kindness shown, a sensitivity respected—in other words, because an American behaved toward Nehru in a manner that showed respect for India's status and conformed to the rules of *dana*. An American's observance of proper place went a long way toward making United States-India relations better overall.

It is easy enough to compile a list of U.S. policymakers with whom Nehru failed to get along: Loy Henderson, Dean Acheson, John Foster Dulles (Nehru called him "nasty"), and John F. Kennedy. The list of Americans whom Nehru liked is equally long, however. It included Chester Bowles, ambassador from 1951 to 1953 and again from 1963 to 1969; Dwight Eisenhower;

Ambassador John Sherman Cooper (1955–1958); and Ambassador John Kenneth Galbraith (1961–1963). With the men in this second group Nehru reached a level of understanding that made doing business easier and disagreements less bitter.

The fundamental difference between the men in these two groups has to do with how they acted toward Nehru, and toward India in general. Nehru frequently made it clear that an individual's behavior, revealing as it did the quality of the person with whom he dealt, mattered very much to him. He wished to be treated with dignity. The Americans with whom Nehru felt he could not work failed this test because they were arrogant. They put on airs; they acted superior to their Indian counterparts; they set conditions for their help; they lacked tact and humility and good manners; and they showed a stupendous ignorance of Indian culture, about which they manifestly cared little. Those on Nehru's undesirable list offended against the protocols of class, caste, and status that Indians felt strongly about. These Americans were patricians who presumed to insert themselves into India's social hierarchy at its highest level. Without benefit of birth or of having earned their position through merit, these American policymakers had arrogated to themselves the privileges of behavior reserved for members of the leading *jati*. Theirs was an outrageous breach of propriety.

By contrast, those westerners with whom Nehru found he could work kept themselves humbly removed from the Indian caste system. They acted respectfully toward Indians, both officials and others, and they adopted an informal style of life that conformed to no prescribed pattern of behavior within the system. That was precisely what ingratiated them to Nehru and the others. As outsiders—non-Hindus, and foreigners—westerners were not to presume that they had a place anywhere inside the social hierarchy. They had to behave as if there were no social expectations of them, as indeed there were not. To act patrician, like Henderson and the others, was to usurp the prerogatives of Brahmins. To act as members of any of the subordinate *jati* was unlikely, but if an American had (for example) substituted obsequiousness for respect, he or she would have been scorned for behaving as a representative of a lower caste, thereby appropriating the dubious privileges of subordination within the system. Informality marked westerners as those without a place in the hierarchy. Remaining outside the caste system was the only legitimate course for those who were genuinely not of it.

Each of the men on Nehru's 'good' list demonstrated respect for the Indian social system by behaving with informality, graciousness, and sincerity toward Indian officials. John Sherman Cooper, by being friendly and forth-right during his term as ambassador, "captured the confidence and admira-tion" of Indians, according to an Indian editor. Dwight Eisenhower seemed to understand the value of respectful behavior. When Nehru came to the United States in late 1956, Eisenhower took the prime minister off to his Gettysburg farm in order to get to know him personally, outside the formal setting of Washington. In India, an invitation to one's home is a gesture of intimacy, and undoubtedly Nehru saw it that way. Ambassador Galbraith seemed to speak to Indians "from the depths of his being," eschewing "lofty" pronouncements (Indians were charmed by the "ehhs" and "uhs" that sprinkled his speech) and putting on a party for four hundred workers constructing a new embassy building in New Delhi, during which the am-bassador and his wife, Kitty, joined in an energetic Punjabi dance.[27]

The most successful American diplomat in India during the Nehru pe-riod was Chester Bowles. Even as he arrived in India in October 1951, the ambassador tasked himself with demystifying the embassy and improving relations between Americans in India and their hosts. He drafted a letter to newly arrived embassy staff, in which he urged Americans to treat Indian staff members considerately, to examine themselves for hints of racial preju-dice, and to drive carefully through crowded Delhi streets. (He also in-cluded a cautionary anecdote about an American woman who worried aloud at a dinner party that her pedigreed dog would be petted by "dirty Indian children" and thereby get an infection.) The Bowleses determinedly re-sisted such imperious behavior. They sent their children to Indian schools, and frequently invited Indians into their home. Dorothy Bowles took Hindi lessons. Chester rode a bicycle. "It is frequently said," wrote an Indian cor-respondent in retrospect, "that Mr. Bowles did a marvellous job of public relations in India—which is true enough. What he really did was to make American informality, American friendliness and American generosity come to life." What Bowles really did, in other words, was to take his proper place outside the Indian social system. He thus approached Indians without any presumptions based on status.[28]

Let it be said, finally, that India was not the only country affected by the American belief that gratitude was a reasonable return on a favor or a gift. Policymakers contrasted Nehru's behavior with that of the Pakistani leaders with whom they dealt. In early 1953, Pakistan faced a food shortage compa-rable to the one faced by India two years before. The Pakistanis asked the Americans for help, and at a meeting on January 28, State Department of-ficials told the Pakistanis that the United States would provide food. The finance minister, Sir Zafrulla Khan, "indicated surprised gratification" at the decision. The United States, he said, "had no obligation to assist them or the rest of the world in the manner in which it had," and "the United States had not received sufficient gratitude from the world" for its previous acts of generosity. There is no need to wonder to whom Sir Zafrulla referred. The Indians spat in America's eye. The Pakistanis said "thank you." It followed that the Americans found the Pakistanis much more pleasant to work with as United States relations with South Asia evolved during the 1950s and 1960s.[29]

PART TWO

Cold War Ambassadors-at-Large

America's "Best Propagandists"
Italian Americans and the 1948 "Letters to Italy" Campaign

WENDY L. WALL

O N APRIL 18, 1948, Italy held its first postwar parliamentary elections. In the months leading up to the vote, tensions between Washington and Moscow mounted. In March 1947, President Harry S Truman unveiled the United States' new policy of "containment," and a few months later he asked Congress for a huge infusion of aid to bring economic and political stability to Europe. That summer, the Soviets walked out of Marshall Plan talks in Paris and formed the Communist Information Bureau to promote their agenda around the globe. In February 1948, with the Marshall Plan stalled in Congress, Communists seized power in Czechoslovakia, toppling leaders greatly admired in the West. Against this backdrop, a well-financed and disciplined coalition of Italian Communists and militant Socialists seemed about to sweep to power in free elections. According to historian James Miller, U.S. government leaders saw the 1948 Italian election as "an apocalyptic test of strength between communism and democracy"—a test that might well determine the fate of democracy on the Continent.[1] The Italian election, Senator Arthur Vandenberg declared, would be "the most important election in the next 100 years."[2]

To the aid of their country rushed Italian Americans. Galvanized by Italian-language newspapers and radio stations, the Catholic Church, fraternal organizations, and community leaders, Italian Americans launched a massive letter-writing campaign to inform their overseas kinsmen of the dangers of voting Communist and the virtues of the "American way of life." In the early months of 1948, thousands of Italian Americans lined up at post offices around the country to mail letters to family and friends abroad. Italian-American newspapers from New York to San Francisco suggested topics for letters, provided writing help, or printed messages that could be clipped and signed. The New England Marshall Plan Committee organized "Freedom Flights" to carry letters from Boston-area Italian Americans overseas. Catholic priests passed out preprinted letters after mass. And radio stations offered free recording time to those who wished to send phonograph records instead: at radio station WOV in New York, which devoted half its time to Italian-language programming, more than four hundred war brides turned up to record phonographs, which were airmailed to friends and relatives in the Old Country. On March 23, *The New York Times* reported that "the volume of airmail letters to Italy had doubled in the last few days," and by April a million extra Italy-bound letters a week were passing through the New York post office.[3]

Commentators later hailed the "Letters to Italy" campaign as a "spontaneous uprising," prompted by Italian Americans' "sentimental attachment" to Italy, their "horror of the Godlessness [sic] of Communism," and their "deep love for America and . . . fervent belief in a political system based on the dignity and importance of the individual."[4] The campaign did tap deep sentiment within the Italian-American community, but it was hardly a grass roots effort. Drew Pearson, the muckraking columnist and liberal anti-Communist, promoted the letter-writing campaign; and it was orchestrated by Italian-American leaders, many of whom had once supported Mussolini and now seized the opportunity both to defeat Old Country leftists and to redeem themselves in American eyes. The campaign also drew strong backing from public officials both within and outside of the Truman administration, who saw personal letters from friends and relatives as a particularly effective form of propaganda. Administration officials coupled praise for Italian Americans' anti-Communist efforts with frequent and vivid reminders of the dire consequences to relatives in Italy should the Communists prove victorious.

The "Letters to Italy" campaign was an early example of a technique used extensively by both the United States and the Soviet Union during the Cold War—popular or public diplomacy. From the late 1940s on, U.S. officials, businessmen, pundits, and others worked to enlist civil society in general, and American ethnics in particular, in defense of the "American Way of Life" overseas. The "Letters to Italy" campaign grew out of an earlier foray into public diplomacy, the Friendship Train of 1947, and it in turn inspired others. In the years that followed, scores of private groups, working closely with the State Department and the U.S. Information Agency (USIA), recruited millions of Americans into student exchanges, pen pal programs, trade group meetings, sister city affiliations, and a massive "Crusade for Freedom" to raise money for Radios Free Europe and Asia. In the 1950s, the USIA billed various "People-to-People" programs as among its most important initiatives, on a par with better remembered projects like the "Family of Man" exhibit and the "Atoms for Peace" campaign.

The "Letters to Italy" effort suggests that such programs should be understood, not simply as weapons in the Cold War, but as part of the complex and ongoing process of constructing a postwar consensus on anticommunism and American identity. During the 1948 letter-writing campaign, millions of Italian Americans were bombarded by—or quite literally handed— the language with which to describe their American blessings. In churches, in community halls, in Italian-language newspapers, street rallies, and radio broadcasts, these first- and second-generation Americans were repeatedly reminded that America was a land of freedom and plenty, a bastion against Godlessness, and the only steadfast ally of their homeland. The minority of Italian Americans who challenged such notions risked not only federal scrutiny, but censure within their churches and neighborhoods.

Finally, the "Letters to Italy" campaign suggests both the dangers and possibilities that the Cold War—and America's newfound internationalism—opened for American ethnics. Those ethnics who questioned the equation of "freedom" and "plenty" with the American status quo—those who challenged the nation's tactics or doubted that communism was inherently antithetical to America's "democratic" values—risked being labeled "un-American." At the same time, Cold War anticommunism allowed many ethnics to reconcile their religious and Old World allegiances with their new American identities and to incorporate themselves more fully into the American "mainstream." The 1948 letter-writing campaign allowed many Italian Americans to position themselves, not as members of a threatening and alien minority, but as U.S. ambassadors and the staunchest of American patriots.

✿   ✿   ✿

Although the idea of using American ethnics to spread U.S. values and burnish the nation's image abroad peaked during the Cold War, it was hardly a Cold War brainstorm. Americans had long realized that immigrants and their children provided the nation's strongest link to the Old World. In the nineteenth century, western land speculators sometimes planted glowing "letters from America" in European newspapers to encourage immigrants to migrate to the American West. And during World War I, George Creel's

Committee on Public Information encouraged General Pershing to send wounded Italian-American soldiers to Italy for convalescence. These ethnic troops, Creel reported, spread the Wilsonian gospel and "turned out to be our best propagandists."[5]

During World War II, commentators across the political spectrum again saw a special role for American immigrants and their children in projecting an "American way of life" overseas. America's ethnic citizens, many liberals argued, had been steeped in a creed of democratic freedom and ethnic co-existence that uniquely qualified them to help their European kindred re-build after the war. "The hour is striking for Lafayette's return and Kosci-usko's too," declared *New York Post* columnist Samuel Grafton. "We need to develop among our own tumbling millions of foreign origin, the new leaders for whom Europe waits."[6]

Some commentators hoped that mobilizing ethnics in a foreign crusade would curb disunity at home. No proponent of this view was more eloquent or persistent than Louis Adamic, the Slovenian-American writer whose best-selling books on labor and the immigrant experience had won him a wide following among liberal intellectuals and in America's ethnic communities. A radical democrat who operated on the margins of the New Deal left, Adamic emerged in the 1930s as an outspoken critic of nativism and racism and a powerful advocate of cultural pluralism. Deeply disturbed by the rise and spread of fascism across Europe, Adamic was equally alarmed by the war's impact at home: the Munich accord, Hitler's invasion of Poland, and the German blitzkrieg across Europe had rekindled dormant loyalties, he warned, turning American ethnics against one another.[7]

The solution to both Europe's and America's problems, Adamic argued, was to use American ethnics to "ignite" an "American revolution in Europe." In his 1941 book *Two-Way Passage*—and in meetings with President Roosevelt, Eleanor Roosevelt, and other administration officials—Adamic urged U.S. policymakers to organize American immigrants and their children into national advisory groups. These ethnic Americans would develop postwar plans for their ancestral homes, then return temporarily to adminis-ter liberated countries after the war. They would bring peace to Europe, not by "policing" the Continent or imposing democracy from without, but by "cut[ting] loose the vicious tentacles of hate, narrow nationalism, oppres-sion and frustration" that kept the *"inherent democracy"* in the hearts of Europeans from flowering. Only the United States could accomplish this task: Europeans would know that the Americans came not as "strangers; not [as] conquerors or invaders, or intruders—but [as] visitors. We are their nephews and second cousins."[8]

This "Passage Back" idea, Adamic suggested, would also help ease America's ethnic tensions, "straighten[ing] out the kinks and quirks in our American innards which come from the 'old country,' from the fact that we're ex-Europeans, escaped Poles and Croatians and Czechs and Scandinavians and Englishmen." Rather than being torn apart by European conflicts, American ethnics would unite around the notion of bringing freedom and democracy to their respective homelands, Adamic predicted. Helping to establish a "United States of Europe" would allow ethnics like himself to be "just plain Americans while we're citizens of the world."[9]

Adamic's vision was that of a cosmopolitan liberal alarmed by rising intolerance both at home and abroad. But some who worried that American ethnics might form a fifth column also called for mobilizing immigrants in a foreign crusade. In a 1942 article entitled "Steam from the Melting Pot," *Fortune* charged that America's foreign-language groups comprised "a replica of explosive Europe on U.S. ground." Given that millions of immigrants "cannot yet get Europe out of their system," the magazine declared, the "only sensible attitude . . . is to transform our foreign stock into the world's greatest task force of political warfare." Such a move would overcome Old World allegiances and animosities by rallying immigrants to America's cause. "There is dynamite on our shores," *Fortune* warned, "and we should explode it in the right direction."[10]

To the editors of *Fortune* and many others, few groups seemed more potentially explosive than America's five million residents of Italian descent. In the decades preceding World War II, many Italian Americans had been alienated from their adopted society by Americanization programs, nativist immigration restrictions, and other forms of informal and institutionalized prejudice. For nearly twenty years, Benito Mussolini had played to this alienation—as well as to Italian Americans' nostalgic patriotism—by waging "one of the most persistent propaganda campaigns ever mounted [in the United States] by a foreign government."[11] Mussolini's appeals to Italian nationalism were widely circulated by Italian-American news and fraternal organizations, and enthusiastically endorsed by the community's conservative *prominenti*. In the late 1930s, while prominent Italian refugees vigorously denounced Mussolini, 80 percent of Italian-language newspapers in the United States and the vast majority of Italian Americans backed Il Duce, whom they saw as "restoring the grandeur of Rome." Italian Americans' "philofascism" contributed to their stunning defection from Roosevelt's New Deal coalition during the 1940 presidential election.[12]

Italy's declaration of war against France in June 1940 dampened Italian Americans' ardor for fascist Italy, and America's entrance into World War II brought the romance to an abrupt end. Community leaders quickly declared their steadfast loyalty to the United States, although, as one study noted, Italian Americans hoped for "a miracle, 'American victory without Italian defeat.'"[13] Still, both federal and private efforts to oust Italian America's conservative *prominenti* from positions of leadership proved largely unsuccessful. During the early years of the war, staunch antifascists, aided by liberals within the Office of War Information (OWI), attempted to win control of Italian-American organizations and news outlets. But the Italian-American masses remained deeply suspicious of both refugee and citizen antifascists from whom they were separated by both "Old-Country social distinctions and educational barriers."[14] Moreover, the Treasury Department buttressed the position of the prominenti by recruiting them to spearhead war-bond drives within the Italian-American community. Finally, the conservative *prominenti* outflanked the OWI and its allies by launching their own nominally "antifascist" groups. By 1943, the OWI had abandoned its efforts to undermine the *prominenti,* and settled instead for trying to unite all Italian Americans in a "broad coalition stressing pro-American themes."[15]

This compromise, which left Italian America's conservative leadership intact, proved crucial once communism replaced fascism as America's chief ideological foe. During the war, however, it limited the federal government's use of Italian Americans for propaganda. The OWI employed exiles on its Italian desk, and some Italian-American politicians appeared on shortwave programs broadcast to the Old Country.[16] State Department officials, however, remained wary of ethnics' political activities and warned that encouraging "political blocs based on race affiliation" would hinder the "integration" of American ethnics.[17] Only the onset of the Cold War—and an onslaught of Soviet-inspired propaganda—would alter the State Department's view.

✿   ✿   ✿

Rarely have global alignments shifted as rapidly as in the months following the close of World War II. In May of 1945, American GIs celebrated victory over the Axis forces alongside Soviet troops. By March of 1947, when President Truman warned a joint session of Congress of a global conflict between "alternative ways of life," allies and enemies had traded places.[18] Alarmed by the march of the Red Army across Eastern Europe—and by the postwar rise of Communist parties in Western European countries like Italy and France—American officials quickly came to see communism, not fascism, as their principal enemy. Embracing the policy that became known as "containment," administration officials spelled out the Truman Doctrine and announced a massive aid program designed to halt the spread of communism across Europe.

Despite such vigorous actions, by the fall of 1947, U.S. foreign policy had stalled on several fronts. In Congress, Republican isolationists blocked the efforts of a bipartisan coalition of internationalists to pass the Marshall Plan. In Europe, the powerful French and Italian Communist parties, urged on by the newly created Cominform, led mounting opposition to "imperialist" U.S. aid. While American politicians bickered over how to counter the Communist propaganda onslaught, the Republican-controlled Congress slashed funding for U.S. propaganda agencies.[19]

This scenario frustrated and appalled many internationalists and cold warriors, both within and outside of the Truman administration.[20] Among them was Drew Pearson, the Washington-based political gadfly whose "Washington Merry-Go-Round" column appeared in some seven hundred daily newspapers and as a commentary on two hundred radio stations. In the fall of 1947, Pearson called for a "Friendship Train" to circle the nation, collecting private donations of food and medicine for the famished millions of Europe. A private committee headed by Hollywood producer Harry Warner answered the call, and in November 1947 a flag-bedecked "Friendship Train" slowly made its way from Los Angeles to New York.[21]

The Friendship Train ultimately provided one of the inspirations for the "Letters to Italy" campaign and it rehearsed some of the letter-writing effort's main themes. A private, scaled-down version of the Marshall Plan, the Friendship Train was designed to stave off communism abroad and strengthen a Cold War consensus at home by mobilizing American citizens into an international humanitarian effort. Most of Europe was suffering in the fall of 1947, but the Friendship Train collected foodstuffs only for Italy and France, the two countries in Western Europe with the largest and most active Communist parties. At an elaborate send-off ceremony in New York, the U.S. delegate to the United Nations stressed the train's "peacemongering" mission, and added that it "should leave no doubt that the policy of the [United States] Government is the policy of the people." When the donated food arrived in Europe, it was not simply distributed. Rather, four Friendship Trains, decorated with American flags and messages in French and Italian, crossed France and Italy, stopping regularly for speeches by Americans and local officials. The European trains, Drew Pearson explained, had been arranged "so [that] the people of those two countries can see them and know where the food came from."[22]

The Friendship Train also suggested the new, if carefully circumscribed, role that the Cold War opened for American ethnics. Ethnic Americans had long attempted to aid their homelands or intervene in Old World politics, but in an era of American isolationism, such efforts rarely received the sanction of American officials and other elites. In the context of Cold War internationalism, however, organizers of the Friendship Train cast immigrants and their children as American ambassadors. At send-off ceremonies in New York City, French and Italian Americans in national dress paraded down Broadway alongside trucks carrying sacks of flour and macaroni. A waterborne parade through New York Harbor carried thirty-three boxcars on railroad floats past the Statue of Liberty.[23]

Similar themes were soon reflected in the "Letters to Italy" campaign, which grew out of the Friendship Train episode. According to one account, Toledo's mayor, Michael V. DeSalle, first broached the idea of an ethnic letter-writing campaign when a section of the Friendship Train stopped in his city. Talking to Drew Pearson, DeSalle suggested that letters from America would provide a perfect complement to the donated foodstuffs: Americans of all ethnicities should write letters to friends and family in Europe telling "how [they were] faring in America and what opportunities were open to [them] here." Pearson liked the idea and plugged it on a December episode of his Sunday-night radio show. Broadcasting from Italy, where he was both overseeing and covering the distribution of Friendship Train supplies, Pearson "urged that Americans with friends or relatives in Europe write them personal letters correcting distorted Communist propaganda about the United States."[24]

Pearson's broadcast coincided with growing fears on the part of American officials about electoral developments in Italy. Italian Communists and left-wing Socialists had reacted to their expulsion from the government in May 1947 and the announcement of the Marshall Plan a month later by staging a series of violent strikes, mass rallies, factory occupations, and assaults on police stations. In the fall of 1947, such actions—together with inflammatory statements by Italian Communist leaders—had convinced American diplomats and military officials that a coup or civil war was imminent. By late December the violence had abated, and all parties had turned their attention to the national elections slated for the following spring. But the focus on free elections proved small consolation to American officials worried about a Communist takeover. In late January, the U.S. ambassador to Italy, James C. Dunn, predicted a sweeping electoral victory for the Left.[25]

A week after Dunn made this prediction, the U.S. chargé in Italy wrote Secretary of State James Byrnes proposing a plan very similar to that advocated by Pearson. "We have been told that Italian language daily newspapers in America have devoted a good deal of space" to America's "tremendous" efforts "to help Italy rehabilitate herself," chargé Homer Byington, Jr., wrote. "The stories in these papers are described as being full, factual, and pregnant with good will toward Italy and with appreciation of America's unselfish motives." Byington urged the State Department to contact the editors of those papers and ask them "to recommend to their readers the practice of clipping stories describing American aid to Italy and sending them to their friends and relatives in Italy." The chargé enclosed a list of newspapers that should be contacted, together with a warning: "[S]ome weekly papers have editorial policies which are critical of American policy of aid to Europe and therefore should not be approached with any plan such as this."[26]

One Italian-American publisher had already taken action. Generoso Pope, the millionaire president of the Colonial Sand & Cement Co., controlled a media empire that included New York's Italian-language radio station WHOM and America's largest and most influential Italian-language daily, the New York–based *Il Progresso Italo-Americano*. Pope's media holdings and his close ties to Tammany Hall made him one of Italo America's most powerful leaders, as well as an influential force within the Democratic Party. In late January 1948, a few days before Byington sent his telegram, *Il Progresso* announced that it was launching a "chain letter plan" to inform Italians of the dangers of communism and of the United States' contribution to world peace, global prosperity, and the Italian nation. *Il Progresso* urged readers to join a "Committee of 100,000" by pledging to write letters to friends and family in Italy and persuading ten other Italian Americans to do the same. To guide readers unsure of what to write, *Il Progresso* printed sample letters daily. It also encouraged readers to enclose copies of *Il Progresso* in the packages they sent to their "far-away loved ones."[27]

How direct a role Drew Pearson or the Truman administration played in inspiring Pope's action may never be known. Certainly, the publisher had close ties to the Democratic Party, and Pope knew Pearson well through their common involvement with the Friendship Train. In late 1947 and early 1948, Pearson contributed a regular column to *Il Progresso* and was named a "special correspondent" of the newspaper.[28] In any case, the "Letters to Italy" campaign also served Pope's political and personal interests. An outspoken supporter and client of Mussolini throughout the 1920s and 1930s, Pope had recanted in 1940 and during the war joined moderate liberals in an American Committee for Italian Democracy.[29] Pope's public *volte-face* helped him survive wartime attacks by ardent antifascists and the OWI.[30] But he never abandoned his fundamental conservatism, and he emerged from the war a strong supporter of Italy's Christian Democratic prime minister Alcide De Gasperi. The "Letters to Italy" campaign thus offered Pope a chance to atone for his past political sins while remaining true to his conservative political beliefs.

✿   ✿   ✿

If Pope catalyzed the "Letters to Italy" crusade within the Italian-American community, he soon had ample aid. In March and early April of 1948, Italian-American newspapers, radio stations, fraternal organizations, and community leaders threw their support behind the campaign. In Italian Harlem, the St. Luke Council of the Knights of Columbus distributed mimeographed fliers exhorting citizens to write their friends and relatives in Italy: "[T]ell them that the Victory of [the Christian Democrats] in Italy will be a Moral Victory for us in the U.S.A. and for the future good of the Italian people" (sic).[31] *Il Voce del Popolo* of Detroit urged readers to join the anti-Communist crusade, as did chapters of the Italian-American War Veterans and the Order of the Sons of Italy. In San Francisco, home of the West Coast's largest Italian-American community, the Columbus Civic Club launched a campaign to send 100,000 letters overseas. Italian-American dignitaries promoted the *"valanga di lettere"* (avalanche of letters) at a rally in North Beach, and a car toured the Italian district broadcasting details of the campaign over a loudspeaker. Those unsure of what to write could turn for instructions to the Bay Area's Italian-language daily, *L'Italia,* or pick up sample letters distributed by the women's auxiliary of the Italian Welfare Agency and through Bank of America branches.[32]

Italian-American leaders weren't alone in promoting the "Letters to Italy" campaign,[33] and in many Italian-American neighborhoods, the Catholic Church became a central conduit of information and support. Urged on by U.S. diplomats, the Vatican in early 1948 "suggested" that the American Catholic hierarchy strongly support private efforts to combat Italian communism, a charge many dioceses took seriously.[34] In Elmira, New York, parishioners at the Italian "national church," St. Anthony's, heard weekly announcements about the campaign at Sunday mass and found writing instructions and sample letters in their parish newsletters; researchers found that the vast majority of Elmira's Italian Americans first learned of the campaign through the church.[35] Meanwhile, priests in Utica, New York, passed out eight thousand prepared letters warning that a Communist vic-

"SI SCOPRON LE TOMBE, SI LEVANO I MORTI" . . .

UNA VOCE: Chi siete? Dove andate? . . .
GLI SCHELETRI: Noi siamo i Martiri dell'indipendenza d'Italia. Andiamo a ricordare
ai dimentichi che noi non siamo morti invano.

FIG. 1. ["THE TOMBS OPEN, THE DEAD ARISE" . . . / A VOICE: Who are you?
Where are you going? . . . / THE SKELETON: We are the martyrs of Italy's independence. We are going to remind the forgetful that we have not died in vain.]

tory would ruin Italy and would trigger world war. And a ready-to-sign letter
distributed throughout the Brooklyn Diocese on Easter Sunday warned that
if Italy embraced communism, it would become simply "another vassal state
of Russia."[36]

As these sample letters suggest, campaign promoters both within and
outside of the Italian American community repeatedly urged letter writers
to stress the threat a Communist victory would pose to Italy's peace and
security. Postcards distributed by the New York–based Committee to Aid
Democracy in Italy (which needed only to be addressed and signed)
stressed that if Italians embraced communism at the polls they would betray
both their ancestors and their long heritage of independence. One postcard
reminded Italians—and perforce Italian Americans—that 1948 was the
centennial of the revolution that freed Italy from foreign oppressors and
created a "free, independent, democratic" nation. A second postcard featured the rising of the dead: "We are the martyrs of Italy's independence,"
intoned one skeleton. "We are going to remind the forgetful that we have
not died in vain"[37] (Figure 1). A model letter published in *Il Progresso* simi-

larly mixed patriotic appeals with religious imagery. Calling the anti-
Communist campaign "this blessed crusade of resistance," the letter called
on all Italians "who truly love *la Patria*" to commemorate the anniversary
of 1948 by "annihilat[ing] the communist snakes that poison with their fatal
bites the nation and render her easier prey for her crucifiers. . . ."[38] Whatever the effect on Italians, such letters clearly played to Italian Americans'
romantic patriotism.

Sample letters and writing instructions also highlighted the dangers to
faith and family of a Communist takeover in Italy. A cut-and-sign letter published in *Il Progresso* warned of the "lies and the perfidious maneuvers of
the Russian tyrants and their hangman's underlings. These [people] do not
want your salvation, but want your ruin, the destruction of your blessed,
beloved family, the banning of your religious beliefs, the renunciation of
your faith and of your devotions."[39] A form letter passed out to parishioners
in Jersey City, New Jersey, went further still. Italians who voted for the
Communists, the letter declared, would drive the pope from Rome and
bring "the malediction of God" down upon themselves and their families.
"Your churches and your homes would be destroyed, your lands devastated,
the Priests and Sisters would be massacred, and your dear ones would be
dragged away as slaves in Russia to be bound to infamous work and to die
of cold and hunger." The Monsignor E. Monteleone instructed his parishioners to sign and address the letters, then return them to the church to be
stamped and mailed.[40]

Those guiding the letter-writing campaign didn't focus solely on the hor-
rors of a Communist victory in Italy. Many sample letters and writing instructions responded to Soviet propaganda by coupling denunciations of
communism with depictions of its implicit alternative: the American Way of
Life. Both Italian- and English-language newspapers printed sample letters
extolling U.S. political and religious freedoms and pointing out that these
were guaranteed by the nation's Bill of Rights. *L'Italia* urged readers to note
that education in the United States was free and that magazines and newspapers weren't censored, a truth which nevertheless belied the temper of
the times. St. Anthony's parish newsletter, *The Antonian*, told parishioners
to write friends and family in Italy about the blessings of democracy and
the rights and privileges Americans enjoyed under a representative government. The ready-to-sign letter attorney Victor Anfuso distributed in Brooklyn on Easter Sunday opened with a joyous picture of American church bells
ringing and "people of every race and creed" living together in "peace and
prosperity." The letter contrasted this American vision—a whitewashed one

to be sure—with Italy's likely fate under communism, closing with "the hope that the Resurrection of Our Lord may always be celebrated in the land that is the center of Catholicism."[41]

No aspect of the "American Way" received more attention than America's material plenty. Newspapers ranging from San Francisco's *L'Italia* to the Order of the Sons of Italy's *OSIA News* urged readers to stress that consumer goods were not rationed in America and that the United States had no clothing shortage. The *New York World-Telegram* reprinted the letter of a young man in the publishing business to his brother, an Italian civil engineer. The American warned his brother against voting Communist, then described conditions in the United States: "We have plenty of everything in this country and, while everything is expensive, wages are high and everyone has a job." Underscoring this prosperity, the American sent canned food and money to pay for a mass for an uncle who had died during the war. The *World-Telegram* also hailed Anthony D'Angelo, a luncheonette owner who reportedly included twelve pounds of English-language newspapers in every package he sent to his family in Italy. "Even Italians who can't read English can recognize the space devoted to amusements and department store advertising and realize that these things are for sale or they wouldn't be spending money advertising them," the newspaper enthused.[42]

Such comments implied that Italians too could enjoy new clothes and washing machines if only they rejected communism at the polls. To some degree, this may have been true, but not simply because of the superiority of America's free enterprise system. Alone among major powers, the United States had reaped an economic bonanza from the war, emerging with the largest share of global GNP in world history. Through the Friendship Train and private care packages, Italians had already profited from American largesse. They stood to gain far more from the Marshall Plan, which the U.S. Congress finally approved in March 1948.

Writing instructions and sample letters stressed this fact, suggesting that the United States, not the Soviet Union, offered Italy true friendship. "From America, money, medicine, packages join you, while Russia asks tributes of war, boats and machinery, and imposes its veto to the damage of Italy in the United Nations," one letter declared.[43] Another ran through a more detailed recounting of America's good deeds and urged Italians to "[h]ave faith in America's proven friendship."[44] The same point was vividly captured in a cartoon that appeared in *L'Italia* just days before the Italian election. Two men stood on a dock next to a huge American freighter and watched a Russian warship steam toward port. The freighter, they noted,

FIG. 2. [Reality is the desire of all Italians. / (from Marcus Aurelius of Rome) / "This is the help from America: [America] brings us grain." / "That is the help from Russia: [Russia] brings us Togliatti."] / Courtesy of the Hoover Institution Library.

was loaded with grain, while the battleship carried the Italian Communist leader Palmiro Togliatti. Scrawled across the top of the cartoon was a quote from Marcus Aurelius: "Reality is the desire of all Italians"[45] (Figure 2).

In the intellectual framework of the campaign, America's blood ties to Italy cinched this friendship. Italian-American newspapers reminded readers that their letters would carry special weight in the Old Country because they were kin. A sample letter published in *Il Progresso* attacked the Communal Council of Taranto (which the paper said was dominated by Socialists and Communists) for refusing to welcome an American squadron on the "pretext" that the Americans threatened Italian independence. "The American boats in the Mediterranean have the blessed and civil mission of protecting the liberty and the independence of the people from Russian aggressions," the letter declared. "Among the marines who are in Taranto, there are sons of Italians and youths who heroically fought in order to liberate

Caro Fratello: e che è successo in Italia?
volete anche voi fare abbassare il SIPARIO DI FERRO?

Se (Dio ne scampi) ciò accadesse, come farò io a continuare ad aiutarvi? . .

FIG. 3. [Dear Brother: and what has happened to Italy? / do you wish also to lower the IRON CURTAIN? / If (God forbid) this should happen, how will I be able to continue to help you? . . .]

Italy from its odious enemy. . . ." The letter not only stressed the kin links between the United States and Italy, but recast Italy as a victim, rather than a perpetrator, of the recent war.[46]

But even American friendship had its limits—as government officials, Italian-American leaders, and sample letters were quick to point out. Truman himself had declared that the Marshall Plan and the Truman Doctrine were "two halves of the same walnut," and U.S. officials made it clear that no aid would flow to an Italy under Communist control. State Department officials and private promoters of the campaign encouraged letter-writers to stress this point, and to cast it in personal terms. A ready-to-send postcard distributed by the Committee to Aid Democracy in Italy showed an Iron Curtain separating Italian Americans and their aid from relatives in the Old Country (Figure 3). The form letter passed out by Monsignor Monteleone in Jersey City noted that, should communism triumph, "America would abandon Italy to her destiny" and would not permit "the shipment of packages to you, our dear ones." And when staffers at *La Tribuna Italiana* in Milwaukee penned letters for readers who could not write, they drove the message home: "[I]f the forces of true democracy should lose in the Italian election, the American Government will not send any more money to Italy and we won't send any more money to you, our relatives."[47]

❋   ❋   ❋

Although it is impossible to determine precisely how many Italian Americans participated in the "Letters to Italy" campaign or how frequently correspondents followed the formulas offered in published instructions and sample letters, participation rates were unquestionably substantial. The campaign was heavily promoted by Italian-American leaders, and U.S. postmasters reported an explosion of Italy-bound mail in the spring of 1948. Some of this can undoubtedly be attributed to bulk mailings by Italian-American individuals and groups to unrelated "kin."[48] But many letters were sent by and to individuals. When Cornell sociologists interviewed Italian-American families in Elmira, New York, in August 1948, more than 40 percent said one or more family members had mailed letters.[49]

What accounted for this apparent outpouring of support for the "Letters to Italy" campaign? In part, it reflected the fierce anticommunism shared by many Italian-American leaders in the postwar period, an anticommunism that was further fueled by the Catholic Church. Unlike most Catholic immigrant groups, Italian Americans had sustained a strong radical tradition in the late nineteenth and early twentieth centuries, but this radical strain largely disappeared in the postwar period. Many of the community's *prominenti* were, like Pope, former philofascists who had emerged from the war chastened, but with their conservative Italian nationalism intact. And under the shadow of communism, even many liberals and former leftists edged to the right. Luigi Antonini, for instance, the first vice president of the International Ladies Garment Workers Union (ILGWU) and president of Italian Dressmakers Local 89, was the dominant figure in Italian-American labor. A reform socialist and staunch antifascist, Antonini had collaborated before and during the war with both liberal New Dealers and leftists. But Antonini was a pragmatist and, like many American social democrats, he was no friend to communism. In 1943 he joined Generoso Pope in forming the American Committee for Italian Democracy. That same year, Antonini created the Italian-American Labor Council, which in the postwar period funneled ILGWU and American Federation of Labor funds to anti-Communists in the Italian labor movement.[50]

The "Letters to Italy" campaign thus played to religious and political allegiances deeply rooted in Italian Americans' ethnic past. At the same time, it gave Italian Americans a dramatic way of displaying their loyalty to their adopted land. When many in the community supported Mussolini in the late 1930s, they did so primarily as Italian immigrants and alienated Americans. But the "Letters to Italy" campaign drew strong support from federal officials, business and civic groups outside of Italian areas, and prominent Americans ranging from New York mayor William O'Dwyer to Hollywood producer James Nasser. "If all the people in the United States of foreign birth or extraction will start movements in each group to write letters to their friends and relatives in the homelands telling how much better freedom and Americanism are than despotism . . . we can win the cold war," declared House Speaker Joseph Martin (R., Mass.) in a speech in Toledo. "[M]illions of lives can be saved . . . rivers of blood can be prevented . . . if we go at it with the earnestness and intensity with which we go to battle."[51]

Such words—which virtually equated letter-writing to military service during the war—underscored the fact that active anticommunism increasingly served both as a loyalty test and as a path to full inclusion in American society. For the many Italian-American leaders like Generoso Pope whose "Americanism" was clouded by former association with Mussolini, the "Letters to Italy" campaign offered a chance to make amends for past transgressions. Addressing one Italian-American group, Pope stressed his *American* motives for launching the campaign, and noted that it placed ethnic Italians squarely in the nation's "mainstream": "I did what I considered to be my duty as an American citizen," Pope declared. "And with us were millions of Americans, regardless of race, color or creed."[52]

Such reasoning probably had a powerful appeal even to those Italian Americans who did not need to seek political absolution. After decades of alienation and discrimination, Italian Americans in the immediate postwar years were poised to enter the American "mainstream." The "Letters to Italy" campaign seemed to offer a way to hasten this process. "[T]he thousands of Italian Americans who responded to the appeal were less interested in the Italian political situation *per se* than they were in achieving status and integration in the American community," argued a University of Illinois sociologist in 1949. "What better demonstration of that desire than to join the anti-Communist crusade at a time when anti-communism was the supreme test of loyalty!"[53]

But if the equation of "Americanism" with anticommunism offered Italian Americans a shortcut into "mainstream" American society, it was a path paved with dangers. The most obvious was the prospect of being cut off from their homeland. The U.S. government announced that, not only would it slash aid to Italy if the Communist coalition won, it would also expel Communist Party members in the United States and refuse immigration visas to any Italian who voted red. With an "iron curtain" falling fast across Eastern Europe, many Italian Americans probably feared Italy would be next. Luigi Antonini, the labor leader, made this point a few days before the election. "Some of our Italian-Americans may have exaggerated in their appeals to the Italian voters," Antonini conceded, "but this was mainly due to their justified fears that their relatives in Italy could have been separated from them by a Communist iron curtain between Italy and America."[54]

Finally, some Italian Americans may have feared for their own status in American society should the Italian Communists triumph. A nota bene attached to the bottom of sample letters published in *Il Progresso* noted that the specific words writers used didn't matter. "What matters are the intentions," the postscript read. "[W]hat matters is the determination to distance from our head the terrible spectre of a monster, that—if it were unfortunately to triumph—would be the destruction of our liberties, the profanation of our families, the eradication of our religious faith, the perversion of our society."[55] The author of this postscript was likely referring to the evils that would befall Italy under communism, but the wording is sufficiently ambiguous to suggest another reading. If Communists triumphed in the Italian elections, then Italian Americans could be tarred by association. Only by wholeheartedly participating in the letter-writing campaign could Italian Americans distance themselves from Communist forces in their homeland and prove their loyalty to their adopted country.

❖   ❖   ❖

Not all Americans agreed with the United States' heavy-handed tactics in Italy or believed that "America" should stand for anticommunism at any cost. Supporters of Henry Wallace, the Progressive Party's presidential candidate in 1948, denounced U.S. intervention in the Italian campaign. And some eighty prominent liberals and leftists—including Louis Adamic, composer Leonard Bernstein, playwright Arthur Miller, and Senator Glen Taylor—sent a telegram to President Truman calling for "an end to all outside interference with democratic electoral procedure in Italy." (Gaetano Salvemini, an Italian refugee antifascist and professor of history at Harvard, drafted the telegram, but later distanced himself from the document, charging that Communists had circulated a "primitive draft" without his permission.)[56]

Although much of the outcry over U.S. actions came from liberals and leftists outside of the Italian-American community, some Italian Americans also braved possible reprisals to voice their opposition to the letter-writing campaign and related U.S. efforts to influence the election outcome. On the Wednesday before the election, some two hundred protesters turned out for a rally at Manhattan Center sponsored by the Committee for Free Elections in Italy. Rep. Vito Marcantonio, a New York leftist with close ties to the Communist Party, condemned U.S. intervention in a speech read to the rally. "The action of our State Department, our former Fascists, and of the former lick-spittles of Mussolini in the City of New York is more evidence that our foreign policy is one of aid to anti-democratic elements throughout the world," Marcantonio declared. "This must be stopped. It must be stopped by free Americans." Committee chairman Fileno de Novellis echoed these sentiments in explaining the event to reporters: "Thousands of Americans of Italian origin feel deeply humiliated by the continuous flow of suggestions, advice and pressure put on the Italians, as though they were unable to decide for themselves whom to elect," Novellis said. "The rally [voiced] the protests of all decent and truly democratic Americans against the interference of any country in the Italian elections of April 18."[57]

Novellis's reference to "truly democratic Americans" hinted at the way anticommunism had redrawn America's political map. Many of the liberals and leftists who now protested U.S. intervention in Italy had, in the late 1930s and early 1940s, argued for staunch U.S. opposition to fascism overseas. Their previous support for U.S. involvement abroad had reflected their belief that New Deal America embodied "democratic" values they held dear: for liberals, those values included ethnic tolerance, and freedoms of speech, press, and religion; for leftists, "democracy" (sometimes cast as "industrial democracy") implied a redistribution of economic power. The Left's appropriation of "democracy" in the late 1930s made many industrialists and other conservatives wary of the term, but they could not afford to reject it during World War II. Rather, conservatives stressed "representative democracy," tying political freedom to religious and economic freedoms under the banner of the "American way of life."[58]

During the war, the united front against Nazism partly concealed *democracy's* multiple meanings. But as the wartime coalition broke apart, the term's internal fractures became clear. Communist and Socialist parties across Europe—including many partisans who had been in the front ranks of the Continent's anti-Nazi brigades—invoked "democracy" in the postwar period, as did embattled American leftists. Meanwhile, U.S. political, busi-

ness, and intellectual leaders continued to portray America as the "democratic" norm, even as the nation slid to the right. During the "Letters to
Italy" campaign, some observers worried that this semantic tug-of-war
would cause confusion. Some Italian Americans "may have used expressions
and methods which could be misunderstood," two observers reflected in a
campaign postmortem. "[S]aying 'Vote democratic,' might mean to an un-
lettered Italian the Democratic Popular Front, the Communist-extreme-
left socialist coalition."[59]

The figure of Giuseppe Garibaldi likely caused even more consternation.
During the "Letters to Italy" campaign, both sample and reprinted letters
invoked the nineteenth-century Italian patriot as a symbol of Italian independence. One Italian-American woman, whose letter to a female relative
was published in the *New York World-Telegram*, reminded her correspondent of "your great uncle, a Garibaldean who fought to liberate Italy from
the yoke of despotism in 1848. Today, one hundred years later, it is up to
you and all women of Italy to free yourselves and Italy from the threat of
communism which menaces your country through agents educated and
trained in Russia," she continued. "You women should rally together and
make your rallying cry the Garibaldi Hymn."[60]

This reasoning had one small flaw: Italy's Communist-dominated coalition had already embraced Garibaldi as their own. A complex and romantic
figure, Garibaldi championed the rights of labor and women's emancipation,
was a religious freethinker, and advocated racial equality far ahead of his
time. A hero of republican revolutions in Italy and Latin America, Garibaldi
was so admired in the United States that Abraham Lincoln offered him a
command during the Civil War. (Garibaldi turned it down.) In the late
1930s and during World War II, many American liberals and government
officials proclaimed Garibaldi an early embodier of the "American idea."
But Garibaldi embraced socialism late in life, and—though Karl Marx dis-
owned him—his views were closer to those of the Italian Communists and
radical Socialists than to the conservative Christian Democrats, who had
close ties to the Vatican. In 1948, it was Italy's Democratic Popular Front
that put Garibaldi's face on their posters.[61]

✿   ✿   ✿

Such confusion ultimately proved inconsequential, for on election day Italy's Christian Democrats stunned all observers, winning 48.5 percent of the
vote and an absolute majority in Parliament. Some observers claimed that
the "Letters to Italy" campaign had a substantial impact on this outcome.

Journalists noted that Italian Communists and left-wing Socialists had denounced the flood of letters, while Italy's ruling conservative coalition both applauded and encouraged the effort. The letter-writing campaign—and particularly its role in publicizing the threat of a U.S. aid cutoff—may have proved particularly important in villages in southern Italy and Sicily, where leftists had made inroads with talk of land redistribution. In such areas, where inhabitants relied heavily on "gift packages from uncles and cousins in the United States," one Christian Democratic official wrote, the letters from America "struck home . . . with the force of lightening."[62]

Whether or not the letter-writing campaign actually influenced the Italian election, it was an important signpost in Italian Americans' efforts to locate themselves within the national community. Politicians of both parties commended the group for its patriotic efforts, and House Speaker Joseph Martin publicly thanked Italian Americans for "helping materially" to stall the "westward march of the iron curtain."[63] The campaign provided former fascists with an opportunity to redeem themselves, offered a litmus test of "Americanism" that excluded radicals, and provided a large group of first- and second-generation Americans with a ready language with which to describe the concrete characteristics of the "American way." In the process, it allowed many Italian Americans to reconcile their religious and Old World allegiances with their new "American" identity.

Finally, the "Letters to Italy" campaign underscored the complex relationship between the construction of an "American Way" at home and abroad during the Cold War. It was a relationship that some U.S. elites were quick to notice. Inspired by the 1948 letter-writing campaign, American business leaders, social workers, and government officials tried in the early 1950s to recruit American immigrants and their children into a far more ambitious, and ultimately less successful, "Letters from America" campaign. Organizers of the second campaign hoped to counter Soviet propaganda and spread American values through a "campaign of truth" far more personal—and thus more effective—than Voice of America broadcasts. At the same time, by recruiting ethnics into the effort to "sell" America to the world, organizers hoped to solidify the allegiance of millions of Americans to a particular vision of the "American Way."

Who's the Real Ambassador?
Exploding Cold War Racial Ideology

PENNY M. VON ESCHEN

I N 1955, WRITING in *The New York Times,* Felix Belair surmised that "America's secret weapon is a blue note in a minor key," and named Louis (Satchmo) Armstrong as "its most effective ambassador."[1] At the age of fifty-four, Armstrong's genius was well established in jazz and American popular music. But his elevation to spokesperson for America as cultural ambassador, fighting a two-front war by symbolizing the superiority of American life to Western Europe and embodying American racial harmony for Ghanaian and other African audiences, was far more than merely an outgrowth of Armstrong's talent.

While Armstrong traveled the world, another internationally renowned artist, Paul Robeson, was barred from leaving the United States. Robeson was deeply admired throughout Africa, Asia, and Europe for his extraordinary gifts as an actor and singer and for his militant stand against racial and economic oppression. Robeson's political activism against racism at home and colonialism abroad led the federal government to revoke his passport in 1950, restricting not only his freedom to travel but effectively blacklisting him in the United States. In rejecting Robeson's appeal, the State Department revealed that it regarded anticolonialism and domestic civil rights activism as interlocking issues that threatened U.S. security. The State Department contended that even if the passport had been canceled "solely because of the appellant's recognized status as spokesman for large sections of Negro Americans, we submit that this would not amount to an abuse of discretion in view of the appellant's frank admission that he has been for years extremely active in behalf of the independence of the colonial peoples of Africa."[2] The government's efforts to silence Robeson signaled a critical shift in its conception of cultural politics. During World War II, the State

Department nervously tolerated Robeson's status as "citizen of the world" and representative of the utopian, democratic promise of the postwar world. By 1950, however, the State Department deemed Robeson a dangerous "political meddler" who, if allowed to travel abroad, might create a terrible "diplomatic embarrassment."[3] The subsequent elevation of Armstrong to goodwill ambassador strikingly underscores the shift from a democratic vision of citizenship to a new public relations appropriate for a dominant global power. If democracies have citizens, empires and leaders of the "free world" have anointed representatives. "Ambassador Satch" was only one of many African American artists promoted around the world by the State Department to advertise U.S. culture and racial progress. These goodwill tours, coming at a time when Jim Crow was still firmly entrenched at home, represented the triumph of a politics of symbolism over a genuine commitment on the part of the U.S. government to protect the rights of its black citizens. Yet as I will argue, a politics of symbolism that relied on the evasion of domestic and global political and economic inequalities, and sought to control and contain the politics of race at home and abroad, was inherently unstable. To the horror of State Department officials, the strategy backfired when Armstrong transgressed his role as ambassador, angrily castigating President Eisenhower following the 1957 school desegregation crisis in Little Rock.

Louis Armstrong and other goodwill jazz ambassadors such as Dizzy Gillespie were only the most visible examples of what was in fact a far-reaching global strategy. As jazz tours by African American artists built on the Voice of America radio broadcasts of Leonard Feather (*Jazz Club USA*) and Willis Conover (*Music USA*), they served a broader State Department strategy in Africa and nonaligned nations.[4] By 1950, the Voice of America and State Department film, radio, and publication programs had been set up throughout Africa to address issues of American "race relations" and U.S. foreign policy. These State Department predecessors to the United States Information Service (USIS), termed "Cultural Affairs, Psychological Warfare, and Propaganda," attempted to defend American foreign policy and manipulate African perceptions of black American life and U.S. "race relations," and sometimes included direct attempts to discredit African American anticolonial and civil rights activists.[5] The fact that many of these programs were in place by 1950 and that they coincided with direct attempts to disrupt anticolonial politics demonstrates that the genesis of the relationship between post-1945 domestic and international racial politics—often noted in the Kennedy administration or seen as an outgrowth of civil rights struggles in the 1950s and 1960s—must be located much earlier. From the prosecution of anticolonial activists to the government's attempts to win the hearts and minds of Africans and Asians, a contest over the meaning of race, the shapes of racial solidarities, and the character and allegiances of new Asian and African states began with the Cold War itself.

The proliferation of these programs, the barring of Robeson from public life, and the elevation of Armstrong illustrate the importance and complexity of contests over race in the U.S. pursuit of global hegemony in the post–World War II era.[6] To understand the significance of this conflict, one must examine America's confrontation with Asian and African nationalism. Between 1945 and 1960, as the United States emerged as the dominant global power, forty countries with a total of eight hundred million people—more than a quarter of the world's population—revolted against colonialism and won their independence. Policymakers in the Truman and Eisenhower administrations wanted to ensure that these new nations remained friendly to the United States. But their efforts were enormously challenged by African American support for anticolonial movements and the persistence of Jim Crow. As the Cold War first emerged, the Truman administration was forced to contend with Africans and African Americans who linked liberation movements in Africa with the struggles of African Americans for civil and economic rights in the United States. During World War II, as European hegemony crumbled before the eyes of an international black press, a broad left and liberal alliance of African American anticolonial activists had forcefully argued that their struggles were inextricably bound to the struggles of African and Asian peoples for independence. In response to Cold War anticommunism, African American liberals began to argue that discrimination at home must be remedied because it undermined the *legitimacy* of U.S. claims as the leader of the "free world." This liberal position also developed a parallel anti-Communist anticolonialism. At the same time, the Truman administration and the State Department, in alliance with African American liberals, sought to ensure that Asia and Africa remained "in the orbit of the West." While working closely with African American liberals such as Walter White and Edith Sampson, who were deemed sufficiently anti-Communist, the Truman administration simultaneously began the systematic repression of those anticolonial activists who continued to oppose American foreign policy.[7]

Several factors made Africa strategically crucial in the transition to the Cold War. During World War II, when Japan occupied much of the Pacific, the Allied Powers had turned to Africa for resources. The United States benefited enormously from the Belgian Congo's increased production of copper, tin, and rubber, as most of the colony's traditional trade with Belgium was diverted to America. The Allies also depended on the Congo's control of two-thirds of the world's industrial diamonds, essential for precision cutting instruments for military weapons, and were even more concerned about controlling the huge supplies of cobalt, essential for jet engines.

African resources were at least as important to the United States during the early Cold War. Industrial diamonds and cobalt continued to be vital. Even more significant, from 1945 to 1952, the Congo's Shinkolobwe mine was the primary source of uranium used in U.S. atomic bombs. Consequently, the large supplies of uranium in the Belgian Congo and South Africa gave the region a unique significance in the eyes of the Truman administration. The CIA was instructed to provide covert surveillance and protection for Union Minière (the Congo's largest producer of uranium), as well as for manganese and chrome complexes in South Africa, southern Rhodesia, and Mozambique.[8] By the late 1940s, following the independence of India and Indonesia and the establishment of a Communist regime in China, the United States and its European allies viewed much of Asia as "lost" to the West, and relied even more on African minerals. With the beginning of the Korean War in 1950, Africa's strategic raw materials became even more critical. The Truman administration also focused more attention on commercially and strategically valuable products of West Africa such as cocoa, manganese, gold, hardwoods, tin, columbite, lead, and zinc, as well as the mineral-saturated south.[9] A 1951 State Department directive emphasized, for example, that "Africa provides a sizable portion of the critical commodities now required by the Free World" and argued that it was imperative to "insure that Africa will remain firmly fixed in the political orbit of the Free World."[10]

The outbreak of the Korean War greatly heightened American policymakers' fears that resentment of American racism might cause Asian and African peoples to seek closer relations with the Soviet Union. The war exacerbated what the historian Melvyn P. Leffler has characterized as the obsession of U.S. officials about the Communist threat in the Third World areas and their exaggeration of the Soviet Union's ability to capitalize on the rising tide of nationalism.[11] As the State Department told the American consul in Lagos in 1951, "no one should doubt for a moment that the Soviet directorate is unaware of the importance of Africa to the Free World. . . . we must never forget that the anti-colonial feeling in certain African territories constitutes a formidable problem because all of the Colonial Governments are aligned on the side of the free World."[12]

Given the increasing strategic and political importance of Africa to the United States, policymakers in the Truman administration walked a tightrope between their allegiances to the colonial powers and their desire to win the loyalty of new Asian and African states. But the projects of anticolonial activists such as Robeson and the Council on African Affairs, of which Robeson was chair, as well as those of indigenous African independence movements, clashed with the explicit aims of the American government to foster pro-Western independence movements in Africa and Asia. The historian Thomas Borstelmann has aptly observed that for most of the peoples of Africa and Asia, "the Cold War and the supposed dangers of communism were merely distractions from the historic opportunity provided by World War II for ending the European colonialism that had long dominated the lives of most of the world's people."[13] As the Truman administration chose to interpret international, national, and even local politics in terms of a fundamental struggle with the Soviet Union, anticolonial activists tried to shift the terms of the debate to colonial people's and working people's control of their labor, their land, and their resources. For Robeson and his allies, the conflict was ultimately over the meaning of freedom. In 1951, for example, in response to Truman's argument that access to vital raw materials would be lost if the "free countries" of Asia and Africa should fall to the Soviet Union, the *African Standard*, printed by the West African Youth League of Sierra Leone, asserted the vacuity of Truman's notion of freedom and its irrelevance for colonized peoples:

> They tell us we are in a Free country . . . yes, we are free. Free to starve, free to live in shacks, free to be idle and unemployed, free to die for want of medical attention. Free to work for low wages, free not to have anything to save . . . It is possible that democracy and freedom have different meaning[s] for different people.[14]

Yet as their allies in Africa and Asia asserted their independence from the Cold War through a politics of nonalignment, anticolonial activists in the United States were unsuccessful in sustaining an opposition to Cold War orthodoxy.[15]

Their failure, as well as the scope and contours of the conflict, can only be understood through the federal government's all-encompassing ideological vision of national security. George F. Kennan observed in 1952 that "national security" is not simply a "negative quality: the absence of something

we call military attack . . . or the successful repelling of it." Kennan argued
that "customs and public policies in race relations" profoundly affect "the
feelings of other peoples toward us and the dispositions they make of their
physical and military resources, and accordingly on the demands we make
of other peoples."[16] Accordingly, the Truman administration saw racial discrimination in America as its Achilles' heel in a propaganda battle with the
Soviet Union to win the allegiance of Africa and Asia. The ensuing propaganda battles mobilized not only State Department personnel but a wide
array of African American spokespersons and representatives, from writers
such as Carl Rowan and J. Saunders Redding, to trade unionists such as
Maida Springer Kemp, to athletes and musicians.

Moreover, this internationalist politics of symbolic representation *replaced,* rather than complemented, commitments on the part of the Truman
and Eisenhower administrations to civil rights at home. As African American liberals traveled the globe extolling the virtues of American democracy,
the Truman administration paid minimal attention to domestic civil rights
programs. With the Truman administration preoccupied with the Korean
War and unwilling to resolutely challenge the southern wing of the Democratic Party, black protest, not segregation itself, became the threat to U.S.
security.[17] And the Eisenhower administration, while broadening propaganda efforts abroad, was certainly no more committed to the enforcement
of civil rights. Mary Dudziak has demonstrated the importance of international criticism of American racism leading to the 1954 *Brown v. Board of
Education* decision to desegregate public education.[18] But just as strikingly,
following the decision, desegregation was not enforced until the 1957 Little
Rock crisis, and then only to counter massive, often violent, resistance to
school desegregation. Indeed, it was not until a full decade after the *Brown*
decision, and *only* after a mass movement of black southerners and their
allies, that the Kennedy administration finally started to set in motion, in
the fall of 1963, events that would lead to the passage of the Civil Rights
Act of 1964.

But while the Truman and Eisenhower administrations refused to genuinely address discrimination, violence, and the denial of rights to black citizens, the State Department was increasingly energetic in propaganda efforts to shape perceptions of America. Courting the loyalty of mineral-rich
Africa, State Department officials in West Africa were deeply concerned
about the impact of prominent anticolonial activists such as Robeson and
W.E.B. Du Bois.[19] The most dramatic example of State Department apprehension about relationships between African Americans and Africans is

revealed in the deliberate attempt to discredit Paul Robeson. As Robeson's biographer Martin Duberman has explained, Robeson had been for many the showcase black American, proof that a "deserving" black person could make it in America, and even better, someone who exuded patriotism and optimism about the country's democratic promise. But with his increasingly forceful opposition to U.S. Cold War foreign policy, he became an unsuitable representative. It became imperative to isolate and discredit him.[20] The revocation of Robeson's passport by the American government drew widespread criticism throughout Asia and Africa.[21] State Department personnel in West Africa were particularly alarmed about the ramifications of the passport case, and were also dismayed by the repercussions of Robeson's criticism of American intervention in Korea. In August 1950, State Department personnel in Lagos, Nigeria, complained that Robeson's criticism of U.S. intervention had been widely publicized in the Nigerian press, arguing that "it is tragic that the most poisonous anti-American propaganda comes from the United States itself."[22]

In 1951, Roger P. Ross, a U.S. official in Accra, Ghana, wrote to the State Department soliciting a disparaging article about Robeson that could be distributed in Africa. Ross wrote:

> [USIS, i.e. the United States Information Service] in the Gold Coast, and I suspect everywhere else in Africa, badly needs a thorough-going, sympathetic and regretful but straight-talking treatment for the whole Robeson episode . . . The universality of its usefulness to us in Africa ought to warrant whatever it costs in time and money. Because there's no way the Communists score on us more easily and more effectively, out here, than on the U.S. Negro problem in general, and on the Robeson case in particular. And, answering the latter, we go a long way toward answering the former.[23]

Ross wanted the story of Robeson "told sympathetically, preferably by an American Negro devoted to his race," as a tragedy. To be convincing, Ross argued, an article must "pay homage to the man's remarkable talents as an artist," and with regret rather than rancor, it must treat his political views as a "spiritual alienation from his country and the bulk of his own people," and as an "illness of the mind and heart" which is "not easily recognized, yet contagious, and thus a deadly danger."[24] Predicting that he could get such an article "serialized in practically every newspaper" in the Gold Coast, Ross requested a printing in booklet form, with pictures. He stressed that to make the article credible, it should be "written by someone independent of the Department, published in an American periodical," and then reprinted.[25] An article of this precise description was published in the November 1951 *Crisis,* the official NAACP, organ as "Paul Robeson—The Lost Shepherd," by Robert Alan. Outlining "the tragedy of Paul Robeson," Alan described Robeson's fall from "a leader of democratic crusades" whose prominence rose from his "great abilities as an artist," to "Moscow's No. 1 Negro." Suggesting that Robeson was deserving of pity rather than hostility, Alan traced this purported change to a personality disorder. Alan was identified only as "the pen-name of a well known journalist."[26]

A struggle over the meaning and significance of race was a critical ideological component in the U.S. pursuit of global hegemony. In addition to attempts to discredit Robeson, the State Department intervened in other ways, culturally and politically, to shape the terms of solidarity among black Americans and Africans, and to shape the world's perceptions of the status of African Americans. The USIS in the Gold Coast (Ghana), Nigeria, Kenya, and South Africa used radio broadcasts, films, and publications to counter the poor image of America abroad stemming from domestic racial discrimination, and to win recognition for the United States as champions of African and black American aspirations. Much USIS effort went into crafting representations of black American life. Citing feelings of solidarity between Africans in the Gold Coast and African Americans, Hyman Bloom of the American consulate in Accra complained in April of 1951 that "the whole issue of race-relations in America" gave the Communists a "perfect theme." According to Bloom, "among Gold Coast Africans, who consider themselves more or less the parent stock of U.S. Negroes, there is deep, wary, almost psychotic concern with the whole issue of race-relations in America."[27] To counter this perceived "psychosis," USIS attempted to project positive images of black American life. Drawing on the economist Gunnar Myrdal's *American Dilemma,* the State Department developed a clear strategy that acknowledged that discrimination existed but hastened to add that racism was a fast-disappearing aberration, capable of being overcome by a talented and motivated individual.[28] Indeed, this Myrdalian twist characterized the dominant liberal discourse on racism in the late 1940s and early 1950s. Thus, in propaganda abroad, a stress on the achievements of prominent black Americans—promoting successful individuals as examples of democracy at work—was promoted over the image of collective advancement. USIS articles such as "Working for World Peace: Dr. Bunche in History," "The United States Negro in Business and Economic Progress," and "Negro Hurdler is determined to win Olympic event" were successfully reprinted in Lagos, Nigeria, in June of 1952.[29]

In one 1953 effort of USIS, the Nairobi-based regional public affairs officer, John A. Noon, and his staff created and broadcast a series of radio broadcasts in Swahili called *The Jones Family of Centerville USA*. Noon explained that this "family serial" was designed to "Broaden understanding of life in the United States; Increase the African's understanding of and appreciation for democratic institutions and processes by presenting democracy in action; Present the role of Negro-Americans in American life." Having secured air time in a twenty-minute spot immediately preceding the 6:00 P.M. news, Noon boasted that the "geographical coverage for these broadcasts includes Kenya, Uganda, Tanganyika and Zanzibar with an estimated listening audience of 3,000,000."[30] In a not very subtle case of revealing anxieties through denying their importance, Noon discussed the "many problems" in scripting the show. "The Jones are Negro-Americans. Should this fact be revealed at the outset or would it be more effective to give ethnic identity at a later time?" After "extensive debate" the staff decided "to avoid ethnic labels for a time in order to impress the audience that this was not a factor defining status in American life" and "to introduce the Negro-American identification most indirectly after the audience had realized that the Jones were able to participate in the full-round of community activities."[31]

But while attempting to defend American racial practices and foreign policy, the USIS itself sometimes became the object of biting criticism and wit. Its arguments, the *Eastern Nigerian Guardian* charged in "Dialectical Hypocrisy," were "calculated to veil the truth and bamboozle Nigerian opinion." Similarly, the *Labor Guardian* attacked USIS:

> To laud to the sky the isolated case of a successful Negro may be tolerated. But to present it to the people as the lot of the Negro community across the Atlantic is a claim tantamount to fraud. We know the lot of our brothers there . . . The Nigerian people cannot afford to have their minds poisoned by a people who though they are free would not allow others to be free.[32]

USIS officers were frustrated by these criticisms and what they considered the alterations or deliberate distortions of their material in the West African press. When the USIS distributed an account of the presentation of an award to the singer and actor Harry Belafonte, praise of Belafonte's "crusade for Americanism" was translated in the Gold Coast *Daily Mail* as "crusade for Africanism."[33] In Lagos, Willard Quincy Stanton complained that Nnamdi Azikiwe's press was using USIS material out of context and charged the *West African Pilot* with an intentional misuse of a USIS release. According to Stanton, Harold Null, the public affairs officer of the American consulate general, had given a series of radio broadcasts celebrating voluntarism in American civil society against statist control in the Soviet Union. Null explained that "when Americans combine toward a common end, the combinations are brief and easily dissolved by other unions." Indeed, anticolonial journalists embellished these broadcasts. In the satirical hands of the *West African Pilot,* Null's defense of civil society was modified into the contention that "the American government has always been an unstable equilibrium of contradictions." Indeed, such instability was offered as an explanation for lynching. "Since American society has moved into the wilderness, it was always well in advance of legal institutions. Vigilantes and lynch law were the frontier's justice when society had to be extemporized on the spot, but they lingered on to become instruments of oppression in the orderly society that replaced the frontier."[34] No wonder USIS officials were furious. In placing racism and violence at the heart of American life and institutions, the *West African Pilot* thoroughly undermined the attempts of the U.S. government to define racism as an aberration, as well as its claim that civil society is necessarily morally superior to the state. Here, civil society was unmasked as a source of terror, an indictment of the state's ineffectiveness as a protector of black rights.

Augmenting these broad cultural and political efforts to capture the sympathies of African peoples, State Department personnel designed programs to justify and defend American foreign policy and win the allegiance of colonized peoples to the side of the "free world." In 1950, the foremost concern of USIS in Africa was reconciling American intervention in Korea with the claim that America was on the side of freedom for colonized peoples. A typical USIS release in Nairobi argued that the "free peoples of the world" were helping the people of "Communist ravaged Korea."[35] During 1950, Twentieth Century–Fox distributed the Department of State's newsreel films *President Truman Reports on Korea* and *United Nations in Korea* in theaters throughout Kenya, Uganda, Tanganyika, and Zanzibar. Angus Ward, American consul general, Nairobi, monitored the showings and sent the Department of State "Town and theater breakdowns of people attending."[36] USIS articles such as "General Ridgway Pleads for Peace in Korea" and "Truman Stresses Aid to Korean People" were reprinted in West and East African newspapers such as the *Daily Success,* Lagos.[37] Along with films and articles addressing U.S. involvement in Korea, USIS officials portrayed the USSR as a nuclear aggressor and the United States as a savior in pamphlets such as *Survival Under Atomic Bombing Attack* in East Africa. (Mombasa, Kenya, 1951).[38]

For consulate staff in Africa, the application of Washington-generated

Cold War hysteria could be awkward. Perceiving that it was a hard sell to make Cold War geopolitics relevant to colonized African peoples, Willard Quincy Stanton, the American consul general in Lagos, wrote to the State Department arguing that they must stress Soviet imperialism over the problem of communism. According to Stanton, material on communism tended to "fall flat." Therefore USIS needed to emphasize "Russian imperialism," and promote the idea that assistance to "Communist agents" would lead to establishment of Russian slavery. Stanton argued that "a line such as this preached in simple terms might be understood by hundreds of thousands, perhaps millions of West Africans who do not like Whites but could perhaps be led to fear Russia."[39] Stanton's proposal materialized later that year. He reported the publication in the local presses of the USIS release "Attempt to Stamp Out Islam in Central Asia," and *Red Star over Islam* was produced as a USIS leaflet and distributed in Muslim areas of Nigeria.[40]

In South Africa the State Department was faced with the dilemma of wanting to court the black majority through the usual means of fabricating an image of American racial harmony, and of simultaneously not wanting to embarrass its white supremacist allies by pretending to believe in this very fabrication. Thus, State Department programs had a much slower start in South Africa than in Nigeria, Ghana, or Kenya. U.S. officials in Johannesburg and Cape Town argued that materials on "the race problem" risked alienating and embarrassing the white minority government and white citizens. Nonetheless, concerned that "the majority, which is black, is frankly skeptical of America's stand on the issue of color," they recommended programs on "Negro culture, or with opera, drama, and music by Negro performers," and again, suggested emphasizing the progress and accomplishments of individuals.[41] By 1955 and 1956, Voice of America and State Department programs highlighting individual achievements and culture were having considerable success in capturing publicity in black South African papers. For example, *The Bantu World*, the largest Soweto-based paper, carried a "Cartoon History of the United States" series, along with extensive reports on music and athletes.

In an African setting, propaganda was often lifted out of its Myrdalian context and was instead interpreted in the context of black solidarity, resistance, and struggles for self-government. In "We Claim Jazz: Listen to Africa," a South African writing in Ghana celebrated jazz and the fact that "the voice of Africa comes to us from thousands of miles away," even "under the splutter and meretricious ornament" of the Voice of America.[42] Moreover, the cartoon histories of revolutionary America or emancipation, portraying the lives of Americans such as Benjamin Franklin, Thomas Jefferson, and Abraham Lincoln, could give momentum and encouragement to local anti-colonial movements, often to the consternation of European colonial powers.[43] South African officials insisted on the cancellation of scheduled USIS-sponsored Fourth of July celebrations in the Belgian Congo. And Belgian officials, complaining that an American compulsion "to be liked" was leading to reckless "sympathy for problems and aspiration of native peoples," halted visits of black American artists and athletes to the Congo when they discerned that Wilbur de Paris and his orchestra "aroused some envy on the part of local Africans."[44]

Indeed, frequently criticized by its British, French, Dutch, Belgian, and South African allies, the State Department saw itself in a bind, "caught in the middle of the jaws of a vice of our own design and fabrication."[45] While the State Department did not want to antagonize its NATO allies, it was convinced that "indigenous disturbances" created conditions favorable to communism, and worried that the excesses of its colonial allies engendered dangerous instability. Moreover, the political and economic interests of the United States would best be served by decolonization. Thus, policymakers saw their task as one of encouraging independent states that would be securely in the Western orbit.[46] A 1951 State Department memo warned against getting trapped into "strong or weak" support of either "African nationalists aspirations" or "colonial policies" and provided "guidance" on measures to "insure the unwavering loyalty of the African to the cause of freedom as we perceive it."[47]

An examination of U.S. officials' readings of African nationalism further illuminates what was at stake in the creation of African policy. Postwar security and State Department documents on African nationalism in many ways echo the story familiar from the more extensively studied Southeast Asia and the Middle East. Of course, the State Department was not monolithic, and differences in readings of nationalist movements had much to do with proximity to these movements. While State Department officials understood nationalist movements through the ideological prism of the Cold War, consulate staff were cognizant of the independence of nationalist challenges and did not often make the mistake of simplistically attributing them to communism. In the early 1950s, for example, USIS in Kenya was targeting the Asian population by planning a radio station in Zanzibar with programs aimed at South Asian audiences.[48] However, with the rise of the Kenya African Union and the Kenya Land and Freedom Movement, popularly known as the "Mau Mau," the USIS realized it needed to be more responsive to indigenous nationalism.[49] State Department and intelligence reports on Kenya in the early 1950s found no evidence of Communist influence in the Mau Mau uprisings, or in the Kenya African Union. Nonetheless they believed that unrest created conditions that Communists could exploit and therefore stressed the importance of courting indigenous leaders to ally with the West.[50] John A. Noon, American consul general in Nairobi, argued that "interest in the Kenya disturbances centers in their reaction to world communism," but he fully acknowledged that Kenyans were not receiving "type one" direct Communist assistance, and that "Kenya authorities are entirely convinced that the subversive movement is entirely propelled from within."[51] Similarly, in Nigeria, State Department political reports focused on the intricacies of nationalist movements, and especially the rivalry between Azikiwe and Obafemi Awolowo. Erwin P. Keeler, American consul general, reported in 1953 that "there is no evidence to indicate any significant Communist participation in the Nigerian agitation and action toward gaining what the Nigerians call 'self-government,' nor any critical danger that they might move in to take over the nationalist movement at this time."[52]

However, the rejection of a monolithic vision of communism by local U.S. representatives did not fundamentally challenge the bipolar paradigm. The racism of U.S. officials, manifest in an inability to view Africans as self-governing peoples, reinforced the fear that movements would be manipulated by communism. William Cole, American consul in Accra, feared that "political emancipation is outrunning [the] economic and social development." Democratic self-government, Cole argued, "is not possible in a country the bulk of whose 4½ million people are 'bush Africans' still essentially animalistic in outlook." Cole feared "a stagnant dictatorship over these primitives by a few well-educated and semi-educated Africans," and argued that in a time of crisis such a government would be "an easy prey of Communists."[53] Ultimately, in a racist and simplistic vision of world affairs, U.S. officials could not see African nation-building projects as anything other than potentially dangerous tools of the Soviet Union. Indeed, for U.S. officials to have recognized the integrity of African and Asian nationalists and nonaligned movements would have required their accepting the legitimacy of African and Asian demands for genuine political and economic equality when in fact officials remained unwilling to challenge the prerogatives of corporate capital or to yield control of military-strategic interests.

Domestically, the same blindness about the nature and allegiances of Af-

rican nationalist movements, and the same determination to control strategic and economic resources, is reflected in government prosecution of
anticolonial activists. In the 1940s and through the early Cold War, activists
in the Council on African Affairs forcefully argued that the struggles of African Americans against Jim Crow were inextricably bound to the struggles of
Africans and colonized peoples for independence. These activists not only
supported anticolonial efforts in Africa and Asia; they also argued that the
independence of new Asian and African nations would help black Americans in their struggles for political, economic, and civil rights. In 1952, two
years after revoking Robeson's passport, and as the United States attempted
to discredit Robeson in Africa, the United States Attorney General's Subversive Activities Control Board charged the CAA with Communist domination and with failing "to register with the Attorney General as provided in
Sec. 7(b) of the Internal Security Act of 1950."[54] However, evidence for the
case rested not on CAA support of the Communist Party, but on its work
on Africa and on its opposition to American intervention in Korea. Asserting
the integrity and independence of anticolonial politics, the CAA's chief line
of defense was to demonstrate the breadth of its work in support of African
liberation movements.[55] Not only was it precisely this support that the government interpreted as Communist influence, but indeed, the next year the
CAA was charged directly for its support of African groups.[56] In a 1953
memo to J. Edgar Hoover, Assistant Attorney General Warren Olney III
implied that the attempts to link the CAA to the Communist Party USA had
been "a mere fishing expedition" and outlined a new case against the Council. Evidence that "the subject is acting as 'a publicity agent' for a foreign
principal" and "soliciting funds for a foreign principal" rested on the CAA's
support of the African National Congress of South Africa, the Nigerian
mine workers, and the Kenya African Union.[57] Olney subpoenaed CAA correspondence with the ANC and South African Indian Congress hoping that
"an examination of the subject's books records and correspondence will reveal the necessary evidence to establish an agent relationship." The FBI
further stepped up its surveillance.[58] The case against the CAA never
reached closure because in 1955, financially crippled by the defense of the
organization and weakened by the restrictions placed on its leaders (Robeson, Du Bois, and W. A. Hunton), the CAA disbanded. The CAA devoted
much of its last months to supporting the 1955 Bandung Conference of
nonaligned nations in Bandung, Indonesia, and embraced the position of
nonalignment. Although the government had successfully contained the

CAA and its leaders, Bandung vindicated their support of the struggles of colonized peoples over bipolar Cold War politics.

*   *   *

The American government's effort to control the politics of race is strikingly evident in its increasing global forays into the world of popular culture, including the promotion of successful black American athletes and musicians. Beginning in the early 1950s the State Department sponsored tours by African American and African athletes. Gilbert Cruter, once a holder of the world high jump record, toured West Africa to help train athletes for regional Olympic trials.[59] Others sponsored by the State Department included the Harlem Globetrotters. Globetrotter appearances between 1951 and 1955 included Berlin, "to combat the popular East German youth rallies being staged by the Communists," and Indonesia, Burma, and Italy.[60] The South African *Bantu World* reported that the Globetrotters have "blended basketball and buffoonery with their own special brand of diplomacy to become one of the United States' most effective weapons in the cold war against communism." Owner-coach Abe Saperstein explained their "unusual role in helping combat the spread of communism" by appearing "at the request of the State Department in areas where communism is a threat."[61]

The "goodwill ambassador" tours by African American jazz musicians were among the State Department's most highly publicized cultural efforts. The tours themselves exemplified the contradictions that beset propaganda efforts. Promoted by both participants and supporters such as Congressman Adam Clayton Powell as part of an antiracist agenda, the tours were opposed by southern segregationists.[62] Yet the tours reinforced an already developed State Department strategy which did not deny that discrimination existed in the United States, but suggested that it was a fast-disappearing aberration capable of being overcome by talented and motivated individuals.[63]

The tours were widely reported in the African American press, which emphasized the challenge to racism presented by the tours. "American jazz," declared *The Afro-American,* "hot, blues, Dixieland, bebop or rock 'n' roll has at last been publicly acknowledged as the principal asset of American foreign policy." According to the Baltimore *Afro-American,* when Powell came up with the idea of jazz ambassadors, "State Department squares first scoffed at the idea," but when "they finally gave up out of sheer exhaustion and shipped the number one be-bopster," Dizzy Gillespie, to the Near

East and Europe, "the result was electric" and the "only problem was find-ing auditoriums large enough to house new converts to the American view-point attracted by Dizzy's bent trumpet, Rhythmic beat, and unorthodox style."[64] Gillespie's USIS tour included Abadan, Iran; Dacca and Karachi, Pakistan; Beirut, Lebanon; Damascus and Aleppo, Syria; and Ankara and Istanbul, Turkey. *The Pittsburgh Courier* celebrated an editorial in a Paki-stani newspaper which proclaimed that "the language of diplomacy ought to be translated into the score for a bop trumpet," and reported a "miracle" in Abadan, Iran, where "these Arabs—who were completely ignorant of what jazz was"—"started to catch the beat" and eventually "the theater was as hot as any American jazz spot where Diz performed for long standing fans."[65] Following the tour, Gillespie did a three week State Department/ANTA (American National Theater and Academy) tour of South America.[66] Defending the tours against critics such as Louisiana's segregationist Sena-tor Allen Ellender, Gillespie argued in a telegram to Eisenhower that "our trip through the Middle-East proved conclusively that our interracial group was powerfully effective against Red propaganda. Jazz is our own American folk music that communicates with all peoples regardless of language or social barriers."[67]

Ironies abound in Gillespie's ambassador tours. For Gillespie, the tours meant a chance to work. An unlikely ambassador as a former draft dodger, Gillespie had once been a card-carrying member of the Communist Party because it enabled him to get gigs in CP run halls. Gillespie later recalled that "I sort've liked the idea of representing America, but I wasn't going to apologize for the racist policies of America." He managed to avoid his offi-cial State Department briefing, noting that "I've got three hundred years of briefing. I know what they've done to us and I'm not going to make any excuses."[68] Deeply aware of the politics of the tours, Gillespie didn't hesitate to defy State Department and local convention while on the tours, promot-ing his own version of America which was considerably more egalitarian than that of the State Department. He later recalled that the tour skipped India because it was nonaligned. His band played instead in Karachi, Paki-stan, where the United States was supplying arms, and Gillespie refused to play until the gates were opened to the "ragamuffin" children because "they priced the tickets so high the people we were trying to gain friendship with couldn't make it."[69]

One does not have to demonstrate that the "jambassadors" endorsed American policy, and for the most part they did not, to see that the State Department got tremendous mileage from these tours. Even jazz artists not sponsored by the State Department were proclaimed "U.S. jambassadors at large" whenever they toured abroad. Lionel Hampton was so designated during his 1956 seven month tour of Europe.[70] Moreover, the enthusiasm for the goodwill-ambassador tours reverberated well beyond the areas visited by artists. Africa-wide *Drum* magazine and *The World,* based in Johannesburg, for example, carried feature articles on Louis Armstrong and his 1956 goodwill tours.[71] Building on the success of the tours, Voice of America broadcast jazz programs in Africa in the fifties and sixties. In South Africa in 1956, for example, the Voice of America aired a two hour jazz program every night along with special programs such as "The Newport Jazz Festival."[72]

❖   ❖   ❖

Already considered by many to be America's most effective goodwill ambassador, Louis Armstrong's 1956 celebrated yet "unofficial" visit to the Gold Coast drew crowds of up to 100,000 and attracted worldwide publicity.[73] The American consulate in Accra reported that Armstrong and his band received an "outpouring of press and public enthusiasm." The government and many private firms even gave employees a half-day holiday to attend an outdoor performance, to which 30,000 showed up. The consulate considered the visit an outstanding success, citing responses such as that by the Ghanaian *Daily Mail,* which applauded the State Department for the visit, praising the "unbiased support for the African's course . . . And they don't just talk thousands of miles away. They come to our land to see for themselves."[74] The tour was deemed such a success that a State Department–sponsored trip through the Soviet Union and South America was planned for the following year, called by *The Pittsburgh Courier* "Satchmo's romp through the land of the Reds."[75] The *Courier* named Armstrong one of the "Brightest Lights" of 1956 for "the easy manner in which he won friends for Uncle Sam overseas."[76]

❖   ❖   ❖

The historian Frank Kofsky observed in 1970 that as a weapon in Cold War propaganda, jazz "may turn out to be a double edged sword."[77] While the State Department no doubt benefited from tours by black American artists, many of the jazz musicians who toured under the auspices of the State Department, such as Gillespie, Armstrong, and later Duke Ellington, not only challenged U.S. policy, but disrupted claims to an exclusively American identity by promoting solidarities among black peoples. Indeed music, and in this era, particularly jazz, became a critical arena in which diaspora identities were elaborated and contested.[78] Ironically, many of Gillespie's ties to Brazilian and South American artists were built partly through his State Department tours. What Gillespie discovered on his government-sponsored tour in Brazil was "a lotta brothers, Africans—and their music is African."[79] And when 100,000 people showed up to see Armstrong in Ghana in 1956, the meaning was clear to him: "After all, my ancestors came from here and I still have African blood in me."[80] Horace Cayton argued in the *Courier* that "there is a deep symbolic meaning underlying the visit of Louis Armstrong to the African Gold Coast last week." Cayton saw this as a "dramatic illustration of the deep bonds of mutual sympathy between American and African Negroes, deeper and wider than the oceans and centuries between us."[81] A veteran journalist who in the 1940s contributed to promoting solidarities between black Americans and Africans, Cayton revisited his argument in the 1950s, not through politics, but through music. Armstrong, Cayton argued, represented not simply America, but black Americans. "The hundreds of thousands of Africans were not only cheering Louis Armstrong as an artist and musician, or as an American. They were cheering Louis Armstrong as the representative of 15 million American Negroes."[82] Thus, the tours encouraged the rekindling of bonds promoted by activists such as Robeson but disrupted by the early Cold War.

The U.S. strategy of promoting black American jazz artists as pro-American propagandists backfired the following year with Armstrong's widely publicized denunciations of Eisenhower and Governor Orval Faubus of Arkansas. When Faubus ordered units of the National Guard to prevent the desegregation of Central High School in Little Rock by blocking entry of black students, Armstrong abandoned his plans for a government-sponsored trip to the Soviet Union, declaring that "the way they are treating my people in the South, the Government can go to hell." Calling Faubus "an uneducated plow-boy," Armstrong said the president was "two-faced" and had allowed Faubus to run the federal government. For Armstrong, "It's getting so bad a colored man hasn't got any country." The impact of Armstrong, regarded by the State Department as "perhaps the most effective un-official goodwill ambassador this country has ever had," not only criticizing and refusing to tour for the government, but declaring that black people in America had no country, sent a very alarmed State Department scrambling to try to get Armstrong to reconsider. (Benny Goodman ended up making the first Soviet tour in 1962.)[83] Armstrong was pressured to retract his harsh criticism of Eisenhower and he refused, despite a flurry of threats and canceled concerts and television appearances. Although Armstrong praised Eisenhower when he finally sent in federal troops to uphold integration, he continued to express outrage over Little Rock. In light of Robeson's blacklisting and his own prior delight in representing America, Armstrong's defiance is especially remarkable. In October 1957 Armstrong said that he'd rather play in the Soviet Union than in Arkansas because Faubus "might hear a couple of notes—and he don't deserve that."[84] E. Frederick Morrow, the only black American on Eisenhower's White House staff, complained that "all of us have been terribly disappointed in the past few months because of Louis's distasteful abuse of the President in the Little Rock Case."[85]

Armstrong's courageous stand surprised a younger generation who, perhaps disapproving of his unabashed pleasure in performing, the manipulation of his image by Hollywood, and his reticence about politics, regarded him as an "Uncle Tom." Indeed, Armstrong was a master of dissemblance. But those who knew Armstrong well knew also his deep awareness of and anger at the daily indignities and humiliations he faced, despite his undisputed and celebrated stature as a protean creator of American music. Moved by the courage of student and community activists in the southern civil rights movement as they crafted new challenges to racism and Jim Crow, and perhaps inspired by his experience in Ghana on the eve of independence, his status as ambassador must have underscored the sense of insult and rejection he felt at the stark demonstration of hypocrisy and the betrayal of a promise he had willingly promoted.

Moreover, there is further poignancy in Armstrong, who had been showcased by the State Department in Ghana, stating a preference for performing in the Soviet Union over the segregationist South. After all, it was only seven years earlier that the State Department had revoked Paul Robeson's right to travel and had expended considerable energy to discredit him in Ghana, insisting in part that his belief that the Soviet Union was less racist than America made him un-American. Indeed, no one was more pleased by Armstrong's castigation of the administration than Robeson, who praised Armstrong for his "heartfelt outburst," and for criticizing the government "in stronger terms than I ever have."[86] And particularly sensitive to the "virtual necessity for the Negro artist" to travel, given the dearth of opportunities for black artists in the United States, Robeson appreciated Armstrong's risk.[87] Indeed, while denouncing black spokespersons who "have set out to calm the clamor of world humanity against racism," Robeson defended performing artists who "went on these government sponsored tours because they needed work and who were out to show the world, as they did, that the American Negro has talent and dignity deserving of respect everywhere."[88]

In an interesting coincidence, just as the Armstrong controversy exploded in late September, the October issue of *Ebony* hit the stands with an interview with Paul Robeson by Carl T. Rowan, "Has Paul Robeson betrayed the Negro?" Noting that one of "the most fabulous characters of our time" had become anathema, Rowan asked, "Why? What caused this almost unbelievable turnabout that sent an international hero plunging into seven years of obscurity?" And "why was the State Department out to get him?"

> "Nobody will ever convince me that the foreign and domestic policies of this country do not come straight from the South," explains Robeson. "This country is run by Jim Eastland and Lyndon Johnson and Richard Russell and that crowd." And Robeson figures that these men feared him, that they saw in him a symbol around which the Negro masses might rally to join hands with "the black power that is now flexing its muscles in Asia and Africa."[89]

For Robeson the issue came back to the American South. The real reason he was silenced was that he challenged colonialism abroad and racism in the South, not for what he considered the false charges of being pro-Soviet. But if there is irony in this story, the imploding of State Department efforts to manipulate perceptions of race was perhaps inevitable. As Robeson told Rowan, "They can keep me from going overseas but they can't keep news of Emmett Till and Autherine Lucy from going over there."[90] The State Department could silence Robeson. The State Department could then promote other black artists in Ghana. But ultimately the State Department, like black artists and all Americans, could not contain American racism, the violence and lawlessness of the American South, or their impact abroad.[91] "By now," Robeson wrote in 1958, "it should be recognized by all that this global advertising campaign has failed in its purpose. Facts still speak louder than words."[92]

Robeson regained his right to travel in 1958. But with his reputation badly tarnished, activists usually saw his efforts on behalf of civil rights as a hindrance. As Robeson's life ended in obscurity, the once internationally renowned artist and civil rights leader anguished by the abandonment and isolation attending his blacklisting, a new generation attempted to expose the inherent instabilities and contradictions in the government's attempts to render racism and its profound inequalities aberrations.

After Armstrong's aborted Soviet tour, he would tour several times for the government, including a six-month African tour in 1960 and 1961, co-sponsored by the State Department and Pepsi-Cola. The cultural arena continued to be a site of political contestation. Dizzy Gillespie used his status as "World Statesman" in his 1964 presidential campaign. However playful his promises to appoint Miles Davis as the head of the CIA and Duke Ellington as secretary of state may have appeared, the campaign provided a venue to voice deep dissatisfaction with America's foreign and domestic policies.[93] And despite his renewed apprearances for the government, Louis Armstrong made a similar departure from his official role as cultural ambassador. In his 1962 collaboration with Dave and Iona Brubeck, "The Real Ambassadors," Armstrong voiced his frustration at continued foot-dragging on civil rights and commented on the dilemma of the American artist in the Cold War era. Observing that "no commodity is quite so strange, as this thing called cultural exchange" the "real ambassador" muses: "I represent the government but the government doesn't represent some policies I'm for." Through satire, the Brubecks and Armstrong exposed once again the impossibility of shielding violent racial discord from audiences at home and abroad.

Any assessment of U.S. cultural Cold War programs in Africa must come back to the sobering context of U.S. intervention on the continent. Indeed, as attempts to mobilize consent were backed up by force, the so-called Cold War has been very hot for many of the world's peoples, costing the lives of millions in military conflicts in Africa, Asia, and Latin America. Throughout, struggles to articulate foreign policies of nonalignment have been undermined by decades of the arming of brutal dictatorships by the United States and the Soviet Union and African mercenaries willing to do the bidding of the superpowers. In 1946, Robeson pointed out that the American government was getting uranium from the Belgian Congo for atomic bombs and that American companies were prospecting for oil in Ethiopia and for minerals in Liberia, and warned that U.S. corporations were increasingly "linked with international cartels which dominate Africa's mineral production."[94] Describing emerging military-industrial alliances, he further warned in 1951 that workers in the Congo were mining tin for guns that would eventually be turned against them. Robeson's prescience in his description of the emerging postwar political economy was tragically illustrated in the death of the prime minister of the independent Congo, Patrice Lumumba, in a 1961 CIA-backed assassination, only two months after Armstrong had performed there as part of his 1960–1961 Africa-wide State Department and Pepsi–sponsored tour.[95] Sadly, the ultimate limitations of

American propaganda programs in Africa are graphically illustrated in covert U.S. military operations, which in Africa have included Ghana, Angola, and Zaire; and apartheid South Africa's American-backed wars in Angola, Zimbabwe, Mozambique, and Namibia.[96] Indeed, if the story of U.S. attempts to control the politics of race in the early Cold War illustrates the subtlety, innovation, and variety of power exercised through cultural programs, it is also a tale of the intimate relationship of these efforts to political, economic, and military power.

The Road to Vietnam
Modernization Theory in Fact and Fiction

JONATHAN NASHEL

IN 1955 WALT WHITMAN ROSTOW, MIT economic historian, former aide to Gunnar Myrdal, and adviser to the Democratic Party, published *An American Policy in Asia.* More of a primer than a monograph, the book's front cover promised "REALISTIC ANSWERS TO MANY BURNING QUESTIONS." Throughout the work, Rostow depicts the classic protocols of Cold War liberalism and proposes an aggressive internationalist posture that would adopt military force when American interests were deemed to be threatened. Rostow is quite direct about the ways that the Cold War has changed the nature of American society and determined its foreign policy responsibilities: "It is an irreversible fact of American life that the fate of our society is now bound up with the course of events throughout the world. The United States as a nation and the American people collectively and as individuals must accept responsibilities in other parts of the world as never before in our history. This is most strikingly true of our relations with Asia."[1] Rostow goes on to make a series of proposals in his short study (only thirty-nine pages) stressing the need for the United States to refashion third world societies into the political and economic structures of modern states. Like other academic theorists of the modernization process, Rostow saw vast sections of the world as a social science laboratory in which "primitive" societies of the underdeveloped world could be guided along an evolutionary path toward their "natural" technological and capitalist fruition. Not incidentally for these theorists, those developing countries would simultaneously act as bulwarks against Communist advances in the third world.

Leaving aside Rostow's breathless prose and his pandering for a major U.S. military presence in Asia (one of the subheadings in the book is

132

"SHOULD THE UNITED STATES INITIATE WAR?"), his argument is indicative of a pervasive Cold War liberalism that had deep roots in the American progressive tradition. Rostow's passion was an American-centered desire to rationalize all global political problems and remake them along American lines. Like Rostow, many other Americans had embarked on the long-term project of exporting this American-style liberalism. Henry Luce, publisher and editor of *Time, Life,* and *Fortune,* probably enunciated most clearly for popular consumption a set of axioms about the nature of America's relation to the rest of the world. His famous declaration of 1941, entitled "The American Century" (later published in book form), remains the classic pronouncement on America's duty to the world. While Luce's title has been reduced to something of a catchall phrase by American historians, it is still the starting point for anyone concerned with the nature of American foreign policy both during and after World War II. As Luce described the situation to his readers, the United States was at a historical watershed; it could either immediately take control of events in the world and create little Americas or miss the opportunity and duty of a lifetime. With no sense of irony, Luce wrote: "Consider the 20th Century. It is ours not only in the sense that we happen to live in it but ours also because it is America's first century as a dominant power in the world."[2] While this statement can be read as a new form of imperialism—one that takes control of time as well as geography—Luce fused this vision with a missionary component when he stated that it was incumbent that America become the "Good Samaritan of the entire world."[3] Luce's call to arms provided a popular base of support, one which led the way for Rostow's Cold War rhetoric a decade later.[4]

At the core of this proposal to export Americana was a fervent belief in modernization theory, a theory predicated on a scientific understanding of world historical development and America's newfound role as mediator of this process.[5] Working from the fields of political science, economics, history, and anthropology, a number of scholars began charting the process of social and technological development on a worldwide scale. Many of these scholars were filled with a genuinely optimistic notion that "traditional" states with "stagnant" economies could be transformed into "modern" states with dynamic economic growth. This understanding of how economic and political development occurred through history became doubly powerful when it was coupled with the argument that the United States must ensure that these transformations take place as rapidly as possible; to delay was tantamount to surrendering to Communist ideology and thus to world chaos. Liberal academics and government officials like Rostow worked to realize modernization theory's goals in everything from flood relief and literacy campaigns to political intrigue and counterinsurgency efforts.

Modernization theory was so popular in the aftermath of World War II that it approximated a civil religion championed by liberal cold warriors.[6] This social science theory was liberalism writ large since it held that American institutions, ideas, and technology not only could but should be transplanted into other areas of the world. It was touted not only as a new version of a Universal History but as one that seemed to offer solutions to two of the most vexing foreign policy problems facing the United States during the Cold War: how to ensure that the newly independent countries of the third world became integrated into a capitalist network of market relations, and conversely, how to prevent these desperately poor countries from becoming communist.[7]

This paper will chart the origins of modernization theory in American Cold War policy as it played itself out in the arenas of policymakers and in American popular culture. In particular, this essay will examine the popularization of American-style liberalism and the way it was exported abroad in the guise of economic and technological development. I use the history, reception, and ultimate policy recommendations of William Lederer and Eugene Burdick's celebrated 1958 novel, *The Ugly American,* as a case study of these interactions at work. Concerning modernization theory's rationale in policy making, the efforts of such cold warriors as Rostow, Robert McNamara, and David Lilienthal will be examined to show how policymakers sought to meld liberalism and modernization theory in Southeast Asia. This combined study of fictional representation with individual actions and motivations will help illuminate the dynamics of liberalism as it was popularized at home and exported abroad.[8]

✿   ✿   ✿

At first glance it may seem a bit of a reach to include a detailed discussion of one middlebrow novel in charting the rise and fall of modernization theory. Yet, William Lederer and Eugene Burdick's immensely popular *The Ugly American* remains distinguished today chiefly because of its overt policy prescriptions concerning U.S. actions abroad and the way it dovetailed with popular concerns at the time. The title alone remains of note and is still used as a catchall phrase to describe unproductive or stupid American actions abroad. The novel was written to directly counter Graham Greene's *The Quiet American* (1955), and to refute his supposed anti-American and anti-interventionist sentiments. In contrast to Greene's account of the tragic consequences of American naïveté and hubris in attempting to refashion other worlds, Lederer and Burdick's "message book" was directed both to American policymakers and to concerned citizens as a treatise on the methods currently used to defeat the Communists in the third world. Its success is easy to measure; as the publisher noted on the paperback edition, the book was "THE BIG BESTSELLING NOVEL THAT CHANGED AMERICAN DIPLOMATIC HISTORY." It was on *The New York Times* best-seller list for seventy-two weeks, sold almost five million copies, was a Book-of-the-Month Club selection, was championed by Senator John F. Kennedy, and was later made into a film starring Marlon Brando, then Hollywood's reigning male icon. President Eisenhower commented on how much he liked the novel and how U.S. foreign policy would benefit from Lederer and Burdick's prescriptions.[9] In short, Lederer (a college professor) and Burdick (a naval officer) succeeded beyond their wildest dreams in influencing American policy toward the third world. Their program of a strong American intervention abroad, one that roundly condemned any hint of isolationism in policy making circles, was to become de facto American policy until the 1970s.

It is of note that the authors had originally intended to write a nonfiction book on these problems and decided instead to spice up their proposals in a fictional format. Yet they made clear that their book was not meant to be read simply as a "story." Or, as they wrote in their "Factual Epilogue," "It is not orthodox to append a factual epilogue to a work of fiction. However, we would not wish any reader to put down our book thinking that what he has read is wholly imaginary. For it is not; it is based on fact." Set in a mythical Southeast Asian country called Sarkhan, the novel's relationship to "fact" consisted of an assortment of pseudonymous characters and events loosely culled from the Philippines and Vietnam of the 1950s and liberally sprinkled with pseudonyms and stereotypes about developing nations. As an example of this merging of fact with fiction, the actual Philippine president at the time the novel was written, Ramon Magsaysay, was the only character in the novel who is referred to by his own name, while many pseudonyms allude to the actual individuals involved, and still other idealized characters, such as the "ugly American" himself, Homer Atkins, appear to be completely fictional.[10]

Lederer and Burdick sift this conglomeration of fact and fiction in the service of a larger ideological purpose that not too subtly drives the novel: "If the only price we are willing to pay is the dollar price, then we might as well pull out before we're thrown out. If we are not prepared to pay the human price, we had better retreat to our shores, build Fortress America, learn to live without international trade and communications, and accept the mediocrity, the low standard of living, and the loom of world Communism which would accompany such a move."[11] This unabashed use of the tenets of Cold War liberalism reveals Lederer and Burdick's ability to tap into a nagging fear of the era: if the United States is so wealthy and powerful, why is it that communism appears as the wave of the future? Furthermore, why is it that many newly decolonized countries are not embracing the tenets of American-style liberalism? *The Ugly American* provided the public with a host of easily applied answers, beginning with the reassuring note that the people of the third world actually want to become more American, but the United States is so poorly projecting its power and image that countries are "falling," à la the domino theory, into the laps of the Communists.

The title of the novel worked against common stereotypes denoting Americans abroad as arrogant, big-spending, loud-talking tourists who had little sensitivity to the people they encountered. This has led to endless misconceptions, since the "ugly Americans" in the novel are in fact the only Americans who are portrayed as positive representatives of Americans abroad.[12] The entire novel is set in dualities between "ugly" Americans, that is, "good" citizens who are not afraid to get their hands dirty and work with peasants, and "beautiful" Americans, that is, State Department officials who know little of the country in which they work and alternatively fear and despise those who are different from them.

One character in the novel is an American military officer, Edwin Hillendale, who is represented as the ideal nation-developer. Hillendale is unique among the other American bureaucrats in that he works with, listens to, and most important respects the nationalistic sentiments of Asians. In turn, the people of Sarkhan deeply admire the ideals of the United States and intuitively reject communism—in short, they want what he wants but they also hope to develop a national cohesion. The fact that Hillendale, unlike his government superiors, is willing to die in order to help them achieve their goals only reinforces the mutual bonds between the Occident and the Orient, which is not surprising since this is one of the major themes of the novel.

True to the novel's Cold War convictions, Hillendale uses a variety of gimmicks and strategies to assist American and anti-Communist forces in Sarkhan. We meet him first in the Philippines, riding intrepidly into a Communist controlled province, armed only with his harmonica and a taste for local cuisine:

> When he arrived in the capital about half-past eleven, the people of Cuenco saw something they had never in their lives seen before. A tall, slender U.S. Air Force Colonel with red hair and a big nose drove into Cuenco on a red motorcycle, whose gas tank had painted on it in black "The Ragtime Kid." He chugged up the main street and stopped at the most crowded part. . . . After waving and smiling at everyone, he took out his harmonica and began to play favorite Filipino tunes in a loud and merry way. . . . Within about fifteen minutes a crowd of about two hundred people surrounded the colonel.[13]

After a group sing-along—where Hillendale also convinces these peasants that he is as poor as they are—the Filipinos begin quarreling among themselves as to who can invite him to lunch. To avoid favoritism, Hillendale suggests that they eat en masse, "And that's where the colonel went, with about ten Filipinos. They ate *adobo* and *pancit* and rice, and they washed it down with Filipino rum and San Miguel beer; and they sang many songs to the accompaniment of the Ragtime Kid's harmonica."[14] Hillendale's triumph is complete when over 95 percent of these citizens vote for the anti-Communist candidate, Ramon Magsaysay, and his pro-American platform.[15]

In a series of vignettes such as these, *The Ugly American* capitalized on the faith that American know-how and an earnest person-to-person diplomacy could solve all problems, be they political, economic, or cultural in nature. Superficially transcultural, the novel insisted that if Americans listen to the people of the third world to learn what they want they will find they simply wish to be Americans. The book made use of this cyclical logic to promote to its readership a popularized version of the academic tenets of modernization theory. However, it is important to keep in mind that the novel was quite scathing about the nature of current development projects, with all of the heroes in the novel—the ones who were "ugly"—opposing large-scale, imported changes, while creating smaller projects that involved working with and listening to the native peoples. In their conclusion, Lederer and Burdick insist: "Most American technicians abroad are involved in the planning and execution of 'big' projects: dams, highways, irrigation systems. The result is that we often develop huge technical complexes which some day may pay dividends but at this moment in Asian development are neither needed nor wanted except by a few local politicians who see such projects as a means to power and wealth."[16] Instead, the novel proposes a mode of American intervention that works to stimulate smaller-scale, local projects, and to follow the lead of local industries and candidates rather than to provide them with an American-dictated direction. A typical example here is when an American woman gets to know her neighbors and notes that their physical problems are caused from sweeping out their huts with inadequate brooms. She then devises longer broom handles made from indigenous reeds, which help keep the Sarkhanese homes clean and prevent stooped shoulders. The purpose of the novel faithfully reflected the basis of modernization theory as it was then being touted; that is, the almost Social Darwinist assumption that the natural evolution of a country will be toward technological progress and democratic reform when protected from deliberately interfering forces such as communism.

What the novel most clearly shared with modernization theories of the day was not the current method of transplanting technological advances into foreign soil, but rather a certainty about the nature of development itself and about America's ability to foster it. Lederer and Burdick write that what the United States should be doing now is developing "chicken and pig breeding, small pumps which did not need expensive replacement parts, knowledge on commercial fishing, canning of food . . ."[17] From this perspective, all countries were either "primitive" or "modern," with the former needing American assistance in their evolutionary progression toward modernity. By translating these larger tenents of modernization theory into popular imagery while insisting on a respect for the "natural" pace of primitive countries, the novel helped to spread and legitimate the ultimate goals of Americanization efforts abroad. Lederer and Burdick's policy prescriptions stemmed from a commonly held view among American commentators in the 1950s that America was losing the Cold War even as its military and economic might was second to none.

The novel was published in 1958, shortly after the Soviets launched Sputnik, when the term "missile gap" animated foreign policy discussions, when Khrushchev announced Soviet support for "wars of national liberation," and when his proclamation "we will bury you" took on ever more ominous tones given the reality that Soviet spacecraft were circling over the United States. The book captured and then reinforced the belief that while America might be winning the war over consumer goods, it was losing the far more important battles over military preparedness, scientific achievement, and the "hearts and minds" of people in the third world. It was the specter of neutralism in the newly formed nations of the third world that caused great alarm to Americans who were fashioning alliances against the Communists.

Even the seeming lull on the European front of the Cold War only heightened American concerns over their perceived losses in Asia, Africa, and Latin America.[18]

While the novel is in a way a case study of the popularization of modernization theory, it also differentiates itself in a variety of ways. First, and most obvious, is the difference between academic theories that were never intended to be read as explicit "how to" manuals and the novel's practical prescriptions; several of the proposals in *The Ugly American* were literally adopted, such as the "small is beautiful" motif, which was later valorized and incorporated into the charter of the Peace Corps. Another key difference between the novel's approach to modernization theory and the approaches of academic theorists of this period was one of scale. The novel proposed local, noninterventionist support of indigenous industries, medical aid, and development of people-led causes, and took a strong stand against large-scale imposition of high-technology projects. Academic theorists, especially before Rostow, were more concerned with noting structural and technological developments, large and small, than with offering specific prescriptions or with limiting the rate of Western intervention. Rostow, though, was simply ahead of the curve, with many other academics turned government officials soon to follow.

More than anything else, the novel represents and helps us understand a climate of American thought in the 1950s. Many Americans shared or were persuaded by the novel's inherent assumption that it was the right and responsibility of scientifically and technologically "advanced" nations to aid the "natural evolution" of less developed societies. And few questioned the notion that American-style scientific and technological prowess was the natural goal of that "evolutionary process." At the same time, it took a combination of the popular appeal represented by the novel and the driving force of academic theorists to create the heyday of modernization theory and the climate of liberal zeal that supported American intervention abroad. However, as the experiences of two practitioners of modernization theory will also show, that very atmosphere of fervent, almost mystical certainty in the efficacy of scientific and technological advancement contributed to an equally fervent and widespread disillusionment when the rewards of American liberalism failed to manifest themselves in Vietnam.

For academic theorists, the possibility of implementing modernization theory, not just as a a category for understanding global change but also as a series of foreign policy directives that could support and enhance the transformation of developing nations through a capitalist, technological framework, was a remote but enticing one.[19] Walt Rostow remains notable among those theorists because his *Stages of Economic Growth: A Non-Communist Manifesto* (1960) was written both as an academic treatise (he traced how and why certain societies grew and others did not) *and* as a political tract (it was an obvious attempt to provide an antidote to the "disease" of communism). In it, Rostow believed that he had uncovered the "laws" integral to economic development: "it is useful, as well as roughly accurate, to regard the process of development now going forward in Asia, the Middle East, Africa, and Latin America as analogous to the stages of preconditions and take-off of other societies, in the late eighteenth, nineteenth, and early twentieth centuries."[20]

While this excerpt points to Rostow's overweening certainty in the inevitability predicated by his own analysis, he was clearly influenced by a host of other writers, and specifically those historians and political scientists who were intent in the immediate aftermath of the Great Depression and World War II on analyzing American history in a way that explained how the country had persevered during these twin crises. The problem that came to naturally occupy such scholars as Richard Hofstadter, David Potter, Daniel Boorstin, and other historians of the "Consensus School" was the analysis of why America did not take the fascist or communist path embraced by so many other countries during this period. In this respect their work coincided with Rostow's concerns, as their mutually approving citations attest. Not surprisingly, then, their collective answer was America's relationship to liberalism. One of the foremost members of this group, Louis Hartz, developed a theory that the United States was a liberal capitalist society from its inception: "the outstanding thing about the American community in Western history ought to be the non-existence of those [feudalistic and religious] oppressions, or since the reaction against them was in the broadest sense liberal, that the American community is a liberal community. We are confronted, as it were, with a kind of inverted Trotskyite law of combined development, America skipping the feudal stage of history as Russia presumably skipped the liberal stage."[21] In Hartz's framework, America's liberalism became the vehicle for Americans not only to explain the idea of their country to one another but also to set the direction in which newly developing countries should be encouraged to progress. Thus, liberalism when it was exported abroad went under the protocols of modernization theory. This projection of an American creed upon other people eventually turned into a melding of religious and secular fervor, in which countries were viewed as either morally good or satanically evil.

Further, during the Cold War, modernization theory became an explicit component of U.S. foreign policy and in this respect it became very much a part of the military-industrial-academic complex that marked this period. First promulgated in American universities like Harvard, MIT, Princeton, Stanford, and Michigan State University, it was put into practice by a host of U.S. government agencies after World War II in increasingly enterprising ways. In Southeast Asia, modernization theorists helped usher in the "Green Revolution," the schemes that were to transform the Mekong Delta into an Asian version of the Tennessee Valley Authority, and equally the rationales for the Strategic Hamlet program. When Lyndon Johnson gave his April 1965 Johns Hopkins Speech, where he told the audience that "the vast Mekong River can provide food and water and power on a scale to dwarf even our own TVA" and that the United States was committed to spending one billion dollars to make this dream into a reality, he was uttering words that modernization theorists had only dreamed of five years earlier.[22] In his memoirs, Lyndon Johnson built on this premise when he stated that the overall purpose of American involvement in Vietnam was less about containing communism than about an entire project of remaking the world: "our struggle there would make sense only if it were part of a larger constructive effort in Asia."[23] The flip side of this beneficent language was LBJ's more earthy boast after he had ordered American warplanes to bomb North Vietnam during the Tonkin Gulf affair. He told reporters, "I didn't just screw Ho Chi Minh. I cut his pecker off."[24]

Even before LBJ announced the practicality of modernization theory, Rostow had been championing it in Washington. His recommendations to President Kennedy in March 1961 speak both to the urgency that policymakers attributed to enacting modernization theory as well as to its overall historical importance: "barring a catastrophe, it is likely that a good many of the countries in the underdeveloped world will, during the 1960s, either complete the take-off process or be very far advanced in it. When take-off is complete a nation may be poor but it is normally in a position to draw its external capital from private commercial sources."[25] Rostow's analysis of recent world trends led him to advocate a more forceful American presence in the third world, which was to guide these countries in their respective "take-offs," or what came to be known as the process of "nation building."[26] Rostow and the other writers who championed modernization theory went to great lengths to argue that their support for sending American funds abroad was not just a case of American altruism—though this was highlighted as well. For Rostow, the United States self-interest was a central reason for bringing aid and encouragement to these countries; it encouraged capitalist integration and the prevention of communism in the third world. Discussions of modernization theory became in turn the type of popular "serious talk" favored by Americans when lecturing about the problems facing the world. America and its form of revolution were the proper paths to emulate, and any deviation from this path met with hostility. This becomes the rationale for Secretary of State John Foster Dulles's notice to the third world that "neutralism was un-American."[27]

In the end, Rostow fervently advocated armed escalation in Vietnam and bombing as the immediate answer to all problems there. No wonder President Kennedy dubbed him our "air marshal."[28] The result of this mind-set had predictably tragic consequences. Rostow's legacy is not that of the man who coined JFK's campaign slogan, "Let's get this country moving again," or later Kennedy's slogan for the space program, "New Frontiers." Instead, Rostow is indelibly marked in studies of the Vietnam War as the fiercest of hawks, a man unable to envision policy prescriptions other than military force. He was reduced, in the end, to explaining the siege at Khe Sanh from a sand-table model, one that President Johnson had had built and placed in the Situation Room in the White House basement.[29] His work, though, remains a key instance of the ways in which an understanding of global and historical change, under the lens of modernization theory, merged into an American Cold War policy that sought to create a global liberalism.

❖   ❖   ❖

Partly due to the influences of academics such as Rostow and their fiction-writing popularizers, Cold War advocacy of modernization theory extended well beyond academic circles and the pages of fiction. In fact, American incursions into Southeast Asia can be representatively portrayed in the persons of two Americans, each of whom advocated a personal application of modernization theory in the third world. These two individuals, Secretary of Defense Robert McNamara, and David Lilienthal, the head of the Tennessee Valley Authority (TVA), were diverse in outlook and temperament but shared a belief in the exportation of American liberalism through the auspices of modernization theory. These two figures are important because of their differing attempts to realize the implications of these academic theories in real world situations.

McNamara was a businessman and academic who represented a new breed of liberal elites after World War II. Throughout his time as secretary of defense, he fully lived out *The Ugly American*'s portrayal of a Washington bureaucrat who makes decisions by numbers. He was consumed with the inviolable certainties promised by statistical surveys and economic studies, and was surrounded by like-minded "whiz kids" who believed that rational, quantifiable cost-benefit analysis could solve all problems. Even when complimentary, as in LBJ's conclusion, "That man with the Stacomb in his hair is the best of the lot," perceptions of McNamara often had a left-handed quality to them.[30] McNamara's commanding belief was that America's overwhelming military superiority guaranteed victory in Vietnam, and that an American victory could usher in a period of unprecedented growth for all of Southeast Asia—assuming, of course, that these countries remained pro-American and anti-Communist in orientation. Because of these assumptions, McNamara became closely associated with the transition from the ideals of modernization theory to their implementation in Vietnam.

McNamara's faith in modernization is epitomized by his efforts to build an electronic barrier between North and South Vietnam. As a form of "intervention" into a developing nation, this high-tech "fence" was exactly the kind of large-scale aggressive import that Lederer and Burdick opposed in *The Ugly American;* in that sense it represents the tragic crux at which modernization projects to aid developing nations were turned to military ends.

When *The Ugly American* was made into a film in 1963, Lederer and Burdick's opposition to large-scale technological interventions was represented through the concept of a "Freedom Road." In the novel, the idea of a modern, cross-country highway system is mentioned simply as one vignette out of many; in the movie, the idea of a road was a cornerstone and used to epitomize the central battle between the Americans, their Sarkhanese allies, and the Communists. The screenwriter for the film, Stewart Stern, wrote in a draft of the screenplay: "THE ROAD: This should be presented as a kind of recurrent visual signature throughout the film: a living, greedy and relentless being that shocks nature and man with its coming: a thing of power that cannot be turned aside or diverted from its blind and hungry destiny."[31] Though Stern does not directly cite the imperialist quality of "THE ROAD," his definition of it seems to evoke the repressive nature of imperialism and its effects. Never mind that in the movie the only car ever seen on this shiny new road is the ambassador's limousine (from which the ambassador and his wife can view friendly peasants waving at them through the safety of their windows). The highway truly is a road that goes nowhere, yet it becomes the key symbol of the central struggle between American interest in the mythical Sarkhan's path of development and Sarkhanese opposition to that interference. When the ambassador, Gilbert

MacWhite, decides to change the highway's direction so that it goes straight into the heart of Communist territory, the objective is not that it is needed there, or that it has ceased to serve the commercial interests it was originally designed for, but that its greater purpose is to penetrate into the heart of communism. In many ways, McNamara's fence took up where the "Freedom Road" left off, since his project united military and technological interests in the effort to literally bifurcate an American-sanctioned South Vietnam from North Vietnamese communism.

Yet for McNamara and others the ironies of this turn were lost in a larger zest for the sheer scale of the electronic fence project. Terrain, logistics, costs—all of these became of secondary concern to McNamara, who was convinced that American technological might could triumph over any foe. Today, McNamara writes of the fence strategy in a cursory fashion:

> In the summer of 1966, I requested a group of distinguished scientists working on contract with the JASON division of the Pentagon's Institute for Defense Analyses . . . to study the problem. They concluded the bombing had indeed been ineffective and recommended building a "barrier" as an alternative means of checking infiltration. This concept, which had first come to my attention in the spring of 1966, would involve laying down a complex belt of mines and sensors across the Demilitarized Zone and the Laotian panhandle to the west. . . . The Joint Chiefs reacted coolly to this idea but did not actively oppose it. Once it was put in place, the barrier was intended to increase infiltration losses. And it did.[32]

When one dissects this techno-non-speak, what McNamara is actually saying is that the fence would have allowed the United States to kill more of the North Vietnamese soldiers who dared to come south. But there is more to this story than McNamara's dismissive account suggests. First, the fence was by no means the triumph that he indicates; the barrier of mines and sensors did not stop the mass infiltration of North Vietnamese troops into South Vietnam. Second, the fence provoked a groundswell of domestic opposition, especially among America's leading scientists, who signed a full page advertisement in *The New York Times* stating that they did not want their expertise used for such goals.

We now know that while McNamara appeared in public as an ardent supporter of the war, he had developed doubts over the conduct of the war, and especially over the intensive bombing of Vietnam that was killing hundreds of peasants indiscriminately every week. Thus his interest in the fence; he was seeking alternatives to a military strategy that placed a premium on killing civilians. In December of 1965, McNamara contacted Carl

Kaysen, an economist from MIT who had worked in the National Security Council during the Kennedy administration. Working with other individuals at MIT and Harvard, Kaysen devised a strategy that would maximize American technological superiority and neutralize the Communists' psychological advantage. Their plan involved installing "a string of new devices—tiny sensors that detected footfalls, air-dropped mines, remotely guided air and ground fire—[which] could be installed starting at the coast, following the 17th parallel, running inland and continuing straight on across the waist of Laos, intersecting the trails that ran north-south there. Along the border between North and South Vietnam, the Marines could build strongpoints to be aided by remote sensing and could kill anything coming across."[33] When presented with this idea, McNamara was enthusiastic. Kaysen recalls: "McNamara was ready and waiting. He just loved the idea. His attitude was: Great. Get me a proposal."[34] Even when others spoke of its impracticality, and pointed out that the amount of resources needed would be enormous— beginning with manpower requirements and including the fact that the Communists could redirect the Ho Chi Minh Trail with ease—their warnings had little impact upon McNamara. When the Joint Chiefs learned of this idea and were asked to comment on its practicality, they noted that it would take up to four years and would require seven or eight U.S. divisions for monitoring and defense purposes. Further, the military cautioned that "operations against North Vietnam and operations in South Vietnam are of transcendent importance."[35]

The issue led to an open disagreement between McNamara and General Westmoreland in October 1966. The conversation became heated, with McNamara arguing:

> I keep asking where did we make a mistake? The first mistake was not putting in a barrier five years ago instead of talking about it today . . . I keep thinking to myself that five years from now I might look back and say it was an error not doing it five years ago. So that is why I want to see this tremendous effort placed. I recognize all the problems; I know all the unknowns. I recognize that it might prove unwise once we get to the point, but for God's sake, let's get lined up so we can do it if we want it.[36]

This passage is terribly revealing as it begins with a search for an original mistake, but does not include any long-range deliberations about changing American Cold War policies and rationales as a result of that mistake. This quote also shows McNamara working within a strict time-frame and using its urgency to propel immediate action despite possible long-term consequences. The only solace one can take from this moment is that McNa-

mara's distress over the nature of the war would eventually lead him to commission the Pentagon's own top-secret internal history of the war, now
known as *The Pentagon Papers*. Finally, in September 1967 he gave a press
conference extolling what came to be called the "McNamara Line." In the
end, the fence would prove to be as unworkable a model as any other con-
jured up in the McNamara Pentagon. Perhaps the most generous reading
of this whole affair is that McNamara simply became consumed by the elixir
of short-term scientific and technological solutions represented by the electronic fence and thus lost sight of the long-range consequences of American
actions abroad.[37]

While the electronic fence failed because of its inability to control South
Vietnam's borders, this failure had a number of components that make it
symptomatic of modernization theory's overarching assumptions. These include the overextension of American policing of the world, the technocratic
impulse carried to extremes, and the unrecognized futility of waging a successful war against the commanding impulse of twentieth-century nationalism. One way in which that overreaching technocratic faith manifested itself
was in the very underestimation of the power and determination of the third
world nationalist movements that *The Ugly American* dramatized. For example, one of McNamara's closest aides, John McNaughton, wrote what
may stand as the definitive rationale of why Americans were in Vietnam.
Written in March 1965, McNaughton discussed in no uncertain terms what
he believed were U.S. goals in South Vietnam:

> 70%—To avoid a humiliating US defeat (to our reputation as a guar-
>   antor).
> 20%—To keep SVN (and then adjacent) territory from Chinese hands.
> 10%—To permit the people of SVN to enjoy a better, freer way of life.
> ALSO—To emerge from the crisis without unacceptable taint from meth-
>   ods used.
> NOT—To "help a friend," though it would be hard to stay in if asked
>   out.[38]

More than a year later, McNamara was melding this purely real politik analysis of American intervention into Vietnam in a quantification of the war
that would sound more palatable to President Johnson. In October 1966 he
wrote to the president:

> The one thing demonstrably going for us in Vietnam over the past year
> has been the large number of enemy killed-in-action resulting from the
> big military operations. Allowing for possible exaggeration in reports, the
> enemy must be taking losses—deaths in and after battle—at the rate of

more than 60,000 a year. The infiltration routes would seem to be one-way trails to death for the North Vietnamese. Yet there is no sign of an impending break in enemy morale and it appears that he can more than replace his losses by infiltration from North Vietnam and recruitment in South Vietnam.[39]

What did not—indeed could not—figure in McNamara's memo or Mc-Naughton's goals was an understanding of why the Communists were willing to take such appalling losses in the field of battle. Ideas like nationalism, anticolonialism, and Communist ideals simply did not figure into these equations, and the results would prove disastrous for all concerned. Leaders of the peace movement, along with select members of the administration like George Ball and even military men like John Paul Vann quickly grasped the importance of Ho Chi Minh's declaration that they had fought the French for a hundred years and were willing to suffer as long as it would take to force the Americans to leave Vietnam—but not McNamara, for statements like these could not be easily quantified. Ho Chi Minh's sense of historical entrenchment, made clear in this declaration, both confounded McNamara's dependence on short-term statistical data and emphasized the extent to which McNamara's ideology underestimated revolutionary nationalism as a counterforce to Western technology.

The classic story involving McNamara's obsession with quantification involved his being briefed by Desmond FitzGerald, a CIA case officer, about current trends in Vietnam. McNamara wanted what he felt mattered—numbers, graphs, telltale symbols of American successes; FitzGerald instead gave him information gleaned from "the man on the street." And when McNamara found this wholly unsatisfactory and demanded statistics, FitzGerald told him that statistics were often meaningless compared with accounts of those who worked with and knew the Communists. FitzGerald soon became a persona non grata to McNamara.[40] To McNamara's critics, stories like the above only confirmed their worst suspicions about the man—that he had no feel for people, let alone what motivated individuals to fight and die for something larger than themselves, be it communism or nationalism. To take another example, in 1963 a South Vietnamese general told Assistant Secretary of State for Far Eastern Affairs Roger Hilsman, "Ah *les statistiques*. Your secretary of defense loves statistics. We Vietnamese can give him all he wants. If you want them to go up, they will go up. If you want them to go down, they will go down."[41]

When the victory in Vietnam that had been assured Americans did not materialize, and instead American involvement dragged on year after year

with the ever-growing amount of destruction and death that naturally followed, much of the criticism focused on Robert McNamara. By 1966, critics
as diverse in political orientation as Bernard Fall and John Paul Vann spoke
knowingly of the futility of American war aims, yet McNamara claims that
the absence of experts was a principal reason for America's misjudging the
nature of the Vietnamese war for independence.[42] What had once been seen
as McNamara's greatest asset, his assuredness of an American victory, began
to ring hollow. Just as McNamara's popularity had been partly due to his
business persona, his grasp of scientific theories, the first critiques of him—
the most notable being David Halberstam's profile in *Harper's*, entitled
"The Programming of Robert McNamara"—made much of his slicked-back
hair, round, shiny glasses, and his middle name, "Strange" (his mother's
maiden name), which they said befitted a man who seemed only able to
speak in numbers and in scientific jargon.

McNamara's love of rational, scientific thought, his fervent belief that
American technology and machines could solve any Cold War problem,
continued to be the reigning American ethos. McNamara's determination
only looks like hubris today because we know the outcome of the Vietnam
War and the limits of 1960s technology. What was not known publicly in the
1960s but is abundantly clear today is that McNamara had turned against
the war even as his press conferences and congressional hearings spoke of
an assured American victory. As McNamara's memoir reveals in some detail,
and was common knowledge to those working with him at the time, he had
come to realize that his calculations did not add up. Thus he began to write
attenuated memos to Johnson explaining the futility of American policy.
And, as already noted, he also commissioned *The Pentagon Papers* chronicling American intervention into Vietnam, including evidence of elite de-
ceptions of and outright contempt for the American people. This from the
man who, when challenged over his overseeing the war in the early years,
proclaimed, "I don't mind its being called McNamara's war. In fact I'm
proud to be associated with it." He would get his wish in ways that he never
imagined.[43] More so than any other U.S. official involved in the Vietnam
War, McNamara still provokes a level of sheer animosity that is simply astonishing. Thus, when he wrote in his recent memoirs about the Vietnam
War that "we were wrong, terribly wrong," his comments were met with
almost universal derision in the press and hostility around the water coolers
of academia.

Notwithstanding the mea-culpa tone of *In Retrospect*, McNamara seems
to have changed little in his vision that the quantification of problems leads

to rational, positive decision-making and that it can be applied to all facets of life. He noted, for instance, in his book that "to this day, I see quantification as a language to add precision to reasoning about the world."[44] That McNamara's desire for good produced so much evil stands as a stark monument to the nature of modern American liberalism as well as to an individual hungry for power. Perhaps this is why when he wept on television soon after the publication of *In Retrospect* in 1995, expressing regret for his actions thirty years earlier, his repentance was met with scorn by so many. Tellingly, *The New York Times* showed no mercy in an editorial published soon after this broadcast:

> It is important to remember how fate dispensed rewards and punishment for Mr. McNamara's thousand days of error. Three million Vietnamese died. Fifty-eight thousand Americans got to come home in body bags. Mr. McNamara, while tormented by his role in the war, got a sinecure at the World Bank and summers at the Vineyard. . .
>
> His regret cannot be huge enough to balance the books for our dead soldiers. The ghosts of those unlived lives circle close around Mr. McNamara. Surely he must in every quiet and prosperous moment hear the ceaseless whispers of those poor boys in the infantry, dying in the tall grass, platoon by platoon, for no purpose. What he took from them cannot be repaid by prime-time apology and stale tears, three decades later.[45]

This editorial, written by Howell Raines, is astonishing in its anger, in its inability to forgive, and in its willingness to lay the entire war on the shoulders of one man. Of course there were many architects to this war, but much of the animus directed specifically against McNamara by the *Times* has to do with his public advocacy of a war he now acknowledges that he did not believe in. The disillusionment that resonates through this editorial, though, should also be understood as a disillusionment with the promises of modernization theory, and the forced recognition of the failure of technology as a liberating force.[46] The death tolls and body bag statistics that Raines marshals here ended up being the determining quantification in American and Vietnamese cultural memory.

✿   ✿   ✿

Another representative of attempts to apply American modernization theories, David Lilienthal, was also a fervent supporter of the tenets of liberalism and technological progress. Unlike McNamara, he was not involved in the military component of American foreign policy; in fact, he spent a lifetime advocating the peaceful uses of American technology and know-how. Yet he worked with McNamara, and his journal entries are filled with glowing adulation of the man and many of his policies. What he shared most with McNamara was an abiding faith in liberalism and a feverish desire to re-make the world. Speaking of development projects around the world, he told Columbia University students in 1964 that:

> We have come to a turning point in economic development. Business or-ganizations operating overseas are becoming increasingly aware . . . that they should center more and more attention on the development of people, as a matter of good, productive business. The international and national public lending and economic aid agencies will more and more, I believe, insist that every undertaking on which they make loans or grants be used imaginatively and efficiently *as a means of developing people.* The role of "education" . . . is simply the process of developing the latent capabilities of people.[47]

He would spend his life bringing this type of education to people in the third world and in the United States. In a curious way he also resembled some of the stock characters in *The Ugly American*—both the "ugly" and "beautiful" ones. He was sympathetic to third world aspirations even as he proposed ever more grandiose development projects.

Lilienthal had a flawless liberal pedigree: in the 1930s he was instrumen-tal in building the TVA into a world-renowned system that brought electric-ity to millions of rural Americans; as the chairman of the Atomic Energy Commission, he was a fierce advocate of the use of atomic energy for peace-ful purposes—under American aegis, of course. He was also a vigorous anti-Communist; thus, his initial support for American involvement in Vietnam. Later, though, his support of the war wavered, and it is this initial commit-ment and eventual disillusionment that mark his relationship to the Ameri-can intervention in Vietnam.

Lilienthal was also a friend of Lyndon Johnson, a like-minded president who was as intent on eradicating poverty and disease as Lilienthal himself. In contrast to Johnson's southern, impoverished roots, Lilienthal was born in Czechoslovakia to lower-middle class parents, excelled in school (and boxing) and went on to graduate from Harvard Law School. At Harvard he came under the influence of Felix Frankfurter and progressivism and developed a lifelong commitment to helping the needy.[48] As a result of this education, he would spend the rest of his life trying to bring modernity to the poor—be they in Maine or Iran—while always advocating the necessity of maintaining American superiority in military and foreign affairs. In his book *This I Do Believe* (1949), Lilienthal pointed out that while the TVA bettered people's lives materially, "this is not the real significance of what has transpired in the Valley of the Tennessee. What is really important is that there has been a change in the spirit of the people themselves, a change in the direction of greater self-confidence. . . . This American experiment has fortified men's confidence that human beings need not be chained to the wheel of technology, but that man can use the machine in the interest of human welfare."[49]

As this suggests, Lilienthal's personal vision of modernization theory was based on an optimistic faith in the power of liberalism and the conviction that material well-being could make spiritual happiness possible.

Lilienthal's life was a series of actions intended to bring America's superior science and technology to bear on the particular problems of third world nations. He traveled the world working with people on a host of issues, ranging from overpopulation to rural electrification. And when he became involved in development projects in Vietnam, he was told by President Johnson: "Dave, you give them some of that philosophy, that good TVA philosophy. . . . As much as you want."[50] Beyond Johnson's flippancy, this aside implies that Lilienthal truly believed that the United States had a responsibility to eradicate poverty and alleviate suffering throughout the world—to bring the TVA system to the world—and that LBJ played upon this concern to ensure that Lilienthal would support his actions in Vietnam.

When Lilienthal was asked by the Johnson administration to participate in a fact-finding mission in Vietnam, he confessed that he knew little of the country and then sought out the counsel of those who did. He turned first to Clark Clifford, who told him: "It isn't winning the war, it isn't the military operations that are closest to the President's mind. It isn't even South Vietnam. It is a pattern for a kind of life that the people of all Southeast Asia can begin to enjoy that is at issue. So what the President wants is to make a *demonstration*, a demonstration in South Vietnam. . . ."[51] It was this type of rationale that made Lilienthal so proud of his responsibilities, and explains why he supported Johnson with such fervor. It also points to how convoluted America's rationale had become in Vietnam as the war dragged on year after year. Yet Lilienthal's enthusiasm led him to urge American technological superiority as a way to bring about a modern Vietnam. Not incidentally, he saw Vietnam as a test case for ushering in a new era for the third world. He also shared with McNamara many of the assumptions that made modernization theory such a powerful ideology of American involvement abroad. Both men believed in the ideal of American democracy, in scientific and techno-logical achievement as the "measure" of an advanced society, and in the responsibility of "modern" nations to intercede in the evolutionary develop-ment of "primitive" countries.[52] However, the fact that Lilienthal tempered his vision with an understanding of human frailties is still of note.

Lilienthal's memoirs are filled with ideas on how the Vietnam "problem" could be solved through a combination of science and American know-how. Even by 1967 he continued to remake Vietnam into a version of America. In his briefing to President Johnson he summarized his comments by stat-ing: "I hope [I] conveyed the spirit of confidence and enthusiasm that I feel about the Vietnamese *people* themselves, and how some of the new young Cabinet members—technocrats—reminded me of the young men of the early New Deal, who were in their early thirties, too."[53] It is this willingness to see the model of American history residing within contemporary Viet-nam politics that marks Lilienthal as both a progeny of American liberalism and one of its fervent champions.

On the other hand, Lilienthal had begun to question American motives abroad by the mid-1960s. It is his wavering, indeed his realization at times that American efforts abroad had an imperialist quality to them, that distin-guishes him from McNamara. Consider the following passage written by Lilienthal in 1967, reflecting on a series of high level meetings he was about to attend between President Johnson and the South Vietnamese. The irony that this "peace conference" was being held in Guam was not lost on Lili-enthal:

> A strange place, Guam to select for a peaceful goals conference. This is the main base for the B-52, the greatest bomber in history; it is from here, on a huge field we shall see today, that these aerial monsters start with their store of bombs to pound North Vietnam. And Guam is as well the home of a fleet of Polaris submarines that patrol the China coast. A mod-ern citadel, extending American power as Singapore once extended the Asian power of the British Empire.[54]

This is an astonishing reflection on Lilienthal's part in its awareness of the dark ironies of modernizing a country by bombing it back to the stone age—all in the interests of fostering American-style revolutions. In this passage, Lilienthal foresees the consequences of American liberalism and its off-spring, modernization theory, upon the third world and in ways that McNa-mara never fully articulated. Part of this reflection can be explained by Lili-enthal's constant need to rethink his and America's motives abroad. In the end he realized that means and ends had become horribly corrupted in Vietnam, with global liberalism standing for little more than the terror-bombing of peasants. His dreams of bringing the TVA to the people of Southeast Asia were being destroyed, literally, by Americans like McNamara and Rostow. He concluded his thoughts on what he had experienced in Guam, where Johnson's dreams were colliding with Westmoreland's announcement that the war might go on for another ten years: "And I find myself sad, sad, sad. Unalterably sad."[55] What needs to be kept in mind, though, is that Lilienthal was also quite adept at public performance, and this quotation no matter how striking, has a calculated quality to it given that he knew that his diaries would eventually be published.

✿   ✿   ✿

By 1968, liberalism, as expounded by McNamara, Rostow, or Lilienthal, had reached a crisis stage. Each responded in his own way: McNamara sought repentance at the World Bank; Rostow retreated to an academic position at LBJ's University of Texas; Lilienthal looked elsewhere to replicate his TVA system. However, none became radicalized by the war as Robert Kennedy did. None of these liberal cold warriors spoke as Kennedy did to a group of students at a Catholic girls' college, after learning that they favored an increase in the bombing of Vietnam, "Do you understand what that means? . . . Don't you understand that what we are doing to the Vietnamese is not very different than what Hitler did to the Jews?"[56]

It is the return of modernization theory that is most intriguing given its failures and loss of influence by the early 1970s.[57] Rostow's *Stages of Economic Growth* has gone through three editions, the most recent being 1991. The major contradictions in the theory—that it constructed a world where all growth patterns mimicked those found in the West, and that it generally neglected the corrosive effects of colonialism upon newly developed countries—have not relegated the theory to an academic curiosity. After reviewing all of the tumult involving this theory, Ian Roxborough wrote that "it would be better to acknowledge . . . and accept that we are all modernization theorists. We all work with some notion of a transition from premodern to modern society. To what extent does this commit us?"[58]

In many ways, the modernization theory of the 1950s can be seen as America's entry into a market-style competition with the tenets of Marxism to win over their Southeast Asian consumers. Modernization theory was an attempt to rewrite Marxist theory, using the Marxist model of an inevitable passage from one economic stage to the next but reversing those stages to one in which consumer capitalism and not communism is the final utopian outcome. Ironically, then, there is still no better definition of what capitalism did—materially and psychically—to Americans' conception of their country and their trading partners than in Marx's history lesson on bourgeois trade:

> The cheap prices of its commodities are the heavy artillery with which it batters down all Chinese walls, with which it forces the barbarians' intensely obstinate hatred of foreigners to capitulate. It compels all nations, on pain of extinction, to adopt the bourgeois mode of production; it compels them to introduce what it calls civilisation into their midst, *i.e.*, to become bourgeois themselves. In one word, it creates a world after its own image.[59]

This is a striking passage, especially Marx's notion of how a bourgeois society like the United States created a world "after its own image." This is exactly what American policymakers sought to do in Asia, and individuals like McNamara and Lilienthal spearheaded this effort by supporting and overseeing newly independent states that were anti-Communist and thus more receptive to American interests. The film version of Lederer and Burdick's *Ugly American* ends with a fascinating scene in which the American ambassador to Sarkhan comes to a supreme revelation (after a coup d'état and much death had ensued) about the need for America to recognize national movements as revolutionary in their own right. In the midst of declaiming this revelation, the ambassador is literally switched off by an American who is watching the speech on television from the comfort of his suburban home. With this warning in mind, we must contemplate the prospect that since our Cold War competitor has not only "failed" but no longer even exists, those Americans intent on refashioning the world will take another look at propounding a theory that proposes a capitalist, technological model of evolutionary social development.

PART THREE

Framing Coups:
Iran and Guatemala

Discursive Subversions
Time *Magazine, the CIA Overthrow of Musaddiq, and the Installation of the Shah*

JOHN FORAN

They [the English] have the wrong notion in their minds that by bringing economic pressure upon Iran, they can make us submit to being longer exploited by them. . .

As you know, the Iranians aim at attaining their liberty . . . I am confident that you will continue in your good course, as before, in spreading reliable information about our country in the U.S. . . . It is our hope that the American people shall come to realize more than ever before the objectives of the Iranian people . . . It is here that we depend upon your support and that of the American people . . .

Please accept my wishes and prayers for your magazine, which is a great factor as far as its services are concerned to world peace.
— MUHAMMAD MUSADDIQ, letter to the editors of *Time*

According to [*New York Times* reporter in Iran in 1953] Kennett Love, from the perspective of some thirty years distance, "More and more, it seems to me that the importance now of what happened was the impact of silence on history; the impact of silence by eminent journals and journalists whose very essence and creed list wrongful and knowing and deliberate silence as the chief sin."
— WILLIAM A. DORMAN AND MANSOUR FARHANG, *The U.S. Press and Iran: Foreign Policy and the Journalism of Deference*

THE CIA-ORCHESTRATED COUP of August 19, 1953, that toppled Prime Minister Muhammad Musaddiq[1] from power had weighty consequences both for Iran and for the United States. From the Iranian point of view, it cut off the most promising experiment in democracy in that coun-

157

try's history, and led to the repressively autocratic regime of Shah Muhammad Reza Pahlavi, which itself ultimately fell in the complex revolutionary
process of 1978 and after.[2] On the U.S. side, the success of this first major
covert action of the Cold War gave policymakers unlimited confidence in
their view of the world and ability to shape events, confirmed a year later in
Guatemala with the deposing of another democratically elected but stub-
bornly independent nationalist government. Finally, it cemented the "special," largely unquestioning relationship of U.S. support for the shah that
would bind together the two countries' fates in tragic ways into the 1980s
and beyond.

The present essay examines the making of these events in the American
popular imagination, exploring the place of Iran in U.S. Cold War discourses during the 1950s, and raising the question of how such discourses
and the practices of foreign policy might be related. Drawing on what I call
the emerging perspective of third world cultural studies, the focus will be
on the construction of the contrasting images of the shah and Musaddiq in
what was arguably the most influential popular press outlet of the day—
Time magazine. Along with consideration of other evidence from the mass
media and the secret diplomacy of the period, this focus will provide us a
window on the deep roots of U.S. intervention in Iran, and on a set of discourses that flowed into and quickened the stream of the Cold War construction of the world. Ultimately, I shall argue, we are here at the proxi-
mate beginnings of a new era in what Tom Englehardt has termed an
American "victory culture," with enormous consequences for the subsequent histories of the third world and its antagonists among the superpowers.[3]

Iran, the United States, and the Cold War

Pinpointing the origins of the Cold War is a risky business, but however
these are measured, Iran plays an important role from an early date. In
1945, a standoff emerged between the Soviet Union and the West in the
northwestern Iranian provinces of Azerbaijan and Kurdistan, which under
the guise of Soviet military occupation had declared their autonomy from
Tehran. As this came to a head in December 1946, Soviet forces withdrew
with extreme reluctance, in part owing to pressures exerted by the Truman
administration. In the course of this crisis, U.S. interests came to be more
sharply perceived in terms of the oil fields of the Middle East and the Soviet
geopolitical threat.[4] On the Iranian side, the twenty-seven-year-old shah at-

tributed the Soviet withdrawal from northern Iran as due, most importantly, to the conviction by all parties to the conflict that the "United States was solidly supporting Iranian sovereignty."[5]

This relationship would be sorely tried in the 1951–53 oil nationalization period, when the British-owned Anglo-Iranian Oil Company (AIOC) would be the prize over which a complex four-sided struggle would take place between the British, the Americans, the shah, and the nationalist government of charismatic prime minister Muhammad Musaddiq. The crisis that erupted in 1951 with the Iranian parliament's nationalization of oil, and its course over the next two years, represents yet another critical juncture in the unfolding of the Cold War and the crystallization of the Middle East as a central place in the strategic imagination.

The seeds of the conflict were planted at the turn of the century in the context of a series of concessions for exploitation of Iran's resources granted by the Qajar dynasty, which ruled Iran from 1796 until the shah's father established the Pahlavi dynasty through a coup in the 1920s. After a British subject discovered significant oil deposits in southwestern Iran in 1908, the British government established an oil company to exploit the fields. Iran was paid a very small amount in royalties compared with British profits, an arrangement that was renegotiated for a somewhat better split of shares by the shah's father, Reza Shah Pahlavi, in 1933, but Britain still made about five times what Iran received, and the duration of the concession was extended by twenty-eight years to 1993. By the late 1940s, several third world states had achieved fifty-fifty profit-sharing arrangements with the West, notably Saudi Arabia and Venezuela with the major U.S. oil companies. In Iran, however, the British refusal to consider matching this led to the selection of Musaddiq as prime minister on a program to nationalize the oil industry, which was duly voted in April 1951 by Iran's parliament, the Majlis, and ratified by the shah on May 1. For the next two years Britain tried unsuccessfully to reverse this decision, while Iran was unable to export oil due to Western support for Britain's claims. The United States was at first a neutral observer of the conflict, then increasingly insistent that Iran must negotiate with the British. Inside Iran, meanwhile, Musaddiq's popularity rose at the expense of the shah, and the two enlisted other political figures and parties in their cause. Among these actors, the most well-organized was the Tudeh (Masses) Party, the Communist party of Iran, which expressed support for the oil nationalization but disdain for Musaddiq. Musaddiq himself tolerated the Tudeh's existence without seeking its support. By 1953 the atmosphere had polarized to the point where Musaddiq had significant popular support and a thin control of the Majlis but faced opposition on a number of significant fronts—from the British, the United States, the shah, and various clerical and secular political rivals. The British gave their plans for a covert operation to overthrow Musaddiq to the newly elected Eisenhower administration, which put them into effect in August 1953. We shall examine the details of the making of the coup at the end of this chapter. Let us now turn to the issue of how to analyze the foundational elements of the perceptions of each of the parties to it.

Third World Cultural Studies

There exist complex relationships among the longer-standing fields of media studies and the sociology of culture, on the one hand, and the newer perspective(s) of cultural studies, on the other. Simply put (to say the least!), media studies and the sociology of culture have pursued practical research agendas aimed at precise measurements of the production and reception of media and cultural objects, often using such methods as content analysis and statistics. Cultural studies originated in England in the 1960s (in another discussable genealogy) out of the union of the new social history from below, Marxism, and literary criticism. Imported in the next decades into the United States, it became many things, as it encountered feminist studies, race and ethnic studies, postmodernism, deconstruction, and other trends in the humanities. In the process, it now seems both more theory-driven and less political in many ways than its English originators. With this essay, I shall attempt to move it further in some old and new directions, under a rubric I will call third world cultural studies.[6]

William Dorman and Mansour Farhang represent the state of the art of the media-studies approach to the construction of the United States–Iran relationship in the period under review here.[7] Their impressive study of *The New York Times, Christian Science Monitor, Newsweek, Time,* and other media coverage of Iran between 1951 and 1978 uses a frame analysis to track the representation of Iran in the American popular press: "Frames are simply constructions of social reality that result from journalistic decision making about what information to include in a news story, what language to use, what authorities to cite, which nuance to emphasize, and so on."[8] They found the link between the press and foreign policy "enormously complex and subtle"—no "simple cause-and-effect relationship. . . .But if the press does not *make* foreign policy or defense policy, in some important ways it helps set the boundaries within which policy can be made."[9] Their major findings on the press and Iran were that the press followed foreign policymakers' cues rather than acting independently—hence, "the journalism of deference" of their title; that both journalists and government officials were prone to being misinformed and ethnocentric; and that the press found itself "deeply rooted in a cold-war mentality that is highly internalized and is more deeply unconscious than willful."[10] The major shortcoming of the press was to ignore Iranian *politics,* due to an assumption "that the political aspirations of Iranians did not really matter. . . . Implicit in such an assumption were the beliefs that the Iranian people were incapable of politics, that they were incapable of self-rule, and that they were incapable of an authentic desire for freedom."[11]

For Dorman and Farhang, press coverage influences public opinion, creating a general "mood" within the electorate, which then shapes presidential foreign policy: "This mood consists of a vague, generalized set of beliefs and hazy understandings and produces a crude context into which even cruder stereotypes are often fit."[12] The authors then suggest that because such understandings/moods are so hazy, they are easily manipulated (by press or government is not specified). So the press frames "a highly generalized *sense of things:* of what is required and of what is not; of who is enemy and who is friend. The press sets the broad limits of our thinking about the 'other'."[13] Such general impressions, rather than specific facts, tend to have an effect on political thinking, up to and including the making and unmaking of governments in elections, as with the terminations of the Johnson and Carter presidencies over foreign problems refracted through the press (a list to which we will add the end of another Democratic administration in 1952). The press, usually quiescent on strategic matters and willing to follow the Washington foreign policy consensus, may become more critical in certain circumstances, such as overwhelming contradictions in policy, open splits among policymakers, uncertainty on the president's part, or evidence of a cover-up of some sort. But the press doesn't initiate any of these circumstances: "To assert . . . that the perceptions of the public, particularly because of their potential impact on electoral politics, set important limits on the formulation and execution of foreign policy, however, is not to argue for the notion that the people through pressure politics somehow *make* foreign policy, and are, therefore, ultimately and conveniently to blame if things go wrong. Rather, it is to reject the contrary notion that the people count for nothing at all, that foreign policy is wholly the product of elites."[14] They go on to say that public opinion influences foreign policy indirectly, not by shaping it, but by allowing it through nonopposition to it. The press's role in this is threefold: 1) to create the general mood discussed above; 2) to (potentially) provide a check on policy elites; and 3) to give or withhold legitimacy from dissenting views, here or abroad: "Are dissenters, either here or abroad, portrayed as worthy of a fair hearing, perhaps even admiration? Or are they depicted as political outlaws whose complaints are as dangerous as they are unfounded?"[15] I find much of this analysis useful to my own account, though against Dorman and Farhang (and by extension, Chomsky and Herman), I will argue that in this case, the press helped make U.S. foreign policy as much as the latter controlled the press.

On the side of cultural studies, Mary Ann Heiss has essayed a new approach to the Musaddiq period in a paper titled "Culture, National Identity, and Oil in the Early 1950s: The United States and Mohammad Mossadeq."[16] Her study of private U.S. and British diplomatic records suggests that their perceptions of Musaddiq were consistent with the popular U.S. press: "Influenced by long-standing Western stereotypes, British and American policymakers consistently employed what Edward Said has termed 'Orientalism' when dealing with Mossadeq, whom they considered inferior, childlike, and feminine."[17] She goes on to qualify her approach:

> Assessing the immediate influence of Western characterizations of Mossadeq on the formation of Anglo-American policy is tricky, because it is not possible to determine a direct causal influence between Anglo-American perceptions and prejudices and specific events. We cannot say, for example, that Western stereotypes led linearly to the coup that removed Mossadeq from office in the summer of 1953. But this does not mean that these stereotypes were unimportant. On the contrary, by shaping the mindset of Anglo-American officials, they were part of the context within which those officials formulated policy. They buttressed claims of Western superiority over Iranian and other Middle Eastern peoples by perpetuating the idea that those peoples were weak and incapable. And their cumulative effect was to paint Mossadeq and others like him in unfavorable ways that rationalized and justified Western control.[18]

Another virtue of Heiss's work is that it suggests the beginnings of a gendered reading of the treatment of Musaddiq by U.S. and British diplomats, noting the British diplomatic correspondence on Musaddiq's "negative and feminine tactics."[19] She also documents "the frequent Anglo-American [diplomatic] references to Mossadeq's childishness and immaturity."[20] The U.S. ambassador in London in October 1951 characterized the British as "saints" in the conflict, and Musaddiq as "'the naughty boy' who needed to be disciplined."[21] Musaddiq was further characterized by the same diplomats in terms of mental illness (and Heiss notes the connection to his characterization as feminine): "The documentary record on the oil crisis is replete with references to Mossadeq as 'crazy,' 'sick,' 'mad,' 'hysterical,' 'neurotic,' 'demented,' 'periodically unstable,' and 'not quite sane'."[22] Such perceptions were carried over to the Iranian people as a whole: in the words of U.S. ambassador Loy Henderson, "Those Iranians who followed Mossadeq were little more than 'mad and suicidal . . . lemmings' who needed to be saved from their folly by Western benevolence."[23]

I would like to build on aspects of both of these approaches. From the media studies and the sociology of culture work of Dorman and Farhang I shall take the notion that there exists a complex relation between cultural constructions and the world. For me, however, this is one in which the press, the public, and elites all share certain conceptions, which, like identities themselves, are complex products, multiple, shifting, and contested. I am also much in agreement with the cultural studies and feminist analysis of Heiss. She is right, I believe, that both policymakers and the press (and the public) drew on a single source, which we may term Orientalism. The question is who influenced whom? I shall argue that the popular press had more influence over the policymakers than most people think; where we agree is that they both tapped a deeper source. The influences worked in various directions, and were cumulatively quite important in what happened. That is, *Time* influenced U.S. foreign policy; both drew on and contributed to Orientalist discourses; Musaddiq and other actors tried to combat these influences; and the coup was a product of this struggle for discursive hegemony, further shaped, to be sure, by the political economy of oil and geostrategic power.

Drawing on the work of Edward Said, Stuart Hall, and Aijaz Ahmad, among others, third-world cultural studies represents an approach to culture that insists on a critical perspective on first-world cultural practices.[24] Peter Chua has defined the perspective in the following terms: "Third World cultural studies explores what culture is in all aspects of life, what we mean by it, what we do with it, and its unique political and historical relations with the 'Third World.' It analyzes and politicizes the ways in which making sense of all parts of the world and of our place as individuals, groups, communities, and nations within it are cultural processes. It examines how cultural meanings are transmitted and considers how the selection and interpretation of cultural messages are essential to the process through which our identities are constructed."[25] A specifically third-world cultural studies then focuses on how political cultures and discourses circulate and compete: "Words *do* have a magical effect—but not in the way that the magicians supposed, and not on the objects they were trying to influence. Words are magical in the way they affect the minds of those who use them. 'A mere matter of words,' we say contemptuously, forgetting that words have power to mold men's thinking, to canalize their feeling, to direct their willing and acting. Conduct and character are largely determined by the nature of the words we currently use to discuss ourselves and the world around us."[26] I am interested in this paper in tracking the meaning and possible impact of U.S. discourses on Iran in hopes of suggesting the existence of a circuit between cultural "knowledges" of the other and foreign policy. The practices of *Time* magazine will loom large in assessing this circuit; the contesting discourses found in *The Nation,* and Iranians' own efforts to portray themselves, will also come in for some attention, as the outcome of their unequal encounter, while not predetermined, says much about the construction of a Cold War hegemony in the United States.

Discourses

Shaping a political culture: Time *magazine and U.S. foreign policy.* The general findings of Dorman and Farhang on the U.S. press and Iran during the Musaddiq period are that the press "followed the lead of official Washington and opted for simple themes that matched Western conceptions of Middle Eastern peoples and neatly fit within the context of the cold war. As a result, Mosaddeq at his political end appeared in the press as a highly irrational and discredited leader, a portrayal that could not help but serve the purpose of those who had planned the coup."[27] They discern several phases in the coverage, each with its dominant theme, and each shift *following* a shift in Washington's assessment. In the first phase of negotiations between Iran and the British, the U.S. press seemed generally supportive of Iranian demands, thereby misleading Iranians about U.S. neutrality. This frame is attributed to U.S. officials' having an interest in gaining a foothold in the oil industry at Britain's expense. As the struggle deepened, U.S. policymakers became alarmed and began to support the British; the press changed its view of Musaddiq "from that of a quaint nationalist to that of a near lunatic to one, finally, of Communist dupe."[28] They are clear in their argument that "For the most part, the press went along with what would prove to be the U.S. State Department's self-fulfilling prophecy that the shah was the only source of stability and continuity in Iran."[29]

My own reading of *Time* magazine suggests that the press played a more significant role in the construction of foreign policy. When *Time* was founded in the 1920s, it conceived its audience as the million or more Americans with a college education.[30] Under Henry Robinson Luce, *Time*'s orientation to the world was Republican, pro-business, and intensely committed to bringing the "serious" issues of world politics to an American audience:

> For him . . . the idea of America's attaining the full zenith of its power was an idealistic one, a true goal. For it was, he thought, an age when America and Americans had to be educated to their power and their responsibilities. To him the idea that the American Century might bring *too much power* was totally alien, to him the danger was of *too little* American power. His American Century was a noble concept, convinced as he was of the rectitude of our culture and our values and our energy; the world would want these same things, on our terms and by our definitions, and it was our clear duty to spread them.[31]

By the 1940s and 50s, *Time* and *Life* had arguably attained the stature of the most influential shapers of opinion in the United States, particularly in Republican and centrist circles, "that is, on American public opinion."[32] In David Halberstam's view, Luce "was, in those grand years of the forties and fifties and early sixties, the most powerful conservative publisher in America, and in the fifties at least as influential as the Secretary of State."[33] Luce's obsession with the "loss" of China to Communist revolution in 1949 would be relayed to the American public in manifold opinions on international and domestic affairs expressed in the pages of his publications as journalistic reporting of fact.

In this context, *Time*'s reporting of events in Iran would go far beyond following the lead of the foreign policy establishment in Washington, particularly under a Democratic administration that had held the reins of power since 1933. *Time*'s coverage of Iran grew in tandem with these international and domestic political struggles: in 1950, before the oil crisis broke, there were only six pieces that mentioned Iran, almost all of them quite short, and usually featured under "People." In 1951, the year Musaddiq became prime minister and the British oil company was nationalized by Iran, the total grew to forty-three pieces in the fifty-two weekly editions, including a cover on Musaddiq and several multipage stories, now more prominently featured under "International News" and "Foreign News." In 1952, as the crisis stabilized, there were twenty-two articles, mostly taking a backseat to more dramatic political-revolutionary events in Egypt. In 1953, the year of the coup, there were twenty-three pieces, of which twelve appeared in the seven and a half months before the coup, and eleven in the four and a half months after. By 1954, the crisis over, there were only thirteen articles, most quite short.

If we turn to the content of *Time*'s analysis of the U.S. position and the situation in Iran, we find a critical stance at odds with Dorman and Farhang's assessment of *The New York Times*. In February 1951, on the eve of the oil dispute, *Time* published a major piece of seven pages, including maps and photos, titled "Background for War." The backing down of the Soviets in 1946 was hailed as a great victory—"the first important postwar setback for Communist aggression"—but a temporary one. The danger in 1951 is greater: "If the Communists grab Iran, they will get an asset far more valuable than Korea."[34] The West depends now on Middle Eastern oil, which is sensible, "provided the Western powers intend to defend the Middle East. Fact is, however, that they show no serious sign of such an intention." The United States and Britain have failed to coordinate their policies, and "Iran no longer believes in the U.S.," turning instead to the USSR for a trade treaty. The analysis concludes:

> **A Turned Back.** So Iran is slipping away—needlessly. A little money (compared to what the U.S. is spending elsewhere) and a lot of leadership might hold it, and with it the rest of the Middle East. It has thousands of well-educated, patriotic men (including [then Prime Minister] Razmara and the Shah) who want their country to have progress and independence. They cannot swing it alone. They need the U.S., and the U.S. gives them only promises, vacillation and contradiction. The U.S., in its turn, needs Iran—but the State Department, in a calamitous failure of foreign policy, has turned its back.[35]

By May 14, 1951, after the oil nationalization decree, *Time* is quite forthright in blaming the State Department.

> In China, the U.S. State Department had chosen to wait "till the dust settles." In Iran, as one State Department official put it last week, State is waiting "for the air to clear." From Teheran, TIME Correspondent James Bell cabled:
> "There must have been a moment in China when it became fully apparent that the West had had it. One day last week such a moment came in Teheran. Suddenly the consequences of Britain's policy of icy commercial hauteur and America's righteous paralysis were starkly obvious."[36]

There follows a description of just what this moment was: a May Day demonstration in Majlis Square attended by 35,000 people cheering a speaker who referred to "the heroic nations of the U.S.S.R. who are at the helm of the democratic front!" Bell comments: "In that roaring crowd, I could hear the voice of the enemy singing one more victory song. Iran is not yet behind the Soviet Curtain, but the Soviets have dangerously softened her up for conquest." *Time* goes on to editorialize:

> In Washington, the State Department was remarkably calm about Iran's nationalization of the Anglo-Iranian Oil Co. and the wave of anti-Western feeling. . . . Said a State Department spokesman: "The only thing that has been lost in this situation as yet is profit to the Anglo-Iranian Oil Co."
>
> It was a dangerously short-sighted view. In fact, the West has all but lost a key strategic position in Iran. . . .
>
> What happened in Iran may happen tomorrow in Iraq, Syria or Egypt; the U.S. State Department has no plan, no ready means to prevent it. When a reporter suggested to a State Department official last week that the U.S. should take decisive action in the Middle East, including pressure on the British to act less clumsily, the State Department man summed up the disastrous weakness of U.S. policy in his reply: "You can't do that kind of thing, as it was done in the 19th Century."[37]

This critique was articulated forcefully again a week later in the pages of Luce's other glossy "news" publication, *Life*, in a piece titled "Our Government's Deplorable Performance in Iran has Contributed to a Great Disaster": "The truth is that the State Department has no policy for Iran and no policy for the Middle East. . . . It may be too late for Iran. It is certainly very late. But it is not too late to appraise the U.S. State Department in the bleak light of Iran, and to bring Secretary of State Dean Acheson to book for a record of neglect and failure which alone is sufficient to justify his dismissal."[38] Calls for the arraignment and dismissal of a secretary of state do not seem to be following the lead of the foreign policy establishment, and indicate that *Time*, at least, stood outside the Washington foreign policy consensus.

This discourse may be contrasted in various ways with that of *The Nation*, a weekly political journal of liberal and progressive opinion, with a much lower circulation than that of *Time* but with a similar aim of influencing Americans interested in world and domestic politics and events.[39] In the pages of *The Nation*, readers were treated to a perspective far more critical of Iran, signaled, for example, by the title "Persia: Rugs Over the Garbage," a July 29, 1950, piece by Andrew Roth, who wrote, "The web of post-war promises [by Iranian politicians] and superficial reforms is like a Persian rug thrown over a garbage heap. It screens the unsightly but does not hide the odor of rottenness."[40] It goes on to describe famine in Azerbaijan, "intensified by the locust-like scourge of officials and landlords' agents who swarmed into the province in the wake of the army which overthrew the autonomous, pro-Soviet 'Democrats' regime in December, 1946. In Persia the right to rule is synonymous with the right to loot." The tone is far more critical than the more mainstream U.S. press, yet one notes the standard preoccupation with corruption ("Persian politics are conducted almost wholly by intrigue"), and the ignorant, if not slightly insulting, use of the term "Persia" (the shah's father had formally asked the West in 1935 to discontinue use of the term in favor of "Iran"). There is more sophisticated analysis, certainly. For example, we learn that "There are four real power groups—the palace, the army, the tribes, and the traditional politicians. The great landowners are represented in all four but work most directly through the politicians. The same tired old faces of the tools of these families appear again and again as Cabinets are made and unmade." It is much more critical as well: media censorship, illegal and unethical repression of the Tudeh Communist party, restrictions on suffrage are openly acknowledged, and linked to an opportunistic move by the shah after an attempted assassination in 1949. This counterdiscourse must be placed in context, however: *The Nation* did not shape popular culture or public opinion because most Americans did not read it, and most policymakers would not agree with it or pay it much attention.

Constructing the Shah: Orientalism-in-reverse? These general discursive orientations may be brought to life with a look at the treatments of the two main protagonists in the Iranian political arena, Shah Muhammad Reza Pahlavi and Prime Minister Muhammad Musaddiq. The context for their portrayal in the pages of *Time* and elsewhere is one in which Iranian politicians are typically depicted as corrupt and venal, with rare exceptions.[41] Iran is a land of "smelly politics";[42] Iranians are generally characterized as "frenetically suspicious"[43] and "explosively chauvinistic."[44]

Time's representation of the shah is noteworthy in that it is generally positive, though not without critical and negative overtones. A good example is the February 1951 characterization of him as "intelligent and devoted to the welfare of his country, around which he pilots his own B-17. This week he announced that he would split up the royal estates, estimated at 1,000 villages of 25,000 people, and sell small farms to the peasants who work the land. But the Shah of Shahs is as insecure and distrustful as all other elements in Persian life."[45] A few months later, in a portrait of the shah in a box among other Middle Eastern leaders, we have the following description:

> **Mohammed Reza Pahlevi** (31), Shahinshah of Iran, is pro-Western and has progressive ideas (last January he began sale of his vast land holdings to peasants on easy installment terms, gave the proceeds to charity). But when the oil crisis flared up, though he was opposed to the fanatical National Front, he did not dare take action. He is now powerless before fragile, faint-prone Premier Mohammed Mossadeq and his National Front.[46]

In another telling phrase, he is "reasonable but ineffectual."[47] On the one hand, he is beloved and serious, "Western" in his tastes and outlooks, wealthy and urbane, capable of standing up to the Soviet Union.[48] On the other, he is fickle and opportunistic in his dealings with the superpowers, and patriarchal within his family.[49] In 1952, *Time* offers a psychoanalytic (as well as paternalistic) reading: the shah is "a nice liberal young man, who likes to call himself a 'working monarch,'" but "The young Shah's sensitivity over his family's short claim to royal legitimacy helps render him indecisive."[50] As the political crisis intensifies in 1953, he is still "earnest but weak . . . the uncertain young monarch."[51] In sum, the shah both does and doesn't fit the stereotype of the Middle Eastern ruler-politician; his class and Western orientation earn him respect in the pages of *Time,* but his youth and lack of decisiveness make him vulnerable to the criticisms of the U.S. media in a major Cold War struggle. We might label this discourse a kind of "Orientalism-in-reverse": the shah possesses the usual vices of the Orient, tempered by his Western education and outlook in a kind of uneasy symbiosis that results in his perception as a weak leader.[52] These representations should be borne in mind when we return to him during and after the coup itself.

The de(con)struction of Musaddiq: From liberal nationalist to irrational fanatic. The shah's nemesis, Musaddiq, receives a decidedly different treatment in the U.S. press. As Dorman and Farhang note in their analysis of *The New York Times,* this shifted from positive to negative in the course of the conflict, although this happened almost immediately in the pages of *Time.* In May and June 1951, the first reports assess his character in terms of his lifelong experience and service to his country. On May 7, 1951, we have the first photo of him, with the punchy caption "The Shah was nationalized too." His first description:

Thin, bald and aging (70) the new Premier is a rich landowner who was
educated in France, has an honorary LL.D. from Oxford. In a country
where political skulduggery is the rule, he has remained an honest man.
He is rated an able orator, often gets so worked up in his speechmaking
that he faints; he is then revived and, after finishing his address, is carried
out feet first. . . .

He is anti-Russian as well as anti-British, only slightly less anti-
American.[53]

A month later, the positive is most strongly stressed once again:

Mohammad Mossadeq, with his faints, his tears and wild-eyed dreams, is
a whirling dervish with a college education and a first-rate mind.
Tried, tested & Worthy. Mohammed Mossadeq spent most of his life
as a fighter for his conception of the right. In the sad history of Iran, a
history of corruption, ignorance and greed, he usually fought on the side
of the angels—the more militant angels. . . .[54]

Reference is made in the same article to his courage in 1925 in voting
against the Pahlavi dynasty's establishment as contrary to law—"the only
prominent man in Iran with the courage to say so." It is noted that he retired
to his farm in 1928 "complaining that the elections were rigged (they
were)." Then comes the first reference to his mental condition: "In 1930 he
went to Berlin for medical treatment, also consulted a psychiatrist about his
worsening nervous condition. The psychiatrist was greatly interested in this
odd case, but Mossadeq refused to continue seeing him." His house arrest
by Reza Shah in 1940 and confinement to his basement for four and a half
months is noted; when he emerged he was unable to walk: "He made a
partial physical recovery, but psychologically, close associates say, he still
bears the injuries of his imprisonment" (it is also noted that this drove his
favorite daughter, seventeen-year-old Khadijeh, to a nervous breakdown
and that she was still in a Swiss sanitarium). His opposition to the Russians
in Azerbaijan in 1945–46 is mentioned as well.

By the end of the year, this grudging respect is dropped and the negative
clearly receives the accent. Musaddiq appeared on the cover of the first
issue for 1952 as *Time*'s "Man of the Year" for 1951. The cover story, titled
"Challenge of the East," opens:

Once upon a time, in a mountainous land between Baghdad and the Sea
of Caviar, there lived a nobleman. This nobleman, after a lifetime of carp-
ing at the way the kingdom was run, became Chief Minister of the realm.

In a few months he had the whole world hanging on his words and deeds, his jokes, his tears, his tantrums. Behind his grotesque antics lay great issues of peace or war, progress or decline, which would affect many lands far beyond his mountains.

His methods of government were peculiar. For example, when he decided to shift his governors, he dropped into a bowl slips of paper with the names of the provinces; each governor stepped forward and drew a new province. . . .

His weapon was the threat of his own political suicide, as a wilful little boy might say, "If you don't give me what I want I'll hold my breath until I'm blue in the face. Then you'll be sorry."

In this way, the old nobleman became the most world-renowned man his ancient race had produced for centuries. In this way, too, he increased the danger of a general war among nations, impoverished his country and brought it and some neighboring lands to the very brink of disaster.

Yet his people loved all that he did, and cheered him to the echo whenever he appeared in the streets.[55]

Musaddiq's name (which does not appear on the cover either; instead we have only the caption "Man of the Year: He Oiled the Wheels of Chaos") is not uttered until the seventh paragraph of the article. More signifiers in this article for Musaddiq include "dizzy old wizard" (this will reappear throughout the year), possessed of a "fanatical state of mind," the "weeping, fainting leader of a helpless country": "Mossadegh, by Western standards an appalling caricature of a statesman, was a fair sample of what the West would have to work with in the Middle East," of a piece with other leaders who "would rather see their own nations fall apart than continue their present relations with the West."

The biography of Musaddiq notes that "The Iranian George Washington was probably born in 1879 (he fibs about his age)." In 1919, "he hardened his policy into a simple Persia-for-the-Persians slogan . . . [and] kept hammering away at his single note. Nobody in the West heard him." This would change in 1951: "The Premier, whose mind runs in a deep single track, was committed to nationalization." Further, "He is not in any sense pro-Russian, but he intends to stick to his policies even though he knows they might lead to control of Iran by the Kremlin. . . . Neither Makki [Hussein Makki, governor of the oil province of Khuzistan], Kashani [the leading cleric in the oil struggle] nor Mossadegh has ever shown any interest in rational plans for the economic reform and development of their country." The piece goes on to assess the geopolitics of the Middle East, concluding that the British position is hopeless and that Iran cannot resolve its own problems, while the United States has no policy in the region: "the U.S. has some dire responsibilities to shoulder. One of them is to meet the fundamental moral challenge posed by the strange old wizard who lives in a mountainous land and who is, sad to relate, the Man of 1951."[56]

In less than a year, the honest, intelligent, patriotic prime minister of Iran has become a demagogic, emotional, childlike fanatic. These themes are hammered away at for the rest of his term in office. Standard qualifying terms for Musaddiq are "frail" or "fragile"; "faint-prone"; "prone to weeping." They are found countless times in the coverage in 1951—virtually no article omits them.[57] As Heiss has noted, this overlaps with treatments of him as childish, intractable, and emotional, as for example, "Better than most modern statesmen, Iran's Premier Mohammed Mossadegh knows the value of a childlike tantrum."[58] He, and his coalition, the National Front, are also regularly represented as "fanatic" and "extremist," and an important equation is made between nationalism and fanaticism, as early as May 28, 1951, when Musaddiq is characterized as "a nationalist fanatic living in fear of assassination by other nationalist fanatics,"[59] or when *Time* notes of the 1952 elections for the Majlis, "The more violently fanatic the candidate, the more votes that candidate polled."[60] At one point, *Time* actually interrogates its own use of the term: "Westerners are apt to call anyone a fanatic whose convictions are stronger and whose behavior is stranger than their own. To call Mossadeq a fanatic may be correct, but it explains almost nothing. Mossadeq is a far more complex character than the most baffling men the West has yet had to deal with, including misty yogis like Nehru and notably unmisty commissars like Joseph Stalin. The biggest single factor that makes Mossadeq different is a religion that the West knows little about: Islam. . . ."[61]

He is, contradictorily, at the same time, a strong man, an image that taps this association of him with Islam (although his politics were quite secular), and which is also a contrast to the shah. This is part of what makes him such a threat to the West. By 1953, when he asked for and was granted extra powers by the Majlis, and as the West's fear that Iran would fall to communism reached a crescendo, he was routinely described in *The New York Times* as a dictator; *Time* sees him already in mid-1952 as "the undisputed strong man of Iran," running the headline "Call Me Dictator."[62]

Efforts to counter these constructions were few in the United States, and difficult to make from Iran. In September 1951, *The Nation* argued that Iranian nationalism is not "self-generated"; that it has been given a boost by the actions of the AIOC and its "fabulous rate of profit."[63] In August 1952, an editorial in *The Nation* commented on Musaddiq's assumption of dictatorial powers, saying he was threatened by the continued poor state of the economy and the growing power (connected to this) of the Tudeh party. Musaddiq had therefore been forced to decree a land reform; the United States should support him on this project of a "democratic agrarian revolution," however remote its prospects for success, for "Revolution crowds on the heels of nationalism, and Russia is waiting at the back door with plans of its own and with a party set to carry them out."[64] This reads today as a more balanced attempt to contextualize Musaddiq's politics than was found elsewhere at the time, but also one which takes quite seriously the Communist threat, and calls idealistically on the United States to support a democratic reformer.

Musaddiq's own efforts to counter the perception of him in the West sought to link Iranian nationalism to U.S. traditions of liberty and independence. In April 1952 he appealed directly to the readers of *Time* in a letter to the editor, a space which is not read as widely as the news and features. *Time* did report the following: "To a U.S. correspondent he once more made clear his feelings: 'Oil nationalization,' he said, 'is Iran's version of the Boston Tea Party.'"[65] But even with his visit to the United States in late 1951, it proved very difficult to break with the dominant representations; indeed, the visit afforded the opportunity for the media to emphasize his weeping, fainting, and other ailments in picture and story. These representations contributed their measure to the coup that was already in the early phases of its making.

Preparing the coup: the shaping of the policy. The covert, secret, diplomatic side of the destabilization that culminated in the coup began with British intelligence as the oil dispute ground on unresolved into 1952, and was transferred to the CIA of the new Eisenhower administration in the first part of 1953. These events will be explored below. The task of this section is to weigh the significance of the public, political, cultural side of the coup through the activities of the American press over this period.

From the early days of the oil crisis, *Time* criticized the Truman administration's actions and placed the dispute in a Cold War context. In January 1951, for example: "Meanwhile, Iran stayed broke and almost defenseless, and U.S. and British diplomats let responsibility fall between them—and the Russians stood ready to pick up the pieces."[66] James Linen, the publisher, referred to the "hopeless resignation" and "ineptitude" of both British and American administrations in Iran since 1946.[67] Intervention was called for as early as June 1951 in an essay in which *Time* purported to speak for the Iranian political class: "Potentially the strongest force for peace and order in Iran is the U.S. Lack of interest in Iran and the Middle East by the U.S. State Department has dissipated much of the good will that existed for the U.S. . . . no matter how loudly Iranian politicos shout against foreign intervention, they would welcome U.S. intervention if they considered it in the country's favor."[68] *Life* echoed this assessment later in the year and drew out the implications of using undemocratic means for the higher goal of reforms. After dismissing the Iranian Majlis as corrupt, wealthy, and xeno-phobic, *Life* goes on: "Nor are the illiterate masses, nor the underemployed intellectuals, much help either. If we wish to start real reform in the Middle East, while maintaining order, we will soon find that our best allies are kings and 'strong men.'"[69] The implication here is that the U.S. public should tolerate undemocratic rulers in the interest of the political order needed to counter Communist insurgencies or subversion.

Attacks on the Democratic administration continued in the election year of 1952, and the theme of a gentle tutelage is sounded once again, as when quoting MacArthur's speech before Congress with approval: "What [the Asian peoples] seek now is friendly guidance, understanding and support, not imperious direction; the dignity of equality, and not the shame of subju-gation." The danger, in *Time*'s view, was that American diplomats would recoil from "the corruption, hatred, fanaticism and disorganization" of the Middle East, just as they had done with Nationalist China.[70] Cold War frames continue to dominate *Time*'s reporting and editorializing (often one and the same): the West is or should be less worried about the loss of Iranian oil on world markets (for this had been made good) than about "the increas-ing danger that Iran, strife-racked, almost bankrupt, and near chaos, will fall into the Red fold."[71] The increasing desperation in U.S. opinion-making circles shows up on September 29, 1952, when *Time* praised the initiative of oil company executive W. Alton Jones, president of Cities Service Co., to help Iran start exporting oil again. To be sure, this went against British pol-icy, but *Time* justifies this because "Iran is becoming a riper and more invit-ing plum for the Reds every week the deadlock continues. Said one Briton last week: 'After all, it might be better to lose Anglo-Iranian and keep Iran.'"[72]

Against this rising tide of Cold War interventionism, *The Nation* tried to add a countercurrent of compromise, not only in its pages but by organizing public forums such as the May 25, 1952, all-day conference at the Waldorf-Astoria Hotel in New York, on the theme of "Freedom's Stake in North

Africa and the Middle East," attended by Eleanor Roosevelt, Senator Estes Kefauver (whose speech was given by his campaign manager), Israeli minister David Gotein, Iranian senator S. R. Shafaq, Ambassador L. N. Palar of Indonesia, and various academics, journalists, publishers, and UN employees, among others. While there were no specific recommendations regarding Iran and the United States, *The Nation* concluded that there emerged a consensus around the following points:

1. That there is need for a revision of [the] policies [of the Western democratic world] in terms of an understanding that security cannot be achieved through military arrangements alone.
2. That security is indivisible: for the Middle East and consequently for the world, security lies in winning the loyalty of the people.
3. That the loyalty of the people cannot be won without a recognition of the profound revolution against feudalism and colonialism which is taking place in that area.
4. That the dynamics of democracy should be applied through an overall plan of assistance to countries of the Middle East, based on recognition of the meaning of that revolution.
5. That the stability of the area, indispensable to security, cannot be achieved unless there is a settlement of the Arab-Israeli war.[73]

This effort to create a fairly visible public forum for the airing of diverse progressive viewpoints was vintage *Nation*. It occupies a dissenting conceptual space, somewhat remote from popular opinion and from real governmental power, but a serious effort to include third world voices and progressive first world ones. It is the minor current in the popular discourse and the struggle to create a counterhegemony in the face of the entrenchment of a Cold War consensus.

Dwight D. Eisenhower would win the 1952 presidential elections, heavily sponsored by Henry Luce, who took credit for getting Eisenhower the nomination over his old conservative friend Robert Taft by issuing a special issue of *Time* during the Republican convention showing the arithmetic of defeat with Taft versus victory with Eisenhower.[74] In 1953, as U.S. plans for intervention in Iran shifted from blueprint to reality, the press also prepared the ground for a coup, building on the calls for U.S. intervention of the previous two years. *Newsweek* anticipated the domino theory in March, with Iran—not Vietnam—as the first domino: "The situation is such that the West may at any instant face the choice of occupying south Iran or watching the entire country go Communist by default. If Iran goes, then

Pakistan—where the Reds have done a remarkable job of infiltration—
would probably be next. This would isolate India, probably topple the rest
of the Middle East within months, and would mean that the West would
have to make the terrible decision whether to begin a fighting war or accept
the loss of the cold war."[75] It was *Time* that made the connection between
Cold War ends and the means required, quoting approvingly the words of
retiring U.S. diplomat J. Rives Childs to the State Department: "On the
basis of my studies and sojourn in Persia, I am convinced that Persia is now
entering a period of chaos and anarchy . . . From the times of Darius and
Cyrus, Persia has known only peace through a strong man . . . To prate of
democracy to the Persians is like advocating prohibition to the denizens of
hell. . . . The U.S. should be prepared, if necessary, to occupy southern Persia and regain possession of [the Abadan oil refinery], preferably at the request of . . . a Persian government sympathetic to the Western world."[76]
Time adds: "if Britain does not back the U.S., Childs says that the U.S.
should act alone."

   This is followed at the end of March with the advice of "One Middle East
oil expert" in a column titled "Iran: The Waiting Game": "Nearest to a stable
element is the Shah, this expert believes: if helped by the U.S., the Shah
might be transformed from the weak ruler he now seems."[77] On July 13,
1953, we have this assessment of Musaddiq as witting or unwitting conduit
for communism in Iran: "the Tudeh infiltration of Mossadegh's government
is now so deep that Communist agents can, in some cases, set government
policy. Said a Westerner: 'We aren't going to have a Communist *coup d'etat*
here. There will be nothing violent about it. We are just going to wake up
one morning and say to ourselves: "Good Lord! We have a pro-Tudeh government!" Then we are going to ask ourselves when did it happen—last
night? Yesterday? Last week? A month ago? And we are not going to be
able to answer.'"[78] A month later, the stage is finally set in the August 17
issue, which came out before the dramatic event of the shah's temporary
flight from Iran on August 16, and is a report on Mossadegh's referendum
on his dissolution of the Majlis, titled "99.93% Pure": "Hitler's best as a
vote-getter was 99.81% *Ja's* in 1936; Stalin's peak was 99.73% *Da's* in 1946.
Last week Premier Mohammed Mossadegh, the man in the iron cot, topped
them all with 99.93%."[79] Musaddiq is now positioned as both undemocratic
and too sympathetic to Communist participation in Iranian public life.

   Columnist Robert S. Allen of the *New York Post* wrote an eerily prescient
article in July 13, 1953, titled "Old Mossy on the Way Out?", in which he
predicted Musaddiq's fall within the year to an army-led coup, and noted

the army's close ties to the United States. He also quoted Secretary of State John Foster Dulles: "Any Iranian government, other than a Communist one, would be better for us than the present government. We have found it impossible to deal with Mossadegh."[80] The implicit chain of logic leading from the U.S. State Department to the Iranian army and a coup was not picked up by other U.S. media, nor referred to after the coup, as we shall see.

What impact did all of this have in preparing the coup? Mark Gasiorowski, who has studied the secret side of the coup in most detail, concludes his assessment of the motives for U.S. action against Musaddiq on August 19, 1953, as primarily the fear of a Communist takeover of Iran, rather than the oft-argued desire to gain a share of Iran's oil production. These concerns seem to have come from "the highest levels of the CIA and the State Department, and were not shared by lower-level Iran specialists."[81] This assessment is echoed by Richard Cottam, another scholar of the period: "The explanation is anti-Communism. . . . [CIA operative Kermit Roosevelt] and Loy Henderson saw Communists everywhere, and found it impossible to believe there might be liberal nationalists in Iran just as there are in the West."[82] That the most knowledgeable U.S. officials in the State Department and in Iran were overruled by their superiors and the CIA, and that the chief concern was the Communist threat to Iran if Musaddiq remained, is at least prima facie evidence that the discourses circulating in the media, led by *Time*'s Cold War view of the world, played their role in the construction of the coup. Let us now examine what is known about the event.

The Coup as Event and Representation

By June 1951 the British Foreign Office had developed plans for a coup.[83] An invasion of Abadan (where the oil refinery lay) was planned for fall 1951 but called off when President Truman said the United States would not support it. Iranian coup plotters centered around retired pro-Nazi general Fazlullah Zahidi, with British support.[84] Musaddiq broke diplomatic relations with Britain when he discovered the plot in the autumn of 1952, making the British even more reliant on the United States in Iran.

The United States tried to mediate the oil dispute several times without success, as feelings soon ran too deep on both sides. The CIA meanwhile had had operations of various sorts directed against Tudeh and Soviet influence in Iran since the late 1940s, including putting out propaganda,[85] organizing anti-Tudeh street fighters, and paying *ulama* (clerics) to attack the Tudeh in sermons. Musaddiq's National Front became an object of CIA disruption after 1951. Gasiorowski believes the CIA did all this without Truman's or the State Department's approval. Anglo-American coup planning began in earnest late in 1952 after the British embassy staff had been ejected from Iran. The British intelligence service, the MI6, put its faith in the newly elected Eisenhower administration, which agreed to develop a plan to overthrow Musaddiq and install Zahidi, code-named "Ajax," in February 1953, just two weeks after the inauguration. The shah was apparently only brought into these concrete plans in the summer of 1953, and even in August remained noncommittal until radioed assurances of official U.S. and British involvement.

The events of August 15–19 still almost eluded the CIA's control. An initial attempt to dismiss Musaddiq through a military-delivered royal decree was foiled by officers loyal to Musaddiq on the night of August 15–16. This prompted Zahidi to take shelter in a CIA safe house and the shah to flee the country on August 16, departing first for Baghdad and then for the pleasures and safety of Rome. On August 17–18 there were numerous anti-shah demonstrations and celebrations in Tehran, some organized by CIA contacts to create chaos in the streets, which were joined by members of the Tudeh and National Front. U.S. ambassador Henderson asked Musaddiq to use the police to break these up, to which Musaddiq agreed. The Tudeh then called its cadres off the streets. On August 19, CIA-organized royalist crowds took over the streets; meanwhile "so much American currency had found its way into the bazaar that the black market exchange rate fell from over 100 rials to the dollar to under 50."[86] The crowds were joined by many police and army units; a nine-hour battle was fought at Musaddiq's home in which three hundred people were killed. By the end of the day, Musaddiq was under arrest and Zahidi was prime minister. The surprised shah prudently waited until August 22 to board a plane back to Iran. In a complex turn of events, the United States had toppled a government by spending $60,000.

How was the coup covered by the press? The mainstream media saw the coup as "a wholly internal matter brought about by widespread dissatisfaction with the ineptitude of Mosaddeq."[87] Newsweek's headline was "Shah Returns in Triumph as Army Kicks Out Mossadegh": "The only mention in the Newsweek piece about the CIA was in a description of the confusion at Rome's Hotel Excelsior among the shah's entourage when news of the successful coup arrived. In an exceedingly cryptic paragraph, Newsweek advised readers, 'Amid the hubbub, Allen Dulles, director of the [CIA], arrived at the Excelsior. No one paid any attention to him.'"[88] *The Washington Post* wrote of "cause to rejoice" (August 20, 1953); *The Christian Science Monitor*'s editorial was titled "Iran Rights Itself," and described the events as "probably the most hopeful that could have happened" (August 20, 1953); *The New York Times* noted "a deep sense of relief in the West" at the demise of the "rabid, self-seeking nationalist" (August 21, 1953).[89]

Due to its publishing schedule, *Time*'s first report was issued on August 31 under the title "Iran: The People Take Over." It notes that by sundown on August 18, "something was stirring in Teheran that could not yet be measured," that perhaps Musaddiq had gone too far too fast and forced the people to choose between him and the shah. *Time* suggested that Henderson's visit to Musaddiq convinced the prime minister to ask the army and police to control the Tudeh demonstrators and clear the streets, calling this "Mossadegh's fatal mistake," for it gave the army courage and angered the Tudeh. August 19 "was the people's day"; the pro-shah crowds are called "mobs," yet "This was no military coup, but a spontaneous popular uprising; individual soldiers joined, but not a single army unit came in. . . . The army had planned to counterattack Mossadegh on Friday, the people beat them to it by two days."[90]

The shah's reaction, when told the news in the dining room of the "showy" Excelsior Hotel in Rome, is characteristic: "The Shah's jaw dropped; his trembling fingers reached for a cigarette. 'Can it be true?' he asked uncertainly. The Queen was quicker on the uptake. 'How exciting,' said Soraya, placing a calming hand on her husband's arm. 'It shows how the people stand,' said the Shah at last. 'I have to admit that I haven't had a very important part in the revolution.'"[91] *Time* comments that though the shah was restored "without having lifted a finger," his flight had been beneficial because it provoked the crisis that led his people, who "had shown more faith in him and in the throne he occupied than he himself suspected," to restore him. In the September 7 issue, the shah is now "fairly confident" of the future: "While returning from Rome in my plane, I had a feeling that I was a completely new man in every respect."[92]

This theme continues in a September 28, 1953, article titled "The New Shah": "'I feel as though I were beginning my second reign,' announced Shah Mohammed Reza Pahlevi five weeks ago when he flew back to Teheran and to the throne of Iran. 'I am older and more experienced, and [now] I know what I must do.'" Now, although *Time* hastened to point out that he is "young," his step is firm, "his shoulders back. He had given up sleeping pills, taken up tennis again and was working hard," conferring daily with

Zahidi and Henderson, and heeding "Iran's ablest and most respected statesman, Court Minister Hussein Ala," having dispensed with "the old meddling palace camarilla" and the "backstairs intrigues" of its leaders, Princess Ashraf and the queen mother, who had not yet returned to Iran.[93] *Time* seems to urge further change in the shah's political demeanor, given the continuing threats of the Cold War: "The Shah, a shy and gentle young man, repeatedly says that he intends to be a conscientiously constitutional monarch, not an authoritarian like his famed father, Reza Shah Pahlevi, father of modern Iran. But the vast reforms needed to ease Iranians' poverty and the decisive acts necessary to check the underground plotting of the Red-led Tudeh and the supporters of old Mossadegh, must be accomplished fast to save Iran from fresh rebellion and capture by Russia. The new Shah's most immutable enemy is time."[94]

These decisive acts followed in short order, with the trial of Musaddiq that condemned him to house arrest until his death in 1967, and the dismantling of the Tudeh networks in the army through a number of executions, all reported in further fascinating Cold War constructions. Thus, the shah is never referred to as a dictator, elections were no more corrupt "than usual," Zahidi is a "strong and able" prime minister, while Musaddiq at his trial is ridiculed in the pages of *Time* as "a wizened old mummer," and by *Life* as "the most uninhibited ham of contemporary politics."[95] An account of the execution of ten Tudeh military men, meant to show their ruthlessness and treachery, reads quite poignantly: "To each of the others in turn, the mullah extended the Koran. Pray and be sent to Paradise, he begged. 'Paradise was the place we were going to make in this country,' said one."[96] *Time* calls the 1954 election "unpleasant and undemocratic, but unusual in its speedy efficiency,"[97] contextualizing it thus: "Though crude and undemocratic by Western standards, the balloting process fits the pattern for Iran, which is backward, deeply infiltrated by a Communist underground and inexperienced at combatting the enemies of democracy with democratic methods."[98] *Life* published a photo essay showing an opposition voter being told his identity card is not in order, and a gang which includes soldiers and police beating up an antigovernment voter, methods condoned as "standard procedures in Iranian elections."[99]

The events of the coup, barely well known even today, leaked out only very slowly. More to the point, they left the American public and most of the world with a misrepresentation (the "silence" in Kennett Love's remarks that head this essay). Love's article in *The New York Times* at the height of the crisis on August 18 mentioned "growing [Iranian] press accusations that the United States and Mr. Henderson himself were involved in the weekend's bloodless stroke and counter-stroke exchanged between the Court and the Government."[100] This lead was never followed up again; Love told Dorman and Farhang that the *Times* did not encourage investigative journalism. Thus he couldn't simply report the "funny" drop in the value of the dollar right after the coup: "If you couldn't say why, you might as well pigeonhole it. And if you didn't, they did":

> . . . the *Times* was *told* [by Love] three separate times of direct American involvement in the affair beginning five months before the story was revealed in the *Saturday Evening Post* in November 1954. Yet according to Love, [foreign editor Emanuel R.] Freedman totally ignored the references, never once mentioning the subject or asking for clarification or further detail. The first major American clandestine intervention of the cold war, therefore, went completely unnoted in the newspaper of record. Equally crucially, the *Times* failed to correct the historical record in the twenty or so years that followed. Although the story came to be treated as accepted fact in a number of books, it was never told in detail in the press until after 1978 and the revolution.[101]

The *Saturday Evening Post* piece referred to was published over a year later under the title "The Mysterious Doings of CIA [sic]."[102] With a number of factual errors, it does credit the CIA with a role in the coup, yet it was never prominently picked up elsewhere again. It was, in fact, prepared with the help of the CIA itself, interested in taking credit for the operation.[103] *The Nation* also made an allusion to an untold story, buried in a piece on Iran a year after the coup: "The inside story of the 'popular revolt' which overthrew the Mossadegh regime in August last year will be known only after the various secret documents involved are made public. One may safely conjecture, however, that the story given to the press did not tell the whole truth."[104] The "true" story, which had some currency inside Iran as a kind of underground counterhegemonic current, found few tellers in the West, journalistic or scholarly, right through the Iranian Revolution that was its indirect legacy a quarter century later.

Conclusions

Viewed in retrospect, Muhammad Musaddiq can be seen as a non-Communist advocate of democracy inside Iran who sought to break with a history of dependency and Western influence in his country's economy and political affairs. Like Sukarno in Indonesia, Gandhi and Nehru in India, Nasser in Egypt, Nkrumah in Ghana, Ben Bella in Algeria, and Ho Chi Minh in Vietnam, he led a movement of national liberation against colonial power. Like most of these leaders and their movements, and even more closely related to those of Arbenz and Arevalo in Guatemala, and later Allende in Chile, his nationalism and democratic aims were fatefully misrepresented in the West, especially in the pages of *Time, The New York Times,* and other U.S. publications. Dominant U.S. constructions of Musaddiq were based on Orientalist and Cold War discourses, and served to further solidify such discourses. I have argued that this contributed directly to the atmosphere—the "structure of feeling"—in which a coup was conceived and made.[105] While *The New York Times* studiously avoided mention of U.S. actions in Iran, Luce's publications *Time* and *Life* were instrumental in castigating the Truman administration's indecisiveness in the region, and contributed to the election of a Republican administration that was more willing to intervene in Iran's internal affairs. The covert policies that produced the coup were in their turn produced by a Cold War discourse that *Time* shaped decisively, and the "success" of the coup forged a precedent that led to further interventions in Guatemala and Cuba, among other places, in the decade that followed.

All the causal links in the chain that produced the coup may never be identified, but I hope that this third world cultural studies perspective on the events has suggested the plausibility of such a chain, and illuminated the events in a new light. Such a perspective insists that the discursive subversion of the Musaddiq administration practiced by the U.S. media played a material role in the history of the Cold War, most fatefully in Iran itself. Against this, we have seen the difficulties of countering this discourse, whether in the pages of *The Nation* or through Musaddiq's own efforts to address the American people.

Having opened with the words of Musaddiq to the American readers of *Time,* it is perhaps fitting to close with his last public speech to Iranians, delivered at his trial: "Since it is evident, from the way this tribunal is being run, that I will end my days in the corner of some prison, and since this may be the last time that I am able to address myself to my beloved nation, I beseech every man and woman to continue on the glorious path which they have begun, and not to fear anything."[106] The opportunity lost to set history on a different course weighs heavily on the world we inhabit today.

Eisenhower's Guatemalan Doodle, or:
How to Draw, Deny, and Take Credit for a Third World Coup

CHRISTIAN G. APPY

[O]ur sister republics to the south feel that the United States pays
too little attention to them. . . .
> — DWIGHT D. EISENHOWER, *Mandate for Change*

There are colorful villages and cities with exotic names. . . . Indians
dressed in hand-woven garments follow customs honored for centuries, and up in the highlands you can still hear the reed pipe and
drum. Crafts are interesting and can be bought inexpensively at village markets. You can dig for your own pre-Columbian artifacts and,
so far, finders keepers.
> — HILDA COLE ESPY, *Another World: Central America*

DWIGHT EISENHOWER was not given to abstraction. The doodles in
his presidential papers are not wild, slashing affairs, or loopy, tangled,
spontaneous gestures, but representational sketches, the kind you might
submit to the Famous Artists Schools. Founded in 1948, this paint-by-mail
art business featured Norman Rockwell as its most famous advisory "fac-
ulty" member and one of its major investors. Eisenhower admired Rockwell, once got some painting tips from him, and even invited the popular
illustrator to one of his black-tie stag dinners. It was rare indeed for an
artist to be invited. Ordinarily these occasions, held every few weeks, were
reserved for wealthy businessmen, high government officials, military officers, and politicians—all-male, all-white, all-American, all-wealthy, and all-
conventional. In this crowd, Rockwell was practically avant-garde. He took
a tranquilizer to calm his nerves.[1]

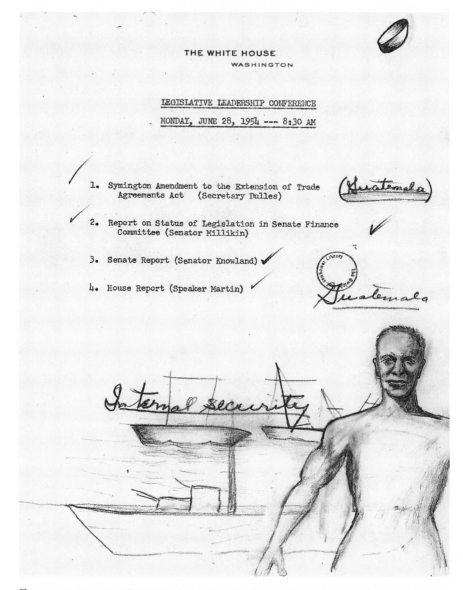

THE WHITE HOUSE
WASHINGTON

LEGISLATIVE LEADERSHIP CONFERENCE
MONDAY, JUNE 28, 1954 --- 8:30 AM

1. Symington Amendment to the Extension of Trade
   Agreements Act   (Secretary Dulles)

2. Report on Status of Legislation in Senate Finance
   Committee (Senator Millikin)

3. Senate Report (Senator Knowland)

4. House Report (Speaker Martin)

FIG. 1. Courtesy Dwight D. Eisenhower Library. Abilene, Texas.

On the morning of June 28, 1954, while meeting with legislative leaders, the president sketched a particularly detailed figure on the bottom of his meeting agenda.[2] It looks remarkably like a self-portrait—a portrait of the artist as a young man. We see the figure from the waist up, his chest bare, his hair close-cropped, his gaze direct. The shoulders are firmly set and the right arm carefully articulated, so muscular it rises away from the body like a weightlifter about to move into a formal pose or a soldier moving stiffly from attention to "at ease." Above the naked male figure, Eisenhower wrote "Guatemala" in two places. He traced over the line of one of them as if it were an exercise in a book on penmanship. In the background are three boats. The largest is some kind of gunboat, though a naval officer might be aghast at the crudeness of the drawing and the distinctly unthreatening rendering of the guns. The other vessels have no apparent military significance. Across their masts are the carefully scripted, doubly written words: *Internal Security.*

This last marking may be the easiest to interpret. "Internal Security" was not listed on the meeting agenda, but the official notes indicate a discussion of a "desirable" "omnibus bill" to address the "anti-subversion program."[3] The president and legislative leaders were almost certainly discussing the Communist Control Act, a law passed in August 1954 to outlaw the Communist Party (it had only been indirectly outlawed by the Smith Act in 1940 and the Internal Security Act in 1950).

Guatemala was another addendum to the agenda. After Eisenhower opened the meeting by urging support for a farm bill, he turned to Secretary of State John Foster Dulles. Dulles informed the congressional representatives that Jacobo Arbenz, the president of Guatemala, had resigned the previous night. Dulles's account, like Eisenhower's doodle, provided no explicit acknowledgement that the United States had orchestrated the coup. Nonetheless, Dulles could not resist claiming the overthrow as "a great triumph for American diplomacy" even as he clung to the passive mode in explaining that "the principal advocate of Communism in the Western Hemisphere [Arbenz] has been eliminated from the government of Guatemala." Then it was on to Indochina, where Dulles called for the creation of a Southeast Asia Treaty Organization to fill the breach created by the recent French defeat at Dien Bien Phu.

But what about that naked man in front of the gunboat? I think of the drawing as Eisenhower's "Guatemalan doodle." It is not a "smoking gun" that links the president to the coup and it is unnecessary to impose such a functional reading. After all, Eisenhower's responsibility for the CIA plot to overthrow the popularly elected government of Jacobo Arbenz has long been established.[4] Rather, the sketch warrants interpretation because it suggests some of the images and assumptions that shaped U.S. Cold War foreign policy.

Here, in Eisenhower's sketch, we have a bare-chested Anglo fronting a flotilla of empty boats; a naked American Adam, presiding in all innocence over a coup that one historian has described as a Cold War version of "gun-boat diplomacy."[5] Eisenhower has clearly been thinking about something called Guatemala, thinking about it enough to write the name twice, to put it in parentheses and underline. But Guatemala is merely a name. In his public narratives, Eisenhower described the coup as a great act of Guatema-lan self-determination, a popular uprising against Communist tyranny. Yet he does not/cannot draw a picture of Guatemalans. We have an American self, backed by military force, but where are the Guatemalan freedom fighters to match the phony narrative of popular revolt? Where are the peas-ant victims of Communist terror turning on their rulers? They cannot be envisioned because they do not exist; but it is also probable that Eisenhower did not care enough about Guatemala even to sketch a fantasy picture of the nation he had invaded. He paid attention to it only to reduce it to a "communist beachhead" that posed a threat to national security. Like a piece in a jigsaw puzzle, Guatemala's distinguishing characteristics were only important so long as they fit into a larger, predetermined design. And if the piece did not fit, Cold War policymakers were not hesitant to file the edges. Of course, even detailed attention to foreign cultures can produce ruthless policy; but we fail to understand a strong strain in U.S. imperialism unless we fully acknowledge the readiness of U.S. policymakers to intervene on the basis of an extraordinarily narrow field of admissible "knowledge." Despite many global interventions, U.S. policymakers have often had strik-ingly little impulse to figure the third world in ways that stretched or chal-lenged their own ideological and cultural claims. Though Eisenhower of-fered much rhetorical support to tourism, international "understanding," and "people-to-people" exchanges, he has left us no evidence of any serious interest in the people of Guatemala.[6]

For Eisenhower, the only information he really needed to know to justify the coup was provided by U.S. ambassador to Guatemala John Peurifoy. After meeting with President Jacobo Arbenz for six hours in December 1953, Peurifoy sent a five-page memo to the State Department.[7] Peurifoy concluded that "normal approaches will probably not work in Guate-mala. . . . The candle is burning slowly and surely, and it is only a matter of time before the large American interests will be forced out completely." Arbenz, he reported, "thought like a Communist and talked like a Commu-nist, and if not actually one, would do until one came along."[8]

In the 1950s and 1960s many Americans regarded Eisenhower as a largely detached, even passive, president who delegated much of his authority, a man less committed to the details of his job than to the pleasures of his many hobbies—golf, bridge, painting, cooking, cattle breeding, fishing. He was, according to this view, a genial, apolitical, grandfatherly caretaker. Some of his liberal champions believed his apparent lack of enthusiasm for politics kept him from being unduly swayed by promoters of the "international communist conspiracy." In the face of Cold War tension, he was, it seemed to many, a man of restraint.

More recent scholars have argued that Eisenhower's public image as a casual statesman masked a man of intense political skill, ambition, energy, and awareness. He was, they claim, an exceedingly competitive and calculating man who artfully disguised his enthusiastic devotion to the machinations of power politics. Indicative of this character profile, we learn that Eisenhower was a compulsive chain smoker who had a four-pack-a-day habit until he decided, with equal fervor, to quit cold turkey in 1949 when his doctor warned that it was hurting his health.[9]

The two views are not entirely contradictory if we understand the intensity with which Eisenhower pursued all his "leisure" activities. The sheer scale of his recreation is staggering. In spite of a heart attack in 1955, abdominal surgery in 1956, and a stroke in 1957, Eisenhower managed to get in eight hundred rounds of golf during his two terms.[10] He made it look a lot more relaxing than George Bush's frenzied outings, but Eisenhower's letters reveal him to be a keen competitor, eager not only to improve his various skills, but to beat others along the way. Even around the putting greens at the White House and Camp David he thrived on competition, drawing friends and visitors into small wagers. He was perhaps even more competitive about bridge and devoted considerable attention to lining up suitable partners at Camp David, Augusta, Georgia, and other venues.

So what? Surely Eisenhower's "personality" or "presidential style" was not itself significant to the Guatemalans who suffered under his policy. But it is worth our attention if it can awaken a better understanding of the way Eisenhower envisioned the world he so profoundly affected. Historians have persuasively demonstrated that Eisenhower was actively involved in establishing the broad outlines of U.S. policy toward Latin America. And he was also well informed of the details of the Guatemalan coup. According to Stephen Ambrose, Eisenhower maintained "tight control" over CIA activities and sought regular briefings on the planning and progress of covert operations. Yet he was also scrupulous about secrecy and left few traces of his role in the overthrow of Arbenz. Many discussions occurred after hours "over cocktails" with Secretary of State John Foster Dulles and during occasional Sunday brunches hosted by Eleanor Dulles for the president, Foster, and Allen Dulles (director of the CIA).[11]

For all of that, there exists scant evidence of any deep or abiding personal interest in the region apart from concerns about national strategic, ideological, and economic self-interest. In Stephen Rabe's book on the subject, *Eisenhower and Latin America,* perhaps the only presidential opinion regarding the people and culture of Latin American was reported by former ambassador to Mexico Robert Hill. Hill recalled that Eisenhower had once waxed nostalgic about his years in San Antonio at Fort Sam Houston (1915–1917) when he often crossed into Mexico on hunting trips. In the course of this conversation Eisenhower said of Mexicans: "You know, they're rascals at heart. You can't trust them and so forth, but they're lovable types, and you know, I sure would like to get away on a holiday and go back to relive that youth of mine in the military, those happy days in Mexico."[12]

Eisenhower left no analogous profession of love for Guatemala. Nor does he seem as "obsessed" with Arbenz as has sometimes been argued of Kennedy with Castro, Nixon with Allende, and Reagan with Ortega. It is certainly likely that Eisenhower followed the Guatemalan operation closely and cared a great deal about its outcome, but it was only one of many concerns. The coup did seem to force one change in schedule. On June 19, the second day of the coup, Eisenhower cut short a trip to Quantico to go back to Washington. According to his press secretary's diary: "Anything [done] by the President [regarding Guatemala] should be done from the White House and not from a military conference at Quantico."[13] Apparently appearances remained important even while conducting a secret war. But Eisenhower was in no rush. First he finished an afternoon round of golf with three generals. And the day before, as the coup began, Eisenhower took the time to write a detailed letter to his friend Clifford Roberts about the U.S. Open golf tournament and his own first eagle:

Dear Cliff:
No matter how the National Open finally comes out, I find this morning that two of my favorite golfers are well up. Billy Jo is leading and Ben is not far off the pace. . . .

While we are talking about good golfers, I should tell you about my eagle. This eagle might not be important to anyone else, but it is my first—and it came on a hole where one day I had an eagle in my grasp and just kicked it out of the window by means of a completely inexcusable putt. I was hitting the ball fairly long and straight the other day and on Burning Tree's #10 banged my second one about six feet from the pin (on the former occasion I was twenty inches away). This time I decided to take no chances so I shut my eyes, gave it a prayerful stab—and sure enough, there it was. . . .

This weekend I have to go down to Quantico for at least one day. Next weekend I will have our British friends on my hands. But maybe some time after that we can fix up a Camp David bridge game. Of course I never plan such things very specifically because minor emergencies are always occurring—but if you are going to be available the early part of July, you might let me know when you get a chance.[14]

Then on June 21, Eisenhower wrote to General Alfred Gruenther, updating him about a marathon bridge game that Gruenther missed:

The day you left Camp David, the three remaining bridge players . . . were left a bit high and dry. After a good workout on my pitching green, in which I won only five bucks to my great chagrin, I challenged the other two to a set game with Mamie as my partner. Out of their generosity and in spite of my violent protests, they insisted on cutting the stakes in half. We played all afternoon, didn't lose a rubber, and came off with forty-seven bucks profit. . . . [15]

And on June 30 Eisenhower wrote his friend George Allen to confirm the details of an elaborate bet (with a possible $700 at stake) designed to encourage both men to lose several pounds in July. Though no doubt conceived out of genuine concern for his friend's health, it is a rather taunting letter: "When such statistics stare you cold-bloodedly in the face, don't you feel heartily ashamed of yourself? You—two inches shorter than I am—weigh a full 60 pounds more!"[16]

These letters, especially when read in their entirety, reveal not just great enthusiasm for golf and bridge, but an intense fascination with the minutiae of competitive score-keeping. Eisenhower relishes the details of his many contests. Even dieting is turned into a competition. The wagers are just another way to keep score. What do we make of such letters alongside the major events that competed for Eisenhower's attention during this period—the Viet Minh victory over the French in Indochina, the recent decision by the Supreme Court to desegregate public schools, the conclusion of the Army-McCarthy hearings just one day before the Guatemala operation began, the visit of Winston Churchill and Anthony Eden, and, of course, the

coup in Guatemala? The point here is not that Eisenhower was insuffi-
ciently attentive to affairs of state. A man of his energy had the capacity to
respond to all kinds of major and "minor emergencies." The real significance of these personal letters lies in what they may suggest about the habits
of mind and character that shaped his public, as well as private, actions.
What was the nature of the attention Eisenhower paid to Guatemala?

There is not much to go on. There are probably more references to golf
than Guatemala in Eisenhower's papers. In part, that is in keeping with a
covert operation that was not intended to leave a paper trail. But it is also
indicative of superpower arrogance. It was simply not thought necessary for
the President of the United States to have a detailed understanding of a
small, relatively powerless Central American nation. And once Eisenhower
had concluded that Guatemala had fallen within the "Soviet orbit," the sat-
ellite's internal life and history was, by definition, rendered largely irrelevant.

Perhaps the most extended presidential description of the Guatemalan
coup comes in Eisenhower's 1963 memoir. While it tells us almost nothing
about Guatemala, it does share the narrative drive and enthusiasm of the
private letters (see pp. 197–98). It also shares their fascination with competition, odds for success, and the final victory. The "plot" is all about the
ability of one adviser to outdo another in persuading Eisenhower to send a
few planes to support the "rebels." Eisenhower makes fun of the adviser
who argued against the intervention, even though the hawkish adviser said
the odds of success were only 20 percent. The overthrow of the Guatemalan
government may be as unlikely as the "prayerful stab" that got him his first
eagle, but by God, it worked. A common trait in male bragging ritual, once
success has been achieved, is to inflate the obstacles to build up the triumph, while diminishing the accomplishment to fend off the charge of con-
ceit (I didn't think I could do it, I closed my eyes, I got lucky).

It is possible that Eisenhower derived more satisfaction from the successful CIA coup in Guatemala than he did from even his best day on the
golf course. But to care about the instrumental outcome of a covert operation is not the same as caring about a nation or its people. Indeed, to the
extent that Eisenhower's "knowledge" of Guatemala focused almost entirely
on the success or failure of the CIA coup, the better able he was to tell a
persuasive cover-story that bore almost no resemblance to Guatemalan reality. We need to confront the simple probability that Eisenhower cared more
about his golf and bridge games than he did about the people of Guatemala,

whose government he was overthrowing and who would live for decades with the brutal legacy of that distant decision.

Historical Overview

According to historian Walter LaFeber, the overthrow of Jacobo Arbenz "is becoming one of the best known" of "Washington's Cold War policies."[17] Perhaps, more accurately, it is one of the few Latin American events that is at least vaguely familiar to most historians of the United States. And it has inspired a substantial body of scholarship. To the general public, however, the coup remains almost as obscure as the CIA intended it to be. When I raised the subject in classes at Harvard and MIT, only a rare student had some knowledge of the story. With that in mind, a brief overview is certainly necessary.

The overthrow of Arbenz in 1954 ended ten years of remarkable reform, a period Guatemalans know as the "Ten Years of Spring." It began in 1944 with a middle-class revolution against the dictator Jorge Ubico. Ubico had perpetuated the brutal exploitation of Guatemalan peasants through a system of vagrancy laws that he introduced to "reform" the debt bondage of the past. Ubico also gave landowners the legal right to do what they had once done as a matter of course—murder any peasant they regarded as a threat to their property.[18] In the 1930s, Ubico cut a sweetheart deal with the United Fruit Company that granted the company extraordinarily low taxes. The Fruit Company returned the favor with a million-dollar loan to Ubico. The contract was drafted by UFCO attorneys at Sullivan and Cromwell (where the Dulles brothers, Allen and John Foster, were partners). Guatemalans called the Fruit Company "El Pulpo"—the octopus—an apt name for a company that had a virtual monopoly on the nation's bananas, railroads, and electricity.

The "October Revolution" against Ubico in 1944 was led by young reformist army officers, students, and professionals and brought the freest elections in Guatemalan history. The new president was Juan José Arévalo (1944–1950), a charismatic intellectual who called himself a "spiritual socialist." He was followed by Jacobo Arbenz Guzmán (1950–1954), a bright young colonel with a passion for social reform. In spite of resistance from local elites and foreign companies like United Fruit, the reformist presidents introduced universal suffrage, a social security system, a central bank, and land reform. They also granted the right to organize labor unions and to strike. By the late forties the Truman administration and UFCO began to characterize these reforms as Communist-inspired. Ironically, this red-baiting was a boon to the Guatemalan Communist Party (which Arbenz legalized in 1951). It allowed them to take more credit than they deserved for popular reforms, thus helping them gain leadership of the major labor union, the Confederación General de Trabajadores (CGT).

The Eisenhower administration came to power promising a more aggressive foreign policy to replace the Democrats' "defeatist" containment. There was talk of rolling back communism and liberating "captive peoples." Most of this was rhetoric. Ending Soviet control of Eastern Europe was a formidable challenge. Guatemala, however, was not nearly so problematic. Here was a winnable opportunity to rollback "communism" in the Western Hemisphere. After all, in Guatemala communism was, at most, a distant prospect, not an entrenched reality backed by a nuclear power.[19]

For both the Truman and Eisenhower administrations the clearest evidence that Guatemala was moving leftward was the effort of the Arbenz government to renegotiate and ultimately void the exploitative contracts Ubico had granted to the United Fruit Company. In 1952 these efforts culminated in the Agrarian Reform Bill, the key element of a program that distributed land to a half-million people (one-sixth of the population). The need for such a reform was dire. Twenty-two owners held more land than almost 250,000 peasant families. The United Fruit Company alone owned 42 percent of the nation's land. The new law expropriated unused land from large plantations and compensated the owners with bonds priced according to the declared value of the land in the most recent tax assessment. The minimal tax rates would now come back to haunt the former beneficiaries. In 1953 the Arbenz administration took 425,000 acres of uncultivated land from the United Fruit Company's total of 3 million acres and offered one million dollars in compensation. UFCO attacked the land reform as Communist-inspired theft and demanded $16 million.[20]

In *Bitter Fruit*, Stephen Schlesinger and Stephen Kinzer stress the centrality of the United Fruit Company in promoting the CIA plot to overthrow Arbenz. They and other scholars have amply demonstrated dozens of close ties between the company and Washington officialdom. If ever there was a shining example of the "revolving door" between corporate, military, and political elites, this is it. The door revolved so quickly, in fact, it is sometimes difficult to keep straight the points at which various actors are employed by the government or the company. Suffice it to say that virtually everyone who shaped Guatemalan policy in the early 1950s had some connection to UFCO.[21]

In *Shattered Hope,* historian Piero Gleijeses argues that Washington would have tried to overthrow Arbenz regardless of UFCO lobbying. "In no country of Latin America had the communists ever been as influential as they were in Guatemala. And no president had ever been as close to the communists as was Arbenz. It required no manipulations by UFCO minions for U.S. officials to appreciate these truths."[22] Though Gleijeses may be right, it is also true that Communists had hardly taken over in Guatemala. Since November 1950 when Arbenz won the freest election in Guatemalan history, Communists had never held more than four of the fifty-six seats in the Guatemalan Congress. Nor had any served on his cabinet. Communists were barred from the police, army, and foreign ministry. Communist Party membership, according to Eisenhower administration estimates, was no more than one thousand. Both Arévalo and Arbenz had supported the United States at the United Nations on the Korean War. Four-fifths of Guatemalan exports went to the United States. Still, Eisenhower was convinced that Guatemala was "openly playing ball with communists" and it could not be tolerated. It was not really a matter of whether his administration was more concerned about protecting the United Fruit Company or more concerned about communism, because they almost surely regarded the two issues as inseparable. The "expropriation" of UFCO land was simply the most convincing "evidence" that Guatemala was moving down a Communist path.[23]

The CIA developed its plan to overthrow Arbenz in the summer of 1953 and code-named it Operation PBSUCCESS, or "Success."[24] Though there had been similar plans during the Truman administration, this one gained momentum in part because that very summer the CIA was celebrating the outcome of another covert operation, the overthrow of Musaddiq in Iran (see John Foran's essay in this volume). That CIA triumph fueled optimism about the chances for a repeat performance in Guatemala. The operation was so secret only a handful of officials were aware of it. Even major figures in the CIA Directorate of Intelligence were not privy to the operation, which was run by the Directorate of Plans.[25]

Under the direction of Frank Wisner, the CIA recruited and armed a small army of roughly two to three hundred, comprised primarily of Central American mercenaries. Operation headquarters were in Opa-Locka, Florida, while supplies and personnel were organized in Panama. The CIA had little hope that this ragtag group could itself seize the capital and remove Arbenz. Rather, the main hope was that the "invasion" and the propaganda surrounding it would persuade the Guatemalan army that Arbenz could not be defended, that he was too vulnerable, that the United States was totally committed to his ouster. The "liberation army" was simply part of a larger effort to create the illusion of significant opposition. To lead the army, the CIA's E. Howard Hunt (of future Watergate infamy) recruited Colonel Carlos Castillo Armas. Castillo Armas had received eight months of training at Fort Leavenworth in 1944 and led a failed coup in 1949.[26]

In May 1954 the CIA discovered a shipment of Czechoslovakian arms to Guatemala. Eisenhower would probably have given the final go-ahead to Operation Success in any case, but the "*Alfhem* incident" (the arms were transported aboard the Swedish freighter *Alfhem*) provided additional and decisive "proof" that Guatemala was moving in the Communist "orbit." *The New York Times* embraced the State Department's characterization of this "grave" development on the grounds that Guatemala had already become "heavily infiltrated by Communists."[27] Wisconsin Republican Alexander Wiley, chairman of the Senate Foreign Relations Committee, described the "massive" shipment of arms as "part of the master plan of world communism."[28] And Democratic minority leader Lyndon Johnson saw it as clear evidence that the Soviets were "seeking to establish a beachhead in the Americas now" and had entered a "military phase of operations." Guatemalan foreign minister Guillermo Toriello defended his nation's right to buy weapons from anyone, especially since they couldn't get any from the United States and its allies. But that was deemed irrelevant. So, too, was the *New York Times* report that appeared a week after the coup, indicating that virtually all of the weapons sent from Czechoslovakia were either damaged or entirely useless for warfare in Guatemala.[29] Operation Success would go forward.

Even before the arrival of "Communist weapons," the CIA began broadcasting radio propaganda from Nicaragua and Honduras (and even made a few transmissions from the U.S. embassy in Guatemala City). Calling itself the *"La Voz de la Liberación,"* this phony radio station claimed to be broadcasting from a rebel stronghold deep inside Guatemala. It would play a key role in persuading many Guatemalans that the nation was experiencing a massive uprising. However, the CIA had no faith that it could actually generate a mass uprising. As Allen Dulles told his brother, Secretary of State John Foster Dulles, the only hope for an overthrow of Arbenz was through the defection of a "large or substantial section of the army."[30]

On June 17 about 150 of the CIA's "rebels" crossed the Honduran border into Guatemala toward the town of Zacapa. Another small group of 100 entered the country at Puerto Barrios. While neither force tried to move more than a few miles, the "Voice of Liberation" reported that several divisions of rebels were rapidly advancing on the capital, Guatemala City. In spite of the invasion and the propaganda, Arbenz was initially quite confident that his military would remain loyal and defeat the invaders. He had accurate intelligence on the small size of the invading force. Civilians, however, were not so sanguine. Local peasant unions began to plead for arms. Arbenz decided not to arm the people, afraid that this would humiliate the army and alienate military officers already concerned that he might establish workers' militias.[31]

Arbenz believed the ground invasion was a sideshow ("we can shoo them away with a hat") that did not require much personal attention. He would remain in the capital and worry about the international context. Though confident that Castillo Armas could be defeated, Arbenz did worry about the possibility of direct U.S. intervention—whether by open military attack, the use of a surrogate attacker such as Honduras, or an economic embargo (Guatemala imported all its oil). He had some hope that the United States would be deterred out of a concern for international opinion. After all, the invasion had already been denounced in demonstrations throughout Latin America as a product of Yankee imperialism. But as the days passed, Arbenz grew increasingly convinced that neither the United States nor his own military would further tolerate his leadership.[32]

A key element of Operation Success was the CIA's air campaign. The CIA had assembled a small air force of aging, rundown planes—the sort of aircraft "rebels" might plausibly purchase on the black market. Though they had only three bombers, "this air force was actually overwhelming by Guatemalan standards, designed to scare, if not bomb, the Arbenz government into submission." The CIA also hired (for $1,000 a month) ten U.S. pilots to join American-exile airmen and CIA pilots of the Civil Air Transport (the CIA air force). In the weeks leading up to the ground invasion the air force dropped thousands of propaganda leaflets from C-47s denouncing the Arbenz regime, encouraging military defections, and promoting a popular uprising.[33]

The CIA air force began bombing raids at roughly the same time as the ground invasion.[34] The lumbering bombers could not carry much payload since they needed to carry enough fuel to get back to Managua, so they dropped few bombs, relying instead on dynamite and other explosives to spread terror and create the illusion of more serious air strikes. The strikes did create panic, especially in the capital city. Along with the rumors, curfews, radio propaganda, and the blackouts imposed by Arbenz in an effort to silence the propaganda, the thundering air strikes persuaded many that an all-out invasion was truly under way.

Effective as this terror campaign may have been in scaring civilians, Guatemalan ground fire destroyed or disabled two of the three CIA bombers within a matter of days. And on June 20 and 21, government troops soundly defeated rebel forces at Gualán and Puerto Barrios. The CIA was pessimistic—more pessimistic, as it turned out, than they needed to be. Allen Dulles requested that Eisenhower supply two more bombers. On June 22, he agreed. While the resupply of planes and the ongoing propaganda were not crucial in military terms, they were important as part of the effort to persuade the Guatemalan military that the United States would not allow Arbenz to stand. By the 23rd it became clear to the military high command that the army had no intention of fighting on. On that day, at Chiquimula, government forces essentially surrendered the town to the rebels. Only a few dozen poorly armed peasants tried to fight off the invaders. According to Gleijeses, many officers were persuaded that the United States stood firmly behind the rebels and would accept nothing less than the overthrow of Arbenz. By June 25 one of Arbenz's trusted officers returned from the countryside to report: "The situation is hopeless. The officers don't want to fight. They think that the Americans are threatening Guatemala just because of you and your communist friends. If you don't resign, the army will march on the capital to depose you. They have already begun to arrest peasants."[35]

On June 27, Arbenz turned over the government to Colonel Díaz. U.S. ambassador Jack Peurifoy quickly orchestrated a transfer of power to Castillo Armas. The coup brought an immediate and shattering end to Guatemala's "Ten Years of Spring." Castillo Armas reversed all the most important reforms, disenfranchising most Guatemalans, banning strikes, revoking land reform, and imposing state-sponsored repression. His regime set the stage for a fifty-year cycle of repression that would result in the loss of more than 200,000 lives.

Calculating the Odds

In his 1963 memoir, *Mandate for Change*, Eisenhower continued to lie about U.S. responsibility for the coup. But he did choose to concede and dramatize one act of U.S. intervention—the decision to provide the "Guatemalan rebels" with two planes once the coup had begun. Eisenhower implies that the bombers provided decisive support and cannot resist claiming at least partial credit for this otherwise secret Cold War victory. "I knew from experience the important psychological impact of even a small amount of air support," Eisenhower crowed. He may even have expected readers to compare this intervention favorably to Kennedy's decision not to use air strikes at the Bay of Pigs in 1961.

Since this story was the key element of Eisenhower's official history of the coup, it warrants some attention. On June 20, Dulles sent a memo to Eisenhower stating that it was "very much in doubt" whether Arbenz could be overthrown. The Guatemalan army had not indicated a willingness to abandon Arbenz, and unless they did, Dulles warned, Castillo Armas "will be defeated."[36] During the first few days of the operation, Guatemalan small arms fire and malfunctions grounded all three of the CIA bombers.[37] On June 22, Eisenhower met with the Dulles brothers and Henry Holland, assistant secretary of state, to consider replacing the planes. Holland was opposed, arguing that it would break international law, expose American involvement, and deeply damage U.S. relations with all of Latin America.[38] Eisenhower then recalls turning to the director of the CIA:

> "What do you think Castillo's chances would be," I asked Allen Dulles, "without the aircraft?"
> His answer was unequivocal: "About zero."
> "Suppose we supply the aircraft. What would the chances be then?"
> Again the CIA chief did not hesitate: "About 20 per cent."[39]

Eisenhower "considered the matter carefully" and determined that it was his "duty" to offer "indirect support to a strictly anti-Communist faction." Then he finished the story, clearly savoring the novelistic details:

> As my visitors prepared to leave the office, I walked to the door with Allen Dulles and, smiling to break the tension, said, "Allen, that figure of 20 per cent was persuasive. It showed me that you had thought this matter through realistically. If you had told me that the chances would be 90 per cent, I would have had a much more difficult decision."
> Allen was equal to the situation. "Mr. President," he said, a grin on his face, "when I saw Henry walking into your office with three large law books under his arm, I knew he had lost his case already."[40]

Eisenhower presents the anecdote as a moment of triumph and humor. There is no hint of concern about the moral implications of killing people with a one-in-five "chance" of success, never mind the morality of con-

structing an elaborate cover story of "indirect" support, or the morality of
the underlying operation. Instead, Eisenhower invites us to laugh at Henry
Holland for opposing intervention on the basis of international law, rather
than "realistic" odds-making. Are we really to believe the president might
have acted differently had Dulles calculated the odds of success at 90 percent? Or is this merely the prideful grin of the cocky bridge player who
wants everyone to know that he can win whatever his partner happens
to bid?

Despite the Cold War mantra of hard-nosed "realism," policymakers often felt an ideological imperative to play the game *regardless* of how poor
the odds. Eisenhower's anecdote recalls the memorandum written by
McGeorge Bundy in early 1965 advocating the systematic bombing of
North Vietnam, euphemistically described by Bundy as "sustained reprisal":

> We cannot assert that a policy of sustained reprisal will succeed in
> changing the course of the contest in Vietnam. It may fail, and we cannot
> estimate the odds of success with any accuracy—they may be somewhere
> between 25% and 75%. What we can say is that even if it fails, the policy
> will be worth it. At a minimum it will drop down the charge that we did
> not do all that we could have done.[41]

As other documents from the *Pentagon Papers* would make amply clear,
American policymakers were far more concerned about the affect of the
Vietnam War on American power and prestige than its devastating impact
on the Vietnamese people. In his 1995 memoir, *In Retrospect,* former Secretary of State Robert McNamara regrets that he did not know more about
Vietnam: "I had never visited Indochina, nor did I understand or appreciate
its history, language, culture, or values. . . . When it came to Vietnam, we
found ourselves setting policy for a region that was terra incognita."[42]
McNamara argues that greater knowledge might have averted a tragic war.
What he will not yet concede is that he and other Cold War policymakers
dismissed as illegitimate any knowledge that challenged their assumptions
about communist expansion. Anyone who presented information that undermined their Cold War orthodoxy, received the same treatment as Henry
Holland, or worse.

Preemptive Coups

The preemptive nature of U.S. Cold War policy has still not been fully recognized. Conventional understanding that American policy was guided by

the goal of "containing" communism has encouraged the assumption that the United States had an essentially reactive policy, only fighting in response to real instances of Communist aggression. In fact, both foreign and domestic policy were often predicated on the conviction—rarely openly acknowledged—that alleged enemies had to be stopped *before* they attacked, at a point when they merely posed a "threat" to international "security."

Even nuclear policy has had a preemptive basis. It is well known that the doctrine of "massive retaliation" asserted the right to retaliate against any act of Soviet-bloc aggression with the full measure of U.S. military power, including nuclear weapons. The United States thus claimed its readiness to use nuclear weapons in response to a nonnuclear attack. But throughout the fifties the policy went even farther. An act of "aggression" might be defined as a perceived *intention* to attack. In 1957 General Curtis LeMay, commander of the Strategic Air Command, said: "If I see that the Russians are amassing their planes for an attack, I am going to knock the shit out of them before they take off the ground." He further claimed his willingness to order a first strike even though official policy required a presidential order.[43] According to the authors of *The Nuclear Predicament*, "in the 1950s *preemption* was the actual national policy—the United States would strike first when there was positive evidence an attack was about to be mounted against it."[44]

Similarly, in domestic policy, public and private authority rooted out alleged subversives they had identified as potentially threatening to "national security." Loyalty and security investigations, HUAC and other committee inquisitions, journalistic red-baiting, all that is now known as McCarthyism, was, as John Lord O'Brian pointed out in his 1955 Godkin lectures at Harvard University, "something like a new system of preventive law."[45] This wholesale attack on the constitutional principle of presumption of innocence had not only a preemptive but a retroactive application. It punished not only those deemed capable of endangering national security *in the future;* it also attacked people who might have endangered it *in the past.*

The coups in Iran and Guatemala both shared this preemptive characteristic. In each case, the administration acted from the conviction that these foreign governments had to be overthrown to prevent their being finally controlled by Communists. And past actions that helped to demonstrate a "pattern" of leftward drift were routinely listed to demonstrate that these nations had become de facto pawns of the Soviet Union. The vilification of the Arbenz government closely paralleled the smear campaigns directed against many domestic victims of McCarthyism.

Varieties of Propaganda

Virtually all media coverage of the Arbenz government and its overthrow ratified the official line provided by Washington policymakers and the press releases distributed by the United Fruit Company in Boston. While the government and the United Fruit Company certainly tried to manage and even manipulate press coverage, it is hard to assess their effectiveness. Journalists generally accepted dominant Cold War assumptions and were therefore predisposed to trust and recapitulate the administration's version of reality. And, as Daniel Hallin has argued in his study of media coverage during the Vietnam War, journalists and their editors were conditioned by the very standards of their profession to report official sources respectfully. The combination of Cold War orthodoxy and "professional" training produced a kind of self-managed censorship of oppositional viewpoints.[46]

It may be, then, that the media required little ideological management. However, events in third world nations were rarely covered extensively, so the real contribution of corporate and state propaganda was to raise the level of public exposure. The media may not have needed much prodding to denounce Arbenz as a dangerous leftist, but UFCO-financed junkets to Guatemala surely paid off in column inches devoted to the "threat." UFCO lobbyists believed this coverage was a vital element in their campaign to persuade Washington to take some action in opposition to Arbenz.

From 1944 through the early 1950s, liberal internationalists were the most active propagandists in constructing a Communist threat in Guatemala—men like Adolph A. Berle (former FDR brain-truster and head of the Council on Foreign Relations), Thomas G. Corcoran (former New Dealer and UFCO lobbyist), former senator Robert La Follette, Jr. (who became a UFCO lobbyist after he was defeated by Joseph McCarthy in 1947), and Edward Bernays (a UFCO lobbyist regarded as the "father of public relations").[47]

These are just a few of the many talented and well-connected men who sought to place stories in the press that were favorable to the United Fruit Company and vilified Jacobo Arbenz. Historian Piero Gleijeses cautions that we should not make too much of UFCO's lobbying efforts. Though every major article about Guatemala in the mass-circulation press cast the government as dangerously pro-Communist, Gleijeses points out that the total number of articles was relatively small, and Guatemala remained "*terra incognita* for the immense majority of Americans," and during the Truman administration it was regarded as a mere "eddy in a sea of worries."[48]

While that may be true, you do not need mass support for a CIA over-throw. Intense private lobbying, along with a few key articles in *The New York Times* and *The Wall Street Journal,* might well be crucial in persuading the president to act. Moreover, even with Truman's "sea of worries," he launched his own effort to overthrow Arbenz in 1952. When Nicaraguan ruler Anastasio Somoza volunteered to lead a strike on the Guatemalan government, the Truman administration gave the green light to the CIA to load a United Fruit Company freighter with arms. The plan went through CIA director Walter Bedell Smith, who later became a board member at United Fruit. He and other administration figures were inundated by letters and requests for meetings from Thomas Corcoran and other lobbyists who encouraged the administration to take action against Arbenz. The freighter was en route to Nicaragua when Truman decided to terminate the operation, perhaps on the advice of Secretary of State Dean Acheson, who belatedly learned of the plot. Richard Immerman believes the cancellation was based on a simple calculation that the possibility of success was too remote, though in this case we don't have a record of any adviser providing specific odds.[49]

When Eisenhower entered the White House, UFCO lobbying redoubled. For example, in March 1953 Adolph Berle wrote a sixteen-page secret memorandum calling for the overthrow of Arbenz.[50] The administration proved sympathetic to the idea but rejected Berle's plan because it depended on José Figueres of Costa Rica to coordinate regional support. Berle regarded him as a more popular and reliable anti-Communist than the right-wing Somoza. But the Dulles brothers regarded Figueres as much too left-wing to trust and they rightly understood that rulers like Somoza would never support a scheme headed by Figueres. U.S. liberals may have supported the coup, but as Gleijeses puts it, "there was no liberal way to overthrow Arbenz."[51] The United States would have to rely on hard-line reactionaries to do its bidding.

Clearly Cold War liberals like Corcoran, Berle, and Bernays were crucial in generating hostility toward the Guatemalan government, and their efforts may have emboldened Eisenhower to act. Hired as a consultant/lobbyist by the United Fruit Company in the early 1940s, Bernays played a key role in developing propaganda against the Arévalo/Arbenz governments. Among his many activities, he organized at least five two-week junkets to Guatemala for U.S. journalists between 1952 and the spring of 1954.[52] *The Christian Science Monitor* even published a series of articles about UFCO written by Ed Whitman, the company's director of public relations (and the husband of Ann Whitman, President Eisenhower's personal secretary).[53]

The prominence of Cold War liberals among UFCO lobbyists reflects, in part, a shrewd corporate decision to hire the kind of men calculated to be effective with the Truman administration. After Eisenhower was elected, the company hired John Clements Associates. Along with his lobbying and public relations work, Clements was an editor at the right-wing *American Mercury* and vice president of the Hearst Corporation. Clements produced several major reports on Guatemala, full of real and imagined treacheries, and distributed them to hundreds of key officials. After the coup, Clements represented Col. Carlos "the Liberator" Castillo Armas in the United States for $8,000 a month.[54]

The reportage of *New York Times* correspondent Sydney Gruson illustrates the narrow parameters within which the media covered Guatemala and the willingness of the U.S. government to intervene when coverage deviated even slightly from official claims. Throughout 1953, Gruson's stories red-baited President Arbenz and accused him of trying to make the United Fruit Company a "pawn in the Soviet's vast conspiratorial design." For this, the Guatemalan government expelled Gruson in February 1954. Protests by the U.S. embassy quickly got Gruson reinstated. However, instead of simply reiterating his prior claims that Arbenz was a "prisoner of the Communists," he wrote a few stories emphasizing Guatemalan nationalism, even daring to suggest that it might be more potent than communism. The Dulles brothers were not amused. Allen Dulles complained about Gruson's coverage to *New York Times* publisher Arthur Sulzberger, who ordered Gruson to go to Mexico City and do his reporting from there. From that point on, his stories may have toed closer to the official line. For example, on the day before Arbenz resigned Gruson wrote: "President [Arbenz's] and the Communists' objectives are one and indistinguishable. The Communists are among his most trusted advisers, and though there is no credible evidence that he is a Communist, he is certainly a strong anti- anti-Communist."[55] But that was cutting it a bit too fine for the administration. At an NSC meeting on the morning this article appeared, John Foster Dulles complained about Gruson's "communist line" coverage.[56]

Many accounts give special significance to the black propaganda of the CIA—its Voice of Liberation broadcasts and leaflet drops. While this may have generated significant concern among Guatemalan civilians, it certainly did not generate popular support for an overthrow of Arbenz. This propaganda tried to create the illusion of a mass uprising, but did not succeed in creating one. The most decisive propaganda in Guatemala was carried out by individual U.S. agents from the embassy, the CIA, and the military in small meetings with Guatemalan military officers. In these meetings, the United States virtually conceded that it was behind the coup and that it would not tolerate failure. The Guatemalans were told that the United States was firmly committed to getting rid of Arbenz; the current show of force was merely a small demonstration of a far greater force that might be brought to bear if Arbenz did not step down. In broadcasts to the world, the State Department vehemently denied a role in Guatemala; in Guatemala itself, U.S. agents made sure that key figures understood that the United States was fully committed to the overthrow of Arbenz.

To the government and army, it was saying in effect: We will not tolerate this government. It will not stand. Come to our side while you still have a chance. Your loyalty to Arbenz may cost you your life. Your future power and security require you to commit treason. CIA bribes, threats, and propaganda surely induced some military officers to abandon Arbenz. Some scholars attribute as many as two hundred defections to CIA efforts, including, most famously, one Guatemalan Air Force pilot who agreed to broadcast an appeal to fellow pilots to join rebel forces.[57] According to Piero Gleijeses, the fear of U.S. intervention was decisive in fomenting treason. "Had they felt free to choose, most Guatemalan officers would have rallied to Arbenz in June 1954 and crushed the rebels. But fear gnawed at them— fear of the United States."[58]

Compliant Media and Narrative Challenges

Providing the kind of coverage Washington wanted required more than uncritical acceptance of the fictional "uprising" carried out by "Guatemalan rebels" or the demonization of Arbenz. At a more basic level, it required that the story be treated as serious news. Given the long tradition of covering Latin American events with dismissive arrogance, this itself may have been the biggest test of the media's Cold War compliance. News accounts periodically instructed readers to distinguish the unfolding Guatemalan story from the typically irrelevant highjinks of Latin American politics.

> In the volatile Republics of Latin America, revolution is as familiar a means of changing governments as balloting in the United States. Accordingly, the coups and caudillos that flash up and down the continent do not generally engage the world's attention. Guatemala is an exception. There the target of the revolutionists is the first Communist-infiltrated regime in the Western Hemisphere. Both the free and the Communist worlds

are following the developments with intense interest; both are heavily involved in the struggle.[59]

Like virtually all U.S. reports, this *New York Times* piece failed to mention that the Guatemalan "regime" under attack was democratically elected.
In May 1954, John Foster Dulles expressed the hope that Guatemalans
would "clean their own house," but no one in the media suggested that they
could already do such a thing at the ballot box.

While both the Arévalo and Arbenz governments had more democratic
legitimacy than virtually all Latin American nations, the media portrayed
them as the signal threat to constitutional government in the region. An
unnamed State Department source was quoted by the *Times* claiming Guatemalan responsibility for Costa Rican labor strikes on its banana plantations. This, he claimed, was "further evidence of the attempts of Guatemala
under Communist guidance to disturb the situation in peaceful neighboring
countries where governments have come to office by constitutional means"
(implying, of course, that the Arbenz government was unconstitutional).[60]

The New York Times imagined people throughout Central America "asking themselves and their neighbors whether now is the time they have been
expecting and dreading—the beginning of all-out Communist expansion
from a Guatemala bridgehead." No evidence is provided other than the
"strong suspicion that Communists infiltrating from Guatemala and El Sal-
vador were guiding" strikes in Honduras. "One way or another, there is not
the slightest doubt in anyone's mind but that the Communist influences in
Guatemala are making themselves felt in all parts of Central America."[61]
One can also find many ponderous news stories on the alleged threat posed
by Guatemala to the security of the Panama Canal, a target separated from
Guatemala by eight hundred miles and four nations.

This Cold War contextualization allowed the media to give the story special significance, unlike the usual fare of Latin American "coups and cau-
dillos." Many accounts of the Communist threat in Central America incited
fears about a literal invasion of Latino subversives. Operation Success coincided with one of the most massive deportations in U.S. history. In June
1954, Attorney General Herbert Brownell, Jr., ordered "Operation Wet-
back" to drive out undocumented workers. More than a million Mexicans
were rounded up and deported. This was merely an intensification of the
policy that had, during the previous four years, deported two-and-a-half
million Mexicans. When asked to explain the justification of Operation Wet-
back, Brownell "cited the illegal entrance of political subversives as the chief
reason for his action."[62]

So, news of "communism" in Guatemala was part of a more general regional fear mongering. However, while that gave stories from the region a tone of seriousness, it was still not exactly clear how the story of the Guatemalan invasion/uprising should be told. The administration faced a tricky literary as well as political problem. They had to construct a story with at least three objectives: (1) it had to deny U.S. involvement; (2) it had to present Guatemala as a dangerous Communist beachhead; (3) it had to show that the *people* of Guatemala opposed their leftist government and were rising in opposition. But all these objectives might be compromised by the obvious fact that there was no evidence of a mass uprising. On June 22, for example, *New York Times* correspondent Hanson W. Baldwin wrote that events in Guatemala seemed less like a war than an "opera-bouffe." That is about as close as any written account came to exposing the phony quality to the "uprising," but it was clear that Castillo Armas's "rag-tag" rebels could not be credibly packaged as a major revolutionary movement. The few visual representations of CIA forces (only a few journalists made it to the "front") showed pitifully few people. In *First Pictures from Guatemala* (a newsreel that did not reach U.S. audiences until after the coup), the camera pans five bedraggled rebels in Esquipulas, making a mockery of the idea of mass uprising.[63] In the *Times,* Baldwin evaded the problem with a Cold War gloss that was commonplace throughout the media. The comic aspects of the revolt, he insisted, "should not conceal the global importance of the struggle." It may look like an opéra-bouffe, but global security hangs in the balance. And besides, Baldwin suggested, the revolt might spread. Though there was no evidence that Castillo Armas had more than three hundred men at most, Baldwin held out the absurd possibility that he might have as many as five thousand.[64] And one front-page *New York Times* article had the following lead: "Guatemalan insurgents under Col. Carlos Castillo Armas are 'marching on the capital' against light resistance and are being joined by 'hundreds' of their countrymen as they advance, according to a 'liberation' liaison unit here." The quotation marks might raise some doubts among scrupulous readers, but the claim remained unchallenged in the article.[65]

However, even if there had been more concrete evidence of an uprising, the Eisenhower administration was a little uncomfortable with the idea of promoting such a revolutionary ethos. John Foster Dulles cautioned Eisenhower against endorsing the phantom "uprising" too enthusiastically for fear that it "would place the President in the dangerous position of appealing to citizens of a foreign country to revolt against their leaders."[66] This caution, along with the insubstantiality of the "revolt" and the absence of a sizable

Guatemalan exile community in the states, meant there would be none of the widespread enthusiasm for the Guatemalan "rebels" that would develop just a few years later in response to Cuba's Fidelistas (see Van Gosse's essay in this volume).

Both before and during the coup, the Eisenhower administration placed more emphasis on the Communist menace than the rebellion. The United States Information Agency sent instructions to officials on how to spin the story: "Deplore bloodshed and violence. Make plain this is an uprising of Guatemalans against terroristic Communist-dominated government."[67] Beginning in May, officials began to insist that in addition to all his other Communist moves (the "expropriation" of land, the Communist advisers, arms shipments from "behind the Iron Curtain"), Arbenz had instituted a "reign of terror" against his own people. The basis of this contention was the fact that Arbenz had declared martial law in response to early CIA propaganda about the impending revolt.

At a June 15 press conference, John Foster Dulles announced:

> No doubt there is going on somewhat of a reign of terror in Guatemala. There is no doubt in my opinion but what the great majority of the Guatemalan people have both the desire and the capability of cleaning their own house. But, of course, those things are difficult to do in face of the communist type of terrorism which is manifesting itself in Guatemala.[68]

During the coup, the press office of the United Fruit Company, from its Boston headquarters, handed out photographs of mutilated human bodies about to be buried in a mass grave and claimed they were victims of the Arbenz regime, a total fabrication.[69] After the coup succeeded, the equivocal "somewhat" in Dulles's statement dropped out and the administration and the House Committee on Communist Aggression patched together retrospective "evidence" of Communist treachery. By the time he published his memoir in 1963, Eisenhower stated without qualification that Arbenz "declared a state of siege and launched a reign of terror."[70]

When evidence did surface that might have challenged the official narrative, the media dismissed it, often doing so by dutifully reporting the most bizarre cover stories. For example, when U.S. pilot William Beall finished strafing the Guatemalan city of Cobán, he ran out of fuel and crash-landed his plane just over the border in Mexico. Surely here was a smoking pilot—an American fighting the "Guatemalan" war. But *The New York Times* put the story in the back pages as a mere allegation by Guatemalan officials. Then it lavished respectful attention on Beall's hilarious claim that his plane had been sabotaged en route to a crop-dusting assignment in Colombia![71]

Once Arbenz was overthrown it was possible to manufacture some retro-active credence to the fiction of a popular uprising. Newsreels showed large crowds gathering in the capital to greet the new junta. Even so, neither the media nor the Eisenhower administration ever presented the "uprising" with as much creativity as the "threat." For example, Eisenhower had Secre-tary of State John Foster Dulles offer the fullest official account of the coup. On the evening of June 30, he gave a fifteen-minute speech (broadcast on television and radio). Most of the talk described the efforts of "international communism" to convert Guatemala into "an official base from which to breed subversion." When he turned to the overthrow itself, Dulles offered only the vaguest possible story of what had happened: "The people of Gua-temala have now been heard from. . . . Led by Colonel Castillo Armas, pa-triots arose. . . . to challenge the Communist leadership and to change it. Thus, a situation is being cured by the Guatemalans themselves."[72]

It was a thin and insubstantial story, but far more satisfying than the archetypal Cold War narrative produced during the Vietnam War. In Gua-temala, Eisenhower had a relatively easy time turning mercenaries into "rebels"—precursors to Reagan's contra "freedom fighters"—and cheering for them in their struggle against a "pro-Communist" "reign of terror." The story was almost wholly fictitious, but because the operation was brief, co-vert, and successful, it produced fewer literary challenges than U.S. sup-port for the French reconquest of Indo-China, the Korean stalemate, the Bay of Pigs invasion, and the Vietnam War. In Vietnam, official storytellers had to turn a right-wing dictatorship into a "democracy" and defend it against the "aggression" of actual rebels. Here Americans were invited to support the overthrow of a "pro-Communist regime" by a "liberation" movement that was reliably conservative, already running on a platform to restore to wealthy landowners the real estate taken by the Agrarian Re-form Law.[73]

Intimations of Involvement

The media's complicity in preserving the secret of U.S. responsibility for the Guatemala overthrow gains significance when we consider the possibil-ity that many political and journalistic insiders surely suspected that Ameri-can agents were playing key, perhaps even decisive, roles. For example, the famous columnist Drew Pearson confided to his diary on June 15, 1954 (just a few days before the CIA launched its operation): "My old friend Jack Peurifoy [U.S. ambassador to Guatemala] has made three attempts at revolution in Guatemala and it looks as if the last one might be successful.

He persuaded six generals to call on President Arbenz and threaten him with revolution unless he gets out."[74]

However, this insider's knowledge and suspicion rarely leaked into public venues. Perhaps the closest a major publication came to suggesting CIA involvement in Guatemala came in a *New York Times* editorial of June 20. James Reston led with the following:

> John Foster Dulles, the Secretary of State, seldom intervenes in the internal affairs of other countries, but his brother Allen is more enterprising. If somebody wants to start a revolution against the Communists in, say, Guatemala, it is no good talking to Foster Dulles. But Allen Dulles, head of the Central Intelligence Agency, is a more active man.[75]

Of course, we never learn what enterprising things Allen might have done to start a "revolution." Reston simply drops the hint of covert action to suggest that foreign aid might be a more effective tool in Latin America. In a more critical age, these suspicions might have been the basis for an exposé of U.S. imperialism. At this zenith of Cold War orthodoxy, however, hints of U.S. involvement, at least before and during the coup, were rare and oblique. The vast bulk of coverage served to deny claims of U.S. intervention.

When such claims did appear they were typically buried in the back pages. On June 22, for example, *The New York Times* reported:

> Although there have been reports that United States agents have been working in Central America since Guatemala received a $10,000,000 arms shipment from Communist Czechoslovakia six weeks ago, the State Department has carefully avoided giving any impression that it is supporting the rebellion, much less the invasion of Guatemala.[76]

When the *Times* then reminded readers that Theodore Roosevelt had promoted a revolt in Colombia to pave the way for the Panama Canal, it hastened to add that even "America's bitterest foes . . . would not compare the situation in Guatemala to that prior intervention."

In fact, some foes did precisely that. The only nearly accurate accounts of what was happening in Guatemala to appear in the U.S. media were the occasional quotations from Soviet and Guatemalan officials, or third world activists. For example: "The 'intervention,' declared a Russian commentator on Moscow radio, had been 'engineered by the Americans in order to put an end to the democratic system established by the freedom-loving Guatemalan people and thus restore the rule of the United Fruit Company."[77]

Claims like these were always discredited as Soviet propaganda, or the "Communist line," and thereby served to foreclose any real debate about U.S. involvement. Communist or third world accusations against the United States were presented as ludicrous by definition and any "Communist" defense of Guatemala was regarded as additional evidence that the Arbenz government was in the Communist camp. And, according to *The New York Times* (citing unnamed sources), the Arbenz government might be using the charge of a foreign plot to invade Guatemala as a justification to liquidate opponents at home. Thus, virtually every statement that accurately identified U.S. responsibility was not only dismissed by policymakers as an obvious Communist lie, but regarded as a retroactive justification for the very operation they were disavowing. The standard State Department response to accurate claims of U.S. complicity was to "refuse to dignify the [Guatemalan/Soviet, etc.] charge with a denial."[78]

Of course, truly curious readers might have wondered why Eisenhower allowed 1,200 U.S. citizens to remain in Guatemala during the uprising. What if Arbenz decided to turn his "reign of terror" against Americans? After all, the Guatemalan government had clearly expressed its concern that the United States was supporting the revolt. Somehow Guatemala posed a threat to the Panama Canal, hundreds of miles away, but not to the U.S. citizens in Guatemala City.

A truly independent press corps might have been equally skeptical. Only a few reporters ignored Castillo Armas's effort to ban journalists from the "war zone." Most stayed in Guatemala City, and apparently quite a few spent the week drinking at the American Club with Ambassador Jack Peurifoy. They couldn't help noticing how cool and calm he was during the air raids. Instead of admiring his courage, they might have guessed that he knew the "rebels" posed no threat. One of Peurifoy's aides even told nervous reporters not to worry about the bomber pilots because "they're well trained and they're doing their jobs." He might just as well have added that they were Americans. After all, Peurifoy had been bragging for months about the need to do something about Arbenz.[79]

How to Take Credit for a Covert Operation

The Cold War produced many scripts that were never meant to be read. The CIA role in overthrowing Arbenz was not intended for global consumption. But the "successful" outcome presented a dilemma. Should the United States deny all responsibility? To do so would be to pass up an opportunity to take credit for a Cold War victory, a roll-back of Communism. Perhaps America could have it both ways—it could celebrate a triumph of indigenous democracy against pro-Communist tyranny *and* claim some responsibility for preserving hemispheric security.

With a friendly regime in power, the media and the Eisenhower administration began to celebrate. But it was equally important to demonstrate that Guatemalans were rejoicing. Newsreel coverage makes clear that the post-coup celebration was much easier to produce than the mass uprising. The initial newsreels from Guatemala are even more confusing than the genre's typically jumpy footage and staccato narration. Because the medium relies so heavily on persuasive local images, the absence of actual "invasion" footage almost by definition raised serious questions about the official story and required the voice-overs to do almost all the narrative work. In a two-minute Pathé Newsreel called *Revolt in Guatemala* (filmed June 19–20, 1954), the only shots we see of Guatemala are twenty seconds of stock footage stuck in the middle—Indian women by a river, volcanoes from the air, and a man leading a donkey. Everything else is shot at the UN, where an emergency session of the Security Council has been called because of "an invasion of Guatemala by anti-communist rebels." The Guatemalan ambassador, "speaking in Spanish," describes the invasion as an "illegitimate international aggression" and claims the "U.S. was involved in the planning." News of the invasion "explodes like a bombshell." "Since its recent purchase of arms behind the Iron Curtain, Guatemala has caused concern here and throughout Latin America." The invaders, we are told, are Guatemalans who have returned to Guatemala "to overthrow its red-infiltrated government." Then come the twenty seconds of local color. Then we're back to the United Nations to hear U.S. ambassador Henry Cabot Lodge telling the Soviet ambassador to "stay out of this hemisphere and don't try to start your plans and conspiracies over here." Lodge calls for a resolution to have the invasion investigated by the malleable Organization of American States rather than by the United Nations. Then the ominous voice-over: "Here now is the Russian negative vote . . . the 60th Russian veto."

Once Arbenz was overthrown, the confusing superpower standoff at the UN could be replaced by more convincing scenes of Guatemala. A few well-orchestrated rallies for the new junta provided the perfect setting for the conventional newsreel bombast that we hear in Pathé's *Peace in Guatemala:* "In Guatemala City, pandemonium and a sense of liberation sweeps the capital. . . . Jubilant crowds greet members of the Liberation Army outside the Presidential Palace!"[80]

The Pathé series of three newsreels on Guatemala did little to imply a U.S. role in the overthrow. Indeed, the omissions are striking. Not one of the newsreels so much as mentions Jacobo Arbenz, the United Fruit Company, the CIA, either Allen or John Foster Dulles, or Eisenhower. However, other reports use the celebratory conclusion as an occasion to suggest a decisive, if ill-defined, U.S. role in producing the overthrow. Just two weeks after the coup, *The New York Times* magazine lionized U.S. ambassador to Guatemala John Peurifoy. Writer Flora Lewis extolled the "ambassador extraordinary" as a "man of courage and action" who places himself "at the very center of the distraught swirl of events." While she does not detail the U.S. role in the coup, she is quite unequivocal in assigning Peurifoy considerable responsibility for making it happen. When Peurifoy was assigned to Guatemala in 1953, she writes, "it was perfectly clear that his instructions and his purpose had one simple theme: 'Get rid of the Reds.'" He arrived with a "timetable" and soon developed a "plan of action." Nor was Peurifoy himself shy about taking credit for the overthrow: "Two days after Arbenz resigned, Peurifoy said jokingly, 'People are complaining that I was forty-five minutes off schedule.'" Lewis concludes:

> No one can say with solemn precision exactly what percentage of the victory came from pure Peurifoy drive and personality. . . . Thinly curtained from the full spotlight by Washington's effort not to appear directly involved in the Guatemalan revolution, his role was at all times important. At some critical moments, it was probably decisive.[81]

Close as this comes to revealing U.S. responsibility, the focus on Peurifoy has a kind of "Our Man in Guatemala" tone, as if this lone ranger were the only American involved. There are intimations of "orders" from Washington, but no effort to link his efforts to a specific plan orchestrated by a Cold War apparatus of covert agents, mercenaries, the CIA, and Eisenhower.

Eisenhower was somewhat more reluctant than Peurifoy to claim credit for overthrowing Arbenz. His initial responses depicted the coup as a triumph of indigenous counterrevolution: "the people of Guatemala, in a magnificent effort, have liberated themselves from the shackles of international Communist direction."[82] However, during the elections of 1954 and 1956 Eisenhower made many vague references to "the saving of Iran and Guatemala from Communism," inviting audiences to believe that his administration deserved significant credit for rolling back the Communist threat.[83]

The role of the CIA in organizing the coup was first exposed in 1964 with the publication of *The Invisible Government* by David Wise and Thomas

Ross. Eisenhower was not one of their key sources. Yet even he, by 1963, made a public speech in which he said of Guatemala: "We had to get rid of a Communist government which had taken over."[84] He wanted to keep the CIA operation secret *and* receive political credit for its success.

Celebrating "Tough Cops"

Post-coup reportage included a great deal of fraudulent hype about the triumph of democracy over the forces of tyranny. That is hardly surprising. What is more striking is the degree to which the press acknowledged and celebrated Castillo Armas's repression. *Time* magazine believed the "crackdown came none too soon." The "leading Reds . . . were hard at work trying to regroup their shattered forces underground." Armas had let them slip away in June, but now his "command decisions" were "finally" striking at "Guatemalan Communism."

"The Reds" were spreading propaganda throughout the world, claiming that the new Guatemalan junta was "a fascist dictatorship imposed by the U.S." In response to these "determined adversaries," Armas "made a decision that shocked his liberal supporters":

> To boss the secret police, Castillo Armas picked Guatemala's toughest cop, Jose Bernabe Linares, 51. As most Guatemalans know, when Linares last ran the secret police under the late Dictator Jorge Ubico his men submerged political enemies in electric-shock baths and perfected a head-shrinking steel skull cap to pry loose secrets and crush improper political thoughts. Whatever else Linares' appointment meant, it suggested that Castillo Armas' latest command decision was not to toy with the enemy forces but to erase them.[85]

The story appears in the last paragraph of page 34, but it is there all the same: a casual endorsement of Guatemala's "liberators" for cracking down on the "enemy" by hiring secret police and torturers. Though the repression is defended—just the sort of thing "tough cops" have to do to erase the Reds—the very mention of it provides an opening to dissent, the empirical material for oppositional readings. And even when the media imposed a script of triumphant democracy, the supporting materials were sorely lacking. For example, one of the first measures of the Armas regime was to deny the vote to 73 percent of Guatemalans (illiterates who had citizenship rights under Arbenz). One reporter used this decree to challenge John Foster Dulles's assertion that the coup represented a successful "housecleaning" by Guatemala: "Do you consider [the denial of voting rights] part of the necessary housecleaning?" Dulles merely repeated that the housecleaning ended the "Communist threat to hemisphere peace and security."[86]

Where cracks in the dominant American story of Guatemalan self-determination began to open, they were either justified, evaded, or denied. And for all the books and articles that challenge the original narrative, we continue to live with its legacy. As a result, the U.S.-orchestrated overthrow of a democratically elected progressive government and the consequences in Guatemala over the next fifty years continue to be, for most Americans, unknown histories.

PART FOUR

Cold War Liberalism, Activist Expatriates, and Third World Revolution

"A World Made Safe for Diversity"

The Vietnam Lobby and the Politics of Pluralism, 1945–1963

JAMES T. FISHER

FROM ITS INCEPTION in June 1954, the government of Ngo Dinh Diem in South Vietnam was ardently supported in the United States by a coalition of liberal internationalists, socialists, and assorted figures on the "non-Communist Left." Diem's propaganda apparatus within the United States was directed by a team of socialists and social democrats, yet the enthusiasm of these and other American leftists for his autocratic regime has never been fully evaluated in various studies of the "Vietnam Lobby."[1]

In the mid-1960s, the non-Communist Left's support for Diem was dismissed by radical journalists and scholars as symptomatic of its ideological bankruptcy, a view that largely prevailed for the next three decades and was reconfirmed in Eric Thomas Chester's *Covert Network* (1995), which examined the role played in CIA operations by the International Rescue Committee, a relief agency whose leadership overlapped with that of the Vietnam Lobby. Joseph G. Morgan's extraordinarily meticulous 1997 study of the American Friends of Vietnam (AFV)—a kind of Vietnam Lobby holding company—offered a sensible corrective to the overheated claims made by critics of the Lobby. The Vietnam Lobby's role in the culture of the Cold War, however, remains shrouded in the mythology surrounding the origins of U.S. intervention in Southeast Asia.[2]

The founders of the Vietnam Lobby were far more than Old Leftists who had lost their nerve. Along with like-minded patrons in the State Department and the intelligence community, they promoted a sophisticated internationalism based on values remarkably similar to those espoused by their harshest critics in the 1960s and beyond. In the early 1950s, Thomas W.

Braden devised a CIA program to combat Communist "front" organizations by supporting artistic and intellectual groups that championed "cultural freedom," typically from a Left anti-Communist perspective ("the idea that Congress would have approved many of our projects," Braden later noted, "was about as likely as the John Birch Society's approving Medicare"). In "I'm Glad the CIA is 'Immoral,'" a notorious 1967 essay for the *Saturday Evening Post*, Braden suggested that his efforts had been intended to transform a world divided, in Winston Churchill's words, "intellectually and to a large extent geographically between the creeds of Communist discipline and intellectual freedom." Braden believed that the CIA's support for international cultural freedom had helped to bridge the void between East and West. "I share the hope," he concluded, "that John F. Kennedy's appeal to the Russians to 'help make the world safe for diversity' reflects the spirit of a new age."[3]

By working toward the creation of that world, non-Communist American leftists of the 1950s enhanced their own interests and cultural authority, because in championing pluralism and "tolerance" in non-Western societies emerging from colonialism, they implicitly demanded the same from those who might view their own ideological lineage with suspicion. In the 1950s the exigencies of "cultural freedom" also linked the work of liberal and leftist anti-Communists to the aspirations of Ngo Dinh Diem and John F. Kennedy, Roman Catholic politicians who responded in very different ways to the counsel of secular-minded Cold War American liberals. While Diem abysmally failed to meet the Vietnam Lobby's minimum standards for tolerance, Kennedy understood that a world made safe for diversity might even include a place for an American Catholic president. The cultural work performed by the Vietnam Lobby on the home front was ultimately more successful than its ill-fated efforts on behalf of the Diem regime.[4]

*   *   *

The muckraking journalists Robert Scheer and Warren Hinckle "named" the Vietnam Lobby in a celebrated 1965 exposé for *Ramparts,* a journalistic mainstay of the New Left. "It is the history," they wrote, "of a small and enthusiastic group of people—including a Cardinal, an ex–Austrian Socialist leader, and a CIA agent—who maneuvered the Eisenhower administration and the American press into supporting the rootless, unpopular and hopeless regime of a despot and believed it actually was all an exercise in democracy." Amid their spectacular charges, Scheer and Hinckle established crucial links between a liberal American humanitarian group, its publicist, and the Diem regime.[5]

In June 1955, the New York public relations firm of Harold L. Oram signed a contract with Ngo Dinh Diem to promote the interests of the Republic of Vietnam in the United States. Diem had assumed leadership of the fledgling state in June 1954, just two months after the French defeat at Dien Bien Phu signaled the beginning of the end of colonialism in Southeast Asia. Diem was a devout Catholic from a mandarin family with roots near Hue, in central Vietnam, but he was also a committed nationalist with far greater prestige in the region than critics such as Scheer and Hinckle claimed, and far stronger links to the Confucian tradition of Vietnam's elite. During a May 14 meeting with the Vietnamese emperor, Bao Dai, a reluctant Diem "yielded . . . to the emperor's appeal to his patriotic duty" and agreed to form a government in Saigon. Diem could not have established his authority, however, without the aid of the U.S. Navy and the CIA, which engineered a massive transplantation of as many as three-quarters of a million Vietnamese Catholics from the North to provide Diem with an instant constituency.[6]

One of Harold Oram's major clients, the International Rescue Committee (IRC), a refugee relief agency with roots in the international socialist, antifascist politics of the 1930s, quickly established relations with Diem and with the American intelligence operatives aiding him in Saigon. Oram's firm was paid a monthly retainer of $3,000 plus expenses to promote the Diem regime in the United States, though by some accounts the contract was much more lucrative than that figure indicates. Oram was a one-time University of Miami reserve quarterback who had "won his spurs raising support for the Loyalists" in the Spanish Civil War. Oram subsequently launched a firm—in partnership with Elliott Newcomb—that provided public relations and fund-raising services for a variety of causes to which he was sympathetic, including Planned Parenthood, the American Civil Liberties Union, and the NAACP Legal Defense Fund.[7]

By the middle of the 1950s Oram remained an unrepentant socialist who enjoyed strong ties to remnants of Trotskyite and assorted leftist groups in New York. Although he had begun to accept work from liberal anti-Communist groups to the right of his own position, Oram's contract with South Vietnam was the product of his socialist connections. Oram won the Diem account largely due to lobbying on his behalf by Joseph Buttinger, a former leader of the Austrian Revolutionary Socialists who had emigrated to the United States in 1939 after marrying Muriel Gardiner, a wealthy American heiress. Buttinger went to Saigon as the IRC's field representative in the autumn of 1954, seeking a postcolonial alternative to communism.

Writing in the liberal anti-Communist periodical the *New Leader* the following year, Buttinger noted that "anti-colonials among the Left parties in France have always supported the originally correct solution of giving independence to the Democratic Republic of Vietnam, headed by Ho Chi Minh, in 1945." He went on to make the dubious claim: "Although the government of Ho Chi Minh was dominated by Communists, this regime had a good chance of developing along democratic lines if French colonial policies had not driven the people of Vietnam into the Communists' arms." But where the non-Communist Left in France had rejected Ngo Dinh Diem as an ineffectual "Third Force" alternative to Ho and Emperor Bao Dai—who was the last best hope of the colonialists—Joseph Buttinger warmly embraced the mandarin during his stint in Saigon. Upon his return to New York in late 1954, Buttinger flatly informed Harold Oram that Diem was committed to a postcolonial, pro-Western, democratic socialist regime for his fledgling nation.[8]

In early 1955, Buttinger planted articles on Diem's behalf in *The Reporter* and *The New Republic;* he also orchestrated a letter-writing campaign to influential newspapers including *The New York Times.* Buttinger lauded Diem as "nobody's pawn," "a man of extraordinary strength, courage, integrity, and political ability," and insisted that "United States interference" in Diem's struggles against Vietnamese sects as well as lingering French interests "is desired by the vast majority of politically conscious people in Vietnam." "U.S. support for South Vietnam will never become effective if we are afraid to oppose the Colonial policy of the French," Buttinger concluded. "We must choose between Paris and Saigon."[9]

The International Rescue Committee and the Diem regime were unlikely allies. The IRC descended from the first organized efforts by American socialists to rescue European intellectuals from fascism, and was the product of a merger between rival leftist groups who comprised part of the byzantine revolutionary socialist movement of the 1930s. As Eric Chester explained, the IRC "can only be understood within the context set by segments of the Revolutionary Left in Germany, Austria, and the United States. Small organizations of revolutionary cadre sought to pursue a strategy far more militant than that of the mass social democratic parties, while remaining independent of the erratic path being followed by the communist International and its member parties." In addition to leading the Revolutionary Socialists in Austria, Joseph Buttinger belonged to a "tiny Leninist sect": in the late 1930s he befriended Karl Frank, a member of a similar group in Germany and an adherent of "the secretive and conspiratorial style characteristic of disciplined, vanguard parties." By 1940, Frank and Buttinger had moved to the United States, where they became the "moving spirits" of the Emergency Rescue Committee, which would merge in 1942 with a relief group linked to the socialist labor leaders David Dubinsky and Jay Lovestone. Joseph Buttinger "remained centrally involved in the ERC, and its successor the International Rescue Committee, for more than three decades."[10]

Buttinger and Frank prevailed upon Eleanor Roosevelt to urge her husband to expedite the "granting of visas to antifascist political refugees." According to Chester, "the government looked sympathetically toward refugees coming from socialist organizations whose leaders had already indicated their willingness to cooperate with government agencies in operations both overt and covert ... most of these recruits soon adapted their politics to the liberal mainstream." For Chester, as for Robert Scheer and Warren Hinckle, the history of the IRC is essentially "the story of an organization initially formed to help socialists under threat of Nazi terror and of that organization's co-optation into the murky world of the covert network." By the early 1950s the IRC had become a fixture in New York's liberal anti-Communist scene; there the organization played a role akin to that of the European socialists utilized by the CIA: "the very people," Tom Braden later explained, "whom many Americans thought no better than Communists—[but who] were the only people who gave a damn about fighting Communism."[11]

Several key figures in the Vietnam Lobby wedded liberal humanitarianism with international entrepreneurship. The chairman and most dynamic figure at the IRC from 1953 through the 1980s, Leo Cherne—the son of a socialist printer—was every bit the capitalist in his role as coproprietor of the Research Institute of America, which sold economic analyses and international market forecasts to American businessmen (Cherne boasted of an accuracy rate of 80 percent for his predictions, and backed that claim by reviewing his performance at an annual luncheon for clients at New York's Waldorf-Astoria). Cherne was often described as a New Deal liberal and a "renaissance man," but he was also a veteran of the byzantine Left political culture of New York City in the 1930s and 1940s. Though he was no ideologue, Cherne often supported candidates from New York's Liberal Party, a political adjunct to David Dubinsky's socialist International Ladies Garment Workers Union (although Dubinsky was a "conservative" socialist, Marvin Liebman, a young ex-Communist who briefly handled the Oram firm's account with the Liberal Party, later argued that the Liberals were at the time "only a bit to the right of the communist-controlled American Labor

Party"). Cherne was also associated with the moderately socialist Jewish Labor Committee, a close collaborator of the IRC in the 1950s.[12]

David Dubinsky's ally Jay Lovestone—a former secretary general of the Communist Party USA turned militant anti-Stalinist—had helped establish the International Relief Association in 1933 as a rival socialist agency to the Emergency Rescue Committee. The merger of the two groups into the International Rescue Committee in 1942, and Leo Cherne's ascension to leadership of the IRC in 1953, signaled a move away from the self-defeating sectarian politics of the non-Communist Left. Cherne had advised the Roosevelt administration on wartime industrial mobilization; in 1946 he drafted a tax plan for Japan designed to redistribute that nation's wealth. Cherne earned access to federal agencies like the National War Fund, which supervised relief activities and "openly financed" the work of the International Rescue Committee in the 1940s, paving the way for an even closer, if often covert, relationship during Cherne's tenure at the helm of the IRC.[13]

Leo Cherne embodied the expansive, progressive, postideological Cold War outlook that was especially attractive to elite figures in the American foreign policy establishment. Like them, Cherne loathed Senator Joe McCarthy, but he actually did something about it in public, squaring off against McCarthy in April 1952 on a television panel show, *The Author Meets the Critics*. Cherne accused McCarthy of leveling "thinly veiled charges of treason" against Dwight D. Eisenhower in his book, *America's Retreat from Victory*. Cherne remained on the offensive throughout the proceedings, utilizing the same intrusive tactics that McCarthy had honed while interrogating hostile witnesses in hearings before his Senate subcommittee. The conventional script for such an exchange would, of course, conclude with McCarthy impugning Cherne's loyalty, but in fact Tailgunner Joe could only sputter that he was certain Cherne was "a very fine young man" who had simply misread his book.[14]

Critics on the Left would later persistently accuse liberal anti-Communists like Leo Cherne of challenging McCarthy's means while endorsing his ends, but the issue was never that simple. In the minds of many Cold War liberals, McCarthyism threatened to unleash forces of authoritarianism, disorder, and irrationality which might destroy not only its putative sectarian target but the non-Communist Left as well. In 1968 Cherne would even claim—during a taping of William F. Buckley's *Firing Line* program—that he had opposed McCarthy as early as 1946 because the Wisconsin Republican "was supported by Communists." Although the comment seemed so bizarre at the time that the FBI pressured Buckley to delete it from the telecast, it revealed a characteristic if largely unexamined aspect of Cold War liberalism's worldview: the habit of linking together all extreme, presumably absolutist ideologies as threats to what Paul Blanshard—an influential 1950s social democrat—called "liberal culture."[15]

Blanshard became a minor celebrity in the late 1940s and early 1950s for his published attacks on Catholicism as the major obstacle to the triumph of "liberal culture" at home and abroad. Ngo Dinh Diem's controversial religiosity required the Vietnam Lobby to directly confront an issue that remained an abstraction for the intellectuals at the CIA-backed Congress for Cultural Freedom. The Vietnam Lobby would in fact prove more effective at championing "cultural freedom" than the much better-known members of the group bearing that lofty goal as its title. Leo Cherne was the point man for the Lobby's campaign to tailor an acceptable image for Diem. A self-made businessman, Cherne was a veteran of the rough-and-tumble diversity of New York life. Though he was rather flamboyant personally, Cherne was also by necessity a mediator between some of New York's most disparate communities: at the Research Institute of America he mentored the young William Casey, a conservative Irish-Catholic lawyer (Cherne told Casey's' biographer: "Bill was to the right of Attila the Hun. He was one hundred percent for Franco and one hundred percent against the Loyalists. To understand this, you had to understand his Catholicism"). During a visit to Saigon in 1954 seeking a role for the IRC among North Vietnamese refugees, Cherne established an enduring bond with Msgr. Joseph Harnett, director of the Catholic Relief Services' effort in Vietnam and a close associate of New York's Francis Cardinal Spellman. While he has been largely ignored by historians of the domestic Cold War, Leo Cherne played a key role, as a liberal anti-Communist, in shoring up the consensus politics of the 1950s that inspired "nation-building" campaigns in Southeast Asia and elsewhere.[16]

After returning from his visit to South Vietnam in the summer of 1954, Cherne convinced the IRC board to assign Joseph Buttinger as a full-time liaison to the Diem regime. In asserting that Buttinger's Catholic background would prove highly beneficial, Cherne indicated his acute awareness of the religious issue as well as his excessive optimism: while Buttinger had been born into an impoverished Austrian Catholic family, by the age of fifteen he "no longer depended on the comfort of religion. This need was gradually replaced by a passion for a world of freedom and equality among all social groups and for lasting peace among all nations." Buttinger's long-standing alliances with various socialist anticlerical groups were hardly ideal credentials for one of the key American handlers of the militantly Catholic Ngo Dinh Diem, but his work advanced the goal of making Diem palatable to American liberals.[17]

In late 1954 Cherne and Buttinger urged Diem to procure an American publicist, apprising the president of Harold Oram's valuable work on behalf of the IRC. Diem began negotiations with the Oram firm to launch the American Friends of Vietnam: "It is my intention," Oram explained, "to do everything possible to aid the government of Viet Nam (South), now headed by Premier Ngo Dinh Diem, to maintain its integrity against the attempts of the Communist Viet Minh to overthrow the government. I believe this to be in the interests of American policy and the Free World." In June, Diem officially hired Harold Oram to handle his regime's public relations in the United States.[18]

The American Friends of Vietnam (AFV) was an impressive if fragile paper coalition of American intellectuals, politicians, and religious figures who pledged to champion Diem's cause before the American public. In addition to Buttinger, Cherne, and Angier Biddle Duke, the patrician president of the IRC, the organization boasted such charter members as Arthur Schlesinger, Jr.; Senators John F. Kennedy and Mike Mansfield; Msgr. Joseph Harnett of Catholic Relief Services; the socialist Norman Thomas; various liberal academics; and for good measure, General John W. "Iron Mike" O'Daniel who, after relinquishing his position as head of the American military advisory group in Saigon, became chairman of the AFV in early 1956.[19]

Another close ally of the Vietnam Lobby in Saigon was Wesley Fishel, a Michigan State University political scientist who had been advising Diem since they first met in Japan in 1950. Fishel used his influence with Diem to win a lucrative contract for his university from the United States Foreign Operations Administration (the precursor to the Agency for International Development). Under the terms of its agreement with FOA, the Michigan State University Group provided dozens of advisers to the South Vietnamese government beginning in 1955. According to historian David L. Anderson, "there were CIA agents in MSUG. How many was secret, and the facts still remain hidden in classified government files." Anderson noted as well that Wesley Fishel himself, "according to various accounts . . . also served the agency." Fishel "emerged as a more influential figure in the AFV" after returning in 1957 from a two-year stint in Saigon.[20]

Ngo Dinh Diem received his money's worth on Madison Avenue. Harold Oram and his young associate Gilbert Jonas carried on the propaganda work begun by Cherne and Buttinger in 1954, planting numerous favorable articles on Diem in liberal and mainstream magazines and newspapers, including *Look*, *The New Republic*, and *The New York Times*. The leadership of the American Friends of Vietnam promoted a brand of tough-minded, flexible realism that CIA liberals and other foreign policy elites particularly appreciated. Perhaps that is why these members of the non-Communist Left were empowered to orchestrate the metamorphosis of Ngo Dinh Diem from Catholic reactionary to cultural democrat. For while Diem was dependent on the fervent support of American Catholics, that constituency was seen by his handlers as unpredictable at best and capable at any moment of reigniting a McCarthyite culture war.[21]

The process of sculpting an acceptable image for Diem was complicated by the fact that the progressives at the Vietnam Lobby were often allied at home with vociferous anti-Catholics. Paul Blanshard, a social democrat, eugenics enthusiast, and frequent contributor to *The Nation*, published a series of best-sellers in the early Cold War years in which he claimed that Roman Catholicism posed the gravest threat to all that the progressives held most dear. In *Communism, Democracy, and Catholic Power*, he echoed the cry of author Philip Toynbee: "We are all too familiar with the facile and vitriolic attacks on liberal and democratic culture by Catholic writers. No educated person could doubt the truth," Blanshard explained, "there are plenty of such attacks on liberal culture by Catholic writers."[22]

A longtime enemy of the Vatican, Blanshard was a close associate of Norman Thomas, a leading socialist and a member of the AFV. In the 1930s American's most prominent Catholic liberal, Msgr. John A. Ryan of the National Catholic Welfare Conference, had resigned from the American Civil Liberties Union after Thomas and ACLU chief Roger Baldwin (another Harold Oram client) "made excuses for the Mexican regime's persecution of the Church." Blanshard's sophisticated anti-Catholicism, however, differed from earlier American versions in several respects, most strikingly in his emphasis on culture: among the Vatican's greatest crimes, he argued, it offered only "a limited culture" to the faithful, while promoting curiosity.[23]

In *Communism, Democracy, and Catholic Power*, Blanshard perfunctorily denounced the Kremlin in order to lend additional credence to attacks on his real target, the Vatican. Although he was not apparently a member of the AFV, his views on socialism were remarkably akin to those of Joseph Buttinger and Harold Oram as well as the liberals at the CIA. Blanshard warned that "free enterprise has already been partially dethroned in Europe and that Communism cannot be defeated on that Continent without the aid of the middle-of-the-road Socialist movement." He ominously added: "An American policy which tied us to a reactionary clerical bloc and to anti-Socialism is destined to defeat no matter how many billions in American relief go with it." Blanshard's central message—which found an extraordinarily large audience among an American intellectual elite—was that Catholicism represented the final obstacle to the complete triumph of a "liberal culture" in America. He called upon American Catholics to examine their own beliefs in the spirit of modern social science, just as after World War II, according to historian Christopher Shannon, American anthropologists had hoped the vanquished Japanese might learn to view their own culture "with a certain scientific detachment and to see their received values as relative and therefore open to revision in the service of consciously chosen ends."[24]

From this theoretical perspective, at least, democratic socialists of the Blanshard school could stake a claim to being the most authentic Americans of the postwar era, including the ex-Communists among their ranks who had not, like Louis Budenz and other well-known Catholic converts, traded one form of absolutism for another. When a young progressive named Marvin Liebman was recommended to Harold Oram for employment in 1951, Liebman "did not lie about my past membership in the Communist party. Impressed that I had confided in him, Oram said that my communist past did not matter so long as I didn't consider myself a Stalinist any longer" (Oram soon assigned Liebman to the IRC account). To Cold War liberals, a rational person could sensibly choose to cultivate a socialist ideology that preserved the positive aspects of Marxism while resisting the lure of totalitarian thought, a feat of intellectual agility that might serve as a model to others.[25]

Paul Blanshard lamented the "perpetuation of mental childhood" found "among the Catholic masses" in countries like Mexico and Italy and warned that the Church was bent on enslaving American minds as well. The Vietnam Lobby proceeded from a conviction that its Southeast Asian client state, despite its Catholic leadership, might be spared the state of "mental childhood" and emerge instead as a full-blown pluralist democracy, complete with a free press and an "open" exchange of ideas. In seeking broad support for Diem at home, the Lobby inevitably became embroiled in the alien world of American Catholic cultural politics. In 1955 Harold Oram hired Peter White, a former OSS officer from a sophisticated Catholic convert family who had met Diem in New York in 1950. White's job, as he later explained, was to steer Diem toward the few influential American Catholics who were "vocal opponents of Senator Joe McCarthy, for whom Cardinal Spellman and powerful Catholics were cheerleaders," preferably opponents "whose clout was unimpaired by McCarthy's downfall."[26]

White and members of the Vietnam Lobby tried hard to manufacture a liberal Catholic constituency for Diem. To plant one pro-Diem essay by White's cousin, Christopher Emmet, in the Jesuits' *America* magazine in early 1956, White mobilized the services of Angier Biddle Duke, Gilbert Jonas, and Fr. Emmanuel Jacques, the Belgian Jesuit who had first introduced Diem to Peter White in 1950. The article was never published, though *America* did run a pro-Diem editorial in March 1956. The problem, as Peter White quickly learned, was that there were simply not enough liberal Catholic internationalists—beyond a small coterie found at such publications as *America* and *Commonweal*—to reward his efforts. In the absence of an internationalist Catholic left, the art of public relations would have to suffice.[27]

For while Cardinal Spellman was blamed by Scheer, Hinckle, and countless others for Diem's ascendance, it was widely recognized in the foreign relations establishment of the 1950s that Spellman was worse than useless as a conspicuous American champion of a free Vietnam. Even General J. Lawton Collins, President Eisenhower's special representative to South Vietnam and no friend of Diem, urged John Foster Dulles in March of 1955 to discourage Spellman from further visits to Saigon, because "the fact that both Diem and the Cardinal are Catholic would give opportunity for false propaganda charges that the U.S. is exercising undue influence on Diem." While Chester L. Cooper's assertion that "Spellman paid little attention to [Diem] until he became Prime Minister" has yet to be challenged by fact, the New York prelate's first visit to Saigon *did* come at the request of the Vatican, ample reason for Diem's handlers to downplay any meaningful links between the two at a time when fears of Vatican interference in American life remained highly potent.[28]

Warren Hinckle and Robert Scheer's sensational *Ramparts* exposé of the Vietnam Lobby promoted an exaggerated appraisal of Spellman's influence at the State Department. As the Jesuit-educated Hinckle conceded in 1974, his magazine's obsession with the Vietnam Lobby "began . . . in an earnest attempt to hang something on the Catholic Church. We set out looking to lay some of the blame for Vietnam at the silken slippers of the Pope; we succeeded only in implicating Cardinal Spellman." *Ramparts* was born amidst the euphoria of the Second Vatican Council (1962–65), and was consumed just as quickly—in its original incarnation—amid the tumult of the immediate postconciliar period. The collaboration between Hinckle and the non-Catholic Robert Scheer thus symbolized, ironically, a short-lived alliance between the Catholic and secular Left, one of the goals of the same Vietnam Lobby whose work they so vociferously condemned.[29]

Though Peter White's campaign to link Diem directly with a "progressive" wing of American Catholicism failed, Diem's handlers continued to trumpet his purported fealty to a broader vision of cultural and political freedom. The IRC and the Oram firm carefully orchestrated Diem's triumphal 1957 visit to the United States, crafting speeches in which the Asian statesman likened his refugee constituents to "the pilgrims and immigrants who, in past centuries, landed on these shores in search for a better life in the framework of Freedom." At a luncheon in his honor hosted by New York mayor Robert Wagner, Diem proclaimed that "New York City has succeeded in uniting in a harmonious community, people coming from different parts of the world, to whom it has offered a haven of peace and prosperity. By this fortunate merger of races and nationalities, your City is also, in this regard, the symbol of America, and, I dare say, of human brotherhood."[30]

At the time, few questioned how a staunch proponent of the divine right of sovereigns could exalt American-style pluralism as the apotheosis of human community, perhaps because Diem's rhetoric merely reflected the seemingly "natural" consensus shared by Americans of all persuasions. After receiving an honorary degree from Seton Hall University in New Jersey, a Roman Catholic institution where, earlier in the decade, he had spent part of his time in exile, Diem affirmed his credentials as a champion of cultural freedom by noting his role in the creation of the university's Oriental Studies department. That program, he declared, would "help to salvage what must be salvaged of the values of Asia in the tornado that befell this large portion of the world." Where conquerors of earlier times had often "bowed to the cultural superiority of the conquered," he noted, "the Communists make a clean sweep wherever they go."[31]

Diem's apparent concern for "culture" offered protection against criticisms that he was an authoritarian Catholic, an absolutist conspiring with Spellman and other coreligionists bent on imposing their particularistic views on the United States if not Vietnam, where "pluralism" had not yet been translated into the local idiom. Diem's American supporters were often exasperated by his remote, haughty demeanor and by his habit of endlessly lecturing them on the history of his people. They seemed to treat him the way an advertising firm would a difficult but important client who thought he knew better than the experts, paid handsomely to save him from himself. Diem repaid their condescension with contempt. "Diem could never understand why the Americans could not control their reporters the same way he controlled his," wrote William Prochnau in his study of American journalists in Vietnam. "But he was philosophical about it. 'If you bring in the American dog,' he said, 'you also must accept American fleas.'"[32]

The leadership of the Vietnam Lobby failed to respect the depth of Diem's conviction that he was divinely ordained to lead his people, a view rooted as deeply in his Vietnamese traditionalism as in his religion. The journalist Denis Warner claimed in 1963 that the most "dogged aspect" of Diem's character, "his rejection of advice, reflects his Confucian, rather than his Catholic, background." Diem had taken a vow of chastity and lived as a kind of lay monk, but according to Warner his brother, Ngo Dinh Thuc, the bishop of Hue, believed that Diem was "too severe" to pursue a career in the Church, "too inflexible to perform the duties of a priest among his own people." Diem's American handlers, however, remained convinced that his authoritarianism was strictly a product of his Catholicism, an issue they felt they could manage.[33]

Diem's flirtation with the avant-garde "Personalist" Catholicism of the French philosopher Emmanuel Mounier was viewed as a hopeful sign. Mounier's religio-political movement—centered around the journal *Esprit*—had turned significantly leftward after 1945. Yet the Americans in Vietnam knew that Diem's brother Nhu was the only real Personalist in the regime, and he merely twisted Mounier's teachings to serve the ends of his own power. Personalism apparently struck Joseph Buttinger as an anticapitalist, anticolonialist "Third Force" ideology not incompatible with socialism, while others at the Vietnam Lobby were content to depict Diem as a sort of honorary urban-American Democrat.[34]

"In light of his concept of divinely appointed leadership," wrote Bernard Fall in 1963, shortly before Diem's demise, "it should hardly be surprising that any Madison Avenue attempt to make a baby-kissing popular leader out of Diem would fail." Years later, in one of the numerous interminable footnotes to his *Vietnam: A Dragon Embattled*, Joseph Buttinger quoted Fall to acknowledge what he must have known about Diem from the start: "he was a spiritual son of a fiercely aggressive and militant faith" rather than, in the Vietnam Lobby's version, an "easygoing and tolerant" Catholic of the "Gallican" variety.[35]

❧   ❧   ❧

Ngo Dinh Diem was a most exasperating client, but his "domestication" into a modern democrat represented a real coup for his handlers, while it lasted. The Vietnam Lobby became vigorously engaged on the domestic cultural front on Diem's behalf: its agents even managed to hijack the production of the film version of Graham Greene's anti-American Vietnam novel *The Quiet American*. The renowned director Joseph L. Mankiewicz acquired the rights to the project in late 1955. The following May, not long after returning from a preproduction research trip to South Vietnam (where he consulted with the CIA's legendary freelancer, Lt. Col. Edward G. Lansdale), Mankiewicz was elected to the IRC board and was also offered membership in the American Friends of Vietnam. The IRC, the Oram agency, and Lansdale—the American in Vietnam with the greatest influence over Diem—collaborated closely with Mankiewicz in the production of the film. Lansdale was a great hero of the Vietnam Lobby's Left-liberals: while assisting Gilbert Jonas of the Oram firm in winning diplomatic clearance to shoot portions of *The Quiet American* in Saigon, he expressed his disdain for vestigial McCarthyism as an impediment to the postcolonial democratization of Southeast Asia (Joseph Buttinger later noted that Lansdale was known in Vietnam for "his pronounced 'anti-colonialist' views").[36]

Lansdale, a former advertising executive, had conducted an ambitious and largely effective psychological warfare campaign on Diem's behalf since the summer of 1954. In *The Quiet American,* a dangerously idealistic young American in Vietnam, Alden Pyle—widely though quite inaccurately assumed to be based on Lansdale himself—supplies plastic explosives to anti-Communist nationalists whom he anoints as a "Third Force" alternative to colonialism and the Marxist Viet Minh. In the novel, a deadly bombing in front of Saigon's Continental Hotel—drawn from an actual incident of January 1952, long before Lansdale's arrival in the country—is depicted as the consequence of Pyle's reckless involvement with Vietnamese nationalists. Lansdale meticulously advised Mankiewicz in a March 1956 letter on ways to reverse the meaning of Greene's novel (in selling his books to Hollywood, the British author routinely surrendered all artistic rights). Lansdale even suggested that Pyle be portrayed not as an intelligence operative but as a private citizen in Vietnam "on a foundation grant from some U.S. foundation"; that is, a figure resembling an agent of the IRC or the AFV.[37]

Mankiewicz got the message; in the film Pyle was depicted as a representative of the "Friends of a Free Asia." Lansdale further advised: "in keeping with your treatment of this [the bombing] actually having been a Communist action, I'd suggest that you just go right ahead and let it finally be revealed that the Communists did it after all." In May 1956, Alfred Katz—a freelance New York publicist and AFV member with social connections to Mankiewicz and his wife, and an IRC volunteer—excitedly informed Harold Oram that Mankiewicz had succeeded in "completely changing the anti-American attitude" of the novel. "The storyline of the Englishman being responsible for the American's death still holds but the Vietnamese girl emerges as a Third Force—the force the American has given his life for."[38]

The cinematic *Quiet American* was essentially an expensive advertisement for the Diem regime and the IRC, which hosted benefit premieres in several cities, the results of which were as dismal as reviews of the film itself. While Greene never mentions Diem in the novel, the movie version has the "quiet American" reverentially credit "a very prominent Vietnamese living in exile" with introducing him to the "Third Force, the Vietnamese people." The American expresses his hope that "if all goes well, if Vietnam becomes an independent republic with a government freely chosen by its people—this man will be its leader."[39]

Joseph L. Mankiewicz was among the most outspoken liberals in Hollywood; he once called Los Angeles "the true threat to the American spirit and the American mind . . . a place where I think it is still against the law to teach your children that the United Nations exits." Though it made perfect sense for Mankiewicz to champion Diem—given his own views and the orientation of the Vietnam Lobby—his biographer, Kenneth L. Geist, reported that a member of the *Quiet American* production staff "contends that at the time Mankiewicz was 'brainwashed' by prominent American Friends of the Diem regime [sic], among them Angier Biddle Duke." (In the 1970s Mankiewicz condemned Diem as "a thoroughly corrupt man" whose regime was abetted by the CIA.) In concluding the Mankiewicz was "duped" into championing Diem, Geist offered yet another testimonial to the enduring mythological power of the Vietnam Lobby.[40]

This "brainwashing" motif was a variant on the model of radical declension journalists Robert Scheer and Warren Hinckle deployed in "The Vietnam Lobby." Since it was inconceivable that men of the Left might have had rational motives for supporting Ngo Dinh Diem, Hinckle and Scheer portrayed the leaders of the Vietnam Lobby as classic McCarthy-era turncoats. They described Harold Oram as "a former promoter of 30s leftist causes, who later became associated with anti-Communist and liberal center groups." They characterized Oram, Buttinger, and Oram's associate Gilbert Jonas as "ex-radicals." Buttinger, they reported, had endured an "embittering experience" as the leader of Austria's socialist underground at the time of the Nazi triumph. In his flight to Paris and then New York, "the certainty of his world of Socialist politics vanished, and so did his ideology."[41]

Buttinger's important financial and intellectual contributions to the socialist *Dissent* magazine in the 1950s were dismissed by Scheer and Hinckle as mere dabbling; they also failed to address the stirring concluding lines of *In the Twilight of Socialism* (1953), in which Buttinger allied himself with those "obstinate socialists" who "feel as close as ever to Marx." Scheer and Hinckle underestimated the flexibility and initiative of Cold War Left-liberals as well as the willingness of the U.S. intelligence community to work with unreconstructed socialists. The CIA did not have to co-opt the International Rescue Committee, for example, because Leo Cherne had actively lobbied Allen Dulles to utilize the IRC's service since at least 1953. Far from being ineffectual dupes of the CIA, the IRC enhanced its own prestige through a variety of collaborative efforts involving certain elements of "the Company," most notably the "Operation Brotherhood" program devised by Landsdale and his Filipino client Oscar Arellano in 1954. In 1955–56 the IRC administered the domestic publicity and fund-raising for Operation Brotherhood, which was "fronted" in the United States by the Junior Chamber of Commerce (on behalf of their phantom "chapter" in Vientiane, Laos), an organization not likely to be implicated in the Left-sectarian political culture of the postwar era. The Jaycees provided the ideal Middle American image to domesticate the nation-building campaign of the Vietnam Lobby. Operation Brotherhood delivered medical aid and political indoctrination to Vietnam via Filipino nurses, doctors, and technicians who were also expected to gather political intelligence.[42]

The IRC's cooperation with the CIA, sufficient evidence for many of the group's hypocrisy, was actually quite consistent with the ideology of the non-Communist Left. The CIA housed more liberals and ex-leftists than any other agency within the executive branch: in 1953 Senator McCarthy assailed the CIA as "the worst yet" when it came to harboring "security risks." As Evan Thomas has demonstrated, one top CIA official whose loyalty had been questioned, Cord Meyer, became "a kind of liberal icon through his writings on behalf of 'world federalism,'" an ideology ardently embraced by at least one key operative in Harold Oram's public relations firm.[43]

Increasingly after 1956, the Vietnam Lobby allied itself with the liberal internationalist wing of the State Department and the CIA. When William Lederer and Eugene Burdick's astoundingly popular novel, *The Ugly American,* was published in 1958, the most fervent defenders of the embattled United States foreign service emerged from the ranks of the Vietnam Lobby, most notably the former leader of the Austrian Revolutionary Socialists, Joseph Buttinger. Buttinger's lengthy critique for *Dissent* of *The Ugly American,* based largely on his contempt for the American mass culture which validated the book, briefly galvanized a counterattack from within the ranks of the foreign policy establishment, members of which lavishly poured out their gratitude to Buttinger on State Department letterheads.[44]

In many ways Buttinger's work anticipated the role advocated for leftists by Seymour Martin Lipset in his 1960 work, *Political Man.* Lipset would argue that "the leftist intellectual, the trade union leader, and the socialist politician" had a place working "with non-Communist revolutionaries in the Orient and Africa." Lipset assumed, as historian Godfrey Hodgson has noted, that such individuals accepted the fact "that serious ideological controversies have ended at home." Yet Lipset readily acknowledged that Western leftists, "by virtue of the fact that they still represent the tradition of socialism and equalitarianism within their own countries . . . can find an audience among the leaders of the non-Communist left in those nations where socialism and trade unionism cannot be conservative or even gradualist."[45]

Lipset did not consider the possibility that such work—while having little impact abroad—might instead confirm the non-Communist Left's compatibility with the ideology of liberal consensus on the home front. For if the core members of the Vietnam Lobby stood for anything in the 1950s, it was a vision of a postsectarian world whose embrace of the "culture concept" ensured universal tolerance and human freedom, the veritable free marketplace of ideas for which expansive Americans had so long yearned. Leo Cherne insisted that the AFV was driven by hopes that "the healthy aspiration of the freedom-loving American liberal and conservative for liberty, independence and a bright economic future may yet be born in Vietnam." In constructing the myth of Ngo Dinh Diem as a cultural democrat, the Vietnam Lobby both internationalized and domesticated a standard of pluralism and tolerance that was echoed by virtually all mainstream social critics of the 1950s. Joseph Buttinger's abiding hostility to "mass culture" represented a standard position at the time among American intellectuals, who feared the "authoritarian personality" that seemed to arise in "mass society." Seymour Martin Lipset, for example, was concerned that members of "extreme moralizing" faiths such as Catholicism were "vulnerable to statuslinked political appeals" that could presumably best be combated by shoring up the bulwarks of "liberal culture" at home and abroad.[46]

The Vietnam Lobby's domestic cultural work was meaningless, of course, to Ngo Dinh Diem. Edward G. Lansdale theorized, in constructing Operation Brotherhood, that the Vietnamese would respond better to their fellow

Asians than to Caucasian operatives, but he failed to first clear the strategy with Diem, who was not schooled in ethnic studies. As Lansdale admitted in his 1971 autobiography: "Diem told me that the Vietnamese did not need the help of a bunch . . . of nightclub musicians (most of the dance bands in Asia at the time were made up of Filipinos)." Vietnam itself often served as a mere backdrop for the work of the Vietnam Lobby: the real inspirations for Joseph L. Mankiewicz in filming *The Quiet American* were fellow countrymen he had observed in action in Vietnam running Operation Brotherhood, "an idealistic bunch of kids . . . who couldn't set off a firecracker on the Fourth of July."[47]

Although the boyish, unassuming war hero Audie Murphy failed to persuasively convey American idealism in his wooden performance as *The Quiet American,* the Vietnam Lobby could still boast of its own real-life folk hero, Dr. Tom Dooley, a former naval officer who had participated in the legendary "Operation Passage to Freedom" in Vietnam during the autumn and winter of 1954–55. At the urging of the Lansdale party within the CIA, Dooley wrote a best-selling account of the transplantation of 750,000 Vietnamese Catholics from the North to the South, but in the spring of 1956 he was suddenly thrown out of the Navy for his homosexuality and just as quickly "rehabilitated" by the IRC, who dispatched him to Laos as a nonsectarian medical missionary. Dooley's celebrated work in Lao villages represented the greatest publicity coup the Vietnam Lobby would ever enjoy. He was a quick study and was more than eager to play the role of "regular-guy" American which the IRC devised for him. It was no fluke that Dooley was a Catholic: he had appealed initially to Lansdale as a potential liaison between Diem and the American public. Dooley came to symbolize everything Diem resisted, if not loathed, as a champion of ecumenism, pluralism, and a postdenominational "brotherhood of man" approach to foreign aid.[48]

Ngo Dinh Diem became an embarrassment to the anti-Communist leftists of the Vietnam Lobby in the late 1950s. His regime had clearly failed to meet minimal standards of democratization, and he displayed no "tolerance" for his adversaries or respect for his handlers. There would be little mourning his demise within the left wing of the Lobby, especially after a schism in the AFV pitted Diem's more militant champions—including Lansdale and retired army general John W. O'Daniel—against the New York publicists and humanitarians Lansdale dismissed as "Madison Avenue eggheads." Angier Biddle Duke later explained that "the organization was moving away from its liberal roots in the world of Wolf Ladejinsky [a controversial "land reform" consultant to Diem] and Joe Buttinger."[49]

Duke had perhaps grown tired as well of defending Diem from attacks by Protestants of his own social class, including the wife of New York's Anglican leader James Pike, who in March 1958 forwarded to Duke an anti-Catholic diatribe from an unidentified but "reputable" source who asked: "I wonder if you are aware of the fact that the present government of Vietnam is completely the handiwork of Cardinal Spellman . . . there he has in effect a virtual gestapo." Duke could only wearily respond that Diem had actually proven "disappointing to the Roman Catholic Church" for failing to "help further his religion in Vietnam." Either way, the "Catholic question" had persistently confounded one of the more unlikely international public relations campaigns in history.[50]

Yet Diem's American handlers had achieved a perhaps unintended feat on the home front: in struggling to depict Diem as a modern, democratic pluralist, they also advanced the cause of a "liberal culture" in their own country. Men of the Left, they found common cause with intelligence operatives who scorned both communism and the tendency of other Americans to link all forms of dissent and "difference" with the dreaded foe. In seeking to make the world safe for liberal internationalism, the Vietnam Lobby also helped secure a viable role for themselves at home. Furthermore, they offered a place in this new consensus as well for individuals from the other side, especially Catholic anti-Communists eager to embrace a complex modern world that the McCarthyites had reviled.

For John F. Kennedy was not, as we have seen, the first American-made Catholic president. As an early and ardent supporter of Ngo Dinh Diem and a charter member of the American Friends of Vietnam, Kennedy was perhaps the greatest beneficiary of the Vietnam Lobby's cultural work. The elaborate campaign to make the Vietnamese Catholic mandarin acceptable to the American populace neatly served his interests as well, especially since unlike Diem, Kennedy genuinely believed that a secular, pluralist democracy represented not only a providential arrangement for the sociopolitical environment he inhabited, but a universal mandate.

Some of Kennedy's critics, on the Left as well as the Right, harbored an enduring suspicion that he was manipulated by a Catholic cabal—headed by his own father and Cardinal Spellman—intent on reviving the sectarian anticommunism of the McCarthy era. Yet Kennedy's ardent participation in the AFV served precisely to *rescue* him from suspicions of McCarthyite tribalism in the same way that support for Diem promised to win non-Communist leftists their own reprieve from charges of disloyalty. It has been largely forgotten that Kennedy's smooth pronouncements on the separation of church and state—delivered with a tone of conviction Diem never bothered to master—deeply upset many theologically sophisticated Catholics in the early stages of his candidacy. As historian Timothy L. Sarbaugh has shown, even such liberal Catholics as newspaper editor Robert G. Hoyt were appalled by Kennedy's promise—in a March 1959 interview with *Look* magazine—that his oath of office would take precedence over his faith. "If this is an American doctrine," Hoyt wrote in 1959, "I'm leaving for Tahiti." Kennedy would assuage the hard feelings, and Hoyt would stay in Kansas City to launch—shortly after Kennedy's assassination—the *National Catholic Reporter,* an organ of the Catholic Left which in time became the American Church's foremost champion of cultural pluralism.[51]

At Washington's Willard Hotel in June 1956, Senator Kennedy had spoken at the American Friends of Vietnam's first national symposium on "Americans' stake in Vietnam." He proclaimed that Vietnam's "political liberty is an inspiration to those seeking to obtain or maintain their liberty in all parts of Asia—and indeed the world," and he reminded his listeners: "The United States is directly responsible for this experiment—it is playing an important role in the laboratory where it is being conducted." "What we must offer them is a revolution," Kennedy continued, "a political, economic and social revolution far superior to anything the Communists can offer—far more peaceful, far more democratic and far more locally controlled." As part of this social revolution, Kennedy stressed the need for the "complete integration" of 750,000 immigrants from North Vietnam who held the key to Diem's success.[52]

The refugees were overwhelmingly Catholic, like Diem, like Tom Dooley, and like Kennedy himself. We can only speculate as to whether the senator viewed these immigrants as akin to his own Irish forebears or simply as subjects of a bold experiment, utilizing the most advanced techniques in the human sciences to ensure the fullest possible integration of the refugees into their new society. We can say with confidence, however, that Senator Kennedy had absorbed a crucial lesson as a participant-observer in the nation-building crusade whose public relations was handled by the Vietnam Lobby: only in a world made truly "safe for diversity" could Roman Catholic Americans and non-Communist leftists alike enjoy the full blessings of freedom and opportunity in a world abundant with new frontiers.

In 1961, former president of the American Friends of Vietnam Angier Biddle Duke was appointed chief of protocol for the Kennedy administration. Duke later recalled that "Kennedy had an ambivalence about Diem . . . He was very, very careful of his own involvement with another

Catholic chief of state. He was very sensitive to that and very conscious of Diem as a Catholic figure." Long after his former colleagues at the AFV had written Diem off as a hopeless despot, Kennedy hoped against the evidence that Diem might institute sufficient reforms to maintain American support for his regime. After Kennedy finally authorized the coup that resulted in the deaths of Diem and his ruthless brother Ngo Dinh Nhu, he took no solace from the remark of a friend that Diem and Nhu were tyrants. "'No,' he said, 'they were in a difficult position. They did the best they could for their country.'"[53]

"We Are All Highly Adventurous"
Fidel Castro and the Romance of the White Guerrilla, 1957–1958

VAN GOSSE

A T THE COLD WAR'S HEIGHT in the late 1950s, a wide range of U.S. citizens enthusiastically backed Fidel Castro's 26th of July Revolutionary Movement. Beginning with Herbert L. Matthews's famous February 1957 articles in *The New York Times,* where he proved that "the rebel leader of Cuba's youth . . . is alive and fighting hard and successfully in the rugged, almost impenetrable fastnesses of the Sierra Maestra," Castro was lionized by the U.S. press. Meanwhile *fidelista* Cuban exiles staged stateside demonstrations and ran guns, and numerous young North Americans tried to get into Cuba to fight alongside the picturesque guerrillas.[1]

This essay begins by considering some of the reasons why this episode was ignored for several decades, placing the seemingly anomalous pro-Castroism of the late 1950s within a longer historical tradition that predates the Cold War. It then examines the types of North Americans who acted upon their identification with the Cuban rebels—journalists, liberal members of the "political public," disaffected youth—and seeks to understand the sources and meaning of their convictions.[2] Having specified who supported Castro and why, I concentrate upon the reasons why the Cuban Revolution, of all the post-1945 third world insurgencies, achieved this singular level of support in the United States, and how the character of "Yankee *fidelismo*" changed after the revolutionary victory. New groups—specifically African Americans—found in Castro a champion both symbolic and real, as others retreated in the face of intensifying U.S.-Cuban hostility. What had been a mainstream, nonpolitical ethos of sympathy and admiration rapidly evolved into a more isolated, New Leftist brand of activism, leading to the founding of the Fair Play for Cuba Committee in early 1960.

The revolution was in power, and the romance was over—though perhaps a new one was beginning.

The Pro-Insurgent Tradition

The sympathetic media coverage of 1957–58, the popular interest that this coverage both reflected and stimulated, and a demonstrable North American presence within the ranks of the tiny Rebel Army all combine to form a unique moment in High Cold War culture. At no other point in the post-1945 period did so many ordinary Americans unabashedly embrace a foreign insurgency of fatigue-clad, gun-toting rebels. However, the public articulation of pro-Castro sentiments was less remarkable at the time than in retrospect, because in the 1950s there was still a residual familiarity with the phenomenon of journalistically driven bandwagons for other peoples' wars of liberation. This long-running custom stretched back to philo-Jacobinism among Jeffersonians during the Republic's earliest days. For the next 150 years, Bolívar, Lafayette, von Steuben, Kościuszko, Kossuth, Garibaldi, Juárez, Zapata, and even Villa were celebrated in sentimental texts and, in the case of the latter three Mexican revolutionary figures, major Hollywood films. Cuba, of course, was the subject of the most intensive public campaign of all in the years leading up to the Spanish-American War, when journalists like Richard Harding Davis produced eyewitness accounts of Spanish atrocities and heroic Cuban resistance, and newspaper magnates like William Randolph Hearst strenuously promoted a military intervention on behalf of the oppressed Cuban people.[3]

The events of 1898, the Mexican Revolution of the 'teens and twenties, and even the tumult in a perpetually revolutionary Cuba during the thirties all seemed much less "past" in the late 1950s than they would even a few years later. The oft-evoked changing of the guard from Eisenhower, a young officer in 1917–18, to Kennedy, a hero of the Second World War, had not yet taken place. Thus, a reassuring sense of continuity underlay Castro's appeal. From 1957 through the first months of 1959, he appeared to be a welcome extension of an established tradition rather than an aberration or a threat.

Historians of the Cold War, to the extent that they are aware of this tradition, have assumed it to be anachronistic and irrelevant to events after 1945. Though journalists and scholars are aware of Castro's popularity in 1957–58, in later years no one has given it more than passing, bemused comment. To most observers, the pro-insurgent disposition vanished with the coming of the "national security state" under the aegis of NSC-68, and was replaced by the manufactured celebration of quasi-reformist strongmen like Ngo Dinh Diem in "South" Vietnam.[4]

There are many seemingly ephemeral episodes involving popular sentiments at odds with the concerns of the political elite, and it is not surprising that they become footnotes in the historical record. Obviously enough, a few years of pro-Castroism in the United States have been forgotten because they were rapidly supplanted by decades of intense, officially sanctioned anti-Castroism. Within months of Castro's triumphal April 1959 tour of East Coast cities, mainstream sympathy toward the Cuban Revolution had largely dissipated, replaced by a bitter war of words and diplomatic sanctions that culminated in the Kennedy administration's humiliation at the Bay of Pigs in April 1961. From that moment on, the hostility toward Castro within the political and journalistic establishment—the sense that he was not only a sworn opponent, but a personal enemy and a betrayer of America's goodwill—overwhelmed the earlier memory of his favorable reception. Other than a brief outpouring of interest in the Fair Play for Cuba Committee in 1960–61, and similar flurries on the liberal Left at later times, the only visible activism on Cuba has been that of the militant and well-organized exile movement based in south Florida, which has actively sought to overthrow the revolutionary leader for nearly four decades.

But this episode's rapid consignment to oblivion cannot be explained only as a result of its submersion by later events and a sea change in American attitudes. After all, "Yalta" as a symbol of Soviet-American rapprochement and liberal folly has remained a fighting word in American politics for many years. Something deeper and more confusing was at work: an inability to remember a moment of promise when it seemed that the United States, not just a few policymakers thinking instrumentally but its own people, could embrace a revolution in a country with a colonial relationship to our own. That this promise was naïve and doomed in the context of the Cold War does not vitiate its significance as a barometer of popular politics during the late 1950s.

In this case, timing was everything. It is inconceivable that Castro could have become a hero among North Americans (indeed, the kind of hero he intended to be) a few years earlier or later. His rise to fame and his fleeting, amused, and always slightly parodied glory captures perfectly the ambience of the late Eisenhower years, when the civil rights movement had first emerged and the Soviet Union began to thaw in the minds of Americans. The moment was ripe for a certain kind of insurgent, one who was sufficiently familiar and politically ambiguous, and above all who passed for "white" and could bridge the ever more tenuous color line.

The Yankee Fidelistas

One does not have to go far to prove that Castro's *Movimiento Revoluciona-rio 26 de Julio* was celebrated in the United States during its two years of hit-and-run warfare against the dictator Fulgencio Batista, a traditional Washington ally. The principal vehicles for this celebration were numerous North American journalists and the eminent institutions they represented, leading some conservatives to accuse the press of selling Castro to an unsus-pecting U.S. public. Witness the notorious 1960 cartoon in William F. Buck-ley's *National Review,* picturing a grinning Fidel with the legend "I Got My Job Through the *New York Times.*"[5]

The naïveté of this view should not prevent us from acknowledging the weight of press support for Castro's hirsute *barbudos,* or "bearded ones," a term relished by newsmen. For two years, their skirmishes were covered in breathless detail by nearly all of the national print media. *Time,* the premier organ of Henry Luce, publicist for the American Century, ran thirty-one stories in less than two years on "This Man Castro," repeatedly evoking America's revolutionary past in homages to Castro's "six hundred wily sharp-shooters." *Life,* the other major Luce organ, ran several full-page spreads, including a remarkably jolly feature on U.S. businessmen and soldiers held hostage in the mountains by Fidel's brother Raul as insurance against Batis-ta's bombing raids (one American airman declared, "I am just like one of them," and *Time* quoted another as saying Raul, "a swell guy," had provided "good food and plenty of it, and beds with clean sheets"). Perhaps most surprisingly, Jules Dubois, star reporter for the *Chicago Tribune,* the beacon of the midwestern Old Right, was Herbert Matthews's closest competitor as a public friend of Castro.[6]

The height of this engagement with the guerrilla *mística* was the May 9, 1957, CBS primetime special, "Rebels of the Sierra Maestra: The Story of Cuba's Jungle Fighters." Placing Fidel and his tiny band amid scenes of mountain rusticity, minus any visible enemy or fighting, it suggested a boy-ishly pure commitment. For American viewers, this spartan scenario was in exemplary contrast to Havana, the hemisphere's synonym for a permanent nightlife of roulette wheels and unmentionable fleshpots. The journalist who made that film, Robert Taber, would found the Fair Play for Cuba Committee in 1960.

One cannot blame the U.S. press for having a field day in Cuba in 1957–58. The tableaux on constant display invited a luxuriant pastiche: foreign revelers carrying on oblivious to a savage conflict only blocks away; bombings, official murders, and assassination attempts denied by a flagrantly corrupt government; Castro's bombastic personality, with his black-framed spectacles, cigars, curly whiskers, and olive-green fatigues complemented by a sniper's rifle with a telescopic sight.

All of the above would have been more distant and objectively rendered, of course, if Cuba were not—as constantly repeated—"only ninety miles away," a quick jaunt from Miami for Americans looking for a wild weekend. It is this last point that has been most forgotten by North Americans (but not of course by Cubans). By the 1950s, Havana was quite literally the whorehouse of the Caribbean. For decades it had stood for a riotous nightlife, "rum and Coca-Cola," the mambo, showgirls, and nightclubs, but by the fifties, under Batista, U.S. organized crime had invested massively. As a consequence, there was nothing like it in the Western Hemisphere. Poised somewhere between the French Riviera and Mexican border towns like Tijuana, Havana was a cornucopia of vice. A young serviceman named Everett LeRoi Jones who visited there in 1956 would later write about its reputation as the "best liberty in the world," and the New Jersey businessman who initiated the Fair Play for Cuba Committee, an inveterate liberal and devotee of I. F. Stone, would explain his admiration of Castro in terms of his revulsion of what Cuba had been formerly: "It's where you went for gambling, drinking, drugs. . . . I wouldn't go to Spain either."[7]

The media's fascination with Cuba's back-alley civil war reflected and spurred two other currents of solidarity. At an elite level, support for Castro grew from Cold War liberals' widely voiced concern that the West was losing the battle for the "developing world" because of its reliance upon outright repression and outmoded despots. As early as 1956, Adlai Stevenson had warned of this danger in his presidential campaign, while Senator John F. Kennedy had scored points with a forceful speech against French policy in Algeria. The most famous example of this perspective was the best-selling 1958 novel *The Ugly American,* in which provincial State Department blockheads and political appointees deliver a fictional Asian nation to the Communists through their racism and refusal to acknowledge local realities.[8]

One retrospective version of how elite opinion functioned as self-criticism and goad in these years is a 1963 *Saturday Evening Post* article, "The Fruit of Castro's Plotting," by the influential columnist Stewart Alsop.

After traveling "10,000 miles through the Caribbean and Central America," Alsop cited approvingly the opinion of an anonymous U.S. ambassador that "Fidel Castro is the best thing the Lord ever did for us." He then explained the four major ways in which "Fidel Castro has served the vital interests of the United States."

> First, he has reminded us North Americans of the existence—and the importance to our nation—of Latin America. Second, he has shown the Latin American "intellectuals" the reality, not the dream, of Communism. In so doing, he has acted as a sort of inoculation against the Communist smallpox in this hemisphere. Third, Castro has thrown a badly needed scare into the Latin-American ruling class. Without such a scare, the Kennedy Administration's Alliance for Progress would not stand a ghost of a chance of succeeding. Fourth, Castro and Khrushchev have given the United States an opportunity to demonstrate, for all the world to see, where the real center for power in this hemisphere lies.[9]

One could scarcely ask for a better indictment of America as a sleeping giant stoking the furnaces of revolution through indifference. But Alsop did not write simply as a journalist, an anonymous observer. With his brother Joseph, he epitomized the well-connected Washington insider, among whom the view was widespread that some form of populistic, managed reform was necessary to head off all-out social revolution. It was such men who pushed the mini-boomlets in the United States for Ramon Magsaysay of the Philippines and Diem.[10]

It is hardly surprising, then, that early in John F. Kennedy's presidential campaign, he spoke of Castro in generous terms, as "part of the legacy of Bolivar," a "fiery young rebel" who might "have taken a more rational course after his victory had the United States Government not backed the dictator Batista so long and so uncritically." In the fall of 1960, however, Kennedy would cut sharply to Richard Nixon's right with the jibe, "If you can't stand up to Castro, how can you be expected to stand up to Khrushchev?" and a coy suggestion that the United States fund a counterrevolution, but his liberal backers preferred to believe the true JFK was committed to the grand promises of the Alliance for Progress.[11]

Under Kennedy, Castro was an in-the-flesh demonstration of things gone awry. In 1957–58, however, he functioned as a credible alternative for some on the outer edges of U.S. diplomacy. The Inter-American Association for Democracy and Freedom (IADF), a group of social democrats and liberals that linked figures like Norman Thomas, Roger Baldwin, and Arthur M.

Schlesinger, Jr., with the hemisphere's "Democratic Left" led by Costa Rica's José Figueres and Venezuela's Rómulo Betancourt, weighed in on Castro's behalf with press conferences, letters-to-the-editor, and lobbying visits denouncing Batista. In Congress, an Oregon Democratic freshman and IADF ally named Charles Porter made a name for himself denouncing U.S. collaboration with Caribbean despots, from the Dominican Republic's Trujillo to Cuba's Batista. CIA officers under diplomatic cover in Cuba funneled a modest amount of aid to the *fidelistas,* and encouraged pro-Castro feeling among U.S. journalists, though the U.S. military mission in Havana remained staunchly pro-Batista. And at a decisive moment in March 1958, Representative Adam Clayton Powell, Jr., weighed in with well-documented denunciations of Eisenhower administration complicity in Batista's atrocities, helping to instigate an embargo on military aid which undercut the Cuban regime.[12]

But no matter how enthusiastic, solidarity with Castro among the elite was always conditional and self-conscious, as indicated by the subtitle of Jules Dubois's otherwise adulatory book, *Fidel Castro: Rebel — Liberator or Dictator?* The dust jacket of this exceptionally topical portrait (published in March of 1959, just two months after Batista's fall; by the fall its author was denouncing Castro) is a balancing act in microcosm. It included a photo of the two men leaning on a small camp table, captioned "Castro grants his first interview after victory to the author, Dubois," and a reproduction of a signed February 14, 1959, letter from Fidel to Dubois:

> Every person in the society of free nations—and even those who are oppressed under the heels of dictators—has a right to express his or her opinion. Under the tyranny of Fulgencio Batista that right was denied to the people of Cuba.
>
> It is the duty of every newspaperman to report the news, for only with freedom of the press can there be political freedom.
>
> Should your book contain errors and should your opinions expressed therein be mistaken or unjust, I shall not hesitate to express my own opinions about the contents of the book when it is published.[13]

Herbert L. Matthews of *The New York Times* also described himself publicly as Castro's "friend" and was a main protagonist in this drama, traveling across the island in a "glare of publicity" to meet with antigovernment groups in the spring of 1957, and publicizing the arrests of 26th of July leaders to save them from execution. But it was Matthews's status as an expert that redeemed his partisanship. Very few North Americans knew

much about Castro, and none had his degree of access. Under these circumstances, the *Times* was prepared to give him his head, but in later years
Matthews would be officially silenced.[14]

Mainstream journalists and the liberals who listened to them did not ex-
haust Castro's support in the United States, and the public's enthusiasm was
notably less modulated.[15] High-minded appreciations of the Cuban lawyer's
abilities mixed with suggestions regarding his anti-Communist utility were
all very well for *Time*. For some significant number of young American men,
however—recent veterans, would-be soldiers of fortune, self-serious undergraduate "liberals," even a few juvenile delinquents—Fidel's derring-do,
his amateurishness and bravado, seemed to set off an internal bomb. Hardly
a decade since the invasion of Normandy, he set off to take the entire island
of Cuba with eighty-two men in an old yacht, only twelve of whom survived
the landing. For reasons that few articulated beyond a desire to get into "a
good fire-fight" and see the world, North American men and boys flocked
into the 26th of July Movement's offices in New York and elsewhere, and
took cheap flights into Cuba; by late 1958 Batista's police were deporting
any Yank wearing combat boots. Most were turned away or sobered up before they could get near the Sierra Maestra, but after Castro's victory twenty
five were reported by *The New York Times* as fighting with the Rebel
Army.[16]

Since there was no organized structure for funneling North American
volunteers into Cuba (the Cubans were bemused by this outpouring,
though Castro and others recognized that it garnered favorable publicity),
we can only study the phenomenon through personal histories and evidence
from newspaper records. The first and most famous case was that of three
youths—fifteen, sixteen, and twenty-one years old—who fled their service
families at the U.S. military's base at Guantánamo in eastern Cuba in early
1957 to join up with Castro. They were featured on Robert Taber's CBS
documentary that spring, and apparently inspired many other U.S. volunteers. Next in visibility came "Captain" William Morgan, who claimed he
was a former U.S. Army paratrooper and in 1957 assumed command rank
with the "Second Front of the Escambray," a revolutionary group tenuously
allied to the 26th of July Movement. Again, it was Herbert L. Matthews
who acted as discoverer, and photos of a bearded, beret-wearing Morgan
were flashed around the world.[17]

The last North American to garner an instant of fame from his exploits
in Cuba was Donald Soldini, a Staten Islander who made up his mind to
fight with Castro upon reading Matthews's initial articles, before news broke

of the runaways from Guantánamo. Soldini, like other eighteen-year-olds then and later, was seeking adventure at any cost, as long as the cause itself fit some general criteria of virtue. It took him many travails to get into Cuba, but once there he fought hard, was wounded in the neck, and escaped from a Batista prison cell. In late 1958, Soldini was back in the States, bringing dozens of former veterans and "screwballs" to Miami to form his own all-Yankee guerrilla column, a plan aborted only by Batista's untimely departure. He ended up on the Jack Paar show in 1959 (as did Castro himself a little earlier, in a live broadcast from Havana).[18]

There are many more of these stray anecdotes, such as the tale of the notorious CIA agent and Watergate conspirator Frank Sturgis (born Fiorini), who was photographed by the AP in January 1959 posing on a burial mound of executed secret policemen.[19] Taken all together, they may seem merely reflective of that aberrant brand of machismo that was typical of the fifties. However, the tale of the Yankees who aspired to become *fidelistas* helps us understand the power of Castroism in this hemisphere, and the social tensions inside the United States at that time.

As Richard Slotkin has pointed out, the problem with the American version of counterinsurgency is that it involved from the beginning "a peculiar kind of identification with the enemy"; through creating a perfect doppelgänger of peasant revolution, the people could be saved for their own (and America's) good. The fierce desire of U.S. men to fight in Cuba indicated long before Vietnam how counterinsurgency packaged as reform would draw in a certain kind of young American and in the end subvert itself.[20] There are numerous parallels, from the fictional hero of *The Ugly American* who beats the Russians at their own game through engineering projects that help the peasants, to the intense interest in the personal story of Dr. Tom Dooley, the American doctor stationed in Vietnam who waged a one-man crusade to heal bodies and win hearts, including overseeing the evacuation of thousands from the North after the French handover of power to Ho Chi Minh's Communists.[21] Recently, the diplomatic historian Lloyd Gardner has demonstrated that such an impulse reached to the very top, as even Lyndon Johnson dreamed of a grandiose Mekong Delta reclamation project to rival the Tennessee Valley Authority and draw all of Southeast Asia, Communist and pro-American alike, together in a new New Deal.[22]

Latin America and the Insurgent Moment

To assert that there was support for Castro does not indicate why this particular third world revolutionary achieved a mass popularity like no other. To make sense of pro-Castro feeling in the United States, it must be situated historically and culturally.

In many ways Cuba stood alone, for reasons ranging from geographical proximity to cultural miscegenation. First is the historical fact of Cuba's relation to the United States, in the larger context of Latin America as a traditional sphere of influence and a largely ignored backwater.

In the ten years since 1945, the focus of U.S. foreign policy had been upon Europe first, and then Asia and Africa, the decolonizing world where Communists seemed poised to spring. Latin America, the land of seedy banana republics, was less threatening and was largely written off as static and easily controllable. In World War II, Americans had fought across Europe and the Pacific, in Burma and in North Africa; a little later, in Korea. In contrast, no GIs had been needed throughout the Ibero-American republics, which seemed to indicate the region's relative unimportance and quiescence. To most North Americans, the Pan-American republics seemed stuck in a primordial ooze of feudal indolence, a place where neither Germans nor Japanese, nor later Russians or Chinese, had ever successfully intruded. Almost completely forgotten were the long-running American military occupations in the Caribbean and Central America earlier in the century, as well as a widespread fascination with the Mexican Revolution among intellectuals and artists throughout the interwar period, and then the brief popular and governmental focus on Latin America in the later 1930s, prompted by concern over growing Nazi influence. From little children to senior citizens, most Americans in the fifties knew far more about Guadalcanal or the Ardennes than they did about São Paolo or the Andes.

North American perceptions of Latin America were given a special twist by Hollywood's long-standing habit of reducing the rest of the hemisphere to a convenient set of stereotypes. Besides the Latin Lover, the Mexican Spitfire, and the Lazy Peasant, there was a constant recourse to the thrills of Latin American revolution as quasi-banditry, with its palpable whiff of gunpowder and individual heroics. From the staged docudramas about Pancho Villa and the Mexican Revolution in the 'teens (for which Villa was paid a considerable sum) through *Viva Villa!* in 1934 and *Viva Zapata* in 1952, Latin America was the preferred site for cinematic rebellions, a commercial and cultural custom that was barely interrupted by the Cold War.[23]

These generalizations took on a special force regarding Cuba since it was closer to the United States than any other Latin American country except Mexico. It was widely understood to enjoy a kind of permanent protectorate status, even though the official right to intervene (codified in a Constitution drawn up under U.S. military occupation) was abrogated by Franklin Roosevelt in 1934. North Americans regarded Cuba as a watering hole for Yan-kees in search of inexpensive luxuries, sexual and otherwise, and as a place where baseball teams trained.

The colonial relationship between the two nations had an unintended political result: the ability of a politicized exile community to build a base of community support impossible for dissidents from Argentina or Brazil, let alone Kenya or Vietnam. The many thousands of Cuban-Americans resi-dent on the East Coast demonstrated vociferously against Batista, held fund-raising banquets for Castro, poured leaflets into the stands at Yankee Stadium, and even ran up their flag at Rockefeller Center, all the time re-ceiving only the bemused tolerance accorded groups from the "captive na-tions" of Eastern Europe. The comparison was driven home by the Cubans, who constantly declared their country "the Hungary of the Americas," a reference with considerable import in 1957.

All of these overlapping contingencies coincided at the moment when Fidel Castro ran the yacht *Granma* ashore in the swamps of eastern Cuba in early December 1956. However, they were given a special piquancy by events specific to the United States itself. At the same time that overturning established orders seemed to be in the air internationally—the Hungarian uprising and the Suez crisis occurred just months before the *Granma's* land-ing—the United States was entering into a period of prolonged confusion about the role of young people.

For many historians, and the general public as well, the litany of "youth culture" happenings in 1955 and 1956—the rise and fall of James Dean, the rise into a world-historical stratosphere of Elvis Presley, the artifacts from *The Wild One* to *Howl*—must seem overdetermined. Material abun-dance and an absence of official restraints are by themselves deemed suffi-cient to explain a quasi-oppositional moment; if a hostile reception by itself can constitute oppositionality, as in the antipathy toward rock 'n' roll of forces ranging from *The New York Times* to the White Citizens Councils.

I would argue that to the extent the youth culture of the fifties was oppo-sitional it was gender-specific and thoroughly racialized: young white men were the presumed subjects who cast themselves as role-players in a con-stantly fictionalized drama. This oppositionality (or at least a form of identity politics) required a universalist, indeed almost Popular-Frontist dismissal of class, ethnic, and regional differences that was quite new within American culture. The "white boy" as such no longer required any other markers, as southern, Irish, Italian, Jewish, or otherwise. Thus there was James Dean and Sal Mineo as a fated couple in *Rebel Without a Cause,* and the embrace of a formerly repugnant type, the white-trash truck driver with slicked-back hair, a figure symbolized by a host of self-consciously vulgar musicians (many of them recording out of Memphis on the Sun label): Jerry Lee Lewis, Carl Perkins, Johnny Cash, Gene Vincent, Eddie Cochran, and Elvis Presley of course.[24]

This was the moment into which walked Fidel Castro, barely thirty. At a time of mumbled frustration and gleeful noise, his ascetic, high-flown braggadocio struck a surprising chord. Thousands read accounts of how at his treason trial in 1953, the young Castro had denounced his judges with the ringing words, "Sentence me. I don't mind. History will absolve me." *Time* writers painted Hemingwayesque word-pictures with acute silences: "Castro is a fighter; 16 months ago he invaded Cuba from a yacht. But he is also an articulate man interested in words, manifestoes, books (he treasures a volume of Montesquieu) and the language of ideas." Yale men debated whether "The United States Should Allow Its Citizens to Give Support to Fidel Castro." Berkeley students who would go on to form SLATE, the pioneering New Left campus party, planned an expedition to Cuba in early 1957 (they described themselves thus: "We consider ourselves liberals . . . we are all highly adventurous . . ."). And to ratify his fame, Castro finally came in person to U.S. campuses in April 1959, where he was cheered by thousands at Harvard and mobbed at Princeton.[25]

The adulation awarded Castro was one piece of a larger fascination with a certain type of male rebel—some combination of drawling, swaggering, uncouth, fey, and inarticulate—which represented a strikingly visible alternative to the clean-cut, middle-class, conventionally handsome WASP, the stolid sort usually played in big-budget Hollywood films by Rock Hudson. So perhaps the best way to decipher Fidel's appeal is to pair him explicitly with the central character in the construction of this alternative: Elvis Presley.

Like Elvis, the key to Castro's charisma was both sexual and racial. Both managed to be "quite a man" (a phrase used by Herbert Matthews in his first article describing Fidel), and yet thoroughly odd. In Elvis's case, it was the sensual, languid, garish character of his face and hair and clothes and his soft, shy-boy manner (which in other circumstances would have marked him as "a queer"), combined with the rutting, thrusting, playful force of his vocal and visual attack.

Castro of course was no rock 'n' roll star, and did not go on the Ed Sullivan show until January 1959, just after he chased Batista out of Havana. But long before that North American boys read about him and gazed at still photographs. What they saw was equally transgressive. On the one hand, he was obviously a big, physically powerful person, and in every photo from late 1956 through the mid-1990s, he is seen wearing military clothing, which marks him as indubitably masculine.

Yet—and it is hard to convey the force of this in 1950s America—he had a beard. And not just a small goatee, like an Italian count or a beatnik painter in the movies, but a thick untrimmed mass, worn as an explicit pledge of faith rather than a stylistic gesture: to abjure shaving until Batista was overthrown. Nor did he take this pledge alone. Many in the Rebel Army were much more unkempt than Fidel, who at least kept his hair short. Particularly notable was his brother Raul, whose "girlish" locks were singled out, even by sympathetic journalists, while some of the earliest anti-*fidelistas* made an explicit comparison between Raul's supposed effeminacy and his vicious attraction to communism.[26]

Here one is forcibly reminded of the negative weight attached to excessive hair of any kind in the Cold War years, if not by national-security managers then by politicians and the adult world. Senator Barry Goldwater summed up the popular view when he remarked after the revolutionary victory that Castro "came over the hills looking like a knight in shining armor, and turned out to be a bum without a shave."[27] Yet there can be little doubt that the sheer hairiness of Castro and his *barbudos* endeared them to North American youth, indelibly associating the Revolution with a generationally inspired insouciance and defiance of convention. A powerfully supportive factor was the constant association of Castro with large cigars—stuck in his mouth, waved in the air, smoked even in combat—a progenitive image that requires no unpacking.

What does need underlining here is that the shabby, hairy Cuban rebels in their cast-off uniforms were quite clearly the polar opposite of the "rebels without a cause," the hipsters and Beats who proclaimed their distaste for politics along with everything else that was organized. The *fidelista* version of hipsterism was something else entirely, not strung out but clued all the way in, so alienated from a corrupt society as to demand an entirely New Man in a new, revolutionary, and liberated nation. The combination of virulent idealism, high-minded bloodthirstiness, and an utter disregard for standards of hygiene and grooming was a potent one. Indeed, to have these wild men also spout Montesquieu, Paine, and FDR at the drop of the hat, while talking about a grisly martyrdom at the hands of Batista's killers as if it were an honor, was almost too much of a good thing. As Barbara Ehrenreich has pointed out, in the fifties Hugh Hefner rhapsodized about living well, even sybaritically, in a world without women other than "chicks." Castro offered the perfect obverse—a vision of living hard and dying well, also in a world without women (other than the nunlike middle-class girls who occasionally cropped up in press coverage of the Rebel Army).[28]

In sum, Castro was "The Outsider," as Colin Wilson would famously put it in a book published the same year as the *Granma*'s landing, like so many culture heroes of the fifties. Yet unlike Elvis or Kerouac or Dean, white boys acting out rebellion on screen, in print, on disc, and through a vastly public private life, Castro was both an actual rebel in the traditional, paramilitary sense—someone who had taken up arms against an established government—and also oddly upstanding, a lawyer and a man of parts who earned a bemused respect from the most respectable of North Americans. How did he pull it off? The final key to understanding the strange breadth of Castro's popularity in the United States lies in his status as a White Man in a Dark Land.

The Rebel as Aristocrat

At the core of Fidel Castro's appeal was the ambiguous racial status assigned to men like him in white North American popular culture. Behind the stirring, sometimes mocking images of Fidel (one young freelancer returned from Cuba called him "a combination Robin Hood, George Washington and Gregory Peck") lay a whole set of racially coded images that drew on North Americans' convoluted thinking about the lands and peoples to their south.[29]

Most obviously, the always implicit questions for most Yankees in dealing with Latin Americans were: Are they white? Which of them is white? And of those who consider themselves white, and whom we accept provisionally as white, how truly white are they? What about the rest—how unwhite are they? Are they like blacks or Indians or something else for which we as yet have no name?

Where did Castro fit in this familiar story? Under the right circumstances, he could be seen as a knight errant transported from Old Spain, fulfilling the familiar part of the aristocratic rebel who overturns locally corrupt authorities at the head of poor but honest peasants (the popular *Zorro* television series was only the latest version of this narrative). Another version of the common story cast him as a much more ambiguous figure, a half-caste bastard aristocrat or "Creole" of uncertain parentage—this was rather closer to the truth, but harder to sell. Both of these were highly fraught personae, but the very confusion between them appealed to the long-standing Yankee fascination with the Latin concept of *mestizaje*, or race-mixing, which defied North America's "one-drop" racial definitions.[30]

Framed by this larger context, the question asked and answered (if only indirectly) about Fidel Castro and his guerrillas is clear. For the U.S. audience, they were treated en masse as fitting into that category of vagueness that, for lack of a better word, we can call "Latin"—meaning something in between, where blanket judgments were suspended, and class and caste were gingerly read into any given social setting without much local assistance.

On occasion, this ambiguity was resolved by an explicit signaling that Fidel himself was white, as Matthews did when he told his readers in that first scoop that Castro's father was an emigrant from Spain, a "Gallego" or Galician like Francisco Franco. But most of the time, U.S. audiences were left to draw their own conclusions. Ultimately, what mattered was not what was said or shown, but the opposite—the omission of any discussion of the racial character of the Rebel Army, let alone the larger context of Cuba's complex politics of color. To put it plainly, there were few if any black faces in this diorama.

Indeed, one could read all of the U.S. coverage of the Cuban guerrilla war in the late fifties and come away with no knowledge at all that very many, even a majority, of Cubans share African ancestry. Only occasional references to Batista's multiracial parentage, and how black Cubans reputedly supported him out of some generalized ethnic solidarity, slipped through this filter.

It would be too easy to indict the Yankee version of *fidelismo* as simply racist, hailing Castro because he was white. In reality, there were more than enough reasons to admire Castro, including the fact that he worked hard to attract North American support. His ambiguous racial status, and his seeming familiarity as a "Spanish" type (the fallen grandee, the matador), were just additional passports to North America. What one can say is that his appeal drew on the long tradition of admiration for semi- or not-quite-white (but never black) heroes, a way of talking about race (and flirting with racial difference) without confronting it. In these situations, a lot depended on how a man looked, plainly enough. So too with Fidel.

Yet North Americans were not so ignorant of Cuba as to think of Castro's followers as simply the equivalent of Spanish, Greek, or Italian "poor whites." Mexicans, Cubans, and other Latins have never been accorded even that lowly status. Castro may have been seen as provisionally white, but not the Cubans as a whole, which is perhaps the most important point to make about the racial politics of North American solidarity: his status was enhanced, not reduced, by his apparent color-blindness, his Robin Hood–like egalitarianism among the *campesinos* of the Sierra Maestra.

Here one uncovers the hidden dynamics of liberal attitudes toward the third world, and the presumed lesson for America. Just as Dixiecrat-style bigotry at home undermined the United States' democratic mission in the Free World, so did narratives of enlightened attitudes elsewhere show the way for right-thinking whites here. Unfortunately for Hollywood, by the 1950s it was impossible to portray in a positive light the British, French, Belgians, or Afrikaners fighting to hold on to imperial privilege premised on the "color bar" in Africa and Asia. There are very few films about the long-running colonial struggles of the fifties, no *Gunga Din* or *Lives of a Bengal Lancer* to stir young imaginations.

In this context, Latin America was an unexpected refuge. Here were men not so different from white Americans (or at least much more "like" them than Ho Chi Minh, Patrice Lumumba, or Kwame Nkrumah), who actually fought to overthrow established privilege, and fought alongside those who were clearly marked as their racial inferiors.

None of this explanation should be construed as suggesting that the U.S. fascination with Castro in the late fifties was manipulated, or insincere in any way. It simply bears repeating that if Fidel had been evidently Afro-Cuban, as so many Cubans are, the character of that solidarity would have been very different, and perhaps much more explicitly radical. In this sense, then, it seems fair to cast Castro as the White Guerrilla, a true-to-life ana-logue of Norman Mailer's famous White Negro—a man who had thrown it all away, and chosen to live dangerously so as to truly live, "a frontiersman in the Wild West of American night life."[31]

The Romance Wears Off: Blacking Up Fidel

One can write about the 1957–58 period as essentially one sustained mo-ment because the character of North American solidarity was constant throughout, waxing and waning only slightly as Castro seemed to advance or recede. The 26th of July's adherents in New York, Florida, and elsewhere picketed, sang, raised money, and tried to pick up guns wherever they could, concocting fantastic schemes to transfer them to Cuba in the manner of their nineteenth-century forebears. Journalists went to the island and wrote about the tropical carnage in breathless prose emulating Matthews. Young gringos of various sorts also went to Cuba (or tried to), modeling themselves upon William Morgan, the three teenagers from Guantánamo, and perhaps Gary Cooper in *For Whom the Bell Tolls.*

In this sense, the "Cuba Story" (as Herbert Matthews called it in a book of that name published in 1960) fully fit the literary model of a romance, in the crassest sense. It entertained and thrilled, and it went on forever; one could always buy another version of the same story. Of course, Fidel's brushes with near-death in the face of Batista's seemingly overwhelming force were heartstopping, and of course readers wanted Fidel to win, but much or most of the excitement depended upon his continuing fight against great odds. Robin Hood must stay in the forest with his Merry Men to assure us that there is always a place to which we can retreat, and from which justice may providentially be summoned forth, not through our own efforts but through the intervention of another.

What changed after Batista's dramatic flight in the early hours of January 1, 1959, as Castro's guerrilla columns closed in on Havana? For a few days, a week perhaps, Fidel was the man of the hour, of the hemisphere. *Life* hailed him as a "liberator," and all of the United States seemed to revel in his victory. Then came the executions of several hundred *batistiano* secret policemen, after public revolutionary trials that inevitably inspired comparisons with the French and Russian Terrors. By the end of January, a chorus of outrage could be heard in the U.S. Congress, even though Castro still merited a pajama-clad appearance live from the Havana Hilton on Edward R. Murrow's celebrity-interview program, *In Person.*

The early months of 1959 continued in this fashion, as a sort of minuet between the North American public's obvious fascination with Castro and his uncontrollable appetite for unseemly radicalism. Clearly, the question was: is he on "our" side or not? The Eisenhower administration, which had only woken up to the reality of a Castro-led revolution too late to stop it, clearly thought not, but it was unseemly to announce this as a bald fact when Castro had been publicly declared a "good guy" by the media, and much else.[32]

Interestingly enough, Fidel seemed well aware that his glow was fading. While committed to a revolutionary transformation of Cuban society, and prepared to do whatever was needed to carry it out, whether a quiet rapprochement with the Cuban Communists in 1959 or later an alliance with the Soviet Union, he still believed in the possibility of convincing the North Americans. His trip to the United States in April 1959 was an "Indian Summer," in all possible senses of that term. Not only were crowds in the streets beguiled, but one Republican Congressman described himself, after meeting Fidel, as a "nuevo amigo," and an awestruck *New York Times* reporter described Castro's presence in Washington as "out of another century—the century of Sam Adams and Patrick Henry and Tom Paine and Thomas Jefferson"—he had "stirred memories, long dimmed, of a revolutionary past."[33]

Castro's ability to overcome doubts through personal campaigning was never more on display, but its effects were short-lived. No matter how convincing his insistence that the Cuban Revolution was *"humanista, no comunista"* (as the Revolutionary Government stamped on mail between the island and the United States during 1959), the Agrarian Reform announced in May 1959 had serious implications for U.S. property holders, and ultimately for the North American position in Latin America. As Castro's popularity receded in the United States during 1959, the language used to describe him changed too. What was formerly seen as a virile outspokenness and dynamism was recast in terms with a distinct racial aura. The use of words like "ranting" and "demagogue" seemed to invoke both Mussolini and darker images, as if he were a Marcus Garvey brought to power, an Emperor Jim brought to life. In *Life*'s view, he had become "the silly egomaniac who runs Cuba . . . just another tinhorn tyrant."[34]

Meanwhile, new constituencies came to the fore within the United States. Castro's victory rapidly attracted the interest of African Americans, who hitherto had paid little attention to Cuba. Black journalists flew to Cuba and reported rhapsodically on the new government even as the white press began decrying its policy of publicly shooting proven killers from the former regime.[35] At Christmas 1959, seventy five African Americans, including various newspaper publishers and Joe Louis, joined a Cuban-sponsored delegation to Havana. Most interestingly, during this period, many in Black America began to see Fidel in a different light. The dissident NAACP leader Robert F. Williams, who had begun practicing armed self-defense in Monroe, North Carolina, wrote in his mimeographed newsletter *The Crusader* that "Castro and all other colored rulers will do well to shun bigoted Uncle Sam's smiling false face and his racial claims of bondage."[36]

In early 1960, stray journalists, honest liberals, and Beat intellectuals would form the Fair Play for Cuba Committee, beginning another chapter of solidarity with the Cuban Revolution. They would rapidly draw in various strands of the Old-into-New Lefts, and after a year of considerable popularity on campuses, suffer an ignominious obscurity that persists to this day.

But behind Fair Play for Cuba, and all the other tangled narratives of the

family feud between Cuba and Uncle Sam, lies the furious, unconsum-
mated courtship of 1957–58. Until Nelson Mandela at the very end of the
Cold War, Castro was the only third world leader ever to walk through
cheering crowds down America's mean streets, the only one to lay a wreath
at the Tomb of the Unknown Soldier, the only one for whom American
boys fought and died as willing, publicly acknowledged recruits. That this
engagement took place not at the height of the sixties but earlier, when the
certainty of American life seemed to stretch to the horizon and beyond,
only indicates how volatile and fecund was the culture of Cold War America,
even at its presumed political nadir.

From Black Power to Civil Rights

Julian Mayfield and African American Expatriates in Nkrumah's Ghana, 1957–1966

KEVIN GAINES

URING THE OFFICIAL FESTIVITIES marking Ghana's independence in 1957, the head of the U.S. delegation, Vice President Richard
Nixon, reportedly asked several bystanders, "How does it feel to be free," only
to be taken aback at their response: "We wouldn't know. We're from Alabama."[1] That incident captures both the bittersweet meaning of the occasion
for African Americans, and its transformative potential for African American
consciousness. At the height of the civil rights movement, from the late 1950s
to 1966, hundreds of African Americans, including intellectuals, technicians,
teachers, artists, and trade unionists, left the United States for Ghana, the
first sub-Saharan African nation to gain its independence from colonial rule.

This extraordinary migration was hardly accidental. Kwame Nkrumah,
Ghana's first president, had studied in the United States during the 1930s.
Nkrumah extended the hand of Pan-African solidarity to black Americans,
including W.E.B. Du Bois, who spent his last years as a citizen of Ghana.
Ghana was a magnet for African Americans whose support for Nkrumah's
politics of nonalignment, African continental unity, and revolutionary Pan-
Africanism was reinforced by their frustration at the racial inequities and
Cold War constraints of U.S. society.[2] The overthrow of Nkrumah in a mili-
tary coup and his death in exile in Guinea in 1972 marked the demise of
Ghana's leadership of struggles for economic and political independence for
African peoples. The fall of Nkrumah's government in February of 1966
occasioned the dispersal of most of the expatriates, whose ties to Nkrumah
made them suspect in the eyes of the new regime.

✻   ✻   ✻

257

Until recently, interpretations of the civil rights era advanced a periodiza-
tion privileging the liberal consensus for civil rights reforms, and the interracial ideal of the beloved community. In this view, the liberal consensus,
having achieved federal antidiscrimination and voting rights laws, and the
social legislation of the Great Society, was shattered on the rocks of black
militancy, urban rebellions, and white backlash.[3] However, recent scholarship, emphasizing virulent white resistance to desegregation in the North,
has revealed this narrative of liberal consensus to be largely an exercise in
nostalgia.[4]

A consideration of the black American expatriates in Ghana, and the
work of the leading intellectual among them, Julian Mayfield, suggests that
white racism was not the only weak link in the civil rights coalition. As much
as racism, the world of Mayfield and the Ghana expatriates was defined by
the Cold War. African American radicals in Ghana struggled against Cold
War ideology and the U.S. government's attempts to impose constraints on
the political language and tactics of black activists and movements.[5]

The importance both the African American expatriates and the U.S. government attached to Ghana as a symbol of black power, and as a platform
from which to criticize U.S. domestic and foreign policy, suggests that the
early civil rights era was marked by contestation, rather than consensus. The
radical promise of Ghana's first republic, and its potential influence on the
tactics and terms of struggle in the United States beyond campaigns for civil
rights and formal equality, led to concerted official strategies of containment.[6] Both in outcome, and in the historical imagination, then, I contend
that black power, understood as the rise of militant black nationalism and
separatism, was not the undoing of civil rights liberalism. Rather, it was Cold
War ideology and politics, in imposing a narrow domestic civil rights
agenda, that proved the undoing of black power. And here, "black power"
is understood, as it was during the early 1960s, as the revolutionary example
of Ghana for black freedom and liberation movements, both at home and
abroad.[7]

Mayfield and other leaders among the Ghana expatriates, including Shirley Graham Du Bois, Sylvia Arden Boone, St. Clair Drake, and Alphaeus
Hunton, thus worked to transform African American political identities by
fostering communication between participants in domestic and international freedom struggles.[8] As part of an international radical expatriate community, they worked to build printed and public forums to advance their
antiracist projects, creating spaces for new critical African American and
diaspora identities to flourish.[9] Besides the expatriates, African American

travelers to independent Ghana were important catalysts for public discussions in the United States of the significance of international black power, or African liberation, on black American consciousness. Malcolm X's well-publicized visit to Ghana and his tour of Africa and the Middle East in 1964 illustrates the significance of African liberation for the potential radicalization of diaspora political identities.[10] Reports of black American travelers to Ghana, including Martin Luther King, Richard Wright, Louis Armstrong, and journalists covering the independence festivities, all suggest variations of the controversy that invariably greeted the assertion of links between African anticolonialism and domestic civil rights issues.

Mayfield, and the African American expatriates in Ghana, are thus critical for an assessment of the impact of the Cold War on black politics and social movements. Indeed, the relative obscurity of Mayfield and the Ghana expatriates is a consequence of the enduring legacy of the Cold War's constraints on black thought and politics, a legacy dismissed by academic and popular declarations that some domestic repression was regrettable, but ultimately justified by the American victory in the Cold War.[11] From U.S. government controls on the freedom and mobility of African American intellectuals and journalists of the postwar period, the most notable examples including W.E.B. Du Bois, Richard Wright, and Paul Robeson, to the state-sanctioned repression against the Black Panthers, to the amnesia with regard to Malcolm X and Martin Luther King's denunciations of the Vietnam War and U.S. counterinsurgency, those antidemocratic legacies of the Cold War and their consequences both here and abroad give the lie to declarations of victory.[12] Mayfield and the Ghana expatriates are instructive precisely because they defied pressure from Cold War liberals to confine their vision of black politics within the domestic realm of civil rights. Justifiably, they were insulted by Cold War liberals' demand that anticommunism take precedence over their commitment to African American and African freedom. They refused to engage in Cold War rituals of disassociation and denial, and vehemently objected to anti-Communist propaganda that portrayed domestic struggles against segregation, and African nation-building projects, as spearheaded by Soviet "outside agitators."

In the late 1950s and into the next decade, Mayfield's support for Ghana joined efforts by African American intellectuals, at home and abroad, to forge an independent black radical politics. Not only did these intellectuals oppose the extremist anti-Communist "states' rights" rhetoric employed by segregationists to discredit the cause of civil rights, but more important, they also insisted on the inherent value of struggles for racial and social

justice, against liberals' tendency to subordinate the domestic issue of civil
rights to Cold War foreign policy imperatives.[13]

As an actor, novelist, and activist intellectual, Mayfield had been at the
center of Harlem cultural life throughout the 1950s. He held a major role
in the Broadway production of *Lost in the Stars,* adapted from Alan Paton's
Cry the Beloved Country. As chairman of the Committee on Negro Art,
Mayfield was an associate of such Harlem-based actors and intellectuals as
Ossie Davis, Ruby Dee, Sidney Poitier, James Baldwin, Rosa Guy, Audre
Lorde, Lorraine Hansberry, and John Henrik Clarke. Almost all were associated with Paul Robeson's *Freedom* newspaper, and later, with the journal
Freedomways, which consistently stressed the close relationship between
anticommunism and massive white southern resistance to desegregation,
and vehemently challenged Cold War liberals' assumptions that black
spokespersons were not entitled to criticize, let alone address, U.S. foreign
policy issues.

                            ✻   ✻   ✻

In Ghana, Mayfield defined black American identities within a dialectic of
domestic and international politics. Mayfield's journalistic writings from
Ghana were prolific and widely circulated throughout anglophone West
Africa and the United States. He adroitly balanced his writing and activism
on both domestic and international fronts, fusing antiracism and anti-
imperialism. Nevertheless, Mayfield was unsuccessful, upon his return to
the States, in publishing three separate manuscripts of his analysis of Ghana
under Nkrumah.[14] It is telling that his only published account of Ghana in
those years is a work of autobiographical short fiction, "Black on Black: A
Love Story," in which events in the fictional African nation "Songhai" were
largely based on his experiences in Ghana. The story concerns the relationship between a Ghanaian politician and an African American woman that is
undermined by popular suspicion of the African American community as a
threat to the nation's stability in the wake of assassination attempts on the
head of state. Although Mayfield's legacy was certainly not helped by his
premature death in 1984 in Washington, D.C., the obstacles he faced in his
repeated attempts to publish suggests the persistence of Cold War limitations on black oppositional thought and politics.[15]

Mayfield's accounts of his work in Ghana, read against his surviving correspondence from that period with other expatriates and colleagues back in
the States, attest to the complexity of the expatriate experience. For those

who voluntarily moved to Ghana, as opposed to those who were political exiles, the enabling condition of exile enjoyed by most of Ghana's expatriates brought forth a critical and largely overlooked perspective on the origins and legacy of black popular movements of the 1950s and 1960s. The many ambiguities of their location in Ghana—being of African descent, yet socially and culturally foreign; remote from the racial controversies of the U.S. scene, yet situated at the center of international anticolonial projects; sympathetic to the politics of African liberation, yet marginal as junior partners of Pan-Africanism, so to speak, within Nkrumah's Ghana—all provided expatriate intellectuals a unique critical perspective from which to reflect on events both near and distant.

Mayfield's account of "our crowd" in Ghana, while suffused with a blend of nostalgia and disillusionment, nonetheless evocatively documents the genealogy and formation of his cohort of black intellectuals. For Mayfield, the crisis of the Negro intellectual was defined by the pressures of U.S. racism, segregation, and Cold War hysteria:

> As Afro-Americans [in Ghana] we were testing the parameters of the Western world. Our heroes, inevitably, were . . . Paul Robeson, the still incredible Jack Johnson, Malcolm X, and most of all, W. E. B. Du Bois, who was still alive, and who lived just around the corner. . . . All of these men had been international in their thinking. They had recognized long ago something that we had to work out for ourselves in Ghana: That being a member of a persecuted minority in a racist nation like the United States almost automatically stunted one's psychological and intellectual growth. Minority thinking limited your vision and scaled down the demands you made on yourself, and on the nation. You asked for one school instead of the whole school system, for a town instead of a country. . . .[16]

Mayfield praised Robeson and Du Bois, who had been victims of Cold War hysteria for their internationalism, specifically their advocacy of African anticolonial struggles.[17] For Mayfield, their radical legacy resisted the political and ideological constraints imposed on black intellectuals within the U.S. context. Ghana, to Mayfield, heralded a revitalized global black identity, rising from the ashes of political persecution and historical erasure. And Nkrumah's project of African liberation offered lessons of struggle to the plight of African Americans in the United States. It was important to the black Americans in Ghana that Nkrumah, in tandem with Nasser's Egypt, exerted dynamic leadership in African affairs, with the first major conferences of African states being held in Accra and Cairo. And, as Mayfield recalled, freedom fighters from the nonindependent territories of the continent came to Ghana for guns, money, and training.

✿   ✿   ✿

The expatriates' experiences went to the heart of the deeply politicized matter of black identity in these years. The Ghana expatriates, and their allies back in the United States, had a considerable stake in debates in the United States around the question of the extent to which African Americans identified with Africa.[18] While this was an old debate, it took new forms in the Cold War context of the 1950s. Following the blacklisting of Robeson, Du Bois, and others, explicit claims of solidarity with anticolonial struggles on the African continent were virtually taboo, perceived as explicit criticisms of the U.S. government. As some commentators maintained that black Americans were completely alienated from their ancestral origins, and others argued that they were as susceptible as many whites to exoticized Western conceptions of a primitive Africa, Ghana expatriates and their domestic allies strongly challenged the establishment view which insisted that African Americans remained unwilling to acquaint themselves with the affairs and struggles of African peoples.[19]

For the expatriates, "home" was where they identified the vanguard of black struggle, and during the late 1950s, this was increasingly understood as Ghana. Relatively unencumbered there by the repressive Cold War climate that branded antiracist dissent "un-American," and scorned attempted linkages of domestic and international struggles for democracy, the expatriates reveled in the expanded horizons of black statehood in Ghana, and for black identity, as well. Some expatriates found there a psychic refuge that made a return to the debilitating forces of U.S. racism for a time unthinkable. The advent of a new era of black power elicited a range of responses among the expatriates, from romantic longings to pragmatic assessments of the obstacles, both internal and external, to nation-building in Ghana, and by extension, to the African revolution.[20]

✿   ✿   ✿

Ghana's potential impact on black American identities, and by extension, domestic politics, made it equally important for the U.S. government to contain, or redefine, its significance. Upon returning from Ghana and five other African countries, Vice President Nixon reported to President Eisen-

hower that Africa was the new site of conflict "between the forces of freedom and international communism."[21] The Eisenhower's administration's
presence at Ghana's independence festivities was to some degree a concession to anger in the black press at the administration's inaction against a
spate of racist bombings throughout the South, while the Soviet invasion of
Hungary remained a matter of intense concern. Black American opposition
seized on the evident double-standard in U.S. policy, effectively making
Ghana an unpredictable phenomenon for a government seeking to mini-
mize its symbolic potential as a catalyst for change.

The Eisenhower administration's post-*Brown* policy of appeasement of
the forces of massive resistance to desegregation led to well-publicized and
embarrassing encounters of diplomats from the new African states with Jim
Crow. Such incidents were detrimental to U.S. attempts to direct emergent
African and Asian states and their development policies, to say nothing of
the objective of managing domestic racial unrest. When the press disclosed
that Ghana's minister of finance, Komla Gbedemah, accompanied by his
assistant, the African American pacifist Bill Sutherland, were insulted and
refused breakfast at a Howard Johnson's restaurant in Dover, Delaware, Eisenhower had "a first-class international incident" on its hands, as E. Frederic Morrow, the lone black on the White House staff, characterized the
event. Morrow's diary of his tenure as presidential aide during this crisis-
ridden period records his frustration: "On top of the Little Rock situation,
this is the kind of thing that makes our country look bad abroad and gives
the world the idea that we are first-class hypocrites when we prate about
our wonderful democracy."[22] Morrow's discomfiture, in the wake of the recent Little Rock school desegregation standoff between Arkansas governor
Orval Faubus and Eisenhower, was eased somewhat by Eisenhower's invitation of Gbedemah and Sutherland to the White House for breakfast. The
inadequacy of the Eisenhower administration's largely symbolic attempts at
reconciliation was abundantly clear as segregationist mobs, clashes between
advocates of "states' rights" and federal authority, continued mistreatment
of African diplomats, and murderous violence would plague the Kennedy
years as well.

If the sight of African diplomats elicited racist responses from benighted
whites, Ghana's image of independent black statehood and Nkrumah's nonaligned foreign policy at the height of the Cold War were inspiring to many
other Americans. Ghana's early alliance with Israel evoked in many African
and Jewish Americans a shared aspiration for an ancestral homeland. Some

blacks lauded Ghana as a refutation of popular myths of Africa as the dark continent. For African Americans, Ghana and the prospect of new African states gave the lie to segregationist assertions that peoples of African descent had no history. Indeed, Ghana was widely seen as a catalyst for southern black college students to make history themselves through the sit-in movement, energizing civil rights struggles in the United States. Upon observing activists at Florida A & M College in 1960, James Baldwin explained that the students were born as Africa was breaking free of European colonialism. "I remember . . . the invasion of Ethiopia and Haile Selassie's vain appeal to the League of Nations, but they remember the Bandung conference and the establishment of the Republic of Ghana."[23]

Like Mayfield, many of the Ghana expatriates had activist backgrounds in civil rights and democratic struggles. Sutherland was imprisoned for refusing to serve in World War II and campaigned against segregation in the armed forces with A. Philip Randolph and Bayard Rustin in the late 1940s. Disenchanted with racism in the United States, Sutherland reached Ghana in 1953, and married the Ghanaian writer Efua Sutherland. Although only a few, such as W.E.B. and Shirley Graham Du Bois, and Dr. Robert Lee, originally from Charleston, South Carolina, went so far as to renounce their U.S. citizenship, generally, the expatriates' embrace of Ghana was reinforced by their abhorrence of American racism.[24]

The expatriates shared Nkrumah's Pan-African conviction that domestic struggles for black freedom were inseparable from African liberation movements.[25] This was not understood as an inevitable racial destiny, but as a position requiring constant practical application and discussion. For example, in 1963 the expatriates staged a demonstration at the U.S. embassy in Accra in conjunction with the March on Washington, enacting their view of solidarity between the struggles of black Americans and African peoples. The Ghana expatriates picketed the U.S. embassy in Accra, carrying placards condemning Kennedy's interventions in Cuba and Vietnam, the administration's appeasement of the apartheid regime in South Africa, and its foot-dragging on civil rights. Such forceful criticism of the Kennedy administration was carefully censored from the officially managed March on Washington. The expatriates' parallel demonstration in Ghana, arguably the most radical of several international demonstrations in sympathy with the March on Washington, accordingly attracted far more U.S. government scrutiny than the others (including those held in Paris, Oslo, Munich, and Tel Aviv). This was evident in the detailed State Department memorandum describing the protest, which included the expatriates' original petition to President Kennedy. Even before this, however, through their links with activists in the United States, they brought their vision of Ghana and internationalism to discussions of black American politics and society.[26]

*   *   *

"Tales of the Lido," Mayfield's final, unpublished account of the period, situates the Ghana expatriates within a radical tradition that challenged not only Cold War anticommunism, but also the Cold War ideology underlying the civil rights establishment, as early as the 1950s. In doing so, Mayfield's analysis complicates narratives that locate the emergence of militancy, indeed, of "Black power," later in the 1960s with the emergence of Malcolm X, black nationalism, and the antiwar movement. Mayfield described his position in the 1950s as one of active dissent from Martin Luther King's status as the preeminent civil rights leader, and the evolving movement's tactical emphasis on nonviolence. With black folk and organizers in the Deep South terrorized by segregationists, Mayfield pointed out that nonviolence enjoyed less than universal popularity.

As Mayfield recalled their arrival in Ghana, "Most of us were leaving something unpleasant behind." Surely this understatement referred to the indignities of U.S. racism. For Mayfield it also alluded to the circumstances of his exile. Mayfield, a journalist, had gotten involved with the armed self-defense movement led by Robert Williams, an NAACP leader in Monroe, North Carolina. In *Commentary*, Mayfield argued the case of Williams, who, though dismissed from the organization, posed to Mayfield a stark challenge to middle-class black leaders incapable of responding effectively to the boycotts, sit-ins, and other forms of black mass protest from below. Before being dismissed from the association by a leadership fearful that he was a liability, Williams had rescued the local NAACP chapter, which had been decimated by white intimidation after the *Brown* decision. He organized a black paramilitary force to thwart resurgent Klan attempts to harass black professionals suspected of supporting the NAACP. Mayfield applauded Williams's efforts to turn the Cold War (and the Second Amendment of the Bill of Rights) to his advantage, putting pressure on the federal government by subjecting antiblack violence to world exposure. Holding black working-class insurgency as the unknown variable in civil rights struggles, and emboldened by the recent revolution in Cuba, Mayfield argued that the legalistic and passive-resistance strategies of the black leadership class failed to address the needs of impoverished blacks. Mass-based leaders such as Williams, "who have concluded that the only way to win a revolution is to be a revolutionary," would then rise to the fore.[27]

Pressured by the FBI to provide information about Williams, Mayfield quit the country, reaching Ghana in 1961. Mayfield reflected on his close call with U.S. authorities in a letter to John Henrik Clarke, suggesting the persistence of the Cold War culture of betrayal and ostracism, putting friendships to the ultimate test: "People who thought I was on my way to jail . . . are feeling their way back. They dropped me cold in September. Well, brother, once burned is enough for me." Mayfield's initial response to Ghana was complicated. Mayfield declared himself no longer able to live in the United States, and held mobility (for those fortunate enough to have it) necessary for his development as an intellectual. Mayfield enclosed photographs of the Ghanaian "outdooring" of his newborn son, Emiliano Kwesi. Born in Greer, South Carolina, and raised in Washington, D.C., Mayfield conveyed the turbulent emotions sparked by leaving the poisonous Cold War atmosphere of racism and distrust, and exchanging the status of a member of a persecuted minority for solidarity with Ghana's black majority society.[28]

In Ghana, Mayfield served as a speechwriter and journalist for Nkrumah. He maintained later that his was a limited influence on the Ghanaian president. Expatriates gathered frequently at the home of Mayfield and his wife, Ana Livia Cordero, a physician from Puerto Rico who ran a public clinic for women in Accra.[29] Through a conversation with Ghanaian journalists, Mayfield inadvertently sparked a corruption scandal, replete with screaming newspaper headlines. Mayfield had mentioned a report in a Nigerian paper that the wife of Krobo Edusei, a prominent CPP (Convention People's Party) official, had purchased a gold-plated bed in London for £3,000.

Mayfield's activities paralleled the deterioration of relations between Ghana and the United States, as Nkrumah's government, along with other radical new states such as Guinea, under Sékou Touré, pursued a policy of nonalignment. By seeking trade-and-aid agreements with Soviet-bloc countries, in effect playing the Cold War antagonists against each other, Nkrumah seemed to confirm the fears of anti-Communists. As Basil Davidson has written, "that sort of non-alignment has become an everyday affair: when Nkrumah embarked upon it, [westerners] saw it as a hostile challenge or a dastardly betrayal."[30] For Nkrumah's information bureau, Mayfield edited a volume on nuclear disarmament, *The World Without the Bomb*, culled from presentations at a conference held in Accra.[31] Mayfield also worked as West African correspondent for the Middle East News, a press agency with bureaus in New York, Cairo, London, and throughout Europe, and as a frequent contributor to the *Accra Evening News.* His articles often discussed Nkrumah's program of African unity and nonalignment across the continent.[32]

Mayfield sought to counter the U.S. policy that supported a limited civil rights agenda primarily as a means of keeping new African states within the West's sphere of influence. Mayfield frequently published in Ghanaian newspapers accounts of U.S. racism and violence, often with graphic illustrations of lynching victims. Mayfield's exposés of U.S. racial atrocities were deployed against the American embassy's propaganda portraying the United States as steadfast in its pursuit of desegregation. Tattered copies of U.S. embassy memoranda located in the Mayfield papers border on hysteria in denouncing Mayfield as the author of several "racist" pieces designed to undermine claims of racial progress and American policies seeking to secure Ghana's membership in the "free world."

Ghana's strategic importance for the United States is further glimpsed in the vigilant concern among the expatriates, found in Mayfield's correspondence and writings, to identify African Americans deemed unfriendly to the cause of independent Ghana. This, too, was an abiding legacy of the Cold War, during which government informants were paid to provide names of real or imagined subversives to the authorities. Among the more immediate causes for Mayfield's and the expatriates' suspicion was the crisis in the former Belgian Congo, sparked by the secession of the resource-rich Katanga province and the assassination of the independent Congo's prime minister, Patrice Lumumba. The overthrow of Lumumba sparked outrage among African American intellectuals, including James Baldwin and Lorraine Hansberry. In a *New York Times* essay, Baldwin warned whites that they were dangerously mistaken in perceiving black Americans' demonstration at the United Nations (whose peacekeeping mission in the Congo was widely believed to be implicated in Lumumba's removal) as Communist-inspired. Indeed, this claim of Communist influence, to Baldwin, was deeply insulting in its suggestion that blacks would otherwise be docile in the face of dreadful conditions, North and South. In a defense of Baldwin against escalating vituperation by black American militants for whom Baldwin's success and his candid writing about homosexuality all but proved his suspect racial credentials, Mayfield reminded the critics that Baldwin, like Hansberry, had taken the unpopular stand in aligning himself with the demonstrators.[33]

The expatriates, along with Baldwin and Hansberry, symbolized a broader tendency among black Americans to view the political status and identity of African Americans through African liberation struggles. Correspondence shows that Mayfield and his cohorts called themselves "Afros," tellingly omitting their American identity, but often with an ironic awareness that blackness in itself was no guarantee of loyalty to Ghana and Nkrumah.[34]

Despite, or perhaps because of, Ghana's post-Bandung challenge of non-alignment, the nation remained beset by Cold War pressures, internally and externally. This state of affairs certainly shaped Mayfield's highly specific notion of the Uncle Tom as the African American enemy of the African revolution. As editor-in-chief of the *African Review,* a magazine published from Nkrumah's ministry of information in his executive offices in Flagstaff House, Mayfield by 1964 found himself floundering in the turbulent politics surrounding Nkrumah. Domestic opposition from conservatives and intellectuals, primarily from the cocoa-producing Ashanti region, had long been strident, and had elicited such controversial policies as Nkrumah's Preventive Detention Act (1958).

Such internal tensions were reinforced by the external pressure of Cold War constraints on Ghana, and black power. Opposition leaders were keen to exploit anti-Communist hysteria at nonalignment. From exile, Dr. Kofi Busia testified before Congress in 1962 that Ghana was the springboard for Communist subversion on the African continent, and thus not a good candidate for further financial aid. Opposition spokesmen such as Busia were effective in characterizing Nkrumah's support for nationalist parties still struggling against colonial rule as Communist-inspired.[35]

The February 1966 coup found Mayfield, like Nkrumah, away from Ghana. Nkrumah learned of the coup in China, en route to North Vietnam on an ill-fated peace mission. Mayfield was on the island of Ibiza, staying in a villa owned by a fellow expatriate. He remained there writing his first unpublished manuscript on Nkrumah, Ghana, and the coup. Almost a year after the coup, Mayfield had concluded that while Nkrumah's flaws certainly contributed to his undoing, the determination of Africa's enemies, as he put it, to prevent African unity was decisive. For Mayfield, the Ghana coup, along with the deaths of Malcolm X, Lumumba, and others, affirmed that "this power struggle is a murderous game. . . . The enemy plays for keeps." Although an authoritative case has been made for the flawed policies of Ghana's first republic, disclosures since the coup have confirmed Mayfield's suspicion of U.S. attempts to destabilize Ghana.[36]

It has been my intention to assess both the impact of black power, as represented by Nkrumah's Ghana, as well as its demise, on African American politics and identity. Although widely understood at the time as an advancement in the struggle, declarations of black power in the United States ultimately reflected the fragmentation of African American politics. Before this fragmentation, the latter careers of Martin Luther King and especially Malcolm X had been transformed in the internationalist image epitomized by Ghana. They had attempted to broaden the civil rights agenda, linking antiracism to struggles for economic justice. They had argued that inequality at home was inseparable from the escalation of the war in Vietnam. Black power rhetoric notwithstanding, the deaths of these martyred leaders virtually enforced civil rights as the normative black political discourse.

From the mid-1960s onward, radical black politics was effectively neutralized by a combination of state repression and increasingly unaccountable, undisciplined leadership that abandoned the movement's strategies of mass mobilization.[37] What remained was in large part a highly rhetorical popular conception of black power, or the new black aesthetic. This new articulation of black power was depoliticized, anti-intellectual, and ineffectual, despite its revolutionary claims.[38] Although from exile Nkrumah managed to publish several perceptive critiques of neocolonialism in Africa, black power rhetoric in the United States tended toward the sort of bourgeois nationalism that Frantz Fanon had identified as the Achilles' heel of independent African states.[39] Undeniably, black solidarities were fragmented from above. In 1957, Vice President Nixon demonstrated anew the U.S. political establishment's vested interest in imposing its own vision of freedom on black Americans. For Nixon, black power was best expressed through promoting small business enterprises in inner cities.[40]

Long after Nkrumah's fall, and Mayfield's passing, Ghana retains its significance, albeit as the locus of profoundly unresolved histories. Ghana and all it stood for potentially undermined for African Americans the racial myths, both imposed and internalized, that trapped them in what Mayfield called minority thinking, and that prevented them from defining and pursuing their independent vision of human freedom. Ghana's socialist project offered African American expatriates, however briefly, an example of independent radicalism that countered the perennial problem of the relationship of African Americans to the white-dominated Left. With the destruction of Nkrumah's vision of an independent, unified African continent, Ghana has come to symbolize unresolved silences and continuing aspirations that are the legacy of the Cold War and the so-called postcolonial condition.

Notes

Introduction: Struggling for the World

1. Ernest R. May, ed., *American Cold War Strategy: Interpreting NSC 68* (Boston: Bedford Books, 1993), 25–26, 81.

2. *Inaugural Addresses of the Presidents of the United States* (Washington, D.C.: Government Printing Office, 1989), 294.

3. See, for example, Amy Kaplan, "'Left Alone with America': The Absence of Empire in the Study of American Culture," in *Cultures of United States Imperialism,* ed. Amy Kaplan and Donald Pease (Durham, N.C.: Duke University Press, 1993).

4. As Burnham indicated, the key to U.S. post-colonial imperialism was not the extension of formal political boundaries, but the quest for global power and control. As H. W. Brands has put it more moderately, "if an essential characteristic of empire is control—the ability to control the activities of the various peoples within the empire—then, in important respects, the American sphere functioned as an empire, regardless of what Americans preferred to label it." *The Devil We Knew: Americans and the Cold War* (New York: Oxford University Press, 1993), 58. The Johnson quote is from his speech at the Johns Hopkins University, April 7, 1965, found in William Appleman Williams, et al., eds., *America in Vietnam* (Garden City, N.Y.: Anchor Books, 1985), 243.

5. The figure of $10.5 trillion is in 1990 dollars and comes from Ann Markusen and Joel Yudken, *Dismantling the Cold War Economy* (New York: Basic Books, 1992), 3. Walter LaFeber puts the figure somewhat lower, at $8 trillion. See *America, Russia, and the Cold War, 1945–1992* (New York: McGraw-Hill, 1993), 1.

6. Tom Engelhardt, *The End of Victory Culture: Cold War America and the Disillusioning of a Generation* (Amherst: University of Massachusetts Press, 1998).

7. Elaine Tyler May, *Homeward Bound* (New York: Basic Books, 1988).

8. There are now, however, a considerable number of diplomatic historians working on cultural questions. For just two important examples see Frank Costigliola, "'Unceasing Pressure for Penetration': Gender, Pathology, and Emotion in George Kennan's Formation of the Cold War," *Journal of American History* 83, no. 4 (March 1997); and Robert D. Dean, "Masculinity as Ideology: John F. Kennedy and the Domestic Politics of Foreign Policy," *Diplomatic History* 22, No. 1 (Winter 1998).

9. Jonathan Schell, "The Gift of Time," *Nation,* February 2–9, 1998, 12.

Culture, Diplomacy, and the Origins of the Cold War in Vietnam

1. T Minutes, 11 November 1943, Subcommittee on Territorial Problems, Division of Political Studies, Box 59, Records of the Advisory Committee on Post-War Foreign Policy (Harley Notter Files, 1939–45), Record Group 59, National Archives, Washington, D.C., 4.

2. See Gary R. Hess, *The United States' Emergence as a Southeast Asian Power, 1940–1950* (New York: Columbia University Press, 1987); Andrew J. Rotter, *The Path to Vietnam: Origins of the American Commitment to Southeast Asia* (Ithaca, N.Y.: Cornell University Press, 1987); Lloyd Gardner, *Approaching Vietnam: From World War II Through Dienbienphu* (New York: W. W. Norton & Company, 1988); Michael Schaller, *The Origins of the Cold War in Asia: The American Occupation of Japan* (New York: Oxford University Press, 1985); William S. Borden, *The Pacific Alliance: United States Foreign Economic Policy and Japanese Trade Recovery, 1947–1955* (Madison: University of Wisconsin Press, 1984); and Robert M. Blum, *Drawing the Line: The Origins of the American Containment Policy in East Asia* (New York: W. W. Norton & Company, 1982).

3. Clifford Geertz, "Ideology as a Culture System," in *The Interpretation of Culture* (New York: Basic Books, 1973), 193–233.

4. Melvyn Leffler, "New Approaches, Old Interpretations, and Prospective Reconfigurations," *Diplomatic History* 19.2 (Spring 1995): 180. For recent examples of pioneering and fascinating studies on gendered discourse and American Cold War diplomacy that nonetheless ultimately leave the precise relationship between culture and the intentions of policymakers unexplained, see Michelle Mart, "Tough Guys and American Cold War Policy: Images of Israel, 1948–1960," *Diplomatic History* 20.3 (Summer 1996): 357–80, and Frank Costigliola, "'Unceasing Pressure for Penetration': Gender, Pathology, and Emotion in George Kennan's Formation of the Cold War," *Journal of American History* 83.4 (March 1997): 1309–39, esp. 1338.

5. Samuel P. Huntington, *The Clash of Civilizations and the Remaking of World Order* (New York: Simon & Schuster, 1996). For a more promising and analytically rigorous approach by political scientists to explore the place of culture in foreign policy making, see Peter J. Katzenstein, ed., *The Culture of National Security: Norms and Identity in World Politics* (New York: Columbia University Press, 1996).

6. My focus on an inherent or instinctual framework for decision making draws upon the work of the philosopher Charles Taylor, who developed this concept to discuss the bases of individual and societal moral choices. See his *Sources of the Self: The Making of the Modern Mind* (Cambridge, Mass.: Harvard University Press, 1989), esp. 3–52, and, for a broader discussion of his approach, "Interpretation and the Science of Man," in *Interpretative Social Science: A Second Look*, ed. by Paul Rabinow and William M. Sullivan (Berkeley: University of California Press, 1987), 33–81.

7. Informing my analysis of the ways in which cultural vocabularies can reveal intel-

lectual predispositions and fundamental assumptions are several theoretical works including Pierre Bourdieu, *Language and Symbolic Power* (Cambridge, Mass.: Harvard University Press, 1991), Raymond Williams, *Keywords: A Vocabulary of Culture and Society* (New York: Oxford University Press, 1976); and J. L. Austin, *How to Do Things with Words* (Cambridge, Mass.: Harvard University Press, 1962). The implications of these approaches for the study of diplomacy have been most satisfyingly explored in the scholarly literature on Chinese foreign policy. See, for instance, David E. Apter and Tony Saich, *Revolutionary Discourse in Mao's Republic* (Cambridge, Mass.: Harvard University Press, 1994), and Michael Schoenhals, *Doing Things with Words in Chinese Politics* (Berkeley: University of California Institute of East Asian Studies, 1992). Daniel T. Rogers's study of the debates surrounding the foundational ideals of American domestic politics is also instructive; see his *Contested Truths: Keywords in American Politics Since Independence* (New York: Basic Books, 1987).

8. Gertude Emerson, "Backwaters of Empire in French Indo-China," *Asia* 23.9 (September 1923): 670.

9. My analysis of the interwar American discourse on Vietnam draws upon more than two hundred books and articles published in the 1920s and 1930s. Journal and newspaper articles were identified through the *Reader's Guide to Periodical Literature* (1919–1940) and the *New York Times' Index* (1919–1940). Books by journalists, missionaries, travel writers, and scholars were identified through a search of the collections held by the Harvard College libraries, the Library of Congress, and the Wason-Echols Collection at Cornell University. Virginia Thompson's *French Indo-China* (New York: The MacMillan Company, 1937) and Thomas E. Ennis's *French Policy and Developments in Indochina* (Chicago: The University of Chicago Press, 1936) were the most sustained and influential American accounts of Vietnam in the interwar period and receive particular attention in my analysis. Thompson, an independent scholar associated with the Institute of Pacific Relations, continued to write on Southeast Asia throughout the World War II and postwar period. Ennis was a professor of history at West Virginia University whose work on Vietnam became required reading for American diplomats in East and Southeast Asia. Examples of consular reporting utilize the following archival collections: Records of the Diplomatic Posts, Saigon, 1889–1940, and Records of Diplomatic Posts, Vietnam, 1936–1940, Department of State, Record Group 84, National Records Center, Suitland, Maryland; Records of the Department of State Relating to the Internal Affairs of France, 1919–1939, Record Group 59, National Archives, Washington, D.C. A fuller exploration of these texts is contained in chapter two of my *Imagining Vietnam and America: Modernity and the Cultural Construction of the Cold War, 1919–1950* (Chapel Hill: University of North Carolina Press, forthcoming), from which the following discussion is drawn.

10. Thompson, *French Indo-China*, 42. At times, American observers and diplomats used the French terms "Tonkinese," "Annamite," and "Cochinchinese" to refer to Vietnamese living in northern, central, or southern Vietnam respectively. More commonly, however, they adopted the broader French term "Annamite" to refer to

the Vietnamese population as a whole. Context usually makes clear if "Annamite" is used in its broader or narrower sense. In quoted material, I retain these appelations to give a better sense of the flavor of this discourse.

11. Mona Gardner, *Menacing Sun* (London: John Murray, 1939), 30; Emerson, "Backwaters of Empire," 673; Thompson, *French Indo-China,* 283; Leland L. Smith, "An SOS in the Jungle of Indo-China," *Radio Broadcast* (May 1923): 44; and Thompson, *French Indo-China,* 43, 45, 51, 284.

12. Thompson, ibid., 259, 260, 44, 47, 252; Emerson, "Backwaters of Empire," 672; Harold J. Coolidge, Jr., and Theodore Roosevelt, *Three Kingdoms of Indo-China* (New York: Thomas Y. Cromwell Company, 1933), 71–74.

13. Gardner, *Menacing Sun,* 16; Thompson, *French Indo-China,* 47. See also Emerson, "Backwaters of Empire," 672; Marc T. Greene, "Shadows over Indo-China," *Asia* 35.11 (November 1935): 676; Gardner, *Menacing Sun,* 22. Vietnamese women, too, were the subject of objectified comment, particularly by male observers who either romanticized their "sinuous" or "supple" shapes and "seductive bosoms" or criticized their "doll-like—usually stupidly doll-like" beauty. See, for instance, Maynard Owen Williams, "By Motor Trail Across French Indo-China," *National Geographic* (October 1935): 503; Thomas Steep, "French Oppression in Indo-China," *American Mercury* 32.127 (July 1934): 330; and Wilbur Burton, "H.M. Bao Dai,"*Asia* 35.12 (December 1935): 723.

14. E. Luro, *Le pays d'Annam* (Paris: Ernest Leroux, 1897), 76–77. Other works in the French sinological tradition often cited by American observers include: Gustave Dumoutier, *Essais sur les Tonkinois* (Hanoi: Imprimerie d' Extrême-Orient 1908); Francis Garnier, *Voyages d'exploration en Indochine,* 2 vols. (Paris: Hachette 1873); Alfred Schreiner, *Les institutions Annamites en Basse-Cochinchine avant la conquête Française,* 3 vols. (Saigon: Claude & Co., 1900); and J. Silvestre, *L'empire d'Annam and et le peuple Annam* (Paris: Félix Alcan, 1889). American observers also drew upon the works of French essayists and journalists who popularized the sinological approach to Vietnam in the 1920s and 1930s, such as Albert de Pouvourville's *L'Annamite* (Paris: Éditions LaRose, 1932). Few scholars have systematically analyzed French writings on Vietnam or the connections between Orientalist writers and agents of French imperialism. Short introductions to the range of available French materials on Vietnam are John Cady, "Bibliographical Article: The Beginnings of French Imperialism in the Pacific Orient," *Journal of Modern History* 14.1 (March 1942): 71–87; and Jean Chesneaux, "French Historiography and the Evolution of Colonial Vietnam," in *Historians of South-East Asia,* ed. by D. G. E. Hall (London: Oxford University Press, 1961), 235–44. More complete bibliographical and descriptive guides to French colonial writings include: H. Cordier, *Bibliotheca Indosinica,* 4 vols. (Paris: Ernest Leroux 1912–15); Paul Boudet and Rémy Bourgeois, *Bibliographie de l'Indo-Chine française, 1913–1926* (Hanoi: Imprimerie d' Extrême-Orient 1929); and Louis Malleret, *L'Exotisme Indochinois dans la littérature français depuis 1860* (Paris: Larose, 1934). For one useful account that begins to analyze the nature of French discourse on Vietnam, see Pani-

vong Nordindr, *Phantasmatic Indochina: French Colonial Ideology in Architecture, Film and Literature* (Durham, N.C.: Duke University Press, 1996).

15. Thompson, *French Indo-China*, 19, 20, 27. See also Ennis, *French Policy*, 56–58; and W. Robert Moore, "Along the Old Mandarin Road of Indo-China," *National Georgraphic* (August 1931): 157, 180–81. Although appearing slightly after the onset of World War II, Alan H. Brodrick's travel narrative *Little China: The Annamite Lands* (London & New York: Oxford University Press, 1942) also focused on the centrality of Chinese cultural forms in Vietnam, arguing that the Vietnamese "have never pretended not to owe everything to China." The French view was also popularized by the accounts of French journalists published in the interwar American popular press. See, for instance, Alfred Meynard, "Sacrifice to Heaven and Earth," *Asia* 28.10 (October 1928): 799; Meynard, "Time's Fresh Budding in Annam," *Asia* 31.2 (February 1931): 105–7; Meynard, "Possessed Annamese on Pilgrimage," *Asia* 31.12 (December 1931): 785–87; and Achille Murat, "In 'The Purple Forbidden City' of Hue," *Asia* 27.5 (May 1927): 383–87, 427–29. The sinological approach to Vietnamese history and society persisted far beyond the interwar period, informing the major American interpretation of Vietnamese history published in the 1950s, Joseph Buttinger's *The Smaller Dragon: A Political History of Vietnam* (New York: Praeger, 1958). Only after 1970 did Western scholars begin to successfully challenge this interpretative framework, using Vietnamese sources to analyze indigenous perspectives on Vietnamese history. Notable examples of this pioneering work include: Keith Taylor, *The Birth of Vietnam* (Berkeley: University of California Press, 1983); John K. Whitmore, *Vietnam, Ho Quy Ly, and the Ming: 1371–1421* (New Haven, Conn.: Yale Center for Southeast Asian Studies, 1985); and Alexander Barton Woodside, *Vietnam and the China Model: A Comparative Study of Vietnamese and Chinese Government in the First Half of the Nineteenth Century* (Cambridge, Mass.: Harvard University Press, 1971).

16. Among the dozens of French works that favor this construction of Vietnamese masculinity, several were mentioned in the narratives of American observers in Vietnam, including Albert Challan de Belval, *Au Tonkin, 1884–1885: Nots, souvenirs et impressions* (Paris: Plon, 1904) and Charles D. M. Rollet de l'Isle, *Au Tonkin et dans les mers de Chine: Souvenirs et croquis, 1883–1885* (Paris: Plon, 1886). For an analysis of these French writings I am indebted to Frank Proschan, "Eunuch Mandarins, Effeminate 'Boys,' and 'Soldats Mamzelles': The Annamite as Androgyne", Unpublished Paper delivered in March 1996 at the Association for Asian Studies 49th Annual Meeting, Chicago.

17. Edward W. Said's *Orientalism* (New York: Vintage Books, 1979), of course, first directed scholarly attention to the significance of Orientalist constructions of non-Western societies, focusing on European and American writings on the Middle East. To date, scholars have not examined European studies of Southeast Asia from the colonial period, but several scholars have drawn upon and expanded Said's analytical framework to explore Western writings on South Asia, including Richard Inden, *Imagining India* (London: Basil Blackwell, 1990); John D. Rogers, "Colo-

nial Perceptions of Ethnicity and Culture in Early Nineteenth-Century Sri Lanka,"
in *Society and Ideology: Essays in South Asian History,* ed. by Peter Robb (Delhi:
Oxford University Press, 1993), 97–109; and Rogers, "Historical Images in the British Period," in *Sri Lanka: History and the Roots of Conflict,* ed. by Jonathan Spen-
cer (London: Routledge, 1990), 87–106.

18. Thompson, *French Indo-China,* 303, 161, 39, 294, 369–70, 24, 248; Gardner, *Menacing Sun* 16. For other examples, particularly on "Oriental" responses to French
conquest, see Ennis, *French Policy,* 20–51, passim.

19. Vietnam was often seen by interwar observers as inferior not only to China but in
relationship to other Southeast Asian societies as well. Mona Gardner's *Menacing
Sun* conveyed much more favorable impressions of Thailand, the Dutch East In-
dies, and British Malaya than of Vietnam, as did works appearing at the end of the
interwar period that were viewed as seminal American accounts of Southeast Asian
societies, such as Virginia Thompson, *Thailand: The New Siam* (New York: The
MacMillan Company, 1941); Amry Vanderbosch, *The Dutch East Indies* (Berkeley:
University of California Press, 1941); and Rupert Emerson, *Malaysia* (New York:
MacMillan, 1937). What appears to separate other Southeast Asian societies from
Vietnam in these accounts is not so much a superior indigenous culture but a belief
that the Thai monarchy and Dutch and British colonialists were more skilled than
the French in following the pracitices that Americans believed should best guide
colonial policies aimed at the development of indigenous peoples. The assumptions underlying this belief are discussed later in the essay.

20. Thompson, *French Indo-China,* 19, 239.

21. See, for instance, Ann L. Stoler, "Making Empire Respectable: The Politics of Race
and Sexual Morality in 20th-Century Colonial Cultures," *American Ethnologist*
16.4 (November 1989): 634–660; Margaret Strobel, "Gender and Race in the 19th
and 20th Century British Empire," in *Becoming Visible: Women in European History,* ed. R. Bridenthal, et al. (Boston: Houghton Mifflin, 1987): 375–96; Helen
Callaway, *Gender, Culture and Empire: European Women in Colonial Nigeria*
(London: Macmillan Press, 1987); John Butcher, *The British in Malaya, 1880–
1941: The Social History of a European Community in Colonial Southeast Asia*
(Kuala Lumpur: Oxford University Press, 1979); and George Mosse, *Nationalism
and Sexuality* (Madison: University of Wisconsin Press, 1985). Also suggestive here
are Edward Said's more recent claims for the overlapping and intertwined nature
of the encounter between the West and non-West in his *Culture and Imperialism*
(New York: Alfred A. Knopf, 1993).

22. See Warren I. Susman, "The Culture of the Thirties" and "Culture and Commitment," in *Culture as History: The Transformation of American Society in the Twentieth Century* (New York: Pantheon, 1984), 150–210; and Frederick Lewis Allen,
Since Yesterday (New York: Harper & Brothers Publishers, 1939), 129–35.

23. Edmund Wilson, *American Jitters: A Year of the Slump* (New York: Scribner's Sons,
1932); Sherwood Anderson, *Puzzled America* (New York: Charles Scribner's Sons,
1935). Selections from the more than sixty thousand images that made up the Farm
Security Administration project were widely disseminated in published works in

the 1930s including Archibald MacLeish, *Land of the Free* (New York: Harcourt, Brace & Company, 1938). On the emergence of this documentary literature in the United States in the 1930s, see William Stott, *Documentary Expression and Thirties America* (New York: Oxford University Press, 1973), and Nicholas Natanson, *The Black Image in the New Deal: The Politics of FSA Photography* (Knoxville: The University of Tennessee Press, 1992). I am indebted to Chris Appy for drawing my attention to the potential utility of these works. American observers of Vietnam may also have been influenced by British authors who chronicled English poverty in the 1930s, a development that suggests the interest in Depression-era poverty was an international, or at least Anglo-American, phenomenon. See, for instance, George Orwell, *The Road to Wigan Pier* (London: Victor Gollancz, 1937); and J. B. Priestley, *English Journey* (London: W. Heineman, 1934).

24. Thompson, *French Indo-China*, 43–44. See also Gardner, *Menacing Sun*, 17–16; Josephine Hope Westervelt, *The Green Gods* (New York: The Christian Alliance Publishing Company 1927), 17–18, 30–31, 66–69.

25. Useful discussions of the interconnections between race, manifest destiny, and American imperialism include: Reginald Horsman, *Race and Manifest Destiny: The Origins of American Radical Anglo-Saxonism* (Cambridge, Mass.: Harvard University Press, 1981); Michael H. Hunt, *Ideology and U.S. Foreign Policy* (New Haven, Conn.: Yale University Press, 1987), 46–91; Walter L. William, "U.S. Indian Policy and the Debate over Philippine Annexation," *Journal of American History* 66 (1980): 810–31; David Healy, *US Expansionism: The Imperialist Urge in the 1890s* (Madison: The University of Wisconsin Press, 1970), 127–43; Healy, *Drive to Hegemony: The United States in the Caribbean, 1898–1917* (Madison: The University of Wisconsin Press, 1988), 58–76; Glenn A. May, *Social Engineering in the Philippines: the Aims, Execution and Impact of American Colonial Policy, 1900–1913* (Westport, Conn.: Greenwood Press, 1980), 9–12; Peter W. Stanley, *A Nation in the Making: The Philippines and the United States, 1899–1921* (Cambridge, Mass.: Harvard University Press, 1974), 163–67; and Robert W. Rydell, *All the World's a Fair* (Chicago: University of Chicago Press, 1984).

26. Paul Giran, *Psychologie du peuple Annamite* (Paris: Ernest Leroux, 1904). For Virginia Thompson's reliance on Giran's analysis, see Thompson, *French Indo-China*, 41–43.

27. See, for instance, John Higham, *Strangers in the Land: Patterns of American Nativism, 1860–1925*, 2d ed. (New Brunswick, N.J.: Rutgers University Press, 1988), 264–330.

28. Ellsworth Huntingon, *Civilization and Climate* (New Haven, Conn.: Yale University Press, 1924), 417–28. Several surveys of scholarly writings on race and climate published in the interwar period also suggest the continuing importance of these ideas in intellectual and policy-making circles. See, for instance, Ellsworth Huntington, *The Character of Races* (New York: Charles Scribner's Sons, 1924); Franklin Thomas, *The Environmental Basis of Society* (New York: The Century Co., 1925); and Robert DeC. Ward, "The Literature of Climatology," *Annals of the Association of American Geographers* (March 1931): 34–51.

29. For American perceptions of French administrators and *colons*, see Steep, "French Oppression in Indo-China," 328–30. See also Ennis, *French Policy*, 59–61; William Henry Chamberlin, "A New Deal for French Indo-China?," *Asia* 37.7 (July 1937): 478; Thompson, *French Indo-China*, 86–88, 419–22, 427–42. On American criticisms of French inability to fully develop the agricultural export market, see Thompson, ibid., 109–43, 173–78; Ennis, *French Policy*, 111–134.

On the inefficiencies of the French colonial infrastructure, see Thompson, *French Indo-China*, 205–13; Ennis, *French Policy*, 126–27; Gardner, *Menacing Sun*, 88, 17. American criticism that the French "couldn't make the trains run on time" was also commonplace among travelers to Vietnam in the 1920s; see, for instance, Coolidge, *Three Kingdom*, 35–36; H. C. Flower, Jr., "On the Trail of Lord Tiger," *Asia* 20.9 (October 1920): 35–36. Americans were also critical of the French tendency to use colonial funds to build what were termed "lavish structures" to house the colonial administration in Hanoi and Saigon. See, for instance, Thompson, *French Indo-China*, 219–20; Steep, "French Oppression in Indo-China," 330 and Emerson, "Backwaters of Empire," 690.

On the reporting of American consuls from Saigon in the 1930s concerning French tariffs and economic policy in Vietnam, see: Henry I. Waterman to Department of State, "Tariff Situation in French Indo-China," May 23, 1930, 651G.113/121, RG 59; Waterman to Department of State, "Propaganda against American Automobiles," January 27, 1931, 651G.1112/11, RG 59; Waterman to Department of State, June 10, 1931, File 800-Saigon-1931, RG 84; and American Consul, Saigon to Department of State, July 7, 1938, RG 59. For the commentary of other American observers on the tariff and its impact, see Thompson, *French Indo-China*, 198–205; Ennis, *French Policy*, 135–37, Wilbur Burton, "French Imperialism in China," *Current History* 39 (January 1934): 428–31; Steep, "French Oppression in Indo-China," 330; Greene, "Shadows Over Indo-China," 680, 682; and Herbert Ingram Priestly, *France Overseas: A Study of Modern Imperialism* (New York: D. Appleton–Century Company, 1938), 234.

30. On the lack of French efforts to include Vietnamese elites in colonial governance, see Gardner, *Menacing Sun*, 34–35; Quincy Roberts (American Consul, Saigon) to Department of State, January 31, 1936, 851G.008/22, RG 84; American Consul, Saigon to Department of State, May 25, 1937, 851G.00, RG 59; Ennis, *French Policy*, 71–72; Thompson, *French Indo-China*, 79–87. On the American criticism of the French colonial tax burden, see Henry I. Waterman to Hester (U.S. Trade Commissioner in Manila), December 1930, File 630-Saigon-1930, RG 84; Thompson, *French Indo-China*, 182–98; Ennis, *French Policy*, 64–65; Greene, "Shadows Over Indo-China," 682; and Priestly, *France Overseas*, 230.

31. On American views of French labor polices, see Chamberlin, "A New Deal," 476–78; "Stepchildren: Indochinese, Forgotten of France, Want Their New Deal, Too," *Literary Digest* 123 (July 3, 1937): 14; Ennis, *French Policy*, 155–61; Thompson, *French Indo-China*, 143–62. On American criticism of French educational policies in Vietnam, see: Steep, "French Oppression in Indo-China," 332; Thompson, *French Indo-China*, 284–307; Ennis, *French Policy*, 169–75. On French medi-

cal policies in Vietnam, see Thompson, *French Indo-China,* 277–83; Ennis, *French Policy,* 149–55.

32. For insightful discussions of inter-European imperialist rivalries and the ways in which colonial norms shaped European critiques of colonialism, see Said, *Orientalism,* 201–25, and his *Culture and Imperialism,* 191–209.

33. Dwight F. Davis (Governor General, Philippine Islands) to Patrick J. Hurley (U.S. Secretary of War), July 15, 1931, File 18868–55, Entry 5, Records of the Bureau of Insular Affairs, RG 350, National Archives. I am indebted to Anne Foster for bringing this document to my attention.

34. Ennis, *French Policy,* 52. See also Ennis, 6–10, 52–72; Priestly, *France Overseas,* 226–32, 337–39; Chamberlin, "A New Deal," 476–78; Thompson, *French Indo-China,* 243, 247–48, 252–53, 294, 399–402, 494.

35. Ennis, *French Policy,* 61–62, 71–72, 176–77; Thompson:, *French Indo-China,* 297–99, 482–85; Gardner, *Menacing Sun,* 34–5; Greene, "Shadows Over Indo-China," 683; Chamberlin, "A New Deal," 478; "Stepchildren: Indo-Chinese, Forgotten of France, Want Their New Deal, Too," 14–15; Quincy Roberts (American Consul, Saigon) to Department of State, January 31, 1936, 851G.008/22, RG 84; American Consul, Saigon to Department of State, January 16, 1937, 851G.00/01, RG 59; and American Consul, Saigon to Department of State, May 25, 1937, 851G.00, RG 59.

36. Thompson, *French Indo-China,* 313, 485–93; Gardner, *Menacing Sun,* 24; Ennis, *French Policy,* 191–92; Foster Rhea Dulles, "French Problems in Indo-China," *Current History* 26 (May 1927): 202; Gardner, *Menacing Sun,* 55; Chamberlin, "A New Deal," 478.

37. On the indigenous nature of Vietnamese anticolonialism and nationalism, see Hue-Tam Ho Tai, *Radicalism and the Origins of the Vietnamese Revolution* (Cambridge, Mass.: Harvard University Press, 1992); Huynh Kim Khanh, *Vietnamese Communism, 1925–1945* (Ithaca, N.Y.: Cornell University Press, 1982); David G. Marr, *Vietnamese Anticolonialism, 1885–1925* (Berkeley: University of California Press, 1971); and his *Vietnamese Tradition on Trial, 1920–1945* (Berkeley: University of California Press, 1981).

38. Ennis, *French Policy,* 185; Henry I. Waterman (American Consul, Saigon) to Department of State, May 16, 1930, 851G.001B/3, RG 59; Thompson, *French Indo-China,* 489–90. Waterman's reporting was criticized within the State Department, with his superiors in the Western European and Far Eastern Divisions arguing that he lacked "discrimination" and that "the French authorities have been stuffing him with a lot of hot air about the communistic menace." But the department did not replace Waterman nor send him instructions to revise his reporting. See John F. Carter (Division of Western European Affairs, WE) to Paul T. Culbertson (WE), Ransford S. Miller (Division of Far Eastern Affairs, FE) and Stanley K. Hornbeck (FE), June 16, 1931, 851G.00B/12, RG 59. For other analyses that focus on the role of external forces in Vietnamese nationalism, see *New York Times,* February 15, 1930; Dulles, "French Problems," 198; "Soviet Light in Asia," *Literary Digest* 108 (February 21, 1931): 14; "France's Colonial Spot of Trouble," *Literary Digest*

110 (August 1, 1931): 15; Greene, "Shadows over Indo-China," 679; Percy Standing, "French Progress in Indo-China," *Contemporary Age* 139 (April 1931): 508;
Priestly, *France Overseas*, 235–37, 243.

39. For penetrating discussions of Japanese wartime occupation of Vietnam and its
impact of French colonial control, see David G. Marr, *Vietnam 1945: The Quest
for Power* (Berkeley: University of California Press, 1995), ch. 1; and Stein Tønnes-
son, *The Vietnamese Revolution of 1945: Roosevelt, Ho Chi Minh and de Gaulle in
a World at War* (London: Sage Publications for the International Peace Research
Institute in Oslo, 1991), chs. 1 and 6.

40. Roosevelt-Stalin Meeting, November 28, 1943, *Foreign Relations of the United
States [FRUS]: The Conferences at Cairo and Tehran*, 1943, 485. See also Minutes
of the Pacific War Council, May 23, 1942, December 9, 1942, and March 17, 1943,
Folder: "Naval Aide's Files, Pacific War #2," Box 168, Map Room File, Franklin D.
Roosevelt Papers as President, 1941–1945, Franklin D. Roosevelt Library; Memo-
randum of Conversation by Harry Hopkins, March 27, 1943, *FRUS 1943, Volume
III: The British Commonwealth, Eastern Europe, The Far East* (Washington, D.C.:
U.S. Government Printing Office, 1963), 39; FDR to the Secretary of State, Janu-
ary 24, 1944, *FRUS: The Conferences at Cairo and Tehran* 1943, 872; Roosevelt-
Stalin Meeting, February 8, 1945, *FRUS: The Conferences at Malta and Yalta, 1945*
(Washington, D.C.: U.S. Government Printing Office, 1955), 770.

41. Minutes of the Pacific War Council, May 23, 1942, Folder: "Naval Aide's Files,
Pacific War #2," Box 168, Map Room File, Franklin D. Roosevelt Papers as President, 1941–1945, Franklin D. Roosevelt Library. The recollections of participants
in the May 1954 Princeton Seminar, which gathered together wartime and Cold
War policymakers such as Dean Acheson, Paul Nitze, and W. Averell Harriman,
also suggest that Roosevelt's critique of French rule in Vietnam was less an attack
on colonialism than on France's inadequacies as a colonial power. In the printed
transcript of the May 15 session of the seminar, an unidentified voice claims: "I
think he [FDR] was much more amenable to the Dutch going back into Indonesian
[sic] than he was to the French going back into Indo-China," to which Dean
Acheson added, "I think he had a higher view of Queen Wilhelmina." See Transcript of May 15 1954, Folder Title: "Reading Copy III: Princeton Seminars May
15–16, 1954 (Folder 2)," Box 84, Papers of Dean Acheson, Harry S. Truman Library, Independence, Missouri, Reel 5, Track 1, Page 8.

42. Minutes of the Pacific War Council, March 17, 1943, Folder: "Naval Aide's Files,
Pacific War #2," Box 168, Map Room File, Franklin D. Roosevelt Papers as Presi-
dent, 1941–1945, Franklin D. Roosevelt Library. See also Edward R. Stettinius,
Jr., *Roosevelt and the Russians* (Garden City, N.Y.: Doubleday & Company, Inc.,
1949), 237; and Elliott Roosevelt, *As He Saw It* (New York: Duell, Sloan and
Pearce, 1946), 115, 165, 251.

43. Roosevelt-Stalin Meeting, February 8, 1945, *FRUS: The Conferences at Malta and
Yalta, 1945*, 770. The sources of FDR's limited knowledge of Vietnamese reinforce
a sense of the president's reliance on the Orientalist paradigm to frame his perceptions. At meetings of the Pacific War Council that included discussions of Indo-

china, Roosevelt often deferred to Chinese foreign minister T. V. Soong to supply the most basic details of Vietnam's population and social organization. Beginning in 1942, Roosevelt did receive regular reports on conditions in Indochina from William J. Donovan, the director of the Office of Strategic Services (OSS). But these reports, which usually focused on Japanese, French, British, and Chinese policies in the region, seldom provided the historical or sociological information on the Vietnamese that OSS field officers were sending on to Washington. For FDR's reliance on Soong at the Pacific War Council, see Minutes of the Pacific War Council, May 23, 1942, and July 21, 1943, Folder: "Naval Aide's Files, Pacific War #2," Box 168, Map Room File, Franklin D. Roosevelt Papers as President, 1941–1945, Franklin D. Roosevelt Library. The majority of Donovan's reports to FDR on Indochina from 1942 to 1945 are contained in Folder: "OSS Report," Boxes 149–152, President's Secretary's Files, 1933–1945, Franklin D. Roosevelt Papers as President, 1941–1945, Franklin D. Roosevelt Library; a few additional reports from 1945 are contained in Folder: "OSS Numbered Bulletin Jan-Apr 45," Box 73, Map Room File, Franklin D. Roosevelt Papers as President, 1941–1945.

It is tempting to believe that Roosevelt's perceptions of the Vietnamese and other Southeast Asian societies might have also been influenced by experiences of Theodore Roosevelt, Jr., Eleanor Roosevelt's first cousin. Theodore traveled to Vietnam in 1928–29 as a coleader of the Kelley-Roosevelt-Field Museum. He also served as the American governor-general to the Philippines in 1932–33. Theodore, however, is unlikely to have had any significant influence in shaping FDR's perceptions. By the early 1920s, a feud between the Oyster Bay and Hyde Park branches of the Roosevelt family pitted Theodore against Franklin and Eleanor. Theodore campaigned vigorously against FDR's vice-presidential bid in 1920. Eleanor's very public opposition to Theodore's campaign for New York governor in 1924 permanently severed any future connection with him. The similarities between FDR and Theodore's perceptions of Vietnamese society more probably reflect the prevailing Orientalist constructions of Asian society. On the Roosevelt feud, see Blanche Wiesen Cook, *Eleanor Roosevelt, Volume One 1884–1933* (New York: Viking, 1992), 278, 351–54; Kenneth S. Davis, *FDR: The Beckoning of Destiny 1882–1928* (New York: G. P. Putnam's Sons, 1972), 621, 771–72; Geoffrey C. Ward, *A First-Class Temperament: The Emergence of Franklin Roosevelt* (New York: Harper & Row, 1989): 532, 540, 700–701.

44. Text of "Radio Address by President Roosevelt, 15 November 1942" contained in appendix to "United States Policy Regarding Dependent Territories, 1933–44 (CDA-246)," February 20, 1945, Box 125, Records of the Advisory Committee on Post-War Foreign Policy (Harley Notter Files, 1939–45), Record Group 59, National Archives of the United States, Washington, D.C.

45. Ibid.

46. Roosevelt-Stalin Meeting, November 28, 1943, *FRUS: The Conferences at Cairo and Tehran*, 1943, 485; FDR Press Conference (#992), February 23, 1945, in *Complete Press Conferences of Franklin D. Roosevelt*, Volume 25 (New York: Da Capo Press, 1972), 70.

47. The place of the Subcommittee on Territorial Problems in the complicated struc-
    ture of the State Department's postwar planning organization is clearly outlined in
    Postwar Foreign Policy Preparation 1939–1945 (Washington, D.C. U.S. Govern-
    ment Printing Office, 1949), 118–19.

48. Biographical information on Kenneth P. Landon is contained in *Biographic Regis-
    ter of the Department of State: September 1, 1944* (Washington, D.C.: U.S. Govern-
    ment Printing Office, n.d.), 125. Landon returned from Thailand in the late 1930s
    to undertake a doctoral program at Cornell University. He became an analyst for
    the Office of Strategic Services just before Pearl Harbor and joined the State De-
    partment in 1942. His writings on Thailand include: *Siam in Transition: A Brief
    Survey of Cultural Trends in the Five Year Revolution of 1932* (London: Oxford
    University Press, 1939) and *The Chinese in Thailand* (London: Oxford University
    Press, 1941). Landon's wife, Margaret, is the author of *Anna and the King* (London:
    George C. Harrup, 1952), the basis for the Broadway musical *The King and I.*
        Amry Vandenbosch's writings on the Dutch East Indies were published in such
    journals as *Amerasia, Asia, Far Eastern Survey,* and *Pacific Affairs.* His best known
    work is *The Dutch East Indies: Its Government, Problems, and Politics* (Berkeley:
    University of California Press, 1942). Melvin Knight's critiques of French colonial-
    ism emerge in his *Morocco as a French Economic Venture: A Study of Open Door
    Imperialism* (New York: D. Appleton–Century Company, 1937).

49. Vandenbosch and Knight's perceptions of French colonial rule and Vietnamese
    society closely followed the views of interwar American observers of Vietnam. In
    several cases, the conclusions of such writers as Virginia Thompson and Thomas
    Ennis are directly incorporated into their reports. See, for instance, "Indo-China:
    Political and Economic Factors (T-398)," November 2, 1943, Records of the Advi-
    sory Committee on Post-War Foreign Policy (Harley Notter Files, 1939–45), Re-
    cord Group 59, 5.

50. T Minutes 56, November 11, 1943, 1–2; T Minutes 55, November 5, 1943, Sub-
    committee on Territorial Problems, Division of Political Studies, Box 59, Records
    of the Advisory Committee on Post-War Foreign Policy (Harley Notter Files,
    1939–45), 2–3.

51. Indochina: Political and Economic Problems (T-398), 6; T Minutes 55, November
    5, 1943, 2; Economic Relations of Indo-China (T-283), n.d., Division of Economic
    Studies, Box 59, Records of the Advisory Committee on Post-War Foreign Policy
    (Harley Notter Files, 1939–45), RG 59.

52. Indochina: Political and Economic Problems (T-398), 4; T Minutes 55, November
    5, 1943, 2–3.

53. T Minutes 55, November 5, 1943, 13; T Minutes 56, November 11,1943, 5.

54. T Minutes 56, November 11, 1943, 1; T Minutes 55, November 5, 1943, 1, 3–4.

55. T Minutes 55, November 5, 1943, 3–4; T Minutes 5, April 11, 1942, Division of
    Special Research, U.S. Department of State, Box 59, Reocrds of the Advisory
    Committee on Post-War Foreign Policy (Harley Notter Files, 1939–45), RG 59, 5.

56. Indo-China: Political and Economic Problems (T-398), November 2, 1943, 4–5.
    See also T Minutes 55, November 5, 1943, 3.

57. French governor-general Albert Sarraut's 1919 speech on the steps of the Temple of Literature in Hanoi was among the most dramatic efforts to employ the metaphors of father and children; the text of the speech is contained in April 27, 1919, *Tribune Indigène*. For a discussion of the familial language used by French colonial officials in Vietnam, see Hue-Tam Ho Tai, *Radicalism and the Origins of the Vietnamese Revolution* (Cambridge, Mass.: Harvard University Press, 1992): 37, 142–43. On American uses of a similar rhetoric, see Stuart Creighton Miller, *"Benevolent Assimilation": The American Conquest of the Philippines, 1899–1903* (New Haven, Conn.: Yale University Press, 1982).

58. See, for instance, Lloyd Gardner, *Approaching Vietnam* (New York: W. W. Norton & Company, 1988), 21–53; Gary R. Hess, "Franklin Roosevelt and Indochina," *Journal of American History* 59.2 (September 1972): 353–68; Hess, *The United States' Emergence as a Southeast Asian Power, 1940–1950* (New York: Columbia University Press, 1987), 47–158; Walter LaFeber, "Roosevelt, Churchill, and Indochina: 1942–45," *American Historical Review* 80.5 (December 1975): 1277–95; and Christopher Thorne, "Indochina and Anglo-American Relations, 1942–1945," *Pacific Historical Review* 45.1 (February 1976): 73–96.

59. "Memorandum of Conversations between Bullitt and Ogburn," May 29, 1947, Box 4, Confidential Records of the Saigon Consulate, Records of the Department of State Foreign Service Posts, 1936–54, Record Group 84, National Records Center, Suitland, Maryland; Reed to Marshall, July 11, 1947, and July 24, 1947; O'Sullivan to Marshall, July 21, 1947; Caffrey to Marshall, July 31, 1947; *Foreign Relations of the United States [FRUS] 1947, VI: The Far East* (Washington, D.C.: U.S. Government Printing Office, 1972), 114–15, 124–25, 121–22, 128; Folsom to Lacy, March 9, 1950, *FRUS 1950, VI: East Asia and the Pacific* (Washington, D.C.: U.S. Government Printing Office, 1976), 758. For a fuller analysis of these discussions, see my "An Improbable Opportunity: America and the Democratic Republic of Vietnam's 1947 Initiative," in *The Vietnam War: Vietnamese and American Perspectives*, ed. Jayne S. Werner and Luu Doan Huynh (Armonk, N.Y.: M. E. Sharpe, 1993), 13–16.

60. For an insightful analysis of Vietnamese Communist military strategy in the war against the French and the primacy of indigenous factors in explaining its increasing success after 1949, see Greg Lockhart, *Nation in Arms: The Origins of the People's Army of Vietnam* (Wellington: Allen & Unwin Australia Pty Ltd, 1989), chs. 5 and 6.

61. Harold R. Isaacs, *Scratches on Our Minds: American Views of China and India* (Armonk, N.Y.: M. E. Sharpe, 1980; reprint of 1958 edition), 227, 229, 238. For a discussion of the transformation of American perceptions of Chinese military capabilities during the Korean War, see Isaacs, *Scratches*, 225–38.

62. Central Intelligence Agency, "National Intelligence Estimate, Indochina: Current Situation and Probable Developments," December 29, 1950; "Analysis Prepared for the Joint Chiefs of Staff by the Joint Strategic Survey Committee," November 17, 1950; *FRUS 1950*, VI, 961, 951. For the sustained discussion among American policymakers in the fall of 1950 on the role of China and the failure of French

military tactics and strategy as the explanation for Vietnamese Communist military victories, see Rusk to Secretary of State, September 11, 1950; Heath to Secretary of State, October 15 and November 1, 1950; Memorandum of the Joint Chiefs of Staff, November 28, 1950; *FRUS 1950*, VI, 878, 894, 914–17, 946. American policymakers offered the same explanatory variables during the spring of 1954 to account for the likely Vietnamese military victory over the French at Dien Bien Phu, a development which effectively brought an end to French rule in Vietnam. See, for instance, Memorandum of Conversation, April 4, 1954; Dillon to Department of State, April 5, 1954; Memorandum of Discussion, National Security Council, April 6, 1954, *FRUS 1952–1954, Vol. XIII, Pt. 2: Indochina* (Washington, D.C.: U.S. Government Printing Office, 1982), 1233, 1237, 1251–66.

63. Reed to Secretary of State Marshall, June 14, 1947, *FRUS 1947, VI: The Far East* (Washington, D.C.: U.S. Government Printing Office, 1972), 103–5; Edwin C. Rendall (Hanoi) to Secretary of State Marshall, June 7, 1948, 851G.01/6-748.

64. Marshall to Embassy in France, July 3, 1948; Marshall to Abbott (Saigon); Marshall to Embassy in France, August 30, 1948, *FRUS 1948, VI: The Far East and Australasia* (Washington, D.C.: U.S. Government Printing Office), 30, 38, 40; and Acheson to Embassy in France, February 25, 1949; Bruce to Secretary of State, June 29, 1949; Acheson to Embassy in France, December 1, 1949, *FRUS 1949, VII, Part 1, The Far East and Australasia* (Washington, D.C.: U.S. Government Printing Office, 1975), 8, 66, 101–2. See also Caffery to Secretary of State, July 9, 1948; Abbott to Marshall, August 28, 1948, *FRUS 1948*, VI, 33, 39; Acheson to Consulate General at Saigon, May 10, 1949; Acheson to Consulate General at Saigon, May 20, 1949; Memorandum by the Department of State to the French Foreign Office enclosed in Butterworth to Bruce, June 6, 1919; Webb to Embassy in India, June 18, 1949, *FRUS 1949, VII, Part 1*, 24, 28–29, 39–45, 60.

65. Acheson to Legation at Saigon, September 1, 1950, Heath (Saigon) to Secretary of State, Acheson to Legation at Saigon, October 30, 1950, and November 28, 1950, Central Intelligence Agency, "National Intelligence Estimate, Indochina: Current Situation and Probable Developments," December 29, 1950, *FRUS 1950*, VI: 868–69, 894, 915, 939, 960.

66. Strum (Hanoi) to Department of State, June 10, 1952, *FRUS 1952–1954, Volume XIII, Part 1: Indochina* (Washington, D.C.: U.S. Government Printing Office, 1982), 177–78. American views on the clash between French and American perspectives on nation building emerge in Indochina Subject Files: 1950–54, Office of Far Eastern Operations, Records of U.S. Foreign Assistance Agencies, 1948–61, Record Group 469, National Records Center; Subject Files: 1950–54, Office of the Director, Mission to Vietnam, RG 469; Memos Sent by Dr. W. W. Winklestein (Regional Director 1952–53), Hanoi Office, Mission to Vietnam, RG 469; Subject Files of J. P. Guttinger (Assistant Agricultural Reform Specialist, 1951–57), Agricultural and Natural Resources Division, Mission to Vietnam, RG 469; "Southeast Asia Files," Papers of John F. Melby, Harry S. Truman Library, Independence, Missouri; "Vietnam Files," Papers of James P. Henrick, Harry S. Truman Library; Records of the French Desk 1941–1955, U.S. Department of State, Record Group 59, National Archives; Records of the Office of Western European Affairs, 1941–

1954, U.S. Department of State, RG 59, National Archives. For an insightful analysis of the American side in these conflicts, see George C. Herring, "Franco-American Conflict in Indochina, 1950–54" in *Dien Bien Phu and the Crisis of Franco-American Relations, 1954–1955*, ed. Lawrence S. Kaplan and Denise Artaud (Wilmington, Del.: SR Books, 1990), 29–48. French views emerge in: "Aide Américaine," Dossier 45, Fonds Conseiller Politique, Dépôt des Archives d'Outre Mer, Archives Nationales, Aix-en-Provence, France; "US Rapports," Dossiers 49 & 57, Fonds Conseiller Diplomatique, Dépôt des Archives d'Outre Mer; "Aide Américaine, Dossier 201-598, and "Comité Franco-Amérique," Dossier 189-566, Fonds Haut-Commissariat de France en Indochine, Dépôt des Archives d'Outre Mer; and "Aid Américaine," Série Asie-Oceanie 1944–1955: Indochine, Archives du Ministère des Affaires Étrangères Diplomatiques, Paris, France.

67. Collins to Dulles, March 29, 1955, Confidential U.S. State Department Central Files: Indochina Internal Affairs, 1955–59, Record Group 59, National Archives, Washington, D.C.

68. Collins to Dulles, April 10, 1955, 757G.00/4-1055, Collins to Dulles, March 22, 1955, 757G.00/3-2255. See also Kidder to Dulles, February 10, 757G.00/2-955; and Kidder to Dulles, February 8, 1955, 757G.00/2-855; RG 59.

69. William Butler Yeats, "The Second Coming," in *W. B. Yeats: The Poems*, ed. Richard J. Tinnerman (New York: The MacMillan Publishing Company, 1983), 187.

70. For a thoughtful discussion of the ways in which modernity sparked both uneasiness and order building among American policymakers throughout this century, see Frank Ninkovich, *Modernity and Power: A History of the Domino Theory in the Twentieth Century* (Chicago: University of Chicago Press, 1994). On the cultural dimension of American interwar visions of international order in Europe, see Akira Iriye, *The Cambridge History of American Foreign Relations, Vol. III: The Globalizing of America, 1913–1945* (Cambridge: Cambridge University Press, 1993), chs. 5–7; Frank Costigliola, *Awkward Dominion: American Political, Economic, and Cultural Relations with Europe, 1919–1933* (Ithaca, N.Y.: Cornell University Press, 1984), chs. 4–6; and Emily Rosenberg, *Spreading the American Dream: American Economic and Cultural Expansion, 1890–1945* (New York: Hill & Wang, 1982).

71. For a probing and original consideration of American liberal order building in the early Cold War period, see Robert Latham, *The Liberal Moment: Modernity, Security, and the Making of Postwar International Order* (New York: Columbia University Press, 1997).

72. One important exception is Andrew J. Rotter, "Gender Relations, Foreign Relations: The United States and South Asia, 1947–1964," *Journal of American History* 81.2 (September 1994): 518–42.

Adoption and the Cold War Commitment to Asia

1. James Michener, "Blunt Truths About Asia," *Life*, June 4, 1951, 96.

2. George Kennan, "Memorandum by the Director of the Policy Planning Staff to Mr. Robert G. Hooker, Staff Member," *Foreign Relations of the United States*,

1949, Vol. I (Washington, D.C.: Government Printing Office, 1976), 404–5. On policymakers' doubts about Americans' willingness to sustain the Cold War, see Guy Oakes, *The Imaginary War: Civil Defense and American Cold War* Culture (New York: Oxford University Press, 1994), ch. 1.

3. NSC 48/5, *Foreign Relations of the United States, 1951, Vol. VI* (Washington, D.C.: Government Printing Office, 1978); A. E. Zimmerman, "A Sense of Responsibility," in *Collective Security,* ed. Marina S. Finkelstein and Lawrence S. Finkelstein (San Francisco: Chandler Publishing, 1966), 241; Roland N. Stromber, *Collective Security and American Foreign Policy* (New York: Frederick A. Praeger, 1963); Frank Darling, *Thailand and the United States* (Washington: Public Affairs Press, 1965), 104; John F. Kennedy, "America's Stake in Vietnam," *Vital Speeches,* August 1956, 618.

4. Loy Henderson, "The United States and Asia," *Vital Speeches,* March 1950, 460.

5. Walter LaFeber, *The American Age: United States Foreign Policy at Home and Abroad* (New York: W. W. Norton, 1989, 1994), 512. On the role of culture in constructing a sense of political obligation, see Robert Westbrook, "'I Want a Girl, Just Like the Girl that Married Harry James': American Women and the Problem of Political Obligation in World War II," *American Quarterly,* (December 1990): 587–614.

6. On the role of education and participation in the process of establishing hegemony, see Michael Denning, *The Cultural Front: The Laboring of American Culture in the Twentieth Century* (New York: Verso, 1996), 63.

7. Dean Acheson, "Relations of the Peoples of the United States and the Peoples of Asia," *Vital Speeches,* January 1950, 238.

8. Dwight Macdonald, "A Theory of Mass Culture," in *Mass Culture: The Popular Arts in America,* ed. Bernard Rosenberg and David Manning White (Glencoe, Ill.: Free Press, 1957), 59–73; Irving Howe, "This Age of Conformity," *Partisan Review,* (January-February 1954): 7–33; Dwight Macdonald, "Masscult & Midcult," *Partisan Review,* (Spring 1960); Leslie Fiedler, *Waiting for the End* (New York: Stein and Day, 1964), 60–61.

9. Joseph Wood Krutch, "Introduction," *The Saturday Review Treasury,* ed. John Haverstick and the Editors of *The Saturday Review,* (New York: Simon and Schuster, 1957), xxi. On high literary culture of the 1950s, see Richard Ohmann, "A Case Study in Canon Formation: Reviewers, Critics, and *The Catcher in the Rye,*" in *Politics of Letters* (Middletown, Conn.: Wesleyan University Press, 1987). I take the idea of a "global imaginary" from Michael Denning, *Cover Stories: Narrative and Ideology in the British Spy Thriller* (London: Routledge and Kegan Paul, 1987) and *The Cultural Front.*

10. Lewis Erenberg, "Things to Come: Swing Bands, Bebop, and the Rise of Postwar Jazz Scene," and Erika Doss, "The Art of Cultural Politics: From Regionalism to Abstract Expressionism," in *Recasting America: Culture and Politics in the Age of the Cold War,* ed. Lary May (Chicago: University of Chicago Press, 1989). Andrew Ross, in *No Respect: Intellectuals and Popular Culture* (New York: Routledge, 1989), discusses the connection between Popular Front and middlebrow culture,

as did many of the New York intellectuals of the 1950s who condemned middle-brow as "Stalinist," but he fails to note the thoroughly anti-Communist nature of much middlebrow culture.

11. Cousins obituary, New York *Times*, December 1, 1990, 31; Henry Seidel Canby quoted in Edward E. Chielens, ed., *American Literary Magazines: The Twentieth Century*, (Westport, Conn.: Greenwood Press, 1992), 301; Mark Starr, "The Coming Revolution in Adult Education," *Saturday Review*, February 8, 1947, 7; Harrison Smith, "Take It Easier," *Saturday Review*, July 20, 1946.

12. Starr, "The Coming Revolution," 7; Stephen Duggan, "Education Under the New Order," *Saturday Review*, September 15, 1945; Norman Cousins, "The Grand Commitment,"*Saturday Review*, May 26, 1956.

13. Norman Cousins, "They Love Us for the Wrong Reasons," *Saturday Review*, January 19, 1952; Cousins, "Tomoko Nakabayashi of the Maidens," *Saturday Review*, June 9, 1956.

14. Henry Luce, "The American Century," *Life*, February 1941; Andrew Rotter, *The Path to Vietnam: Origins of the American Commitment to Southeast Asia* (Ithaca, N.Y.: Cornell University Press, 1987), 108.

15. The Advertising Council in 1952 sponsored "The American Roundtable," a group of nine business, labor, and education leaders, supported by the Ford Foundation and John D. Rockefeller III , whose stated purpose was to "develop a restatement, in modern terms, of the ideals, beliefs, and dynamics of the American Society"; discussed in Lewis Galantiere, "Just What Is America?" *Saturday Review*, January 19, 1952, and W. D Patterson, "Search for America," *Saturday Review*, May 31, 1952. NSC 48/5, *Foreign Relations of the United States, 1951*, Vol. VI, 44; Frederick Lewis Allen, "The Unsystematic American System," condensed in *Reader's Digest*, August 1952, originally published in *Harper's;* Bradford Smith, "We're Selling America Short," condensed in *Reader's Digest*, December 1952, originally published in *The American Scholar;* Norman Cousins, "The Incomplete Power," *Saturday Review*, December 1, 1951.

16. Smith, "We're Selling America Short."

17. Acheson, "Relations of the Peoples of the United States and the Peoples of Asia," 240.

18. Dwight D. Eisenhower, "Commencement Address at Baylor University, May 1956," in *Papers of the President, 1956*, (Washington, D.C.: Government Printing Office, 1957), 533, 529.

19. Michael Hunt, *The Making of a Special Relationship: The United States and China to 1914* (New York: Columbia University Press, 1983).

20. Larry E. Tise, *A Book About Children: The World of Christian Children's Fund, 1938–1991*, (Falls Church, Va.: Hartland Publishing, 1993), 64. Edmund W. Janss, *Yankee Si! The Story of Dr. J. Calvitt Clarke and his 36,000 Children*, (New York: William Morrow & Company, 1961). John C. Caldwell, *Children of Calamity*, (New York: John Day, 1957).

21. Janss, *Yankee Si!*, 182, 126.

22. *The Saturday Review*, November 29, 1952.

23. *The Saturday Review,* August 14, 1954.

24. Caldwell, *Children of Calamity,* ch. 2.

25. H. W. Brands, *Inside the Cold War: Loy Henderson and the Rise of the American Empire, 1918–1961* (New York: Oxford, 1991), 223–24.

26. Barbara Ehrenreich, *The Hearts of Men: American Dreams and the Flight from Commitment* (New York: Anchor, 1983), ch. 3. I am grateful to Christian Children's Fund librarian Mrs. Joan Losen for sharing with me material from the CCF library.

27. Jeanine Basinger, *The World War II Combat Film: Anatomy of a Genre* (New York: Columbia University Press, 1986), 176–88.

28. Macdonald, "Masscult & Midcult," 39.

29. Philip D. Beidler, "*South Pacific* and American Remembering; or, 'Josh, We're Going to Buy This Son of a Bitch!'" *Journal of American Studies* 27 (1993); Frederick Nolan, *The Sound of Their Music: The Story of Rodgers and Hammerstein* (New York: Walker and Company, 1978); James Robert Parrish and Michael R. Pitts, *The Great Hollywood Musical Pictures* (Metuchen, N.J.: Scarecrow, 1992). The figure on aid to Vietnam is derived from George Herring, *America's Longest War: The United States and Vietnam, 1950–1975* (New York: Knopf, 1986, 2d. ed.), 57.

30. John P. Hayes, *James A. Michener: A Biography* (Indianapolis: Bobbs-Merrill, 1984).

31. Ibid., 9, 233, 3; "Michener of the South Pacific," *Newsweek,* January 25, 1954, condensed in *Reader's Digest,* April 1954, 20.

32. Hayes, *Michener,* 110–11; *Congressional Record,* September 17, 1962, 19683; James Michener, *The World Is My Home: A Memoir* (New York: Random House, 1992), 464.

33. James Michener, *Tales of the South Pacific* (New York: Macmillan, 1945), 112, 113.

34. Mary L. Dudziak, "Desegregation as a Cold War Imperative," *Stanford Law Review,* (November 1988): 111–12.

35. Michener, *Tales of the South Pacific,* 108.

36. Philip Wylie, *Generation of Vipers,* (New York: Rinehart, 1942).

37. Richard Brodhead, "Sparing the Rod: Discipline and Fiction in Antebellum America," in *Cultures of Letters: Scenes of Reading and Writing in Nineteenth-Century America* (Chicago: University of Chicago Press, 1993).

38. Kennan, "Memorandum by the Director of the Policy Planning Staff to Mr. Robert G. Hooker, Staff Member," 404.

39. Frederic Jameson, "Reification and Utopia in Mass Culture," *Social Text* 1:1 (1979) and Jameson, *The Political Unconscious,* (Ithaca, N.Y.: Cornell University Press, 1981); Richard Dyer, "Entertainment and Utopia," in *Genre: The Musical,* ed. Rick Altman (London: Routledge & Kegan Paul, 1981).

40. Benedict Anderson, *Imagined Communities,* (London: Verso, rev. ed., 1991).

41. Michener, *The World Is My Home,* 149.

42. Hayes, *Michener,* 66.

43. "The 1957 Anisfield-Wolf Awards," *Saturday Review,* June 28, 1958, 22.

44. Rochelle Girson, "Welcome House," *Saturday Review,* July 26, 1952, 21.

45. Peter Conn, *Pearl S. Buck: A Cultural Biography* (Cambridge: Cambridge Univer-

sity Press, 1996); Hayes, *Michener*, ch. 10; Hugh Fordin, *Getting to Know Him: A Biography of Oscar Hammerstein II* (New York: Random House, 1977), 115, 284–85; Norman Cousins, "Earle Reynolds and His *Phoenix*," *Saturday Review*, October 11, 1958, 21.

46. Fordin, *Getting to Know Him*, 335.

47. Anne McClintock, *Imperial Leather: Race, Gender and Sexuality in the Colonial Contest* (New York: Routledge, 1995), 45.

48. Herring, *American's Longest War*, 60–62.

49. John F. Kennedy, "America's Stake in Vietnam," *Vital Speeches*, August 1956, 618.

Class, Caste, and Status in Indo-U.S. Relations

1. Dennis Merrill, *Bread and the Ballot: The United States and India's Economic Development* (Chapel Hill: University of North Carolina Press, 1990), 60–74; Memo of Conversation by P. L. Kelser, Dec. 16, 1950, Dean Acheson Papers, Box 65, Harry S. Truman Library (HSTL), Independence, Mo.; Memo by J. Robert Fluker, Jan. 15, 1951, Department of State, *Foreign Relations of the United States* (*FRUS*), 1951, vol. 6, "Asia and the Pacific" (Washington, D.C.: U.S. Government Printing Office, 1977), 2085–87; "India's Request for Food Grains: Political Considerations," Jan. 24, 1951, *ibid.*, 2103–6; Acheson to the Embassy in Egypt, Mar. 28, 1951, and Editorial Note, *ibid.*, 2132–33; Memo by Charles Murphy, Feb. 6, 1951, David Lloyd Papers, Box 4, HSTL; Acheson to the Embassy in Egypt, Mar. 28, 1951, and Editorial Note, *FRUS* (1951), vol. 6, 2132–33; U.S. House of Representatives, *Congressional Record* 87/1, 1951, 5651, 5842–43, 6182–84.

2. Robert J. McMahon, *The Cold War on the Periphery: The United States, India, and Pakistan* (New York: Columbia University Press, 1994), 101; Memo of Conversation by T. Eliot Weil, Dec. 29, 1950, Acheson Papers, Box 65; George McGhee to Acheson, Jan. 25, 1951, 611.91/1-2551, Box 2858, Department of State, Decimal File, Record Group 59, National Archives (NA), Washington, D.C.; Elbert G. Mathews to David Lloyd, Feb. 4, 1951, Lloyd Papers, Box 4; House, *Congressional Record*, 1951, 1403, 5736, 5823–27; Senate, *Appendix to the Congressional Record* 87/1, 1951, A314-A315.

3. The Secretary of State to the Embassy in India, Jan. 24, 1951, *FRUS* (1951), vol. 6, 2090; *Washington Post*, Apr. 1, 5, 22, May 1, 1951; House, *Congressional Record* 87/1, 1951, 5615, 5618, 5741.

4. Loy Henderson to the Secretary of State, Feb. 3, 1951, *FRUS* (1951), vol. 6, 2112.

5. Dean Acheson to Loy Henderson, Apr. 21, 1950, *FRUS* (1950), vol. 5, "The Near East, South Asia, and Africa" (Washington, D.C.: U.S. Government Printing Office, 1978), 1464; Jawaharlal Nehru to Asaf Ali, Dec. 21, 1946, Sarvepalli Gopal, ed., *The Selected Works of Jawaharlal Nehru* (*SWJN*), 2nd series, vol. 1 (New Delhi, 1984), 556–57; George Allen to John Foster Dulles, June 8, 1954, Foreign Service Posts: India General Records, Box 66, RG 84, Washington National Records Center (WNRC), Suitland, Md.; Taya Zinkin, *Reporting India* (London: Chatto & Windus, 1962), 212.

6. Harold R. Isaacs, *Scratches on Our Minds: American Views of China and India* (New York: John Day, 1958), 388; *Hindu* (Madras), Oct. 26, 1961.

7. Gerald D. Berreman, "Stratification, Pluralism and Interaction: A Comparative Analysis of Caste," in Anthony de Reuck and Julie Knight, eds., *Caste and Race: Comparative Approaches* (Boston: Little, Brown, 1967), 45–73; Raymond Williams, *Keywords: A Vocabulary of Culture and Society* (New York: Oxford University Press, 1983), 60–9; Edward B. Harper, "A Comparative Analysis of Caste: the United States and India," in Milton Singer and Bernard S. Cohn, eds., *Structure and Change in Indian Society* (Chicago: Aldine, 1968), 59.

8. Isaacs, *Scratches on Our Minds*, 387–88; Louis Dumont, *Homo Hierarchicus: The Caste System and Its Implications* (Chicago: University of Chicago Press, 1980), 16–19; *Times of India (TOI)* (Bombay), Nov. 27, 1956; Hans Mattson (Calcutta) to John Davis, Mar. 30, 1883, *Despatches of U.S. Consuls in Calcutta*, microfilm, Doe Library, University of California–Berkeley.

9. Stephen A. Tyler, *India: An Anthropological Perspective* (Prospect Heights: Waveland Press, 1986), 147–52; Erving Goffman, *The Presentation of Self in Everyday Life* (Garden City: Doubleday, 1959), 36–7; M. N. Srinivas, "Mobility in the Caste System," in Singer and Cohn, *Structure and Change,* 189–90; Arjun Appadurai, "Putting Hierarchy in Its Place," *Cultural Anthropology,* 3. 1 (Feb. 1988): 36–49.

10. Tyler, *India,* 147–48; Sudhir Kakar, *The Inner World: A Psychoanalytic Study of Childhood and Society in India* (New Delhi: Oxford University Press, 1978), 123–24.

11. Michael Brecher, *Nehru: A Political Biography* (London: Oxford University Press, 1959), 2; Jawaharlal Nehru, *Toward Freedom: The Autobiography of Jawaharlal Nehru* (New York: John Day, 1941), 353.

12. G. Morris Carstairs, *The Twice-Born: A Study of a Community of High-Caste Hindus* (Bloomington: Indiana University Press, 1961), 48.

13. R. Smith Simpson to DOS, Oct. 20, 1953, 611.91/10-2053, Box 2858, Decimal File, RG 59, NA.

14. Memo of Conversation by T. Eliot Weil, Nov. 6, 1950, 611.91/11-650, Box 2857, Decimal File, RG 59, NA; Sarvepalli Gopal, *Jawaharlal Nehru: A Biography,* vol. 2 (Delhi: Oxford University Press, 1979), 189–90, 255.

15. Memo of Conversation by Dean Acheson, June 2, 1950, 611.91/6-250, Box 2859, Decimal File, RG 59, NA. Despite their admiration for hierarchy, the British agreed; on May 12, 1950, the secretary of state for the commonwealth relations, P. C. Gordon-Walker, wrote of the Kashmir dispute: "I think it is worse than useless to engage upon a policy of 'gestures'." See doc. FL 10118/106, file 84255, Foreign Office (FO) File 371, Public Record Office (PRO), Kew, England.

16. Roland, *In Search of Self,* 66.

17. M. R. Masani, "India: Dos and Don'ts for Americans," *Foreign Affairs* 30. 3 (April 1952): 412–25; *SWJN,* 1st ser., vol. 14 (1982), 440–42, vol. 15 (1983), 519, 562; ser. 2, vol. 1, 471–76; Jawaharlal Nehru, *Speeches,* vol.1, 1946–1949 (New Delhi: The Publications Division, Ministry of Information and Broadcasting, Government of

India, 1949), 25–7; Proceedings of the 54th Indian National Congress, Nov. 23–24, 1946, and address by D. B. Pattabhi Sitaramayya, Indian National Congress, 55th session, Dec. 18, 1948, All India Congress Committee (AICC) Papers, NMML.

18. Jawaharlal Nehru to M. C. Chagla, Oct. 3, 1946, File 36, M. C. Chagla Papers, NMML; K. P. S. Menon, diary entries for Oct. 7, 1946, Jan. 23, 1951, K. P. S. Menon Papers; SWJN, 2nd ser., vol. 1, 542–43.

19. Progress Report on U.S. Policy Towards South Asia (NSC 5409), Mar. 30, 1956, FRUS (1955–1957), vol. 8: "South Asia" (Washington,D.C.: U.S. Government Printing Office, 1987), 1–10; Oral History Interview with Elbert G. Mathews by Richard D. McKinzie, June 13, 1975, 64, Oral History Collection, HSTL.

20. New Delhi Embassy to DOS, Apr. 28, 1959, Papers of the Council on Foreign Economic Policy, Office of the Chairman, Randall Series, Box 6, Dwight D. Eisenhower Library (DDEL), Abilene, Kans.

21. Memo of Conversation by William L. S. Williams, June 26, 1950, 611.91/6-2650, Box 2857, Decimal File, RG 59, NA; Donald D. Kennedy to DOS, Sept. 28, 1954, 611.91/9-2854, Box 2859, Decimal File, RG 59, NA.

22. Loy Henderson to Secretary of State, Apr. 12, 1950, 611.91/4-1250, Box 2857, Decimal File, RG 59; TOI (Bombay), May 20, 1961.

23. Subimal Dutt, With Nehru in the Foreign Office (Columbia, Mo.: South Asia Books, 1977), 239–41; John Foster Dulles to Henry Byroade, Nov. 15, 1954, released to author under Freedom of Information Act request; Chester Bowles, "New Delhi Diary," entry for Sept. 3, 1963, Box 392, folder 159, Chester Bowles Papers, Yale University Library, New Haven, Conn.

24. TOI (Bombay), Dec. 29, 1950; Clifford Manshardt to Chester Bowles, June 12, 1952, Bowles Papers, Box 99, folder 327.

25. John Kenneth Galbraith, Ambassador's Journal: A Personal Account of the Kennedy Years (Boston: Houghton Mifflin, 1969), 126.

26. McMahon, Cold War on the Periphery, 97; Memo of Conversation by Loy Henderson, Feb. 20, 1951, and Henderson to Secretary of State, Mar. 24, 1951, FRUS (1951), vol. 6, 2118–27, 2130–32; Report on Interview, Jawaharlal Nehru and Edgar A. Mowrer, Mar. 22, 1951, Bowles Papers, folder 323, Box 98; House, Congressional Record, 87/1 1951, 5830; Gopal, Nehru, vol. 2, 137; Introduction of Daniel Patrick Moynihan by Loy Henderson, Mar. 25, 1975, Loy Henderson Papers, Box 8, Library of Congress.

27. Memo by Henry Byroade for the Secretary of State, Nov. 4, 1954, FRUS (1952–1954), vol. 11, "Africa and South Asia" (Washington,D.C.: U.S. Government Printing Office, 1983), 1772–73; TOI (Bombay), Dec. 12, 1959, and May 14, 1961; John Kenneth Galbraith to the Secretary of State, Dec. 7, 1962, John F. Kennedy Papers, National Security Files, Country Series, Box 111, John F. Kennedy Library (JFKL), Boston; Galbraith, Ambassador's Journal, 362.

28. Letter from Ambassador Bowles, n.d. [early 1953], Bowles Papers, folder 504, Box 112; Chester Bowles to Donald Kennedy, May 5, 1952, Bowles Papers, folder 266, Box 95; Bowles's "New Delhi Diary," July 22, 1963, Bowles Papers, folder 159, Box

392; Chester Bowles, *Ambassador's Report* (New York: Harper & Brothers, 1954), 32; M. V. Kamath, "Our Coca Cola Culture: An Indian View," *Current History* 31. 184 (December 1956): 321–27.

29. Memo of Conversation by Peter Delaney, Jan. 28, 1953, *FRUS* (1952–1954), vol. 11, 1822–24.

Italian Americans and the "Letters to Italy" Campaign

Financial support from the Social Welfare History Archives, the National Endowment for the Humanities, and Duke University aided in the preparation of this essay. Special thanks to Irving Elichirigoity and Anthony Cashman for their help in translating articles from the Italian-language press.

1. James E. Miller, "Taking Off the Gloves: The United States and the Italian Elections of 1948," *Diplomatic History* 7 (1983): 35–36.
2. Quoted in Richard Robbins, "Letters to Italy—A Reconsideration," *Common Ground* 10 (Autumn 1949): 40.
3. "Italian 'Freedom Flight'," *New York Times* (March 27, 1948): 3; "One Thing and Another," *New York Times* (March 28, 1948): II-11; "Italians Warned of Red 'Slavery'," *New York Times* (March 23, 1948): 2.
4. Sylvan Gotshal and Halsey Munson, "Letters to Italy," *Common Ground* 9. 3 (Autumn 1948): 4, 6, 11.
5. Quoted in David M. Kennedy, *Over Here: The First World War and American Society* (New York: Oxford University Press, 1980), 65.
6. Samuel Grafton, "I'd Rather Be Right" column, *New York Post* (July 28, 1941).
7. "Louis Adamic (1989–1951): His Life, Work, and Legacy," *Spectrum* (a newsletter of the University of Minnesota's Immigration History Research Center) 4 (Fall 1982): 1–2; Robert F. Harney, "*E Pluribus Unum:* Louis Adamic and the Meaning of Ethnic History," *Journal of Ethnic Studies* 14 (Spring 1986): 29; Louis Adamic, *Two-Way Passage* (New York: Harper and Brothers, 1941), 17, 134, 149.
8. Adamic sent copies of his book to Eleanor Roosevelt and Assistant Secretary of State Adolph Berle, and tried to push his ideas at a private White House dinner with the Roosevelts and Winston Churchill. Adamic followed up on the dinner with a long memo to Eleanor Roosevelt, which was subsequently circulated within the administration. Louis Adamic, *Two-Way Passage*, 266–68, 290; Lorraine M. Lees, "Louis Adamic and American Foreign Policy Makers," an unpublished paper presented at the symposium on "Louis Adamic: His Life, Work, and Legacy," held May 29–30, 1981, at the Immigration History Research Center, University of Minnesota.
9. Adamic, *Two-Way Passage*, 270, 286, 311.
10. "Steam from the Melting Pot," *Fortune* (September 1942): 134, 137.
11. James Miller, "A Question of Loyalty: American Liberals, Propaganda, and the Italian-American Community, 1939–1943," *The Maryland Historian* 9 (1978): 50.
12. John P. Diggins coined the term "philofascism" to suggest a support for fascism rooted in nostalgic and romanticized patriotism. Diggins offers the most compre-

hensive account of Italian Americans' relationship to Mussolini before World War II in *Mussolini and Fascism: The View from America* (Princeton, N.J: Princeton University Press, 1972), 77–143. See also John Morton Blum, *V Was for Victory: Politics and American Culture During World War II* (New York: Harcourt, Brace, Jovanovich, 1976), 147–55. A particularly dramatic demonstration of Italian-American support for Mussolini came after Italy's invasion of Ethiopia in 1935. As Diggins recounts on p. 302, tens of thousands of Italian Americans attended rallies in America's major cities, and many women contributed their gold wedding rings to the war effort, "receiving in turn steel rings from Mussolini which were blessed by a parish priest." Although most Italian Americans supported Mussolini, an anti-fascist segment also existed, centered around the Italian-American labor movement and the radical Italian-language press.

13. Blum, *V Was for Victory,* 152. For a personal recollection of the ambivalence within Italian-American communities, see Studs Terkel, *"The Good War": An Oral History of World War Two* (New York: Ballantine, 1984), 135–40.

14. Diggins, *Mussolini and Fascism,* 142.

15. Miller, "A Question of Loyalty," 59–63.

16. Ibid. 63. Diggins, *Mussolini and Fascism,* 401. Diggins notes that New York's garrulous mayor, Fiorello La Guardia, "became as popular on the *marciapiedi* of Italy as he was on the sidewalks of New York; one town, Torre Annunziata, adopted him as a patron hero."

17. Lorraine Lees, "National Security and Ethnicity: Contrasting Views During World War II," *Diplomatic History* 11 (1987): 114, 118–119, 123.

18. For a fascinating study of some of the implications of this switch, see Christopher Simpson, *Blowback: America's Recruitment of Nazis and Its Effects on the Cold War* (New York: Weidenfeld and Nicolson, 1988).

19. Many Republicans feared that a peacetime propaganda agency would be used to help reelect President Truman or to spread New Deal tenets around the globe.

20. For example, see Ken W. Purdy, "We're Losing the Propaganda War," *Parade* (January 18, 1948): 5. Mr. Purdy had served in the OWI during the war and in 1948 was editor of *Parade.*

21. "Pearson Go-Round," *Newsweek* (November 22, 1948): 58; Drew Pearson, "The Washington Merry-Go-Round" column, *Washington Post* (December 20, 1947): 15B; "Friendship on Wheels," *Newsweek* (December 1, 1947): 22; Edward J. Nickel, "Generosity: An American Tradition," *Parade* (December 21, 1947): 5. Drew Pearson's role in catalyzing this and other private Cold War propaganda campaigns has been virtually overlooked by historians. In addition to the "Friendship Train" and "Letters to Italy" campaigns, Pearson helped launch the "tide of toys" for European children. He also engineered a famous Cold War publicity stunt: floating thousands of balloons, each bearing a message of "peace" and "democracy," on easterly winds into Czechoslovakia. See Jack Anderson with James Boyd, *Confessions of a Muckraker: The Inside Story of Life in Washington During the Truman, Eisenhower, Kennedy and Johnson Years* (New York: Random House, 1979), 8–9, 230.

22. "City Hails Friendship Train; Food Total is Put at 270 Cars," *New York Times* (November 19, 1947): 1; Drew Pearson, "Washington Merry-Go-Round" column, *Washington Post* (December 12, 1947): 15C, and (December 30, 1947): 12B. The hoopla surrounding the train's passage across the United States—and the coverage given the distribution of food in Europe—suggests that its intended audience was not simply foreign.

23. "City Hails Friendship Train."

24. Gotshal and Munson, "Letters to Italy," 6; Robbins, "Letters to Italy—A Reconsideration," 43; Drew Pearson, "Washington Merry-Go-Round" column, *Washington Post* (March 30, 1948) and (April 24, 1948): 15B. Although Pearson urged all Americans to write friends and relatives in Europe, this suggestion clearly had the strongest resonance for those Americans only recently removed from the Old Country.

25. Miller, "Taking Off the Gloves," 40–45.

26. Byington's confidential dispatch of January 28, 1948, is printed in U.S. Department of State, *Foreign Relations of the United States,* 1948, vol. 3 (Washington, D.C.: U.S. Government Printing Office 1974), 822–23 (hereafter cited as *FRUS*). Although Byington did not cite Pearson specifically, he did note that the idea was "suggested by several Americans in Italy who are not connected with the Government." Most news organizations, and Pearson himself, credited the columnist with launching the "Letters to Italy" campaign. Pearson covered it extensively in his columns.

27. John Diggins, *Mussolini and Fascism,* 84; "Il Progresso Propone L'Invio D'Un Milione Di Lettere In Italia Per Combattere La Manaccia Del Comunismo," *Il Progresso Italo-Americano* (January 19, 1948): 1; "To Tell Italians of Gifts," *New York Times* (January 24, 1948): 4. *Il Progresso* ran articles on the campaign, as well as sample letters and writing instructions, regularly on p. 5.

28. "Friendship Train Gets Pledges Here," *New York Times* (November 15, 1947): 4.

29. Italian fascist authorities helped Pope acquire his newspaper empire, and he accepted free telegraph service and other special privileges from them throughout the 1930s. Pope, in turn, hailed both Mussolini and "Il Corporativismo all'Estero" in the pages of his papers, and raised vast sums for Italy during the Ethiopian War. Only after President Roosevelt warned Pope personally in 1941 did the publisher repudiate Mussolini. During the war, Pope endorsed the Italian-American Labor Council's call for a national conference to unify Italian-American groups. John Diggins calls the resulting American Committee for Italian Democracy "an expedient fusion of ex-Fascist sympathizers and anti-Fascist fighters: the former seeking new democratic respectability, the latter trying to organize for a coming showdown with the Stalinists." John Diggins, *Mussolini and Fascism,* 84–86, 109, 303, 347–48, 401, 404–5.

30. James Miller, "A Question of Loyalty," 57–59.

31. Undated flier addressed to "Citizens of Harlem," in "International Relations; Italy, Assistance To" folder, Box 51, Vito Marcantonio Papers, New York Public Library (hereafter Marcantonio Papers).

32. Gotshal and Munson, "Letters to Italy," 6–8; "Italian 'Freedom Flight'," *New York Times* (March 27, 1948): 3; "La Campagna Delle Lettere All'Italia," *L'Italia* (March 2, 1948): 1; "100.000 Lettere All'Italia," *L'Italia* (March 26, 1948): 2; "L'Inizio Della Campagna Per L'Invio Di Lettere In Italia," *L'Italia* (March 30, 1948): 2.

33. For instance, the *Denver Post* and the Broadway, a local Denver theater, paid the cost of cablegrams sent to Italy, as did the Chamber of Commerce in St. Petersburg, Florida. Alexander Smith and Sons Carpet Co. of Yonkers, New York, offered to send airmail letters to Italy. And in Syracuse, New York, form letters were circulated by the Republican Club in cooperation with the Catholic Church. Gotshal and Munson, "Letters to Italy," 10; "Pleas to Italy Ask Vote Against Reds," *New York Times* (April 8, 1948): 3; E. Edda Martinez and Edward A. Suchman, "Letters from America and the 1948 Elections in Italy," *Public Opinion Quarterly* 14 (Spring 1950): 113.

34. James Edward Miller, *The United States and Italy, 1940–1950: The Politics and Diplomacy of Stabilization* (Chapel Hill: University of North Carolina Press, 1986), 244. In "Taking Off the Gloves," p. 44, Miller notes that the Vatican—though firmly anti-Communist—was initially "ambivalent about Italy's nascent democracy." With American encouragement, however, "the Church edged toward full participation in the anti-Communist coalition."

35. Martinez and Suchman, "Letters from America and the 1948 Elections in Italy," 121–23.

36. "Group to Aid Italians to Fight Communists," *New York Times* (March 17, 1948): 5; "Lawyer Here Fights Communism in Italy," *New York Times* (March 28, 1948): 15.

37. Martinez and Suchman, "Letters from America and the 1948 Elections in Italy," 117–18.

38. *Il Progresso Italo-Americano* (January 24, 1948): 5.

39. *Ibid.*, (January 21, 1948): 5.

40. Martinez and Suchman, "Letters from America and the 1948 Elections in Italy," 113, 115. The widespread use of form and sample letters during the campaign clearly undermined its personal nature, and suggests that organizers were not sure individual Italian Americans could be counted on to send the "right" message. It also suggests that the intended audience for the campaign was as much domestic as foreign: U.S. officials, Catholic priests, and conservative Italian-American leaders may have hoped to convert the majority of Italian Americans to active anticommunism. At the same time, Italian-American *prominenti* probably hoped to prove the loyalty of their community.

41. "La campagna delle lettere all'Italia," *L'Italia* (March 2, 1948): 1; Martinez and Suchman, "Letters from America and the 1948 Elections in Italy," 114–15, 122.

42. "La campagna della lettere all'Italia," *L'Italia* (2 March 1948): 1; Gotshal and Munson, "Letters to Italy," 5, 7–8.

43. *Il Progresso Italo-Americano* (January 19, 1948): 1.

44. Martinez and Suchman, "Letters from America and the 1948 Elections in Italy," 114.

45. *L'Italia* (April 14, 1948): 8.

46. *Il Progresso Italo-Americano* (January 23, 1948): 5.

47. In early March, Ambassador Dunn sent a telegram to the State Department suggesting that American letter-writers tell their friends and relatives that they would no longer be able to send gift and food packages if the Italians voted the Democratic Front into power. Stephen E. Ambrose, *Rise to Globalism: American Foreign Policy Since 1938,* fourth rev. ed. (New York: Penguin Books, 1985) 90; *FRUS,* 1948, 3:842; Martinez and Suchman, "Letters from America and the 1948 Elections in Italy," 115, 118; "Letters to Be Sent to Italy," *New York Times* (March 22, 1948): 4.

48. For instance, Monsignor Monteleone, the same priest who passed out form letters to his parishioners, sent an additional five thousand form letters to friends in Rome, Naples, Turin, Milan, and Genoa to be distributed in factories there. Martinez and Suchman, "Letters from America and the 1948 Elections in Italy," 113.

49. Martinez and Suchman, "Letters from America and the 1948 Elections in Italy," 123.

50. Ronald L. Filippelli, *American Labor and Postwar Italy, 1943–1953: A Study in Cold War Politics* (Stanford, Calif.: Stanford University Press, 1989), 21–26.

51. Martinez and Suchman, "Letters from America and the 1948 Elections in Italy," 113; Robbins, "Letters to Italy—A Reconsideration," 43.

52. Pope's address to the Citizen's Committee of the Columbus Scholarship Fund is quoted in Martinez and Suchman, "Letters from America and the 1948 Elections in Italy," 112.

53. Robbins, "Letters to Italy—A Reconsideration," 41.

54. Miller, "Taking Off the Gloves," 48; "Pleas to Italy Ask Vote Against Reds," *New York Times* (April 8, 1948): 3; "Salvemini Denies Protest on Italy," *New York Times* (April 16, 1948): 9.

55. See, for instance, *Il Progresso Italo-Americano* (January 21, 1948): 5.

56. The fact that Louis Adamic joined this appeal suggests the ways in which the shift from antifascism to anticommunism altered America's political landscape. "Sets Founding Day of Wallace Party," *New York Times* (April 12, 1948): 15; "Appeal to Voters in Italy Assailed," *New York Times* (April 15, 1948): 8; "Salvemini Denies Protest on Italy," *New York Times* (16 April 1948): 9.

57. Some news accounts referred to the committee sponsoring the rally as the *Italian-American* Committee for Free Elections in Italy (emphasis added). "Appeal to Voters in Italy Assailed," *New York Times* (April 15, 1948): 8; undated typescript in "Speeches and Press Releases, Misc." folder, box 68, Marcantonio Papers; "Pleas to Italy Ask Vote Against Reds," *New York Times* (April 8, 1940): 3.

58. An example of this approach is the "Tripod of Freedom" public relations campaign, which the National Association of Manufacturers launched in 1940. The campaign is briefly described in Richard Tedlow, "The National Association of Manufacturers and Public Relations During the New Deal," *Business History Review* 50. 1 (Spring 1976): 34.

59. Gotshal and Munson, "Letters to Italy," 11.

60. Ibid., 5.

61. The symbol of the Democratic Popular Front was Garibaldi's head, backdropped by a red star. In an interesting twist, the Christian Democratic party issued a propaganda leaflet that refashioned the symbol. When the leaflet was turned upside down, Garibaldi's head became the head of Joseph Stalin. See *New York Times* (April 1, 1948): 3.

62. "U.S. Letters Anger Leftists," *New York Times* (April 1, 1948): 3; "I Comunisti Italiani Protestano Per La Valanga Di Lettere Dall'America," *L'Italia* (April 2, 1948): 1; "Letter Campaign Denounced," *New York Times* (April 9, 1948): 17; Martinez and Suchman, "Letters from America and the 1948 Elections in Italy," 120; Miller, "Taking Off the Gloves," 51. A letter reprinted in *The New York Times* in late April suggests that some Italians may have resented American advice, even as they followed it: "Following your suggestion, most of my neighbors and my family have agreed not to vote the Communist ticket," Conolato Luvera wrote his brother Paul of Anacortes, Washington. "I understand you people will be having an election soon. We all hope that you and your neighbors don't mind if we tell you how you should vote."

63. Martinez and Suchman, "Letters from America and the 1948 Elections in Italy," 120.

Exploding Cold War Racial Ideology

I wish to thank Kevin Gaines and Chris Appy for valuable criticism and advice throughout the preparation of this article. Parts of this article have appeared in a modified form in Penny M. Von Eschen, *Race Against Empire: Black Americans and Anticolonialism 1937–1957*, (Ithaca, N.Y.: Cornell University Press, 1997).

1. Felix Belair, *New York Times*, November 6, 1955, 1.

2. W. A. Hunton Papers, Box 1, Folder 19, Organizational, the Council on African Affairs, 1945–55, MG 237, Schomburg Library, New York City. Martin Bauml Duberman, *Paul Robeson* (New York: Alfred A. Knopf, 1988), 388–90.

3. W. A. Hunton Papers, Box 1, Folder 19, Organizational, the Council on African Affairs, 1945–55, MG 237, Schomburg Library, New York City; Duberman, *Paul Robeson*, 434.

4. On the early VOA music programs and Leonard Feather's Jazz Club USA, see Leonard Feather, "Music Is Combatting Communism: Voice of America Shows Bring Universal Harmony," *Down* Beat, October 8, 1952, 1, 19. For an excellent exploration of U.S. Cold War cultural programs in a European context, see Reinhold Wagnleitner, *Coca-Colonization and the Cold War: The Cultural Mission of the United States in Austria after the Second World War* (Chapel Hill: The University of North Carolina Press, 1994). On jazz, see pp. 201–15.

5. The United States Information Agency was established as an agency separate from the State Department in 1953. Before this, it was directly under the auspices of the State Department. Records are held in State Department General Files, RG 59, Class 500: Cultural Affairs, Propaganda, and Psychological Warfare.

6. I have explored aspects of this argument in Penny M. Von Eschen, *Race Against*

Empire: Black Americans and Anticolonialism, 1937–1957 (Ithaca, N.Y.: Cornell University Press, 1997). Mary L. Dudziak has explored related issues in "Josephine Baker, Racial Protest, and the Cold War," *The Journal of American History* (September 1994): 543–70.

7. For a further development of these points, see Von Eschen, *Race Against Empire*. See especially ch. 5, "Domesticating Anticolonialism," and ch. 6, "Hearts and Mines." On anticolonialism and African Americans and U.S. foreign policy in this era, see also Brenda Gayle Plummer, *Black Americans and U.S. Foreign Affairs, 1935–1960* (Chapel Hill: University of North Carolina Press, 1996).

8. Thomas Borstelmann, *Apartheid's Reluctant Uncle: The United States and Southern Africa in the Early Cold War* (New York: Oxford University Press, 1993), 44–46, 96–99, 181, 198–99; William Minter, *King Solomon's Mines Revisited: Western Interests and the Burdened History of Southern Africa* (New York: Basic Books, 1986), 116–17. For an example of increased wartime production see the report on rubber production in the Congo: Office of the Special Representative, Few Mission, Belgian Congo, Leopoldville, Belgian Congo to Sidney Scheuer, Director Foreign Development and Procurement, Bureau of Supplies, Foreign Economic Administation, Washington, D.C., Feb. 16, 1944; RG 234 a-284218, National Archives.

9. Borstelmann, *Apartheid's Reluctant Uncle*, 139; William Roger Louis and Ronald Robinson, "The United States and the Liquidation of the British Empire in Tropical Africa, 1941–1951," in Prosser Gifford and William Roger Louis, eds., *The Transfer of Power in Africa: Decolonization,1940–1960* (New Haven, Conn.: Yale University Press, 1982), 45–46. For reports on West African resources, see AMCONSUL Lagos, Nigeria to Department of State, NEA Letter dated April 23, 1951; Sujct: Political, Economic and Social Survey of Nigeria; RG 59: 745H.00/6-951 and Amconsulate, ACCRA to Department of State, Combined USIE Semi-evaluation Reports; RG 59: 511.45G/2-1552.

10. E. H. Bourgerie, Director, Office of African Affairs to A. W. Childs, Esquire, American Consul General, Lagos, Nigeria, April 23, 1951: RG 745H.00/4-2351.

11. Borstelmann, *Apartheid's Reluctant Uncle*, 143, 161; Melvyn P. Leffler, *A Preponderance of Power: National Security, the Truman Administration, and the Cold War* (Stanford, Calif.: Stanford University Press, 1992), 506–9.

12. Bourgerie to Childs, April 23, 1951.

13. Borstelmann, *Apartheid's Reluctant Uncle*, 195.

14. *New Africa* 10. 2 (March 1951): 1. The Truman statement that the West African Youth League refers to is from Truman's State of the Union Address, January 8, 1951, and is also quoted in Borstelmann, *Apartheid's Reluctant Uncle*, 162–63.

15. Paul Gordon Lauren, *Power and Prejudice: The Politics and Diplomacy of Racial Discrimination* (Boulder and London: Westview Press, 1988), 209.

16. George F. Kennan, "Notes for Essays," Box 26, Kennan Papers, Spring 1952, Seely G. Mudd Library, Princeton University. Thanks to Anders Stephanson for this document.

17. Borstelmann, *Apartheid's Reluctant Uncle*, 64–65, 141–42, 161; Lauren, *Power and Prejudice*, 164, 192–95.

18. Mary L. Dudziak, "Desegregation as a Cold War Imperative," *Stanford Law Review* 41 (November 1988): 61–120.

19. The arrest of Du Bois and other Peace Information Center officers led to "urgent" requests from State Department personnel in Lagos for information to quell publicity on the case, and a 1953 U.S. intelligence report on the Mau Mau uprising in Kenya linked Jomo Kenyatta to Paul Robeson. Telegram from Crowle, Lagos to Secretary of State, April 5, 1951; and Acheson to Amconsul, Lagos, Nigeria, April 6, 1951, "Cleared in substance by phone with Foley, Justice Department," RG 59: 745H.011/4-551 and 745H.111/4-551. Department of State, Intelligence Report no. 6307, June 12, 1953, Reel VII, Frame 1055.

20. Duberman, *Paul Robeson*, 342–43.

21. On criticism in India, see Carl T. Rowan, *The Pitiful and the Proud* (New York: Random House, 1956), 21, 162–63.

22. From Am Consul, Lagos to Department of State, August 8, 1950, RG 59:511.45H/8-850.

23. Roger P. Ross, Public Affairs Officer, American Consul, Accra to Department of State, Subject: USIE, Request for a Special Story on Paul Robeson, Jan. 9, 1951; Department of State, RG 59: 511.45K21/1-951, National Archives; Duberman, *Paul Robeson, 349.*

24. Ross to State, Jan. 9, 1951.

25. Ibid.

26. Robert Alan, "Paul Robeson—The Lost Shepherd," *Crisis,* November 1951, 569–73. The quotes are from pp. 569–70. On the article's publication and other attacks on Robeson including Walter White's "The Strange Case of Paul Robeson," published in *Ebony,* see Duberman, *Paul Robeson,* 395. See also "Paul Robeson: Right or Wrong: Right: says W. E. B. Du Bois: Wrong: says Walter White," *Negro Digest,* March 1950, 8–18.

27. Hyman Bloom, American Consul, Accra, to the Department of State, April 2, 1951: RG 59: 511.45K5/4-251.

28. Gunnar Myrdal, Richard Stern, and Arnold Rose, *An American Dilemma: The Negro Problem and Modern Democracy* (New York: Harper, 1944).

29. American Vice Consul, Lagos, Nigeria to the Department of State, Washington, July 30, 1952: Subject: Major Releases from the USIS Office, Lagos. Published in the local press during the period June 1–30, 1952: Department of State General Files: 511.45H21/7-3052.

30. The scripts were written by Noon and the RPAO and translated into Swahili by Mr. Symons W. Onyango, the translator for the information office. Edmund J. Dorz, American Council General, Nairobi to Department of State, August 5, 1953; and enclosure, John A. Noon, Regional Public Affairs Officer, *IIA Nairobi Introduces Family Serial Program for African Audience,* State Department General Files, RG 59, 511.45R5/8-553, National Archives.

31. Edmund J. Dorsz, American Consul General, Nairobi to Department of State, August 5, 1953; and enclosure, John A. Noon, RPAO, *IIA Nairobi Introduces Family Serial Program for African Audience,* State Department General Files, RG 50: 511 511.45R5/8-553, National Archives. Programs focused on the following themes:

Ethnic accommodation as the American way; Democracy in Action; Education opportunities and getting ahead; Projections of American life; and Advantages of scientific training.

32. To: Department of State, from Lagos, April 25, 1950; Subject: *left-wing Labour Champion* Attacks United States Information Service, RG59:511.45H/2-1551.

33. From: AmConGen: Accra, To: The Department of State, January 31, 1957, Subject: Current Developments in the Gold Coast January 16–31, 1957, RG 59 745K.00/1-3157.

34. To: Department of State, Washington, D.C., From: Lagos 342 November 24, 1950; Subject: Out of Context Use by Zik's Press of USIS Broadcast Material, RG 59: 511.45H21/11-2450.

35. Robert W. Stookey, American Vice-Consul, Nairobi to Department of State, November 22, 1950: Subject Publicizing USIE Film Acquisitions: Enclosure: Specimen copy of November 24 issue of the ISIE Nairobi newsletter, p. 3: Department of State, RG 59: 5111.45R5/11-2250.

36. For example, between August 29 and October of 1950, *President Truman Reports on Korea* was seen in twenty theaters by 12,677 people. In August and September, *United Nations in Korea* (35 mm) was seen by 36,158 people in twenty-eight theaters. Another 16 mm version of *United Nations in Korea* was seen by 1,745 people in nineteen theaters in August and September. Angus Ward, Am consul General, Nairobi to Department of State: January 5, 1951: re: Further Commercial Distribution and audience data on newsreel films "President Truman Reports on Korea," and "United Nations in Korea." RG 59 511.45R5/1-55-1.

37. Robert W. Ross, American Vice Consul, Lagos Nigeria to the Department of State, June 2, 1952; Major Releases from the USIS Office, Lagos. Published in the Local Press during the period April 1–30, 1952. The Department of State General Files, 511.45H21/6-252.

38. Mombasa to Department of State, January 29, 1951, RG: 59: 511.45T21/1-2951.

39. Willard Quincy Stanton, American Consul General to Department of State, November 13, 1950, RG 59: 511.45H/10-3050.

40. Willard Quincy Stanton, American Consul General Lagos, to Department of State, January 17, 1951, Subject: Major Releases from the USIS Office, published in the local presses during the period November 30 - December 31, 1950, Department of State General Files, 511.45H21/1-1751. A. W. Childs, American Consul General, Lagos Nigeria to the Department of State, Washington, Dec. 13, 1951, Department of State General Files, 511.45H21/1-352.

41. American Consulate General, Johannesburg to Department of State, March 24, 1952 (reference Department's Confidential Airgram, February 6, 1952), re "Radio Programs Dealing with the American Negro," RG, 511.45A4/3-2452; W. J. Gallman, American Embassy, Cape Town to Department of State, April 3, 1952 (reference February 6 Airgram) re "Projected Transcribe Radio and Television Series," RG 59, 511.45A4/4-352.

42. "We Claim Jazz: Listen to Africa," *Voice of Africa*, Accra, July 1962.

43. See "The Life and Times of Benjamin Franklin," by Verus, *The World*, Johannes-

burg, June 2, 1956, 4; and "True Tales—Abraham Lincoln," by Verus, *The World,* Johannesburg, June 23, 1956, 4.

44. Memorandum from the Representative at the Trusteeship Councils (sears) to the Secretary of State, Feb. 15, 1956, Department of State, IO/ODA Files: Lot 62 D 225, *FRUS,* 1955–1957, Volume XVIII, 37–40. Amcongen, Leopoldville to the Department of State, Wasington, March 6, 1958, RG 59: 511.55A/3-3158.

45. Memorandum by the Consul General at Leopoldville (McGregor) December 28, 1955, *FRUS,* 1955–1957, Volume XVIII, 25.

46. Borstelmann, *Apartheid's Reluctant Uncle,* 143–44. Borstelmann's work is a very important corrective to scholars such as William Roger Louis and Ronald Robinson. Louis and Robinson have argued that U.S. policy in the immediate postwar period played a crucial indirect role in the decolonization of Africa but they suggest that this came from a top-down U.S. pressure on the British and had little to do with pressure from African anticolonial movements. Louis and Robinson, "The United States and the Liquidation of the British Empire in Tropical Africa, 1941–1951," 45–46. Even if one accepts their stress on U.S. pressure in colonial reform and independence, their conclusion that the role of nationalist movements was relatively insignificant begs the question of what animated the "instability" in the colonies that so concerned the United States.

47. E. H. Bourgerie, Director, Office of African Affairs to A. W. Childs, Esquire, American Consul General, Lagos, Nigeria, April 23, 1951: RG 59 745H.00/4-2351.

48. Mombasa 187 to Department of State, January 23, 1951: RG 5111.45T2/1-2351.

49. See John A. Noon, Regional Public Affairs Officer, Consulate General Nairobi to Department of State, January 8, 1953: Subject: Semi-Annual evaluation report for the period ending December 31, 1951: RG: 511.45S/1-853.

50. In the past decade there has been a tendency among scholars of the Cold War to get away from a bipolar fixation on U.S.-USSR relations. Scholars have begun to look at the interplay of local politics and bipolar relations and have argued that local forces (classes, elites, parties, and individuals) played an active and in some cases crucial role in unfolding events. See for example, Bruce Cumings, *The Origins of the Korean War* (Princeton, N.J.: Princeton University Press, 1981), and Robert J. McMahon, "The Cold War in Asia: Toward a New Synthesis?" *Diplomatic History* 12 (Summer 1988). See also Robert J. McMahon, *Colonialism and the Cold War: The United States and the Struggles for Indonesian Independence, 1945–49* (Ithaca, N.Y.: Cornell University Press, 1981), 319, and Richard H. Immerman, *The CIA in Guatemala: The Foreign Policy of Intervention* (Austin: University of Texas Press, 1982), 82–100.

51. Noon to State, January 8, 1953.

52. Erwin P. Keeler, American Consul General, Lagos, Nigeria, to Department of State, Washington; Subject: Communism in Nigeria today, September 9, 1953, RG 59: 745H.001/8-1453.

53. William E. Cole, Amconsulate, ACCRA to the Department of State, Washington; USIE Field Reporting, February 15, 1952, RG 59: 511.45G/2-1552.

54. FBI report NY 100–19377, June 3, 1952: Papers of W. E. B. Du Bois, University

of Massachusetts Amherst, Box 377, Folder 136. On charges, see alsoGerald Horne, *Black and Red: W. E. B. Du Bois and the Afro-American Response to the Cold War, 1944–63* (Albany: State University of New York Press, 1986), 187–88; and Hollis R. Lynch, *Black American Radicals and the Liberation of Africa: The Council on African Affairs, 1937–55* (Ithaca: Africana Studies and Research Center, Cornell University, 1978), 50.

55. Outline of proposed testimony, W. A. Hunton, October 23, 1953, W. A. Hunton papers, Box 1/Folder 19, MG 237, Schomburg Library, New York City.

56. Warren Olney III, Assistant Attorney General, Criminal Division to the Director of the Federal Bureau of Investigation, File 146–28-376, 1953. W. E. B. Du Bois Papers, U. Mass, Amherst, Group 2/3, Section 23, Box 379, Folder 60, 1–3.

57. Ibid.

58. Ibid., W. A. Hunton Papers, Organizational, Council on African Affairs, Legal, 1945–1955, Box 1/Folder 19; MG 237 Schomburg Library, New York City; To: SCA NY 100–19377 From Director, FBI, 100–69266, July 19, 1954, W. E. B. Du Bois Papers, U. Mass. Amherst, Group 2/3, Series 23, Box 376, Folder 31.

59. "Gil Cruter, ex–high jump ace, big hit in West African tour," *The Afro-American,* March 3, 1956, 15.

60. Dave Zinkoff with Edgar Williams, *Around the World with the Harlem Globetrotters* (Philadelphia: Macrae Smith Company, 1953), 109, 169. "U.S. Basketball Team See World: The Harlem Globestrotters Spread Goodwill," Supplement to *Bantu World,* July 2, 1955.

61. "U.S. Basketball Team See World."

62. For a discussion of congressional and conservative opposition to State Department support of abstract expressionism, see Jane de Hart Matthews, "Art and Politics in Cold War America," *American Historical Review* 81 (1976): 762–87.

63. Dizzy Gillespie with Al Fraser, *Dizzy: To Be or Not to Bop* (London, Melbourne, New York: DaCapo Press, 1982), 413.

64. "Jazz Wins U.S. Friends," *The Afro-American,* editorial, July 21, 1956.

65. "Indians Dizzy over Gillespie's Jazz," Parts I and II, *Pittsburgh Courier,* June 2, 1956, 22; and June 9, 1956. On the tour, see also "Gillespie's Band a Hit in Beruit," *New York Times,* April 29, 1956, 24.

66. "Diz Set for Tour of South America," *Pittsburgh Courier,* July 21, 1956, 23.

67. "Dizzy Urges Ike to Back Jazz Tours," *Pittsburgh Courier,* August 4, 1956, 21. On the tours see Frank Kofsky, *Black Nationalism and the Revolution in Music* (New York: Pathfinder Press, 1970), 109–11, 119–21.

68. Gillespie, *To Be or Not to Bop,* 414.

69. Ibid., 415–18; "Indians Dizzy over Gillespie's Jazz"; Andrew Ross, *No Respect: Intellectuals and Popular Culture* (New York and London: Routledge, 1989), 242.

70. *Pittsburgh Courier,* July 21, 1956, 23.

71. "Modern Jazz Is Here to Stay," *The World,* January 28, 1956, 5; *Drum,* four-part series on Louis Armstrong: "Satchmo's Own Story: The Modern Pied Piper," April 1956; "The Louis Armstrong Story: Satchmo on the Streets," May 1956, 71; "Satchmo's Big Break," June 1956, 67; and "Satchmo Blows Up the World," August 1956, 40.

72. The programs were very popular in South Africa, and information and publicity was carried by local papers. "Enjoys Jazz Program," *The World*, Johannesburg, November 17, 1956, 4; "Jazz Corner," *The World*, Johannesburg, February 1, 1958, 6.

73. "100,000 Dig the King: Armstrong 'Axe' Gasses Ghanese Fans," *Pittsburgh Courier*, June 2, 1956; "Modern Jazz Is Here to Stay," *The World*, January 28, 1956, 5; "Satchmo Blows Up the World," *Drum*, August 1956, 40; Gary Giddins, *Satchmo* (New York: Doubleday, 1988), 159–60.

74. American Consulate General, Accra to Department of State, Washington, June 4, 1956, RG 59:745K.00/6-456.

75. "Armstrong to Tour Russia, S. America," *Pittsburgh Courier*, August 10, 1957, 22. See also "Satchmo Blows for Hungary," *Chicago Defender*, editorial, December 22, 1956, on Armstrong's benefit concert with the Royal Philharmonic in London, for Hungarian refugees.

76. "Brightest Lights," *Pittsburgh Courier*, December 29, 1956, 4, magazine.

77. Kofsky, *Black Nationalism and the Revolution in Music*, 121.

78. On Duke Ellington's extensive State Department tours, see Edward Kennedy Ellington, *Music Is My Mistress*, (Garden City, N.Y.: Doubleday & Company, Inc., 1973), 301–89. On the 1960s, see also Ronald M. Radano's discussion of an African-inspired cultural nationalism in the Chicago based Association for the Advancement of Creative Musicians. *New Musical Figurations: Anthony Braxton's Cultural Critique* (Chicago and London: The University of Chicago Press, 1993), 95–103.

79. On Gillespie's South American tour, see the chapter on samba music in Gillespie, *To Be or Not to Bop*, 428–33. The quote is from 428.

80. Gary Giddins, *Satchmo*, 159.

81. Horace R. Cayton, "World at Large," *Pittsburgh Courier*, June 9, 1956, 9.

82. Ibid.

83. "Louis Armstrong, Barring Soviet Tour, Denounces Eisenhower and Gov. Faubus," *New York Times*, September 19, 1957, 23; "Satchmo Tells Off Ike, U.S.," *Pittsburgh Courier*, September 28, 1957; Gary Giddins, *Satchmo*, 160–65. For advance praise of the canceled tour, see "State Department Pipes Up With 'Satchmo for the Soviets,'" *Variety*, July 31, 1957.

84. Giddins, *Satchmo*, 163.

85. E. Frederic Morrow, *Black Man in the White House* (New York: MacFadden-Bartell, 1963).

86. Paul Robeson, *Here I Stand* (Boston: Beacon Press, 1988), originally published 1958, 72.

87. Ibid., 70–71.

88. Ibid., 82.

89. Carl T. Rowan, "Has Paul Robeson Betrayed the Negro?" *Ebony* 12.2 (October 1957): 31–42; the last quote is from p. 33. See also Rowan's reflections on the piece over three decades later in Carl T. Rowan, *Breaking Barriers: A Memoir* (New York: Harper Perennial, 1991).

90. Rowan, "Has Paul Robeson Betrayed the Negro?", 42.

91. Musicians continued to comment on the State Department tours in terms of the South. In an interview published in September 1962, Miles Davis said of Arm-

strong: "People really dig Pops like I do myself. He does a good job overseas with his personality. But they ought to send him down South for goodwill. They need goodwill worse in Georgia and Alabama and Mississippi than they do in Europe." Miles Davis interviewed by Alex Haley, September 1962, in *The Playboy Interview*, ed. G. Barry Golson (New York: Playboy Press, 1981), 10.

92. Robeson, *Here I Stand*, 82.

93. Gillespie, *To Be or Not to Bop*, 452–61.

94. Paul Robeson, "Anti-Imperialists Must Defend Africa," Address at Madison Square Garden rally sponsored by the Council on African Affairs, June 6, 1946, in *Paul Robeson Speaks*, ed. Philip S. Foner (New York: Citadel Press, 1978), 169.

95. William Blum, *Killing Hope: U.S. Military and CIA Intervention Since World War II* (Monroe, Me.: Common Courage Press, 1995), 156–62.

96. Ibid., 156–62, 198–200, 249–56, 257–62, 280–89, 148–52.

Modernization Theory in Fact and Fiction

1. Walt Rostow, with Richard Hatch, *An American Policy in Asia* (Boston: Technology Press of MIT, 1955), 1.

2. Henry Luce, *The American Century* (New York: Farrar & Rinehart, 1941), 27.

3. Henry Luce, *The American Century*, 37.

4. While Luce and Rostow represented the dominant Cold War liberal voice, others disagreed with their vision of America and its relationship with the world. Perhaps the most nuanced conservative voice was George Kennan, the father of containment. He argued that America's problems were more internal than external. Furthermore he came to doubt "whether America's problems were really soluble at all by operation of the liberal-democratic and free-enterprise institutions traditional to our country." [George Kennan, *Memoirs: 1950–1963* (Boston: Little, Brown, 1972), 85.] His voice was in the distinct minority, and his general revulsion toward modern America and toward mass society and consumerism in general led to his being viewed as something of a throwback, even a crank.

5. The origins of modernization theory stem from nineteenth-century German sociology and its interest in the revolutionizing quality of capitalism upon traditional societies. It has long been a model favored by American historians in understanding the development of the United States from an economic outpost to a world power. See Dwight Hoover, "The Long Ordeal of Modernization Theory," *Prospects* 11 (1986). He wrote: "modernization became the single most important theory of social change in American if not Western social science" (408). Rostow may have been influenced by the work of historical sociology as well, such as David Reisman's *The Lonely Crowd* (New Haven: Yale University Press, 1950), with its trajectory of societies that evolved from "inner directed" to "outer directed." Reisman's case studies of countries that shared this cycle of development ranged from India, to the Soviet Union, to the United States.

6. The classic works on modernization theory include Daniel Leaner, *The Passing of Traditional Society: Modernizing the Middle East* (New York: Free Press, 1958);

Walt Rostow, *The Stages of Economic Growth: A Non-Communist Manifesto* (Cambridge: Cambridge University Press, 1960); Cyril Black, *The Dynamics of Modernization: A Study in Comparative History* (New York: Harper & Row, 1966); S. N. Eisenstadt, *Modernization: Protest and Change* (Englewood Cliffs, N.J.: Prentice-Hall, 1966).

7. The phrase "Universal History" is taken from Francis Fukuyama's *The End of History and the Last Man* (New York: Free Press, 1992), 68. He sees proponents of modernization theory as following in the footsteps of other Universal Histories (e.g., Hegel and Marx). There is much truth to Fukuyama's historical analysis here, for modernization theorists were quite confident that liberalism was the "end" of human history.

8. For a representative sample of fictional works that touch on this problem, see Mark Twain's *Innocents Abroad* (1869), Henry James's novel *The American* (1877), and Gore Vidal's *Empire: A Novel* (1987). Nonfictional critiques include Charles Beard's condemnation of Franklin Roosevelt's foreign policy in *The Open Door at Home* (1934), William Appleman Williams's *Tragedy of American Diplomacy* (1959), and C. Wright Mills's dissection of American military officials in *The Power Elite* (1956). Finally, Garry Wills's searching yet sympathetic critique of Richard Nixon in *Nixon Agonistes* (1970) pays considerable attention to the nature of exporting American values abroad.

9. Michael Hunt, *Lyndon Johnson's War: America's Crusade in Vietnam, 1945–1968* (New York: Hill and Wang, 1996), 3.

10. Perhaps Lederer and Burdick used Magsaysay's name to give the novel historical veracity (or, considering that so few Americans had ever heard of Magsaysay, his name may have seemed to add an "authentic" Filipino touch). It is curious, though, that the novel begins with the classic disclaimer: "The names, the places, the events, are our inventions. . ." It appears that even when fictionalized, the Orient is nothing but historical footage.

11. William Lederer and Eugene Burdick, *The Ugly American* (Greenwich, Conn.: Fawcett Publications, 1958), 229, 240.

12. This misunderstanding continues to this day. In a discussion of the metamorphosis of the concept of the "ugly American," David Sanger wrote that the ambassador in the novel and film version of *The Ugly American* was "ugly" because he was "meddling [and] culturally obtuse." David Sanger, "Winning Ugly: Bashing America for Fun and Profit," *New York Times*, October 5, 1997, sec. 4, 1.

13. Lederer and Burdick, *The Ugly American*, 93. The *New York Times* review of the book was used by the publisher to sell the novel. It was reprinted on the front cover, and in capitals: "IF THIS WERE NOT A FREE COUNTRY, THIS BOOK WOULD BE BANNED. DEVASTATING."

14. Ibid., 95.

15. Lederer and Burdick's character bears some resemblance to Edward Lansdale, a CIA operative who worked under the cover of an Air Force officer, in the Philippines and Vietnam throughout the 1940s, 1950s, and 1960s. Unlike academics such as Rostow, Lansdale spent a great deal of time in Southeast Asia, and in contrast

to Lederer and Burdick's fictional Sarkhanese setting, he interacted with the real peoples and political movements in the Philippines and Vietnam. For a fuller discussion, see Jonathan Nashel, "*Edward Lansdale and the American Attempt to Remake Southeast Asia, 1945–65*" (Ph.D. dissertation, Rutgers University, 1994).

16. Lederer and Burdick, *The Ugly American*, 237.

17. Ibid., 237- 38.

18. True, by 1958 the Cold War had achieved some form of stability in Europe given that Austria was allowed to become neutral in 1955 and the German problem would not resurface again until 1961. But these events did not take place in Asia or Africa or Latin America—where most of the Cold War battles took place.

19. Stephen Sanderson, *Social Transformations: A General Theory of Historical Development* (Cambridge: Blackwell, 1995), 205.

20. Rostow, *Stages of Economic Growth*, 139. Rostow uses the word "disease" when describing communism on p. 162.

21. Louis Hartz, *The Liberal Tradition in America: An Interpretation of American Political Thought Since the Revolution* (New York: Harcourt Brace Jovanovich, 1955), 3.

22. Lloyd Gardner, *Pay Any Price: Lyndon Johnson and the Wars for Vietnam* (New York: Dee, 1995), 6, 321.

23. Lyndon Johnson, *The Vantage Point: Perspectives of the Presidency, 1963–1969* (New York: Holt, Rinehart, and Winston, 1971), 356.

24. David Halberstam, *The Best and the Brightest* (New York: Random House, 1972), 414.

25. Cited in Michael E. Latham, "Ideology, Social Science, and Destiny: Modernization and the Kennedy-Era Alliance for Progress," *Diplomatic History* 22. 2 (Spring 1998): 199.

26. For a full discussion of the origins of the U.S. attempt at "nation building" in Vietnam, see David Anderson, *Trapped by Success: The Eisenhower Administration and Vietnam, 1953–1961* (New York: Columbia University Press, 1991).

27. Dulles actually said, on June 9, 1956, that America's security arrangements "abolish. . .the principle of neutrality, which pretends that a nation can best gain safety for itself by being indifferent to the fate of others. This has increasingly become an obsolete conception, and, except under very exceptional circumstances, it is an immoral and shortsighted conception." *Department of State Bulletin*, June 18, 1956, 999–1000.

28. In Roger Hilsman, Jr., Interview, 8/14/70, John F. Kennedy Library Oral History Program, 23.

29. Neil Sheehan, *A Bright Shining Lie: John Paul Vann and America in Vietnam* (New York: Random House, 1988), 707.

30. Henry L. Trewhitt, *McNamara: His Ordeal in the Pentagon* (New York: Harper & Row, 1971), 257.

31. Kent Brown, *The Screenwriter as Collaborator: The Career of Stewart Stern* (New York: Arno, 1980), 153.

32. Robert S. McNamara, *In Retrospect: The Tragedy and Lessons of Vietnam* (New

York: Vintage, 1996), 246. McNamara adds a footnote to his discussion of the electronic fence which is, again, revealing of problems he encountered: "My account of the anti-infiltration barrier (or McNamara's Line, as it came to be called by some) is based on recollection rather than the contemporaneous record—largely because the August 1966 JASON study has yet to be declassified."

33. Deborah Shapley, *Promise and Power: The Life and Times of Robert McNamara* (Boston: Little, Brown, 1993), 362–63.

34. Ibid., 363.

35. William Gibbons, "The U.S. Government and the Vietnam War: Executive and Legislative Roles and Relationships, Part IV, July 1965–January 1968," Committee on Foreign Relations, United States Senate (Washington, D.C.: GPO, June 1994), 454–55.

36. Ibid., 457.

37. In a revisionist account of the Vietnam War, Harry Summers, *On Strategy: A Critical Analysis of the Vietnam War* (Novato, Calif.: Presidio Press, 1982), argues that the United States could have won the war using something akin to an electric barrier. His argument has come under extensive criticism for many of the reasons noted above (e.g., it would be a massive building project, it would place American troops on an ever more defensive posture, and the Communists could have circumvented it with ease).

38. Cited in Godfrey Hodgson, *America in Our Time: From World War II to Nixon; What Happened and Why* (Garden City, N.Y.: Doubleday, 1976), 239.

39. Cited in Tom Engelhardt, *The End of Victory Culture: Cold War America and the Disillusioning of a Generation* (New York: Basic Books, 1995), 211.

40. Halberstam, *The Best and the Brightest*, 348–49.

41. Cited in Ward Just, "McNamara's Complaint," *Diplomatic History* 20. 3 (Summer 1996): 463. Just goes on to note, "in an atmosphere whose context was progress, there was no in-box for retrogression or stasis" (465).

42. McNamara makes much of the lack of experts as a primary reason for America's failure in Vietnam, and places some of the blame for this failure on the "Witch hunts" generated by McCarthyism. See McNamara, *In Retrospect*, 32, 322. This view has come under extensive criticism. See, especially, Thomas L. Hughes, "Experiencing McNamara," *Foreign Policy* 100 (Fall 1995): 155–71. Hughes's review of McNamara's book is the most detailed to date and particularly incisive concerning the brutal and cunning ways that McNamara responded to those who questioned either his or the Pentagon's analysis of the war. This leads Hughes to note that McNamara has now "produce[d] his own strange retrospective-without-introspection" (155).

43. Shapley, *Promise and Power*, 299.

44. McNamara, *In Retrospect*, 6. It is somewhat curious that McNamara's book provoked so much furor given that McNamara has been saying essentially the same thing since he left the Johnson administration in 1968. For instance, his doubts were made clear in a series of memos to Johnson, which were made public with the release of *The Pentagon Papers* in 1971. And during the CBS-Westmoreland

libel trial in 1984, he stated in his deposition that "I did not believe the war could be won militarily." He said he came to this view in 1966, "if not earlier." He later said that it might have been 1965 (*New York Times*, May 16, 1984, 24). Concerning McNamara's politics, Deborah Shapley in her biography of McNamara refers to him as a "secret dove and dissenter" (Shapley, *Promise and Power,* 429).

45. "Mr. McNamara's War," *New York Times*, April 12, 1995. In some ways a more perceptive analysis of McNamara comes from the novelist Robert Stone. He wrote:

> . . . any judgment of McNamara ends up being conditioned by one's personal experience and political perspective, and even by one's temperament. Some people like to forgive, others enjoy not forgiving. There's another factor involved as well. If Ho Chi Minh and Vo Nguyen Giap had lost their war, they'd be universally condemned today as monsters who sent millions of their countrymen to the slaughter. We're all anti–Vietnam War now, with the possible exception of Ronald Reagan. As Churchill once observed, anyone who organizes a war would be well advised to win it. (Robert Stone, "Maximum Bob," *The Village Voice*, June 6, 1995, 76)

The reception of McNamara's book became a spectacle of opinions. Perhaps the angriest, after *New York Times* editorial, was David Halberstam's condemnation of McNamara as "a man so contorted and so deep in his own unique self-delusion and self-division that he still doesn't know who he is and what he did at that time" (*Los Angeles Times*, April 16, 1995). See also the roundtable discussion in *Diplomatic History* (Summer 1996) for a wide-ranging and altogether unsympathetic discussion of the man and his book.

46. Ronald Steel, "When Worlds Collide," *New York Times*, July 21, 1996, Sec. 4, 15.
47. David E. Lilienthal, "The Road to Change: Some Pages from Experience in the Practical Art of Getting Things Done," 24. In Lilienthal Papers, Seely Mudd Library, Princeton, N.J.
48. "David E. Lilienthal Is Dead at 81; Led U.S. Effort in Atomic Power," *New York Times*, January 16, 1981, 1.
49. David Lilienthal, *This I Do Believe* (New York: Harper & Brothers, 1949), 49–50.
50. Gardner, *Pay Any Price,* 320.
51. David E. Lilienthal, *The Journals of David E. Lilienthal: Volume VI: Creativity and Conflict* (New York: Harper & Row, 1976), 352, emphasis in original.
52. The concept of "measuring" is taken from Michael Adas, *Machines as the Measure of Men: Science, Technology, and Ideologies of Western Dominance* (Ithaca, N.Y.: Cornell University Press, 1989).
53. Lilienthal, *Journals: Volume VI,* 529.
54. Ibid., 417.
55. Ibid., 418.
56. Arthur Schlesinger, Jr., *Robert Kennedy and His Times* (Boston: Houghton Mifflin, 1978), 855.
57. Given the cyclical nature of so much of academic writing, it should come as little surprise that there has been a recent resurgence of interest in modernization the-

ory. See Francis Fukuyama's *The End of History and the Last Man,* 133, for his half-hearted approval of the theory. Also see Lucien Pye, "Political Science and the Crisis of Authoritarianism," *American Political Science Review* 84. 1 (1990), for a more vigorous defense of the theory.

58. Ian Roxborough, "Modernization Theory Revisited: A *Review Article,*" *Comparative Studies in Society and History* 30. 4 (October 1988): 755.

59. Karl Marx and Friedrick Engels, *Manifesto of the Communist Party,* in *The Marx-Engels Reader,* 2d. ed., ed. Robert C. Tucker (New York: Norton, 1978), 477.

Time, CIA Overthrow of Musaddiq, and the Shah

My thanks to research assistants Judi Kessler, who gathered all the data on the U.S. press for the period covered in this study—a Herculean feat—and Joe Bandy, who tirelessly tracked down references in the latter phases. Editor Chris Appy made numerous suggestions, large and small, for the improvement of this essay, as did an anonymous reviewer, and colleagues Arvind Rajagopal and Nikki Keddie.

1. Due to the complexities of transliterating Persian words and names, Musaddiq's name (and many others) can be spelled in a variety of ways, variants of which the reader will encounter in these pages.

2. General histories of Iran that cover this period include Ervand Abrahamian, *Iran Between Two Revolutions* (Princeton, N.J.: Princeton University Press, 1982); John Foran, *Fragile Resistance: Social Transformation in Iran from 1500 to the Revolution* (Boulder: Westview Press, 1993); Homa Katouzian, *The Political Economy of Modern Iran: Despotism and Pseudo-Modernism, 1926–1979* (New York: New York University Press, 1981); and Nikki Keddie, *Roots of Revolution: An Interpretive History of Modern Iran* (New Haven, Conn.: Yale University Press, 1981). Specialized studies of the period include Fakhreddin Azimi, *Iran: The Crisis of Democracy* (New York: St. Martin's, 1989); James Bill and Roger Louis, eds. *Musaddiq, Iranian Nationalism, and Oil* (Austin: University of Texas Press, 1988); Farhad Diba, *Mohammad Mosaddegh: A Political Biography* (London: Croom Helm, 1986); Mostafa Elm, *Oil, Power, and Principle: Iran's Oil Nationalization and Its Aftermath* (Syracuse: Syracuse University Press, 1992); Mark J. Gasiorowski, "The 1953 Coup d'Etat in Iran," *International Journal of Middle East Studies* 19 (August 1987): 261–86; Mary Ann Heiss, *Empire and Nationhood: The United States, Great Britain, and Iranian Oil, 1950–1954* (New York: Columbia University Press, 1997); Homa Katouzian, *Musaddiq and the Struggle for Power in Iran* (London: I. B. Tauris, 1990); Sussan Siavoshi, *Liberal Nationalism in Iran: The Failure of a Movement* (Boulder: Westview Press, 1990); and Sussan Siavoshi, "The Oil Nationalization Movement, 1949–53," in John Foran, ed., *A Century of Revolution: Social Movements in Iran* (Minneapolis: University of Minnesota Press, 1994), 106–34.

3. Tom Engelhardt, *The End of Victory Culture: Cold War America and the Disillusioning of a Generation* (New York: Basic Books/HarperCollins, 1995). Engelhardt's thesis is that a "victory culture" dates back to seventeenth-century captivity

narratives and began its *decline* with the blurring of victory and defeat after Hiroshima. I believe that the Cold War significantly recast the meaning of a victory
culture around a new set of conceptions of enemy and self. I thank Chris Appy for
clarifying these points in the argument.

4. A 1946 State Department memo from Loy Henderson (who would later become
U.S. ambassador to Iran in the Musaddiq years) to Dean Acheson (Secretary of
State from 1949), notes that the Joint Chiefs of Staff "hold the view that all the oil
fields of Iran, Saudi Arabia and Iraq are absolutely vital to the security of this country": U.S. National Archives (hereafter USNA), October 8, 1946, Office Memorandum, 891.00/10-846.

5. USNA, U.S. ambassador Allen, Tehran, to Secretary of State, Telegram 1597, Secret, December 17, 1946, 891.00/12-1746.

6. Third world cultural studies has affinities with postcolonial studies, subaltern studies, Marxist literary criticism, and other trends. I have not seen this label attached
to it by others. I teach a course with this name in which graduate students and I
have been trying to articulate its dimensions.

7. William A. Dorman and Mansour Farhang, *The U.S. Press and Iran: Foreign Policy
and the Journalism of Deference* (Berkeley: University of California Press, 1987).

8. Ibid., 8, with reference to Gaye Tuchman, *Making News: A Study in the Construction of Reality* (New York: Free Press, 1978), and Erving Goffman, *Frame Analysis:
An Essay on the Organization of Experience* (Cambridge, Mass.: Harvard University Press, 1974).

9. Dorman and Farhang, *The U.S. Press and Iran,* 2. This perspective is close to
Noam Chomsky's many works criticizing U.S. foreign policy and dissecting its in-
fluence on the media; see, inter alia, Noam Chomsky and Edward S. Herman,
Manufacturing Consent: The Political Economy of the Mass Media (New York:
Pantheon, 1988).

10. Ibid., 13, 2.

11. Ibid., 13.

12. Ibid., 19.

13. Ibid.

14. Ibid., 27–28.

15. Ibid., 30.

16. Mary Ann Heiss, "Culture, National Identity, and Oil in the Early 1950s: The
United States and Mohammad Mossadeq," paper presented at the Organization of
American Historians, Chicago (March 1996). See now also her book, *Empire and
Nationhood: The United States, Great Britian, and Iranian Oil, 1950–1954* (New
York: Columbia University Press, 1997).

17. Ibid., 1.

18. Ibid., 11.

19. Ibid., 4, quoting Ramsbotham to Logan, August 20, 1951, FO 371, 91580/
EP1531/1391.

20. Ibid., 5.

21. Ibid., 6, quoting Walter S. Gifford, Tel. 1698 to State Department, October 5,

1951, *Foreign Relations of the United States, 1952–1954* (Washington,D.C.: U.S. Government Printing Office, 1989), vol. 10, 205.

22. Ibid., 6, citing various U.S. and British diplomatic sources.

23. Ibid., 7, quoting Henderson, USNA, Tel. 377 to State Department, July 24, 1952, RG 59, 788.00/7-2452.

24. See, for example, Edward Said, *Culture and Imperialism* (New York: Vintage, 1994), and Aijaz Ahmad, *In Theory: Classes, Nations, Literatures* (London: Verso, 1992). The works of Stuart Hall are too numerous and hopefully well known to list here.

25. Peter Chua, "Third World/Cultural Studies Research Proposal," Department of Sociology, University of California, Santa Barbara (Fall 1996), 11.

26. Aldous Huxley, "Words and Their Meanings," in Max Black, ed., *The Importance of Language* (Englewood Cliffs, N.J.: Prentice-Hall, 1962), 1–2.

27. Dorman and Farhang, *The U.S. Press and Iran*, 33.

28. Ibid., 34.

29. Ibid., 36.

30. John Tebbel and Mary Ellen Zuckerman, *The Magazine in America 1741–1990* (New York: Oxford University Press, 1991), 161.

31. David Halberstam, *The Powers That Be* (New York: Alfred A. Knopf, 1979), 47–48; see also 46, and Tebbel and Zuckerman, *The Magazine in America,* 161, 174.

32. Stephen J. Whitfeld, *The Culture of the Cold War* (Baltimore: The Johns Hopkins University Press, 1991), 160; cf. Halberstam, *The Powers That Be,* 86. In a survey conducted in 1971–72, of some five hundred "leaders" (business executives, labor leaders, congressmen and senators, civil servants, mass media executives, party leaders, and heads of voluntary associations), *Time* was the most widely read magazine in the United States: read by 70 percent of industrial executives, 56 percent of nonindustrial executives, 57 percent of "owners of large wealth," 66 percent of congressmen and senators, 36 percent of high civil servants, 58 percent of political party leaders, 48 percent of heads of voluntary associations, 31 percent of labor leaders, and 76 percent of media executives and professionals. It was just ahead of *Newsweek* in most of these categories. It was virtually tied with *The New York Times* in most of these categories. Carol H. Weiss, "What America's Leaders Read," *The Public Opinion Quarterly* 38. 1 (Spring 1974): 6, table 2, 8, table 3.

33. Halberstam, *The Powers That Be,* 58.

34. *Time* (February 5, 1951), 20.

35. Ibid., 26.

36. *Time* (May 14, 1951), 28.

37. Ibid. The last sentence, ending the article, echoes the caption to the whole article: "You Don't Do That."

38. *Life* (May 21, 1951), 38.

39. Writing of *The Nation* in the late nineteenth century, Tebbel and Zuckerman note its "trickle-down influence on large numbers of people. It was quoted frequently in pulpit and press, and its ideas were sometimes the subject of debate in Congress" (*The Magazine in America,* 122).

40. *The Nation* (July 29, 1950), 108.

41. Thus Musaddiq's predecessor, Ali Razmara, is described as having "a reputation for honesty and selfless service rare among Iranians politicos." *Time* (July 10, 1951), 24.

42. *Time* (March 19, 1951), 37.

43. *Time* (August 27, 1951), 30.

44. *Time* (October 12, 1953), 30.

45. *Time* (February 5, 1951), 25.

46. *Time* (September 10, 1951), 36.

47. *Time* (August 27, 1951), 30. Cf. *Life,* which calls him "a young man who has always meant well"; (May 21, 1951), 38.

48. *Time* (January 9, 1950); (July 31, 1950), 25; (February 19, 1951), 80.

49. *Time* (November 27, 1950), 33; (April 24, 1950), 92; (February 5, 1951), 25.

50. *Time* (August 4, 1952), 22, 25. The same piece refers to the shah as "weak" and "too timid," in contrast with Musaddiq, "the undisputed strong man of Iran"; 27.

51. *Time* (March 9, 1953), 35.

52. The term "orientalism-in-reverse" is taken from Sadiq al-Azm, who uses it in a different way to offer a Left critique of Edward Said's influential book, *Orientalism.*

53. *Time* (May 7, 1951), 35.

54. *Time* (June 4, 1951), 30. He is on the cover of this issue, and the article is titled "Dervish in Pin-Striped Suit."

55. *Time* (January 7, 1952), 18.

56. Ibid., all quotes from 18–21.

57. Examples are found in *Time* (June 11, 1951), 32; (November 26, 1951), 38; (June 25, 1951), 33. This last piece contains a wonderful anecdote: "[U.S. Ambassador Henry Grady] sent a go-between to the bedside of frail, faint-prone Premier Mohammed Mossadeq, who was so weak that the doctors gave him a transfusion (seeing that it was American plasma, Mossadeq cracked: "Do you think it will make me more reasonable?")."

58. *Time* (December 31, 1951), 25. See also (September 17, 1951), 34; (October 15, 1951), 34; and Heiss, *Empire and Nationhood,* passim.

59. *Time* (May 28, 1951), 34.

60. *Time* (February 18, 1952), 41.

61. *Time* (June 4, 1951), 30.

62. *Time* (August 4, 1952), 27; (August 11, 1952), 32. On *The New York Times,* see Dorman and Farhang, *The U.S. Press and Iran,* 41–44.

63. The *Nation* (September 8, 1951), 183.

64. The *Nation* (August 23, 1952), 143.

65. *Time* (September 17, 1951), 34. Musaddiq's letter to the editor is quoted in the epigraph to this essay.

66. *Time* (January 8, 1951), 24.

67. *Time* (June 18, 1951), 17.

68. *Time* (June 4, 1951), 32.

69. *Life* (November 12, 1951), 36.

70. *Time* (January 7, 1952), 20.
71. *Time* (September 8, 1952), 40.
72. *Time* (September 29, 1952), 24.
73. The *Nation* (June 7, 1952), 553.
74. Halberstam, *The Powers That Be*, 90–92.
75. Dorman and Farhang, *The U.S. Press and Iran*, 45, quoting *Newsweek* (March 9, 1953), 27.
76. *Time* (February 16, 1953), 32.
77. *Time* (March 30, 1953), 29.
78. *Time* (July 13, 1953), 42.
79. *Time* (August 17, 1953), 27.
80. *New York Post* (July 13, 1953).
81. Gasiorowski, "The 1953 Coup d'Etat in Iran," 276, 275.
82. Cottam is quoted by Thomas Powers, "A Book Held Hostage" (review of Kermit Roosevelt's *Countercoup: The Struggle for the Control of Iran*), pp. 437–40 in *The Nation* (April 12, 1980), 439.
83. I rely in this section largely on Gasiorowski, "The 1953 Coup d'Etat in Iran." The standard accounts cited in note 2 are also all worth consulting, as they put the coup in the context of Iranian internal politics—and its interaction with the external forces—more than I can here.
84. British diplomat Sir George Middleton dates meetings of Zahidi with British and American officials as early as September 1951. The shah was brought into these conversations in the fall of 1952, and the plans included making Zahidi prime minister. Interview by Habib Ladjevardi, London, October 14, 1985, in the Iranian Oral History Project, Harvard University, 11–12, 15–16.
85. The use of the Iranian media in shaping the political culture of the period would be a fascinating study in itself.
86. Gasiorowski, "The 1953 Coup d'Etat in Iran," 285 note 67.
87. Dorman and Farhang, *The U.S. Press and Iran*, 47.
88. Ibid., 48, quoting *Newsweek* (August 31, 1953), 31.
89. All quotes in Dorman and Farhang, *The U.S. Press and Iran*, 48. A year later, *The Christian Science Monitor* editorialized: "It is now the estimate of responsible officials that Premier Mossadegh's regime was so infiltrated with Communists at the time it was overthrown by Gen. Fazlullah Zahedi, that if it had lasted two weeks more the Communists would have seized control of Iran. It was a close shave" (August 5, 1954), quoted in ibid., 65.
90. *Time* (August 31, 1953), 14. On September 14, *Time* does refer to "the anti-Mossadegh coup," interestingly enough.
91. *Time* (August 31, 1953), 15.
92. *Time* (September 7, 1953), 32.
93. *Time* (September 28, 1953), 28.
94. Ibid.
95. *Time* (November 30, 1953), 40; *Life* (November 23, 1953), 37.
96. *Time* (November 1, 1954), 37.

97. *Time* (February 15, 1954), 27.

98. *Time* (March 22, 1954), 38.

99. *Life* (March 22, 1954), 38.

100. *New York Times* (August 18, 1953).

101. Dorman and Farhang, *The U.S. Press and Iran,* 61, 55. The *Times* apparently did not report it until 1971, "and then only in passing": David Detmer, "Covering Up Iran: Why Vital Information Is Routinely Excluded from U.S. Mass Media News Accounts," pp. 91–101 in Yahya R. Kamalipour, ed., *The U.S. Media and the Middle East: Image and Perception* (Westport, Conn.: Greenwood Press, 1995), 94, referring to Dorman and Farhang, *The U.S. Press and Iran,* 54, 119–20. The October 12, 1971, *Times* editorial "In the Footsteps of Cyrus?" reads: "Shah Pahlevi, who was put on the throne by the British during World War II and who retained it only after C.I.A. intervention during the Mossadeq uprisings in 1953, is no Cyrus. Nor should he aspire to be, beyond emulating the ancient ruler's reputation for tolerance and justice." A passing reference indeed, leaving the reader imagining that Musaddiq had led some sort of insurrection in 1953!

102. Richard and Gladys Harkness, "The Mysterious Doings of CIA," part two, *Saturday Evening Post* (November 6, 1954).

103. Dorman and Farhang, *The U.S. Press and Iran,* 49.

104. A. Kessel, "Iran's Fabulous Oil and Some Popular Fables," *The Nation* (September 11, 1954), 212.

105. The phrase is that of one of the English founders of cultural studies, Raymond Williams.

106. Quoted in Diba, *Mohammad Mosaddegh,* 189.

Eisenhower's Guatemalan Doodle

1. Rockwell met Eisenhower in 1952 when he painted a portrait of the Republican presidential candidate for the *Saturday Evening Post.* Eisenhower had taken up painting a few years before while president of Columbia and took the opportunity to ask Rockwell for some tips. He asked Rockwell if he used black on his palette. Rockwell advised Eisenhower to make his black from softer hues. *Saturday Evening Post,* June 11, 1955. On the proliferation of art as a popular hobby, television and mail-order art classes, and the paint-by-numbers craze, see Karal Ann Marling, *As Seen on TV: Visual Culture of Everyday Life in the 1950s* (Cambridge, Mass.: Harvard University Press, 1994), 50–84. The stag party invitation lists are available at the Eisenhower Library. A stag party held in the midst of the CIA-sponsored coup in Guatemala on June 24, 1954, is typical. Of the seventeen guests, there were ten corporate executives, three retired generals, one admiral, two government leaders, and the head of a right-wing foundation (Freedom's Foundation). I include Arthur Vandenberg as a government leader though he was by then teaching at the University of Miami. Eisenhower Library, Ann Whitman File, DDE Diary Series, Box #7.

2. After finding this sketch in the Eisenhower Library, I discovered that Robert Ferrell had published the document as an illustration in his edited compilation of Ei-

senhower's diaries. However, Ferrell makes no mention of the Guatemalan coup, thus perpetuating the silence surrounding not only covert operations, but historical questions that leave few documents. See Robert H. Ferrell, ed., *The Eisenhower Diaries* (New York: W. W. Norton, 1981), 283.

3. Ann Whitman Files, Legislative Meeting Series, Box 1, 1954 (3), Eisenhower Library.

4. Important books on the subject include: Stephen Schlesinger and Stephen Kinzer, *Bitter Fruit: The Untold Story of the American Coup in Guatemala* (New York: Anchor Books, 1982); Richard H. Immerman, *The CIA in Guatemala* (Austin: The University of Texas Press, 1982); Piero Gleijeses, *Shattered Hope: The Guatemalan Revolution and the United States, 1954* (Princeton, N.J.: Princeton University Press, 1991); Jim Handy, *Gift of the Devil* (Boston: South End Press, 1984); Blanche Wiesen Cook, *The Declassified Eisenhower* (Garden City, N.Y.: Doubleday & Co., 1981); Nick Cullather, *Secret History: The CIA's Classified Account of its Operations in Guatemala, 1952–54* (Stanford, CA: Stanford University Press, 1999). I completed my essay prior to consulting Cullather's valuable work. While it provides some important new details, it does not alter the substance of my argument.

5. As Blanche Wiesen Cook put it: "The events that occurred in Iran and Guatemala during 1953 and 1954 globalized that aspect of United States foreign policy known as 'gunboat diplomacy.'" *The Declassified Eisenhower,* 218.

6. By contrast, Christina Klein's recent work demonstrates an abundance of "middlebrow" cultural texts such as musicals and travel narratives that emphatically seek to construct cross-national and cross-racial feelings of obligation, mutuality, and personal commitment. These works serve to garner consent for U.S. Cold War assertions of international power by coding it in nonimperial rhetoric and representation. See her essay in this volume, along with Christina Klein, "Cold War Orientalism: Musicals, Travel Narratives, and Middlebrow Culture in Postwar America," Yale University Ph.D. dissertation, 1997. She also points out that Eisenhower was a great advocate of international "understanding," tourism, and "People-to-People" exchanges.

7. Though Eisenhower had initially approved the coup several months earlier, the prominence he gives the Peurifoy report in his memoir suggests that it may have been decisive in persuading Eisenhower to go forward with the plan.

8. Eisenhower does not quote the original Peurifoy memo, but a retrospective summary. The lines about "normal approaches" and "the candle" come from the original memo and are not quoted in Eisenhower's book *Mandate for Change*. "Talked like a Communist" is a slight rephrasing of the original memo and is the version Eisenhower quotes. For the original memo see Schlesinger and Kinzer, *Bitter Fruit,* 137–39. For the retrospective summary quoted by Eisenhower see Dwight D. Eisenhower, *Mandate for Change* (Garden City, N.Y.: Doubleday, 1963), 422.

9. The first important scholarly works to present this revised view of Eisenhower were Fred I. Greenstein, *The Hidden-Hand Presidency* (New York: Basic Books, 1982) and Blanche Wiesen Cook, *The Declassified Eisenhower.*

10. Curt Sampson, *The Eternal Summer* (Dallas: Taylor Publishing Group, 1992), 5.

11. Stephen E. Ambrose, *Eisenhower: The President* (New York: Touchstone, 1984), 111, 193; Immerman, *The CIA in Guatemala*, 134.

12. Stephen G. Rabe, *Eisenhower and Latin America* (Chapel Hill: The University of North Carolina Press, 1988), 26–27.

13. James C. Hagerty Papers, Diary, Box 1, Eisenhower Library.

14. Ann Whitman File, DDE Diary Series, Box 7, Eisenhower Library.

15. Ibid.

16. Ibid.

17. Walter LaFeber, *Inevitable Revolutions: The United States in Central America* (New York: W. W. Norton, 1984), 111.

18. Gleijeses, *Shattered Hope*, 13.

19. Cole Blasier, *The Hovering Giant: U.S. Responses to Revolutionary Change in Latin America* (Pittsburgh: University of Pittsburgh Press, 1976), 205.

20. Jim Handy, *Revolution in the Countryside: Rural Conflict and Agrarian Reform in Guatemala, 1944–1954* (Chapel Hill: University of North Carolina Press, 1994), 86–92, 170–73.

21. John H. Coatsworth provides a convenient chart of the links between U.S. officials and UFCO in *Central America and the United States* (New York: Twayne, 1994), 87. The Dulles brothers, for example, had been partners at Sullivan and Cromwell in the 1930s, the firm that cut the sweetheart contract between UFCO and Ubico. Leonard Mosely, *Dulles: A Biography of Eleanor, Allen, and John Foster Dulles and Their Family Network* (New York: Dell, 1978), 92; Handy, *Revolution in the Countryside*, 173.

22. Gleijeses, *Shattered Hope*, 362.

23. For a cogent summary of this evidence and the Eisenhower's "penchant for mistaking nationalism for communism," see Chester J. Pach, Jr., and Elmo Richardson, *The Presidency of Dwight Eisenhower* (Lawrence: University of Kansas Press, 1991), 89–93; Rabe, *Eisenhower and Latin America*, 46–7.

24. According to Richard Bissell, covert operations often had arbitrary two-letter prefixes, so PB may be meaningless. See Gleijeses, Shattered Hope, 243.

25. Gleijeses, Shattered Hope, 244.

26. Immerman, *The CIA in Guatemala*, 133–43.

27. *New York Times*, May 18, 1954, p. 10.

28. *New York Times*, May 19, 1954, p. 1.

29. *New York Times*, July 9, 1954, p. 1, 4.

30. Papers of John Foster Dulles, Telephone Calls Series, Box #2, Telephone Conversation with Mr. Allen Dulles, May 19, 1954, 8:56 A. M., Eisenhower Library.

31. Gleijeses, *Shattered Hope*, 320–22.

32. Ibid., 323–24.

33. Schlesinger and Kinzer, *Bitter Fruit*, 115–16.

34. The *Times* reports on possible strafing as early as June 15; other sources date the beginning of the air operations on June 18.

35. Gleijeses, *Shattered Hope*, 332–33.

36. Cited in Richard M. Bissell, Jr., *Reflections of a Cold Warrior* (New Haven, Conn.: Yale University Press, 1996), 85.

37. The planes were old and vulnerable because the operation planners had insisted on plausible deniability, thus requiring that the CIA use planes the rebels might have reasonably purchased on the black market. Bissell, *Reflections of a Cold Warrior* 87.

38. When Holland first heard of the operation in early April 1953 (after replacing John Moors Cabot in March), he briefly considered resigning in protest. Holland stayed on in hopes of preventing the operation from going forward, though once the operation succeeded he became a strong advocate of CIA operations. Gleijeses, *Shattered Hope*, 245.

39. Eisenhower, *Mandate for Change*, 425–26.

40. Ibid.

41. *The Pentagon Papers: The Defense Department History of United States Decisionmaking on Vietnam: The Senator Gravel Edition,* 4 vols. (Beacon Press, 1971), 3:312–15.

42. Robert S. McNamara, *In Retrospect: The Tragedy and Lessons of Vietnam* (New York: Vintage Books, 1996), 32.

43. Fred Kaplan, *The Wizards of Armageddon* (New York: Simon and Schuster, 1983), 134.

44. Peter R. Beckman, et al., *The Nuclear Predicament* (Englewood Cliffs, N.J.: Prentice Hall, 1992), 76.

45. John Lord O'Brian, *National Security and Individual Freedom* (Cambridge, Mass.: Harvard University Press, 1955), 22.

46. Daniel Hallin, *The "Uncensored War": The Media and Vietnam* (New York: Oxford University Press, 1986).

47. Peter Grose, *Gentleman Spy: The Life of Allen Dulles* (Boston: Houghton Mifflin, 1994), 171.

48. Gleijeses, *Shattered Hope*, 130–33.

49. Immerman, *The CIA in Guatemala*, 118–122.

50. Gleijeses, *Shattered Hope*, 240–42.

51. Ibid., 242.

52. Schlesinger and Kinzer, *Bitter Fruit*, 87.

53. Ibid., 88–89.

54. Ibid., 94–95.

55. *New York Times*, June 27, 1954, Section IV, p. 4.

56. Peter Grose, *Gentleman Spy*, 380; Harrison E. Salisbury, *Without Fear or Favor: An Uncompromising Look at the New York Times* (New York: Times Books, 1980), 478–82.

57. Burton Hersh, *The Old Boys: The American Elite and the Origins of the CIA* (New York: Charles Scribner's Sons, 1992), 348.

58. Gleijeses, *Shattered Hope*, 335. According to Gleijeses, on many occasions in the spring of 1954 American military officers and embassy officials approached Guatemalan officers with an ultimatum—get rid of Arbenz or the United States will intervene and do it themselves. Especially important to his case are several interviews with former Guatemalan officers and former U.S. deputy chief of mission Bill Krieg (see p. 305). Historian Jim Handy offers a somewhat different interpreta-

tion. He believes significant elements of the military and economically privileged moved against Arbenz primarily out of their own antipathy toward Arbenz rather than from U.S. pressure, though that pressure may have acted as a trigger. Handy, *Revolution in the Countryside*, 169.

59. *New York Times*, June 27, 1954, IV, p. 1.

60. *New York Times*, May 27, 1954, 6.

61. *New York Times*, May 23, 1954, 9.

62. Matt S. Meier and Feliciano Rivera, *The Chicanos* (New York: Hill and Wang, 1972), 227.

63. "First Pictures from Guatemala," Pathé News, June 22, 1954, Sherman Grinberg Film Library, Library No. D-6182, Issue 90.

64. Hanson W. Baldwin, "Opera-Bouffe, But Crucial," *New York Times*, June 22, 1954, p. 4.

65. *New York Times*, June 20, 1954, 1.

66. Wiesen Cook, *The Declassified Eisenhower*, 277.

67. Ibid., 278.

68. Carl W. McCardle Papers, 1953–57, Series II: Dulles' Statements and Press Conferences, Box 6, Eisenhower Library.

69. Thomas McCann, *An American Company: The Tragedy of United Fruit* (New York: Crown, 1976), 60. McCann, who worked for twenty years in public relations for the United Fruit Company, admitted in this book that they had no idea what the photographs showed. They were just looking for gruesome pictures and supplied the captions.

70. Immerman, *The CIA in Guatemala*, 180–82; Eisenhower, *Mandate for Change*, 425.

71. *New York Times*, June 21, 1954; Schlesinger and Kinzer, *Bitter Fruit*, 172;

72. *New York Times*, July 1, 1950, 2. Dulles's redundant emphasis on the behavior of the "Guatemalans *themselves*" is reminiscent of the way American officials during the Vietnam War continually invoked the "Vietnamese themselves." While it gave lip service to the importance of third world people charting their own destiny, it really was defensive rhetorical camouflage thinly hiding the fact that the United States was *not* allowing the Vietnamese to make their own history. See Jonathan Schell's excellent gloss of this issue in his introduction to *The Real War* (New York: Pantheon, 1986), 5–8.

73. Designated as "the supreme chief of the movement of national liberation," Castillo Armas announced in a June 17 interview that he was pledged to drastically revise the Agrarian Reform Law to offer landowners fair compensation for their land. In fact he returned most of it. *New York Times*, June 21, 1954, 3.

74. Tyler Abell, ed., *Drew Pearson Diaries: 1949–1959* (New York: Holt, Rinehart and Winston, 1974), 321. While Pearson offered tacit support for Peurifoy, his own Guatemalan proposal was to establish a "summer camp in Guatemala with perhaps the sending of a thousand young Americans, 4-H Club members, people of all religious groups, to work with Guatemala and show them that we are real human beings, and not all executives of United Fruit Company." Ibid., 297.

75. *New York Times*, June 20, 1954, Section IV, p. 8.

76. *New York Times*, June 22, 1954, 2.

77. *New York Times*, June 22, 1954, 8.

78. *New York Times*, May 18, 1954, 10.

79. *New York Times*, June 22, 1954, 8; Schlesinger and Kinzer, *Bitter Fruit*, 186.

80. *Revolt in Guatamala*, Pathé News, June 19–20, 1954, Issue 89; *The First Hours of Peace in Guatemala*, Pathé News, July 2–6, 1954, Sherman Grinberg Film Library, Library No. D-6209, Issue 94.

81. Flora Lewis, "Ambassador Extraordinary: John Peurifoy," *New York Times* Magazine, July 18, 1954.

82. Cited in Immerman, *The CIA in Guatemala*, 178.

83. Eisenhower, *Mandate for Change*, 435.

84. Cited in David Wise and Thomas B. Ross, *The Invisible Government* (New York: Random House, 1964), 166.

85. *Time*, August 23, 1954, 34; Immerman, *The CIA in Guatemala*, 200.

86. *New York Times*, July 9, 1954, 4; Wendy Kozol has argued that even in the darkest years of the Cold War, *Life* magazine sometimes provided grounds for dissenting interpretations. See *Life's America* (Philadephia: Temple University Press, 1994).

The Vietnam Lobby and the Politics of Pluralism

1. I use "non-Communist Left" to designate those individuals whose politics ranged from activities on the left wing of the Democratic Party to the various socialist groupings found in the United States between the 1920s and the 1950s. Most but not all of the non-Communist leftists at the Vietnam Lobby had socialist backgrounds: few had been Communists, as far I know, and fewer still could have been considered repentant ex-leftists as of the mid-1950s. Robert Scheer and Warren Hinckle, in "The Vietnam Lobby," *Ramparts* (July 1965), 16–24, established the enduring model for New Left critiques of postwar American cultural imperialism. An equally influential work utilizing the same approach was Christopher Lasch's essay, "The Cultural Cold War," originally published in *The Nation* in September 1967, and reprinted in Christopher Lasch, *The Agony of the American Left* (New York: Knopf, 1969), 63–114.

2. Eric Thomas Chester, *Covert Network: Progressives, The International Rescue Committee, and the CIA* (Armonk, N.Y., M. E. Sharpe, 1995); Joseph G. Morgan, *The Vietnam Lobby: The American Friends of Vietnam, 1955–1975* (Chapel Hill, University of North Carolina Press, 1997); other valuable works that discuss aspects of the Vietnam Lobby include William Conrad Gibbons, *The U.S. Government and the Vietnam War: Executive and Legislative Roles and Relationships, Part I: 1945–1960* (Princeton, N.J.: Princeton University Press, 1986), 301–5, and David L. Anderson, *Trapped by Success: The Eisenhower Administration and Vietnam, 1953–1961* (New York: Columbia University Press, 1991), 158–62.

3. Thomas W. Braden, "I'm Glad the CIA is 'Immoral,'" *Saturday Evening Post* (May 20, 1967), 19–12.

4. For a fascinating treatment of the emerging discourses of "difference" and "tolerance" among American social scientists, see Christopher Shannon, "A World Made
Safe for Differences: Ruth Benedict's *The* Chrysanthemum *and the Sword," American Quarterly* 47 (December 1995), 659–80.

5. Scheer and Hinckle, "The Vietnam Lobby," 17–21.

6. Robert Scheer conducted extensive research in Vietnam and the United States for
a study of the origins of American intervention commissioned by the Center for
the Study of Democratic Institutions. In that report, *How the United States Got
Involved in Vietnam* (Santa Barbara: Center for the Study of Democratic Institutions, 1965), Scheer did not repeat the most glaring error from the *Ramparts* article, a claim that Diem, as of 1950, "was in the seventeenth year of a self-imposed
exile" (18). Diem had in fact remained in Vietnam through the entire period in
question and was a prominent figure in at least some important nationalist circles.
While the Scheer-Hinckle essay was remarkably perceptive in many ways, the authors' inability to take Diem at all seriously was echoed in subsequent writing by
others. In a 1972 essay Scheer described Diem as "this former French colonial
official, who had been plucked out of the obscurity of a life in the Maryknoll Catholic Seminary in New Jersey." See Robert Scheer, "The Language of Torturers," in
Thinking Tuna Fish, Talking Death: Essays on the Pornography of Power (New
York: Hill and Wang, 1978), 139; for Diem as Confucian, see Denis Warner, *The
Last Confucian* (New York: Macmillan, 1963), 68–69, 72; Ellen Hammer, *A Death
in November: America in Vietnam, 1963* (New York: Oxford University Press,
1987), 47–49; for Diem's ascent to power see Anderson, *Trapped by Success*,
53–56; Bernard Fall, *The Two Viet-Nams* (New York: Praeger, 1963), 244; Neil
Sheehan, *A Bright Shining Lie: John Paul Vaan and America in Vietnam,* (New
York: Random House, 1988), 175.

7. Aaron Levenstein, *Escape to Freedom: The Story of the International Rescue Committee* (Westport, Conn.: Greenwood Press, 1983), 9; interview with Harold L.
Oram, August 12, 1986.

8. By far the most thorough and reliable account of the roles played by Oram, Buttinger, and other leftists in the Vietnam Lobby is to be found in Morgan, *The Vietnam Lobby*, 19–20, 62–92; Joseph Buttinger, "Are We Saving South Vietnam," *New
Leader* (June 27, 1955): S13; Oram recounted Buttinger's hopes for a socialist
South Vietnam in the August 12, 1986, interview. In *Vietnam: The Unforgettable
Tragedy* (New York: Horizon, 1977), Joseph Buttinger reported that he told Diem
in 1954: "You must undo the harm the French did that strengthened the Communists; you must build a socially progressive society through a radical land-reform
and through rapid economic progress with American aid; and you must let all non-
Communist parties, groups, spokesmen, the politically concerned students and intellectuals participate in the country's political life" (46). Buttinger claimed that he
had his first "serious disagreement" with Diem over land reform in December
1954, but that by the time "Diem visited the United States in May, 1957, I was still
far from realizing that behind a pseudo-democratic façade his policy had become
the very opposite of what I considered the only justification for American support

of a non-Communist regime in Saigon" (48). By August 1958, however, Buttinger had completely lost faith in Diem: in 1962 he became "a really active and determined opponent of the Diem regime" (50).

9. Morgan, *The Vietnam Lobby*, 22.

10. Chester, *Covert Network*, 6, 12–13.

11. *Ibid.*, 5, 16–17, Braden, "I'm Glad the CIA is 'Immoral,'" 10.

12. Leo Cherne's background is discussed in Joseph E. Persico, *Casey: From the OSS to the CIA* (New York: Viking, 1990), 40–43, and Roberta Ostroff, *Fire in the Wind: The Life of Dickey Chapelle* (New York: Ballantine, 1992), 180–81, 187; for Cherne's annual predictions see William F. Buckley's column in the *New York Daily News*, September 6, 1991; Marvin Liebman, *Coming Out Conservative* (San Francisco: Chronicle Books, 1992). 83.

13. Chester, *Covert Network*, 6–19: Morgan, *The Vietnam Lobby*, 17, Levenstein, *Escape to Freedom*, 51–2, *Washington Times*, July 15, 1991.

14. "TV Panel Makes More Noise Than Sense," *Life* (April 14, 1952), 101–10.

15. Natalie Robins, "Inside the FBI," *National Review* (May 11, 1992), 44; Paul Blanshard, *Communism, Democracy, and Catholic Power* (Boston: Beacon Press, 1951), 129. For an excellent treatment of the troubled relationship between Catholicism and twentieth-century American liberalism, see John T. McGreevy, "Thinking on One's Own: Catholicism in the American Intellectual Imagination, 1928–1960," *Journal of American History* 84 (June 1997): 97–131.

16. Warren Hinckle's *Ramparts*, ironically, was largely responsible for the intensive scrutiny paid to the Congress for Cultural Freedom at the expense, perhaps, of further inquiry into the Vietnam Lobby. *Ramparts* broke the story of CIA funding for the National Student Association in March 1967. Since by that time most American intellectuals were opposed to the Vietnam War—and because the funding trail leading from the NSA to the CIA and back to such groups as the Congress for Cultural Freedom was easier to trace than that connecting the agency with the Vietnam Lobby—a wave of indignation quickly broke out in the New Left. Christopher Lasch's celebrated 1967 essay "The Cultural Cold War" was remarkably similar in tone to Scheer and Hinckle's original exposé of the Vietnam Lobby, yet Lasch's targets at the CCF were but relatively ineffectual Cold War intellectuals, especially compared with Diem's retainers in the Vietnam Lobby. For a more realistic if partisan treatment of the CCF see Peter Coleman, *The Liberal Conspiracy: The Congress for Cultural Freedom and the Struggle for the Mind of Postwar Europe* (New York: Free Press, 1989); for Leo Cherne's relationship with William Casey, see interview with Leo Cherne, December 7, 1990; Morgan, *The Vietnam Lobby*, 56–62; Persico, *Casey*, 42.

17. Leo Cherne to Daly C. Lavergne, October 13, 1954, Box 32, Cherne Papers, Special Collections and Archives, Boston University; Muriel Gardiner, *Code Name Mary: Memoirs of An American Woman in the Austrian Underground* (New Haven,Conn.: Yale University Press, 1983), 70.

18. Morgan, *The Vietnam Lobby*, 24–26.

19. *Ibid.*, 34–35, 39.

20. *Ibid.*, 47; Anderson, *Trapped by Success*, 141–47.

21. Morgan, *The Vietnam Lobby*, 91–93; Scheer and Hinckle, "The Vietnam Lobby," 19–22.

22. Blanshard, *Communism, Democracy, and Catholic Power*, 129.

23. Richard Gid Powers, *Not Without Honor: The History of American Anticommunism* (New York: Free Press, 1995), 109–10; Blanshard, *Communism, Democracy, and Catholic Power*, 105.

24. Blanshard, *Communism, Democracy, and Catholic Power*, 297; Shannon, "A World Made Safe for Differences," 660.

25. Liebman, *Coming Out Conservative*, 82.

26. Blanshard, *Communism, Democracy, and Catholic Power*, 234; telephone interview with Peter White, January 28, 1993; Peter White, personal correspondence, February 13, 1993.

27. Peter White, personal correspondence, February 23 and March 11, 1993; Angier Biddle Duke to Emmanuel Jacques, S. J., January 4, 1956; Gilbert Jonas to Father McLuskey, S. J., January 9, 1956; Angier Biddle Duke to Christopher Emmett, January 9, 1956; Fr. Emmanuel Jacques, S. J., to Angier Biddle Duke, January 11, 1956, Box 12, American Friends of Vietnam Papers, Center for the Study of the Vietnam Conflict, Texas Tech University, Lubbock, Texas; "Diem Firmly in the Saddle," *America* 94 (March 24, 1956): 680.

28. Memorandum of a conversation between the Special Representative in Vietnam (Collins) and Bishop Ngo Dinh Thuc, Saigon, March 25, 1955, *Foreign Relations of the United States, 1955–1957, Vol. 1, Vietnam* (Washington, D.C.: U.S. Government Printing Office, 1985), 145–46; John Cooney, *The American Pope: The Life and Times of Francis Cardinal Spellman* (New York: Times Books, 1984), 243–44; Chester L. Cooper, *The Lost Crusade: America in Vietnam* (New York: Dodd, Mead, 1970), 124–25.

29. Warren Hinckle, *If You Have a Lemon, Make Lemonade: An Essential Memoir of a Lunatic Decade* (New York: 1974), 145; Hinckle's collaboration with Robert Scheer neatly paralleled the unlikely intercultural alliance enshrined in the Vietnam Lobby. "I had never met anyone quite like Scheer," Hinckle wrote in his memoir. "I also came to understand Scheer's deep-rooted competitiveness (which made him a damn good journalist) in terms of his four-year survival course in the left-wing Jewish intellectual Olympics at New York's City College, with its constant one-upmanship and leftist backstabbing. I was unable to even imagine the conditions of such a combatant world. But if I thought Scheer was from Mars, he thought I was from Pluto, with my imperious, fat-dumb-and happy Irish attitude toward everything" (102).

30. "An Address by His Excellency Ngo Dinh Diem," Waldorf-Astoria Hotel, May 13, 1957, UA 1269, Box 5, Wesley Fishel Papers, Michigan State University Archives and Historical Collections.

31. "Reception Speech by His Excellency Ngo Dinh Diem," Seton Hall University, South Orange, New Jersey, May 12, 1957, UA 1269, Box 5, Fishel Papers, MSU.

32. Interview with Gilbert Jonas, September 19, 1991; William Prochnau, *Once Upon a Distant War* (New York: Times Books, 1955), 17.

33. Denis Warner, *The Last Confucian* (New York: Macmillan, 1963), 68–69, 72–73.

34. Frances Fitzgerald, *Fire in the Lake: The Vietnamese and the Americans in Vietnam* (Boston: Atlantic–Little, Brown, 1972), 127–28.

35. Bernard Fall, *The Two Viet-Nams: A Political and Military Analysis* (New York: Praeger, 1963), 237, 246–52; Fall is quoted in Joseph Buttinger, *Vietnam: A Dragon Embattled, Vol. II, Vietnam at War* (New York, Praeger, 1967), 1095–96, n. 2.

36. Alfred Katz to Harold Oram, February 13, 1956, and May 2, 1956, Box 12, American Friends of Vietnam Papers, Center for the Study of the Vietnam Conflict, Texas Tech University, Lubbock, Texas; Minutes of Executive Committee of the American Friends of Vietnam, February 14 and May 8, 1956, courtesy of Brother Joseph G. Morgan; Jonathan Nashel, "Edward G. Lansdale and the American Attempt to Remake Southeast Asia, 1945–1965," Ph.D. dissertation, Rutgers University, 1994, 282–96; Gilbert Jonas interview. Buttinger quoted Donald Lancaster on Lansdale in *Vietnam: A Dragon Embattled*, 1113, n.95.

37. Graham Greene, *The Quiet American* (New York: Viking Press, 1955); Edward G. Lansdale to Joseph L. Mankiewicz, March 17, 1956, Box 35, Edward G. Lansdale Papers, Hoover Institution on War, Revolution and Peace, Palo Alto, California.

38. Lansdale to Mankiewicz, March 17, 1956; Alfred Katz to Harold Oram, May 2, 1956; Stephen Whitfield, in "Limited Engagement: *The Quiet American* as History," *Journal of American Studies* 30 (April 1996): 69, accurately debunks the Lansdale-as-Pyle theory, though Whitfield was apparently not aware of Lansdale's role in the cinematic version of *The Quiet American*.

39. *The Quiet American*, directed by Joseph L. Mankiewicz, produced by Samuel Goldwyn, screenplay by Joseph L. Mankiewicz (Figaro, Inc./United Artists, 1958).

40. Kenneth L. Geist, *Pictures Will Talk: The Life and Films of Joseph L. Mankiewicz* (New York: Scribner, 1978), 275–76; Nashel, "Edward G. Lansdale," 294–95.

41. Scheer and Hinckle, "The Vietnam Lobby," 20–21.

42. Ibid., 24; Joseph Buttinger, *In the Twilight of Socialism: A History of the Revolutionary Socialists of Austria* (New York, 1953), 549. Joseph Buttinger figured prominently in the intergenerational drama concocted by members of the New Left to distance themselves from their elders. Todd Gitlin, in *The Sixties: Years of Hope, Days of Rage* (New York: Bantum Books, 1987), 171–75, recounted a difficult meeting between several SDS members (Gitlin included) and Buttinger, Irving Howe, and other *Dissent*-style socialists. "Generations crystallize around their memories," wrote Gitlin. "So do political rifts." At the end of the meeting, held in Buttinger's elegant Manhattan town house, the socialist elder presented Gitlin and Tom Hayden with a copy of *In the Twilight of Socialism*. Gitlin was "both moved and uneasy" about the title, although it is not clear whether he read the book to discover how misleading was its title. "But through no fault of his own," Gitlin recalled thinking, "history had condemned him to be a loser." Gitlin did acknowledge, however, that his cohort's dismissal of Buttinger "didn't stop us from going to Buttinger's family foundation" the following year to request a grant for the SDS's Economic Research and Action Project, "a request he graciously granted." The SDS-*Dissent* summit meeting is recounted as well in Maurice Isserman, *If I Had a Hammer: The Death of the Old Left and the Birth of the New* (Urbana: University

of Illinois Press, 1993), 216. Isserman's study is more attentive to continuities within the Left than other works on the topic. Allen W. Dulles to Leo Cherne, May 9, 1953, Box 56, Allen W. Dulles Papers, Seeley Mudd Library, Princeton University; for the IRC's role in Operation Brotherhood see Leo Cherne to Wesley Fishel, April 17, 1955, UA 1269, Box 7, Fishel Papers; Chester, *Covert Network,* 153–54; see also Cecil B. Currey, *Edward Lansdale, the Unquiet American* (Boston: Houghton Mifflin, 1988) 159, 165, 342.

43. Evan Thomas, *The Very Best Men: Four Who Dared: The Early Years of the CIA* (New York: Simon and Schuster, 1995), 100–101.

44. Joseph Buttinger, "Fact and Fiction on Foreign Aid," *Dissent* 6 (Summer 1959): 316–67; for the tributes of Foreign Service personnel to Buttinger, see C. Alphonso Smith to Joseph Buttinger, July 17, 1959, Loy W. Henderson to Joseph Buttinger, June 29, 1959, and Elbridge Durbrow to Joseph Buttinger, July 1, 1959, Box 9, Joseph Buttinger Papers, Harvard-Yenching Library.

45. Seymour Martin Lipset, *Political Man: The Social Bases of Politics* (Garden City, N.Y.: Doubleday, 1960), 516–17; Godfrey Hodgson, *America in Our Time* (Garden City, N.Y.: Doubleday, 1976), 95.

46. Morgan, *The Vietnam Lobby,* 159; McGreevy, "Thinking on One's Own," 118.

47. Lansdale quoted in Currey, *Edward Lansdale,* 165; Geist, *Pictures Will Talk,* 275.

48. For Dooley see James T. Fisher, *Dr. America: The Lives of Thomas A. Dooley, 1927–1961* (Amherst: University of Massachusetts Press, 1997).

49. Edward G. Lansdale to Maj. Gen. John W. O'Daniel (ret.), August 5, 1963, Box 39, Edward G. Lansdale Papers, Hoover Institution on War, Revolution and Peace, Palo Alto, California.

50. Esther Pike to Angier Biddle Duke, March 24, 1958, Box 12, AFV Papers, Lubbock; Draft letter, Angier Biddle Duke to Esther Pike, April 23, 1958, Box 12, AFV Papers, Lubbock.

51. Timothy J. Sarbaugh, "'No Catholic in the White House': John Fitzgerald Kennedy, the Catholic Vote, and Presidential Politics, 1959–1960," unpublished manuscript, 34.

52. Sen. John F. Kennedy, "America's Stake in Vietnam," in *A Symposium on America's Stake in Vietnam* (New York: HarperCollins, 1956), 8–14.

53. Gerald S. and Deborah H. Strober, *"Let Us Begin Anew": An Oral History of the Kennedy Presidency* (New York: 1993), 419; Ellen J. Hammer, *A Death in November: America in Vietnam, 1963* (New York: 1987), 300–301.

Fidel Castro and the White Guerrilla

1. *New York Times,* February 24, 1957, 1. This is the lead sentence in the top left hand, front page article, next to a grainy closeup of Matthews and Castro conferring together on a hillside. Castro had landed in Cuba with a small force in early December 1956 and had come under immediate attack by the army of the dictator Fulgencio Batista. The Cuban government's claim that it had killed Castro was widely reported, so much so that Matthews' proof of his existence caused a great sensation, with thousands of reprints smuggled into the island by pro-Castro exiles.

2. It draws mainly upon Van Gosse, *Where the Boys Are: Cuba, Cold War America and the Making of a New Left* (New York: Verso, 1993), incorporating some additional perspectives.

3. A key text here is Richard Harding Davis, *Cuba in War Time* (1897), with its Remington drawings of a picturesque Cuban *jacquerie*, brutal Spanish officers, and heroic *insurgentes* facing the firing squad as sweethearts and parents look on.

4. Since the late sixties, an explicitly oppositional anti-imperialist "solidarity" has revived on the Left, but this was an adaptation of socialist internationalism in concert with a radicalized Christianity. These activists look to Cuba, but it is the post-1961, socialist Cuba they see, the beacon of an intransigent third world liberation. A mass response to Castro and his guerrillas outside of, and prior to, an organized "New Left" politics is received by most activists (and activist scholars) as something archaic and quaint, a relic of the fifties. I would argue that this demonstrates the narrow premises of most left-wing thinking about political dissent in the United States, and an unwillingness to recognize continuities and affinities with conventional politics and common passions.

5. Reprinted in George Black, *The Good Neighbor: How the United States Wrote the History of Central America and the Caribbean* (New York: Pantheon, 1988), 105. See also William E. Ratliff, ed., *The Selling of Fidel Castro: The Media and the Cuban Revolution* (New Brunswick, N.J.: Transaction Books, 1987).

6. *Time,* October 28, 1957; *Life,* April 14 and July 14, 1958; *Time,* July 14, 1958. Carlos Franqui, *Family Portrait with Fidel* (New York: Random House, 1964), 11.

7. Interview with Alan Sagner, June 25, 1990.

8. Jules R. Benjamin, *The United States and the Origins of the Cuban Revolution: An Empire of Liberty in an Age of National Liberation* (Princeton, N.J.: Princeton University Press, 1990), 137.

9. Stewart Alsop, "The Fruits of Castro's Plotting," *Saturday Evening Post,* March 16, 1963, 75–76.

10. See Joseph G. Morgan, *The Vietnam Lobby: The American Friends of Vietnam, 1955–1975* (Chapel Hill: University of North Carolina Press, 1997).

11. John F. Kennedy, *The Strategy for Peace,* ed. Allan Nevins (New York: Popular Library, 1961), 167–68; Kevin Tierney, "American-Cuban Relations, 1957–1963" (Ph.D. dissertation, Syracuse University, 1979), 133.

12. See Gosse, *Where the Boys Are,* 23–24, 48–49, 77–79. On the split within the U.S. embassy, see Hugh Thomas, *Cuba: The Pursuit of Freedom* (New York: Harper & Row, 1971), 964–67; Mario Lazo, *Dagger in the Heart: American Policy Failures in Cuba* (New York: Funk and Wagnalls, 1968), 139–40, 233–35; Morris Morley, *Imperial State and Revolution: The United States and Cuba* (Cambridge: Cambridge University Press), 66–71; plus correspondence in the Herbert L. Matthews Papers at Butler Library, Columbia University, concerning different foreign service officers.

13. Jules Dubois, *Fidel Castro: Rebel — Liberator or Dictator?* (Indianapolis: Bobbs-Merrill, 1959). The first printing was in March 1959, with a second in April.

14. See Gosse, *Where the Boys Are,* 71–75 for an extended discussion of Matthews's role.

15. The only available polling data is from May 1959, when there had been months of negative news coverage: by that time 88 percent of those asked knew Castro, and 31 percent regarded him favorably (*New York Times,* May 18, 1959).

16. Neill Macaulay, *A Rebel in Cuba* (New York: Quadrangle, 1970), 13, where Macaulay meets a new acquaintance just returned from fighting in Cuba at the 26th of July's Manhattan headquarters: "Soldini said he could tell I was a guy just like him—a guy who liked a good fire-fight"; *New York Times,* September 6, 1959.

17. See *New York Times,* April 4, 1958, for Morgan's statement "Why I Am Here" and photos.

18. Interview with Donald Soldini, June 3, 1992.

19. For an adulatory account of Fiorini/Sturgis as gunrunner and combatant, see *Chicago Sun-Times'* correspondent Ray Brennan's *Castro, Cuba and Justice* (Indianapolis: Bobbs-Merrill, 1959), 189 *passim.*

20. Richard Slotkin, "Gunfighters and Green Berets: *The Magnificent Seven* and the Myth of Counter-Insurgency," *Radical History Review* 44 (April 1989): 75.

21. See James T. Fisher, *Dr. America: The Lives of Thomas A. Dooley, 1927–1961* (Amherst: University of Massachusetts Press, 1997).

22. Lloyd Gardner, *Pay Any Price: Lyndon Johnson and the Wars for Vietnam* (Chicago: Ivan R. Dee, 1995).

23. Allen Woll, *The Latin Image in American Film,* revised edition (Los Angeles: UCLA Latin America Center Publications, 1980).

24. Doubtless, one could argue about the particular effect of any of these cultural productions, and cite all of the young whites who continued to buy Patti Page records and signed pledges to abstain from rock 'n' roll as they would from premarital petting.

25. *Time,* April 14, 1958; letter from Yale Political Union President to Herbert L. Matthews, November 12, 1958, asking him to moderate the debate, and letter from Hank di Suvero to Matthews, March 9, 1957, both in Herbert L. Matthews Papers, Butler Library, Columbia University.

26. See Nathaniel Weyl, *Red Star over Cuba: The Russian Assault on the Western Hemisphere* (New York: Devin-Adair, 1960).

27. Quoted in an editorial in the New York *Daily News,* September 21, 1960, while Castro was visiting the city and causing an enormous furor.

28. Barbara Ehrenreich, *The Hearts of Men: American Dreams and the Flight from Commitment* (New York: Anchor/Doubleday, 1983). That the Rebel Army as a homosocial space was part of its (and Castro's) gender-specific attraction should not be too surprising. As Tom Engelhardt emphasizes in *The End of Victory Culture: Cold War America and the Disillusioning of a Generation* (New York: Basic Books, 1995), men and boys at this point in U.S. history were deeply absorbed in a variety of war stories. Too little work has been done to date on what dreams and images preoccupied young women and girls, though it seems clear that they were quite different. Both Sara Evans, *Personal Politics: The Roots of Women's Liberation in the Civil Rights Movement and the New Left* (New York: Vintage, 1979), and, in a

very different way, the chapters by Marjorie Melville in Thomas and Marjorie Melville, *Whose Heaven? Whose Earth?* (New York: Knopf, 1971) are useful here in describing the faith-based inclination toward self-sacrifice and self-abnegation among middle-class white women (Marjorie Melville entered the Maryknoll order of missionaries in the early 1960s and was sent to Guatemala, where she became close to the revolutionary movement and was expelled in 1967).

29. *New Leader,* September 30, 1957.

30. For extended discussions of North American interest in how race operated differently in Latin America, see Fredrick B. Pike, *The United States and Latin America: Myths and Stereotypes of Nature and Civilization* (Austin: University of Texas Press, 1992).

31. Norman Mailer, "The White Negro," reprinted in Gene Feldman and Max Gartenberg, eds., *The Beat Generation and the Angry Young Men* (Secaucus, N.J.: Citadel Press, 1958, 1984), 344.

32. For accounts of U.S. diplomatic policy toward Castro before and after January 1, 1959, see Benjamin, *The United States and the Origins of the Cuban Revolution,* and Wayne S. Smith, *The Closest of Enemies: A Personal and Diplomatic Account of U.S.-Cuban Relations Since 1957* (New York: W. W. Norton, 1987).

33. *New York Times,* April 18 and 20, 1959.

34. *Life,* November 16, 1959.

35. See "The African American Press Greets the Cuban Revolution," in Lisa Brock and Digna Castaneda Fuertes, eds., *Between Race and Empire: African Americans and Cubans Before the Cuban Revolution* (Philadelphia: Temple University Press, 1998).

36. *The Crusader,* November 28, 1959.

Julian Mayfield and African American Expatriates

I would like to thank Chris Appy, Martin Kilson, Nell Painter, and Penny Von Eschen for their comments and suggestions.

1. Nixon's gaffe is recounted in David Rooney, *Kwame Nkrumah: The Political Kingdom in the Third World* (New York: St. Martin's Press, 1988), 133, and in Erica Powell, *Private Secretary (Female)/Gold Coast* (New York: St. Martin's Press, 1984).

2. Kwame Nkrumah, *I Speak of Freedom: A Statement of African Ideology* (New York: Praeger, 1962).

3. This idealized view is to be distinguished from Bayard Rustin's formulation "From Civil Rights to Black Power," which was an apt description of the new character and location of activism. Struggles against racial segregation in the South had given way to campaigns for economic democracy in northern ghettoes.

4. Gary Gerstle, "Race and the Myth of Liberal Consensus," *Journal of American History* 82, no. 2 (September 1995):579–86; Thomas Sugrue, "Crabgrass-Roots Politics: Race, Rights, and the Reaction against Liberalism in the Urban North,

1940–1964," Ibid.: 551–578; Arnold Hirsch, "Massive Resistance in the Urban North: Trumball Park, Chicago, 1953–1966," Ibid.: 522–550.

5. Although it generally does not address the experiences of African American expatriates, much of the literature on the civil rights movement addresses the conflict between black activism and Cold War perceptions and policy. See Clayborne Carson, *In Struggle: SNCC and the Black Awakening of the 1960s* (Cambridge, Mass.: Harvard University Press, 1981); Taylor Branch, *Parting the Waters: American in the King Years, 1954–1963* (New York: Simon and Schuster, 1988); Manning Marable, *Race, Reform and Rebellion: The Second Reconstruction in Black America, 1945–1982* (Jackson: University Press of Mississippi, 1988); and Godfrey Hodgson, *America in Our Time: From World War II to Nixon* (New York: Vintage Books, 1976). On federal surveillance of black intellectuals and activists, see Kenneth O'Reilley, *Racial Matters: The FBI's Secret File on Black America* (New York: The Free Press/Macmillan, 1989).

6. Richard Mahoney, *JFK: Ordeal in Africa* (New York: Oxford University Press, 1983).

7. Indeed, the phrase "Black Power" described the emergence of the newly independent nation from the British-ruled Gold Coast colony; see Richard Wright, *Black Power: A Record of Reactions in a Land of Pathos* (New York: Harper and Brothers, 1954); and Paul Robeson, *Here I Stand* (Boston: Beacon Press, 1988).

8. The radical black journals *Freedomways* and the *Liberator* published accounts by the expatriates as did the Nation of Islam weekly tabloid, *Muhammed Speaks.*

9. Ghana's expatriate sympathizers included Conor Cruise O'Brien, Immanuel Wallerstein, Thomas Hodgkin, Geoffrey Bing, and H. M. Basner.

10. Leslie Alexander Lacy, "African Responses to Malcolm X," in Leroi Jones and Larry Neal, eds., *Black Fire: An Anthology of Afro-American Writing* (New York: William Morrow and Co., 1968), 19–38.

11. For the debate on the legacy of Cold War repression, see "Right or Wrong to Name Names," Letters, *New York Times* (August 2, 1999) 14. For the conflict between Cold War anticommunism and black dissenters, see Cedric Robinson, *Black Marxism: The Making of the Black Radical Tradition* (London: Zed Press, 1983), Penny M. Von Eschen, *Race Against Empire: Black Americans and Anticolonial Politics* (Ithaca, N.Y.: Cornell University Press, 1997).

12. Kenneth O' Reilley, with David Gallen, ed., *Black Americans: The FBI Files* (New York: Carroll and Graf Publishers, 1994); Clayborne Carson, *Malcolm X: The FBI File* (New York: Carroll and Graf Publishers, 1991); O'Reilley, *Racial Matters.*

13. James Baldwin, "A Negro Assays the Negro Mood," *New York Times Magazine* (March 12, 1961): 25, 103–6; Lorraine Hansberry, "Congolese Patriot," Ibid. (March 26, 1961): 4; Hansberry, "A Challenge to Artists," *Freedomways* 3, no. 1 (Winter 1963): 33–35.

14. Mayfield's unpublished manuscripts are preserved in Box 14, "Ghana manuscripts," in the Julian Mayfield collection at the Schomburg Center. The first, "The Lonely Warrior," written immediately after the coup, is divided between a political biography of Nkrumah and an analysis of the coup. Journalistic and anecdotal, it

presents a balanced assessment of Nkrumah's flaws and failed policies within a critique of the continued dominance of foreign economic interests in post independence Ghana. The second, "When Ghana Was Ghana," is a revised version of the first manuscript, maintaining the validity of Nkrumah's project of African unity while seeking to strengthen this analysis with more documentation and research. The final manuscript, "Tales of the Lido," was evidently written between the late 1970s and Mayfield's death in 1984. In its surviving fragments, this memoir of Mayfield and the Ghana expatriates abandons the scholarly tone of the previous works, interspersing historical and political analysis with a more informal, gossipy, and sexualized remembrance of Ghana.

15. Julian Mayfield, "Black on Black: A Political Love Story," in Mayfield, ed., *Ten Times Black* (Toronto: Pathfinder Books, 1972), 125–49; "Julian Mayfield, Novelist and Actor, Dies at 56," *Washington Post* (October 23, 1984), B-6.

16. Julian Mayfield, "Tales of the Lido," unpublished manuscript, Box 14, Julian Mayfield collection, Schomburg Center for Research in Black Culture, New York City.

17. Von Eschen, *Race Against Empire;* W. E. B. Du Bois, *The Autobiography of W. E. B. Du Bois* (New York, International Publishers, 1968).

18. Harold Isaacs, *The New World of Negro Americans* (New York: The Viking Press, 1963).

19. On the Cold War repression of black American anticolonial politics, see Von Eschen, *Race Against Empire;* on official claims that African Americans took no interest in new African and Asian states, see Robeson, *Here I Stand,* 86–88; on the various degrees of African American identification with Ghana and African affairs, see Marguerite Cartwright, "African Odyssey: Ghana," *Negro History Bulletin* 20.8 (May 1957): 175–78; Phaon Goldman, "The Significance of African Freedom for the Negro American," *Negro History Bulletin* 24.1 (October 1960): 2, 6; Shirley Graham Du Bois, "The African Personality," *Political Affairs* 39 (September 1960): 13–19; Horace Mann Bond, "Howe and Isaacs in the Bush: The Ram in the Thicket," *Negro History Bulletin* 25.3 (December 1961): 66–70.

20. For black expatriates' memoirs, see Maya Angelou, *All God's Children Need Traveling Shoes* (New York: Vintage, 1984); Leslie Alexander Lacy, *The Rise and Fall of a Proper Negro* (New York: MacMillan, 1970); Mayfield, "Tales of the Lido," and William Gardner Smith, *Return to Black America* (New York: Prentice-Hall, 1970).

21. Mahoney, *JFK: Ordeal in Africa,* 34–35.

22. E. Frederic Morrow, *Black Man in the White House* (New York: McFadden, 1963), 126–27.

23. James Baldwin, "They Can't Turn Back," reprinted in Baldwin, *The Price of the Ticket: Collected Nonfiction, 1948–1985* (New York: St. Martin's/Marek, 1985), 228.

24. Ernest Dunbar, *The Black Expatriates: A Study of American Negroes in Exile* (New York: E. P. Dutton, 1968), 69–109.

25. Nkrumah, *I Speak of Freedom.*

26. An account of the demonstration is given in Ronald Walters, *Pan Africanism and the African Diaspora* (Detroit: Wayne State University Press, 1993), 119–20.

27. Julian Mayfield, "Challenge to Negro Leadership: The Case of Robert Williams," *Commentary* (April 1961): 297–305. The Xerox copy in the Mayfield papers at the Schomburg carries a 1971 note with instructions to have sixty copies of the piece made for Mayfield's students, indicating Mayfield's commitment to acquainting younger generations with prior, forgotten struggles.

28. Julian Mayfield to John Henrik Clarke [1962], Julian Mayfield folder, John Henrik Clarke papers, Schomburg Center for Research in Black Culture.

29. Angelou, *All God's Children Need Traveling Shoes*, 8.

30. Basil Davidson, *Black Star: A View of the Life and Times of Kwame Nkrumah* (London: Allen Lane, 1973), 172.

31. Mahoney, *JFK: Ordeal in Africa*, 180.

32. Julian Mayfield, "What Nkrumah Means by a United Africa," *Egyptian Gazette* (July 22, 1964); Mayfield, "Ghanaian Sketches," in Roger Klein, ed., *Young Americans Abroad* (New York: Harper and Row, 1962), 176–204; Mayfield, "Congo Is a Lesson for the Apologists," *Muhammed Speaks* (U.S.)(March 19, 1965), 11; Mayfield, "Malcolm X: A Tragic Loss," *Ghanaian Times* (February 24, 1965), 6.

33. James Baldwin, "A Negro Assays the Negro Mood," *New York Times Magazine* (March 12, 1961), 25, 103–4; Julian Mayfield, "And Then Came Baldwin," *Freedomways* (Spring 1963): 143–55.

34. Mayfield, "Uncle Tom Abroad," *Negro Digest* (June 1963): 37–39.

35. On Busia's testimony, see Davidson, *Black Star*, 174.

36. For a detailed analysis of the political and economic strategies that contributed to Nkrumah's downfall, see Bob Fitch and Mary Oppenheimer, *Ghana: End of an Illusion* (New York: Monthly Review Press, 1968). Mayfield to John Henrik Clarke, February 1, 1967, in Mayfield correspondence folder, John Henrik Clarke papers, Schomburg center. On the role of the CIA station in Accra in the coup, see John Stockton, *In Search of Enemies* (New York: Norton, 1978); for a general discussion of CIA interventions in Africa, see Ellen Ray, et al., eds., *Dirty Work 2: The CIA in Africa* (Secaucus, N.J.: Lyle Stuart Inc., 1980).

37. Clayborne Carson, "African American Leadership and Mass Mobilization," *The Black Scholar* 24.4 (Fall 1994).

38. Jennifer Jordan, "Cultural Nationalism in the 1960s: Politics and Poetry," in Adolph Reed, ed., *Race, Politics, and Culture: Critical Essays on the Radicalism of the 1960s* (New York: Greenwood Press, 1986), 29–60.

39. Nkrumah, *Class Struggle in Africa* (New York: International Publishers, 1970); Frantz Fanon, *The Wretched of the Earth* (New York: Grove Press, 1963).

40. On Nixon's co-optation of black power, see Daniel Schechter, Michael Ansara, and David Kolodney, "The CIA as an Equal Opportunity Employer," in Ray, et al., eds., *Dirty Work 2*, 50–69.

Contributors

CHRISTIAN G. APPY is the author of *Working-Class War: American Combat Soldiers and Vietnam* (University of North Carolina Press, 1993). A former associate professor of history at MIT, he is now a freelance writer working on an oral history of the Vietnam War era to be published by Viking. Appy also edits "Culture, Politics, and the Cold War," a book series published by the University of Massachusetts Press. He lives in Sharon, Massachusetts.

MARK BRADLEY is associate professor of history at the University of Wisconsin-Milwaukee. He is the author of *Imagining Vietnam and America: Postcolonial Modernity and the Cultural Construction of the Cold War, 1919–1950* (University of North Carolina Press, forthcoming). He is currently working on a project that explores the emergence of internationalism in the twentieth century.

JAMES T. FISHER is professor of history and theological studies at Saint Louis University. He is the author of *The Catholic Counterculture in America, 1933–1962* (University of North Carolina, 1989) and *Dr. America: The Lives of Thomas A. Dooley, 1927–1961* (University of Massachusetts Press, 1997). He is currently working on a history of American religion since 1945, and a study of Jesuit labor priests and the New York waterfront in the 1940s and 1950s.

JOHN FORAN is professor of sociology at the University of California, Santa Barbara. He is the author of a number of studies of social change in Iran, including *Fragile Resistance: Social Transformation in Iran from 1500 to the Revolution* (Westview, 1993). He is currently writing a book on the origins of social revolutions in the third world.

KEVIN GAINES teaches history and African American studies at the University of Michigan, Ann Arbor. He is the author of *Uplifting the Race: Black*

Leadership, Politics, and Culture during the Twentieth Century (University of North Carolina Press, 1996). His contribution to this volume is drawn from the book he is completing, "From Black Power to Civil Rights: African Americans in Kkrumah's Ghana, 1957–1966" (University of North Carolina Press, forthcoming).

VAN GOSSE is an editor of the *Radical History Review,* and the author of *Where the Boys Are: Cuba, Cold War America and the Making of a New Left* (Verso, 1993). He has taught at Wellesley College, Trinity College in Connecticut, and George Mason University. He was formerly Executive Director of the Center for Democracy in the Americas, and is currently Organizing Director of Peace Action.

CHRISTINA KLEIN is assistant professor of literature at MIT. She is currently completing a book entitled "Cold War Orientalism," based on her dissertation in American Studies at Yale University.

JONATHAN NASHEL is assistant professor of history at Indiana University South Bend. He received his Ph.D. in History from Rutgers University. He has published articles on CIA agent Edward Lansdale, Graham Greene's *The Quiet American,* and popular images of the CIA. He is completing a cultural history of Lansdale and American intervention in Vietnam.

ANDREW J. ROTTER is professor of history at Colgate University. He is the author of *The Path to Vietnam: Origins of the American Commitment to Southeast Asia,* and the editor of *Light at the End of the Tunnel: A Vietnam War Anthology.* His book *Comrades at Odds: Culture and Indo-U.S. Relations, 1947–1964,* from which this essay is taken, is forthcoming from Cornell University Press.

PENNY M. VON ESCHEN teaches history and African American studies at the University of Michigan, Ann Arbor. She is the author of *Race Against Empire: Black Americans and Anticolonialism, 1937–1957* (Cornell University Press, 1997). She is currently writing a book entitled "Satchmo Blows Up the World: Jazz, Race, and Empire during the Cold War."

WENDY WALL is assistant professor of history at Duke University. She completed her dissertation at Stanford University, "'The Idea of America': Democracy and the Dilemma of Difference, 1935–1965."

Index

Note: page references in italics indicate a photograph or an illustration.

333